PEACE and WAR

A PROJECT OF THE INSTITUTE FOR WORLD ORDER

Introductory readings assembled by a
student/faculty group at Colgate University

Michael F. Altschul '71
Charles R. Beitz '70
Thomas C. Chase, III, Psychology
Theodore Herman, Geography
Mark Landau '71
Charles R. Naef, Political Science
Andrew Schneidkraut '73
Andrew Swatkovsky, Russian
Sherry A. Swirsky '73
Huntington Terrell, Philosophy
Franklin W. Wallin, Provost and Dean of Faculty
Clarence W. Young, Psychology

Contents

PEACE

AND

WAR

EDITED BY
Charles R. Beitz and Theodore Herman

With a foreword by Alan Geyer, Colgate University

W. H. FREEMAN AND COMPANY
San Francisco

Library of Congress Cataloging in Publication Data

Beitz, Charles R   comp.
  Peace and war.

  "A project of the Institute for World Order."
  Includes bibliographies.
    1. Peace.   2. War.   I. Herman, Theodore, 1913–
      joint comp.   II. Title.
JX1937.B43   327'.172   73–4511
ISBN 0–7167–0787–X
ISBN 0–7167–0786–1 (pbk)

Printed in the United States of America

1   2   3   4   5   6   7   8   9

Foreword

For many student generations Colgate University has made the study of world affairs a central part of its liberal education. In 1970 that tradition combined with a rich fund of experience in transdisciplinary learning and a robust student concern for world peace to create the peace studies program.

In the background of the new program were the following: an informal extracurricular war/peace seminar that evolved into an experimental course; a 1969 proposal for an interdisciplinary "core" course titled "Problems of War and Peace"; and a 1970 summer workshop, with moral and material aid from the Fund for Peace and the Institute for International Order, to plan the course and produce a syllabus and book of readings.

In the next two years the core course was offered four times, engaging the talents of more than a dozen faculty in half a dozen disciplines, enrolling several hundred students, bringing outstanding lecturers and films to the Colgate campus, and preparing the way for an expanded peace studies program. The latter now offers a major concentration and is directed by the first full-time professor of peace studies at the undergraduate level in the United States.

In addition to Problems of War and Peace, the university now offers such courses as Problems of World Community, Politics of Peacemaking in the United States, Nonviolence and Conflict Resolution, International Ethics, International Politics and American Foreign Policy, International Organization and Law, Arms Control and Disarmament, Cross-Cultural Communication, and International Politics—not to mention many other courses in international relations, area studies, and related fields.

At the heart of the Colgate program is a commitment to *empowerment:* equipping persons to be effective and influential peacemakers. This commitment must be seen as a direct and deliberate challenge to the feeling of impotence shared by many students—indeed by most of us—who are concerned about the persistence of war, the arms race, and overextended military establishments. This feeling of impotence tends to make students more vulnerable to alienation, cynicism, and privatism. But it can also generate a powerful motivation to focus critical intelligence and creative imagination on the war system and to seek humane alternatives. Surely there is no greater challenge to liberal learning in our time.

The readings in this volume, selected for the course in Problems of War and Peace, were assembled as instruments of empowerment for the individual student. They are designed to help the student ask throughout: "What do I think and what can I do about the problems of war and militarism? What peaceful alternatives can I support? What vision of the world's future makes sense to me?"

These questions cut across all the traditional academic disciplines. At Colgate such diverse fields as philosophy and geography, psychology and history, and political science and economics have been enlisted in the teaching team for Problems of War and Peace. Beyond these disciplinary differences we have discovered profound, but welcome, varieties of personal opinion. It is especially appropriate for peacemakers to accept and even welcome the conflicts of specialization and conviction in a truly liberal community; for as teachers and students together learn to cope humanely with conflict, they become better equipped to cope with all the variety and tension of the whole human community.

This is a conspicuously varied volume. It is a characteristic fruit of the academic style of Colgate University. It is the first of what we hope will be a series of empowering publications from our peace studies program. It represents substantial revision through experience and will profit greatly from suggested improvements by its readers.

November 1972   *Alan Geyer*

Preface

The course this book documents originated during the late 1960s, when the Vietnam war escalation and increasingly widespread military violence in the Middle East created in many of us a renewed awareness of the extent to which war and its threat were a fixed part of our expectations of international politics. We believed that a social institution having such immediate relevance to students' lives should not go unexamined, and that only by examining the war system could we provide a background against which all of us could make responsible choices to participate in war or to protest against it. We also recognized that the questions of war and peace are far more profound than the traditional questions asked of international relations; they are bound up with the roles that each individual must choose to play in the world, with his or her personal fate and moral identity.

Our experience in designing the course has indicated that to do justice to the "war problem," a wide variety of factors needs to be taken into account. War prevention is one of a number of social goals—including protection of human rights and the earth's ecological balance—the relationships of which must be noted and in some cases explored, if we are to project coherent visions of a more peaceful world.

Consequently, this collection aims less to achieve an understanding of how the world political system works—although such an understanding is clearly an important part of our work—than to discover its fundamental assumptions, examine them, and explore alternative possibilities for a peaceful world. Part one begins with a consideration of the moral dimension of the problem of modern war, because we believe that moral terms are essential in coming to grips with pressing human concerns. It proceeds with examinations of some commonly discussed rationales, functions, and causes of war and concludes with a discussion of whether human nature makes war inevitable. Part two is organized around the notion of change from the world today to a more peaceful world in the future. In it we can examine various proposals for changing the war system and ask what action each requires at the levels of national policy and individual action. The entire volume focuses on the question, "How can we as individuals be effective peacemakers?"

Although this book is based on readings assembled for a course on the problems of war and peace, it is not in itself such a course. It would be more accurate to say that these are the source materials for a group inquiry about some important aspects of these problems. Their purpose is not to supply answers but to raise questions not asked in conventional courses on world politics or international relations. We assume that these materials will be used by others as they were used at Colgate: as fodder for small group discussions that leads to further inquiry by making crucial global problems relevant to the experience and interests of students. This, we believe, is the function of interdisciplinary learning in the field of peace and world order.

In assembling this book, we have attempted to suggest directions for discussion and further inquiry. The readings are organized in nine consecutively related sections. Each section has an introduction that gives an overview of the section and raises significant questions about the readings included. The introductions also relate the readings to one another and with other readings in other sections of the book. Finally, each introduction is followed by a brief list of books useful in pursuing interesting questions beyond the superficial consideration they receive in the limited space this book allows.

November 1972   *Charles R. Beitz*

Part ONE

THE WAR SYSTEM

1
THE MORALITY OF WAR

Introduction

Virtually all major religious and moral systems are based on the principle of respect for human life, and killing as a method of resolving human conflict is almost universally condemned. Yet war—the mass killing of soldiers and of innocent civilians as well—is not only permitted but also glorified in many modern cultures, and in most modern cultures war is accepted as an effective and justifiable way of protecting national interests and achieving diplomatic goals.

The two selections reprinted here explore the moral dilemma of war and question some of the assumptions on which its acceptance is usually based. Ralph Potter's remarks, originally presented as a lecture to students of Occidental College in Los Angeles, are a contemporary statement of the traditional Christian approach to the morality of war. The theory of the "just war," first enunciated by St. Augustine, holds that a war is justified only when it is fought for a just cause, there is reasonable likelihood that it can achieve its just objectives without disproportionate cost, the means used to prosecute it are themselves morally acceptable, and it is genuinely a last resort. Underlying this view is the perception that war and injustice are closely related: sometimes the weight of oppression can be so great that even violence can be justified as a way of righting wrongs. Thus, in Augustine's view, going to war may be justified as an act of charity, a tragic but inevitable necessity done out of love to restore the possibility of decent human life to people who have been wrongfully made to suffer.

To stop here would make Potter seem to be a hawk, since similar rhetoric has been used to justify practically every war in recent history. As is clear from his later remarks, however, Potter is certainly not a hawk. He argues that even in the presence of a just cause, there are a variety of strict conditions that must obtain before a war could morally be undertaken, and even then, combatants may use only those weapons and strategies that discriminate between the killing of soldiers and the killing of innocent civilians. Potter claims that it is this feature of the just war doctrine—the immunity of civilians from direct, intentional attack—that is most limiting, especially in the case of the counterinsurgency warfare in Vietnam, which, because of the nature of guerrilla warfare, cannot always distinguish between soldier and civilian. The reader must decide whether, given modern military technology and the development of weapons of mass destruction, any side in any war could be justified in view of this rule.

H. J. N. Horsburgh's book, *Non-Violence and Aggression,* from which the next selection is reprinted, explores the possibility of replacing existing military systems of defense with programs of civilian, nonviolent, unarmed defense, resembling resistance movements that developed in some parts of Europe during the Second World War, and patterned after Ghandi's nonviolent campaign to free India of British domination. His moral position is similar to Potter's: if war can be justified at all, it can be justified only as a last resort in the defense of human life and liberty. Since nonviolent systems for defense have never even been tested on a large scale, we have no clear grounds for supposing that military defense is ever a necessary last resort. Horsburgh's book suggests a plan for civilian defense and gives reasons why it might be expected to work. (See section 8 for further readings on this subject.)

The selection reprinted here is Horsburgh's argument that military force should not be regarded as a morally acceptable instrument of justice. In this he relies heavily on the Ghandian critique of violence. War, Horsburgh holds, is first of all irrational. It is a vastly inefficient, costly, unreliable, divisive way of settling conflicts. Secondly, war is morally erosive, that is, the atmosphere generated in a country at war is usually charged with such hatred and bitterness toward the opponent that objective moral judgments about strategies become all but impossible. "Each war," Horsburgh says, "traces a path of moral descent." Finally, and most critically, Horsburgh contends that war violates the moral principle of respect for persons. This most basic moral principle holds that every human being has the right to be treated as a person capable of his or her own fulfillment, with legitimate desires and needs, and with values and preferences that are just as valid as anyone else's. As Emmanuel Kant put it, we should always treat others, not only as means, but also as ends in themselves, that is, as subjects with intrinsic moral worth. Horsburgh contends that war compels us to see soldiers as objects to be destroyed—as "gooks," "krauts," etc.—and hence defies the most basic of all moral rules. It substitutes force for reason and destroys the possibility of calm dialogue about the sources of conflict.

Horsburgh claims to be making a moral case against all war, yet he often uses qualifying terms like *modern, total,* and *major.* It can be asked of Horsburgh, as of Potter, how much of his case against war depends on the weapons and strategies employed, and whether war at the end of the twentieth century is likely to be morally more objectionable than in previous periods of history. On this point, Horsburgh is quite emphatic: "to continue to justify wars in a way that demands moral discrimination in the choice of means is radically dishonest."

While there are certainly areas of disagreement between these authors, especially in the religious and moral principles from which they begin their arguments, some important conclusions can be drawn to which both would probably assent. Most obviously, war is tragic whenever it occurs. Sometimes it seems necessary to prevent injustice, since peace and justice cannot always coexist. Yet many questions must be answered before any war can be justified: Is there a just cause? Is war the last resort? Are the weapons and tactics clearly directed only against military targets? How do modern and previous wars differ in scale and tactics? Could a just war actually be fought under modern circumstances?

Modern doctrines regarding the justifiability of war raise some other problems as well. For example, What is the moral status of guerrilla wars in which guerrilla fighters claim to be fighting for social justice? What is the moral status of deterrence, which uses the threat of large-scale devastation as the principal mechanism for preventing war from actually breaking out? These problems are discussed further in other sections of this book.

Horsburgh suggests one avenue of escape from the moral dilemma of war: it is the creation of new systems of defense that promote and protect justice while not themselves partaking in the evils of military defense. Another way out is the creation of a world order in which people agree to guarantee just social conditions, thus eliminating injustice as a cause for war. These alternatives to war are also considered in subsequent sections.

SUGGESTIONS FOR FURTHER READING

Hannah Arendt, *On Violence*. New York: Harcourt, Brace and World, 1969.

Roland H. Bainton, *Christian Attitudes Toward War and Peace*. New York: Abingdon Press, 1960.

Joan V. Bondurant, *Conquest of Violence: the Ghandian Philosophy of Conflict*. Berkeley: University of California Press, 1965.

J. Glenn Gray, *On Justifying Violence Philosophically*. New York: Harper and Row, 1970.

Edward LeRoy Long, Jr., *War and Conscience in America*. Philadelphia: Westminster Press, 1968.

Peter Mayer, ed., *The Pacifist Conscience*. Chicago: Henry Regnery, 1967.

Ralph B. Potter, *War and Moral Discourse*. Richmond, Va.: John Knox Press, 1969.

Paul Ramsey, *The Just War*. New York: Scribner's, 1968.

Richard Wasserstrom, ed., *War and Morality*. Belmont, Calif.: Wadsworth, 1970.

The Moral Logic of War

RALPH B. POTTER, JR.

All of us are aware that our life together in society depends upon our mutual respect for the principle that we must do no harm to our neighbor. Each of us is extremely vulnerable; our safety and welfare are secure only so long as the temptation to kill and to commit mayhem, to destroy property and to plunder are suppressed both internally by moral instruction and externally by the severe sanctions of law. In civil society those who inflict severe injuries upon their neighbors are condemned, convicted and confined.

Our common life is sustained by a strong moral and legal presumption against the use of force. It is remarkable, therefore, that there is a way of thinking and talking that can transmute the act of killing into an act of heroism. By what logic can it happen that if a young American gunlover kills fourteen strangers from the top of the tower on the University of Texas campus in Austin, he is summarily slain and denounced as a psychopath, while another young American who kills fourteen strangers in a village in Vietnam is decorated, welcomed at the White House, and acclaimed a model for the youth of the nation?

Clearly, some powerful moral logic is here at work to enable us to make distinctions and to respond in a strikingly different manner to acts which share many outward characteristics. The term *war* can be used

Excerpts from the Remsen Bird Lecture at Occidental College, Los Angeles, Calif., November 19, 1969. Reprinted by permission of the author. Potter is Professor of Social Ethics at Harvard Divinity School.

to excuse conduct that would, under other circumstances, be condemned as an inexcusable assault upon the life and property of fellow human beings. It grants to warriors an immunity from punishment and blame.

A concept or word with such potency should be examined with care. For if it could be invoked promiscuously it would be dangerous to us all. . . .

The first task is to explain how the institution of war could be morally condoned under any circumstance. If there is a general rule against inflicting harm upon our neighbor, a rule that is indispensable for the existence of peace and good order among men, on what grounds can we legitimate such a colossal and brutal exception as the organized use of violence by one political community against another? Three circumstances have perennially been claimed to establish justifiable grounds for resort to war. In each case, the claim must be qualified by a series of conditions we will touch upon later. But, broadly stated, the just causes of war are:

1. To protect the innocent from unjust attack.
2. To restore rights wrongfully denied.
3. To reestablish an order necessary for decent human existence.

A just cause of war can only arise out of the necessity to restrain and correct a wrongdoing of others on behalf of the public good. . . .

. . . When one reflects upon the person of Jesus, his simplicity and gentleness and willingness to suffer, and then surveys the history of military actions conducted by those who claim allegiance to his name, it is impossible to avoid a grotesque sense of incongruity. How has the presumption against the use of force, established by his word and deed, by his life and death, been overcome?

In the early church it was not overcome. The early Christians were pacifists in practice, [but] a transformation in thought and practice eventually took place. In the age of the emperor Constantine, in the early fourth century, Christianity was first tolerated as a legal religious community and soon after established as the official religion of the Roman Empire. Christians were no longer members of a small, persecuted sect on the fringe of society. They now were invited to help guide the policy of the state. . . . But exercise of political rule entailed the responsibility to protect the innocent and to punish wrongdoers, tasks which, then as now, seemed to require forceful and violent actions not easily made compatible with the example of Jesus.

The travail of Christian conscience, formed by the example of Christ but confronted with the obligations of political responsibility, can be seen most vividly in the writings of St. Augustine. As a youth, Augustine had received a classical education which instilled in him a deep appreciation for the culture and civil order of the Roman Empire. After his conversion to Christianity, he served, until his death in 430, as Bishop of Hippo, an important metropolis in North Africa. The region was beset by the invasion of barbarian tribes who threatened to destroy the fabric of community. In 410 the imperial capital of Rome was sacked by barbarians who inflicted great loss of life and destruction. Augustine wrote his book, *The City of God,* in response to the charge that Christians, by their indifference to civil affairs and hostility to the martial virtues of the pagan heritage of Rome, were responsible for undermining the state which preserved the order and security necessary for the very continuation of the life of the churches and the values of civilization.

Augustine confronted a severe dilemma. The Gospel in which he was nurtured established a firm presumption against the use of violence. Yet, as a leader in ecclesiastical and communal affairs, he recognized that the high virtues and values he prized could not flourish in the midst of chaos and anarchy. Love and justice both demanded that order be preserved. But with barbarians at the gates, the protection of the innocent and the preservation of a just order of society required that armed resistance be made to those who would kill and plunder and rape.

Augustine wrestled with the dilemma. He determined that, out of obedience to the high calling of the Gospel, he himself would foreswear, abjure the right of self-defense. If he were traveling alone on the desert and were beset by brigands intent upon taking his life and his goods, he would not kill even in self-defense. Following the example of Jesus, he would rather suffer death than inflict it. Life in this passing world is not so precious as to be purchased at the price of slaying even an unjust attacker. Augustine was clear, however, that the moral formula is transformed when a third party is introduced. If he were traveling upon the desert in the company of women and children and again they were set upon by brigands, Augustine reasoned that the same unselfish love for others would this time demand that he sacrifice himself in defense of the innocent victims of unjust attack. He would fight, and if need be, die in their defense. On this occasion, resort to violence was to be seen . . . as a work of charity. . . .

The logic of St. Augustine enables us to understand the awesome ambivalence men experience in reflecting upon war and upon the calling of the soldier. War is an evil in the sense of being a human calamity. . . . But war, when viewed as a necessary measure undertaken with reluctance as the only means of protecting the innocent from an unjust attack, is not evil in the second sense connoting that which is "wicked," morally reprehensible and deserving of moral censure and legal penalty. Under such severe necessity, the lesser evil of war takes on the aspect of the morally preferable act. It is tragic but not wicked. Our sense of justice seems to demand that the innocent not be abandoned to the sword of invaders. . . .

The first cause of war requires the least argument. The institution of war can most plausibly be justified when it is necessary to provide immediate, direct defense of the innocent victims of unjust attack. This commonly accepted case entails certain corollaries which expand the number of those whose participation can be justified. The immediate victim of unjust aggression is entitled not only to repel force by force but also to avail himself of assistance in making his just defense. Those bound to him by treaties and alliances are under strong moral obligation to fulfill their promises by coming to the aid of a nation wrongfully attacked. The right of intervention may be claimed even by other states not bound by treaty or alliance who, nevertheless, perceive that the international community has a common stake in preserving and imposing sanctions against flagrant violations of the rights of others. Failure to intervene, the refusal to give all possible aid to a beleaguered victim, may be viewed as the default of a moral obligation and a disservice to the nascent community of nations.

The second just cause of war was to restore a right wrongfully denied. The wrongdoing which occasions such wars may be less visible than a blitzkrieg sweeping across international boundaries. But a war of intervention to correct a flagrant and persistent denial of justice may, nevertheless, be justified as a defense of the innocent. If, for example, in response to revolutionary stirrings among blacks in South Africa, the racist regime of that nation should launch an indiscriminate and deadly assault upon the black community within its boundaries, a minimal sense of justice would compel neighboring states to intervene to halt the slaughter. In effect, the international boundary would not only be overlooked but erased. A state which persistently denies equal protection of the laws and as a matter of policy does not seek the consent of the governed or allow participation of the majority in the decision-making processes, is not properly to be considered a sovereign state. It is morally indistinguishable from a band of brigands devoted to exploitation and plunder rather than to the common good. Those who undertake to protect the victims of the brigands are fighting a justifiable war for the defense of the innocent even though their action entails the first crossing of an international boundary.

The third instance in which war may be justified is when it is the only means of reestablishing an order necessary for decent human existence. Human lives are formed in a social and political context that shapes or misshapes personality. Where oppression and tyranny reign, human lives are distorted. Governments are constituted among men "in order to form a more perfect Union, establish justice, insure domestic tranquility, provide for the common defense, promote the general welfare, and secure the blessings of liberty. . . ." Where these purposes are not served, a right devolves to the people to reconstitute the political organs of their society, by force, if necessary. . . . The United States of America was "the first new nation." We can hardly deny that the use of force in revolution may, under certain conditions, be justified as a defense of the innocent against the "structural violence" imposed by a despotic and exploitative regime. The assault upon the innocent is more subtle and slow and concealed, but it nonetheless demands correction in the name of justice.

We have been answering the question, "Why should any exceptions at all be allowed to the general ban upon the use of force in human relations?" The justifications for the institution of war rest upon its presumed utility as a necessary means of serving the common good by protecting the innocent from unjust attack, restoring rights wrongfully denied, or reestablishing a social order necessary for decent human existence. . . . But war is clearly a clumsy, inefficient, unpredictable, wasteful, and hideous form of sanction, a very faulty instrument of enforcement. . . . There can be no guarantee that the side conscientiously contending for justice will prevail in battle. Villains may gain victory at arms and consolidate their position, increasing their capacity to work mischief. Moreover, violence is a paradoxical means of enforcing justice. For the indiscriminate nature of the processes of violence offends the very justice it may seek to serve. In domestic society, the verdict decreed by a judge and implemented by the police can, with due caution, be applied discriminately and precisely upon the malefactor alone. In war, however, the judgment falls severely upon the innocent child as well as the guilty politician and warrior.

The violence of war always threatens to escape control. The psychological effects of the use of violence are devastating. It engenders ferocity and a spirit of revenge and thus generates a cycle of retaliation. It tends towards relentless escalation beyond the limits originally envisioned. War is, indeed, a very faulty instrument for the enforcement of justice.

War cannot be justified without a just cause. But even with a just cause, the instrument of enforcement is so faulty that further restraints upon the right to wage war must be imposed. Not every just cause is to be prosecuted. There may be situations in which a just cause is undoubtedly present but conditions are such that resort to force would not serve the welfare of the national or international community. Hence, other criteria of the justifiable use of force are required in addition to the certitude of a just cause.

We come, thus, to our second major task of defining the conditions under which it is . . . permissible to prosecute a just cause. Violence is costly. Once states contemplate the price of violence, they suffer under the temptation to recoup some economic, political, territorial, or psychological gain beyond the narrow legitimate benefit of restraining wrongdoers for which the exceptional right to wage war may be conceded. Being aware of such temptations, we can forearm ourselves with specific criteria that will enable us to separate rationalizing pretexts from justifiable causes of war and to detect when the boundary between proper use and improper use of force has been passed. . . .

One way of recounting the basic logic concerning the right and wrong use of force in war would be to say that war can be a justifiable exception to the general ban against doing violence to fellow men only when it is both necessary and effective in serving the public good. It follows that war is unjustifiable when it is not necessary, not effective, or not for the public good. Arguments in defense of a particular war must meet all three of these criteria. Arguments against a war must show merely that it fails on one or more counts.

In expounding the criteria to be used in determining when a just cause may be rightfully prosecuted through war, I wish to depart from this tidy formulation and employ the language found in the classical sources provided by those who have elaborated the Augustinian logic through fifteen hundred years.

The first criterion that both tests and limits the right to wage war in a just cause is the requirement that there must be a due proportion between the good to be accomplished through war and the harm predictably to be suffered by all parties. It is clear that war is dangerous: dangerous for every member of a warring state. It is the responsibility of political leaders to see that those placed in their care are not recklessly exposed to danger for trivial reasons. Hence, there must be a proportionality in the gravity of the cause for which war is waged and also a proportionality in the means employed.

A second criterion . . . seeks to forestall any resort to war from the motives of vengeance, hatred, ambition, cruelty, greed, or hysteria. War must be waged with just intentions, that is, with a mournful sense of tragic necessity in the service of universal norms of justice. In battle and in victory no other intention can be harbored. . . .

A third requirement is that war must always be a last resort. Every peaceable means of obtaining redress must have been tried and exhausted. Only strict necessity can legitimate resort to force. Thus, a "preventive war" cannot be justified.

A fourth safeguard is the provision that war may be conducted only by lawful authority. War is an armed conflict between states, an affair in which the entire political community, every man, woman, and child, is brought into severe jeopardy. No one other than the sovereign authority within a state has the right to commit the entire community to undergo the risk of killing and being killed. Members of the community must be protected by clear procedures which focus responsibility for the initiation of war and permit the fullest possible representation of sentiment. If the due processes are not observed, citizens are effectively disenfranchised and war becomes not an act of the political community but an enterprise of a usurping minority upon whom guilt must rest.

The provision that war can be conducted only under lawful authority reinforces the requirement that violence can be justified only when it is politically purposeful, that is, when it can be claimed to serve the public good by establishing or preserving an order of justice in which the impartial application of general laws replaces arbitrary personal rule. . . . Thus, the violence of bandits and looters, who serve only their own interest, is to be distinguished from that of would-be patriots organized in guerrilla bands in the service of a provisional government or a government in exile intent upon establishing or reestablishing a political constitution. Bandits and looters who employ violence in their selfish enterprise are punishable under civil law as common criminals. Guerrilla fighters are properly to be treated as Prisoners of War acting wrongfully, perhaps, but, nevertheless, in good conscience as officers of a new commonwealth struggling to be born.

A fifth condition necessary to justify resort to war is that a clear declaration of the causes and aims of war be made generally known at home and abroad. There are three purposes of such a declaration.

First, to indicate to a potential enemy the conditions upon which a settlement might be made and war thereby avoided.

Second, to give notice to all other nations so that they may assess the justice of the cause and conduct themselves accordingly.

Third, to establish with certainty that war is being waged not on the initiative of a small clique but by the will of the people of the contending states.

A sixth condition is that there must be reasonable hope of success. This criterion flows from the moral ban upon suicide and the fundamental principle that political leaders are stewards of the welfare of the nation and the life of each citizen. Lives and goods are not to be squandered. War must be a politically purposeful act made barely tolerable by the necessity of defending the innocent. It can never be justified by the vain desire to avoid admitting an error in past judgment, a refusal to acknowledge changed circumstances, or an extravagant and misplaced sense of heroism. It is immoral to expose other men to death to save one's political face.

All of the above conditions suggest questions that ought to be asked in formulating a response to the question, "When is it permissible to wage war?" These criteria constitute the principles of the *ius ad bellum,* that is, the law governing the resort to war.

Another basic question may be asked by those contemplating war: "What acts may be committed in the conduct of war?" The principles which determine the response to this question constitute the *ius in bello,* that is, the law governing conduct in war. A seventh condition, then, is that the *ius in bello* must be observed, or, as it may be said, only just means must be employed in combat and in conquest.

. . . Reflection upon the just means of warfare must be guided by the principle of the moral immunity of noncombatants from direct attack. The principle is a simple corollary of the logic we have unfolded. We live by the presumption that men must do no harm to their neighbors. That presumption can be overridden when it is necessary to restrain wrongdoers from inflicting harm. It is only this necessity that can grant to any man an excuse to kill. It follows that those who need not be restrained must not be killed. This is the heart of the moral logic of war. In seeking to prevent men from doing harm to those who deserve no harm, we cannot ourselves rightfully inflict harm upon those who deserve no harm.

We are allowed to use force only to restrain. In this mission we cannot ignore the obligation to respect human life even in the person of our enemy. We must employ only the least amount of force effective to restrain. On occasion, it may be that we cannot prevent a foe from doing injury except by killing him. It is then permissible to do so. But the rightful purpose remains only to restrain. Once that has been accomplished the right to kill is forthwith revoked.

Only those immediately and actively engaged in the bearing of hostile force in an unjust cause are properly subject to direct attack. Civilians living in the cities of the enemy's homeland or in villages near the scene of battle cannot purposefully be harmed. An enemy soldier who has dropped his weapon to surrender, or has suffered a wound, or is captured unaware, or by any other circumstance is rendered incapable of inflicting harm, reverts immediately to the status of a fellow human being whose life is surrounded by the protection of the principle that we must do no harm to our neighbors. No one can claim an excuse to do him violence. Neither vengeance, nor expediency, nor the need for information, nor the desire to terrorize others, nor fear of future betrayal, nor any other reason can override the restraint embedded in the very logic by which we can barely justify war as itself a measure of restraint.

It is the task of . . . every just and thoughtful citizen to make this logic have binding effect in the conscience of every policy maker . . . and every soldier we train to kill and maim and to destroy in the name of America. . . . To fail to speak out clearly concerning the immorality of the use of indiscriminate weapons, the execution of prisoners, the use of torture and political assassination and other acts commonly known to be practiced or condoned by American forces in Vietnam can be explained only by gross moral ignorance, political cowardice, or despicable negligence in the fulfillment of the common obligations of citizenship. . . .

We have been searching for the principles that can aid us in discerning right from wrong in the use of force. I suspect that many of you have become impatient with the explication of abstract principles. Moral principles have not been in style of late. We have suffered a fad for contextualism or situationalism in ethics. The "new morality" gained popularity, if not plausibility, as a weapon in the campus crusade for liberation from conventional sexual mores. Many have lapsed into a crude form of intuitionism, the very purpose of which is to foreclose the possibility of inquiring into the right and wrong of another person's behavior. The claim that every situation is utterly unique and impervious to moral illumination prior to the moment in which one is immersed in the totality of the context means that we must be left to follow our inclinations and intuitive judgments concerning that which is "fitting." . . .

In Vietnam we are inheriting the political consequences of the new morality. Slowly, young and old are becoming aware that some things are too important to be left to impromptu decisions and that the inclinations and intuitions of some men are not to be trusted. At this moment, Americans need to talk to one another about what is right and wrong. But the vocabulary itself has been forgotten, the intellectual framework within which words of moral criticism have meaning and power has been allowed to decay. An indispensable national resource has been squandered. Moral discourse represents the most peaceable, nonviolent mode of influencing others. When it is no longer possible, we wield influence upon others by cruder means of political invective and threat, billy club and tear gas, assassination and terror.

The task of the college, its primary contribution to society, must be to rebuild the intellectual apparatus which makes the distinction between war and murder, between justifiable and unjustifiable use of violence meaningful. . . .

Critique of Armed Force as an Instrument of Justice

H. J. N. HORSBURGH

I shall review the main deficiencies of war under three heads. Such classifications are always unsatisfactory in one way or another. All that I should claim for my own is that, although it creates some untidy overlaps, it does enable me to bring out the manysidedness of the moral problems which war involves.

WAR AS IRRATIONAL

All social conflicts are disruptive in some degree. But the disruptiveness of most of them is limited by one or more of the following: (1) a framework of more fundamental agreement such as usually exists when the disputants are all members of the same community; (2) one party's recognition of the superior power of the other; (3) the superior power of a third party which would intervene if the conflict passed beyond certain limits, e.g., the awareness of both sides in an industrial dispute that government action will occur if their conflict leads to an outbreak of violence; (4) awareness of the precise issues at stake; (5) a steady awareness of the limited importance of these issues; (6) the fears which

From *Non-Violence and Aggression* by H. J. N. Horsburgh, pp. 5–19. Copyright © 1968 by Oxford University Press. Reprinted by permission of the publisher. Horsburgh is senior Lecturer in the Department of Moral Philosophy at the University of Glasgow, Scotland.

the disputants inspire in one another; and (7) renunciation by at least one party to the dispute of the use of certain methods of gaining one's ends.

The fourth and fifth of these are less obvious limiting factors than the others; and therefore it is perhaps in order to say rather more about them. Let me begin with the claim that awareness of the precise issues at stake in a struggle tends to limit its disruptiveness. As I understand it, this has two aspects. The less important of these is connected with the fact that awareness of the issues at stake acts as a counter to the tendency for these issues to widen in the course of the ensuing struggle. Such a tendency is quite general owing to the hostility which a conflict is liable to engender and to the stupid or malicious actions in which this hostility is likely to be expressed. And clearly, the more issues there are to settle the more difficult it will be to reach a settlement. The more important aspect has to do, not with the multiplication of disputed issues, but with loss of definiteness as to the basis of the conflict. Such loss of definiteness has most serious repercussions on the effects of the dispute. To begin with, it means that actions and policies can no longer be directed by precise ends. This involves an obvious loss of rational control over means; and such control is vital if the disruptive effects of conflict are to be minimized. Again, a firm grasp of the basis of a dispute is essential if the contestants are to be steadily aware of its limited importance. Also, as the basis of a dispute loses its definiteness the attention of the contestants fixes itself upon the gross fact of their opposition and at once seeks to explain it by reference to some objectionable quality or qualities in the other party. These prejudiced assessments add to the mutual hostility of the parties to the dispute, making them less accommodating and better disposed towards extreme or relatively destructive measures. Finally, when mutual hostility becomes the dynamic basis of the conflict, as is inevitable once the original issues in dispute have ceased to dominate the minds of the antagonists, no course of events is likely to be regarded as satisfactory which stops short of the injury, or even the destruction, of one's enemies.

I now turn to the claim that the disruptiveness of any social conflict is controlled by steady awareness of the limited importance of the issues which have given rise to it. The significance of this factor is difficult to overestimate. In the last analysis it is usually awareness of the relative importance of different ends which restrains us from the wilder and more destructive manifestations of hostility towards our enemies. Indeed, some of the other factors limiting the disruptiveness of conflict are best thought of as special forms taken by this more general factor when it operates in situations of certain kinds. Once it ceases to operate altogether, it is all too likely that the conflict will descend to the level of unrestricted savagery—unless mutual fear still acts as a restraint upon the antagonists; and intense hatred "casteth out fear" almost as effectively as perfect love.

I must now consider whether any of the above factors place significant limits upon the evils of warfare.

The disruptiveness of war is not limited by a framework of more fundamental agreement; on the contrary, a resort to arms clearly testifies to the absence of such a framework. Nor is it significantly limited by one party's recognition of the other's superior power. Faced with an overwhelmingly powerful enemy an armed state has three choices: avoidance of war on the best terms available, token resistance, and full-scale military resistance. Military disparities have sometimes helped to preserve the peace. If, however, they fail to prevent hostilities, they only reduce their destructiveness in those cases in which no serious military resistance is offered. But such cases are necessarily very rare since token resistance neither serves to improve the enemy's terms nor satisfies a nation's pride or will to independence. Again, the disruptiveness of war is seldom limited by the superior power of a third party. There are exceptions, however. Thus, at the time of the Suez crisis American opposition to the Anglo-French attack upon Egypt (probably reinforced by the fear inspired by Soviet threats) proved sufficient to end the war and may well have restrained the British and French Governments from carrying out a still more ruthless and brutal assault. But this factor is seldom important even in the case of relatively minor wars; and it would be difficult to find instances in which it has played a significant part in limiting major wars. Thus, although the U.S.A. was already a major—though not a super—power at the outbreak of the First World War, American protests do not seem to have exercised a marked effect upon either side in the conduct of the war at sea. It would be an exaggeration to assert that neutral opinion has no restraining effect upon the conduct of belligerents. But its main influence is exerted prior to the commencement of hostilities. There are several reasons why this should be so, including the following: the assurances which prospective belligerents often receive from important neutral powers prior to the outbreak of war; the fact that a decision to make war is often tantamount to a decision not to be influenced by the opinions or actions of neutrals; and the inherent lawlessness of war itself.

Is the disruptiveness of armed conflict limited by awareness of the precise issues that have led to an outbreak of war? Warfare is impossible

in the absence of hostility. Consequently, prospective belligerents must
do all they can to arouse and intensify their feelings of antagonism. The
resulting mutual hostility progressively blurs the war aims of both sides,
setting them free to express their hatred without restraint. But it may
be doubted whether one needs to stress the operation of this general
tendency in order to show that awareness of the issues at stake does
little or nothing to limit the destructiveness of war. What I have in mind
is the fact that such awareness is an effective limiting factor only when
the issues of which a firm grasp is to be retained have a certain general
characteristic, namely, detachment from unfavourable estimates of the
qualities or intentions of the other party to the disagreement. Consider,
for example, a dispute between two groups of city councillors as to
whether a municipal golf course should be used as the site of a new
housing estate. Even if the council is divided over the issue along party
lines and local politics are fairly bitter the issue retains a sturdy independence and can be discussed in nearly all its aspects without tempting
the opposing sides to concentrate attention on one another's characters
and allegedly evil designs. Typical war aims are quite different. Save
in the case of an aggressor with a clear but limited programme of expansion, such as Prussia under Bismarck, war aims tend to be predominantly negative in character, and are directly concerned with unfavourable estimates of the enemy's qualities and intentions. In a word, typical
war aims are largely a product of enmity. Thus, the fundamental objectives of the Western Allies in the Second World War were those of halt-
ing German aggression, destroying Germany's military power, and bringing down the Nazi regime. Such objectives are consistent with the per-
petration of any barbarity and impose no significant limits upon the
disruptiveness of a conflict. To this it may be objected that wars often
have such positive objectives as maintaining a certain way of life, preserving national independence, and so on. This is true. Indeed, I shall
have occasion to stress this aspect of war aims later in this chapter. But
it does not affect the issue. For once the struggle is joined these positive
ends are said to depend upon the realization of such negative objectives
as the destruction of the enemy's military power; and in the confusion
and bitterness of war any injury which one inflicts on the enemy can be
represented as a contribution to the achievement of this objective. Thus,
however positive the ends to which one's propaganda pays lip service,
one's operative aims are of a kind which does not exercise any limiting
effect upon one's choice of means.

Again, although belligerents in minor wars sometimes retain an awareness of the limited importance of what is at stake, as Britain and France
can be said to have done in their brief war with Egypt, a major war is

always represented as a struggle to the death, victory being regarded as an essential step towards the realization of *all* national objectives. It follows that whether or not the stakes in a major war *are* of limited importance, such limits as they have exercise no control over the destructiveness of the struggle.

There is room for disagreement over whether the fears which belligerents inspire in one another have significantly affected—or may still significantly affect—the course of major wars. (It is clear that it has affected the conduct of belligerents in minor wars.) For example, did the Germans abstain from the use of gas in the Second World War through fear of reprisals? Again, if a Third World War breaks out, will nuclear weapons be directed only against carefully selected targets from fear of reprisals? In answer to these questions I shall content myself with three remarks. First, this factor would only be important if one or more of the following exceptional conditions were fulfilled: the weapon system in question were such that its use was unlikely to be decisive at any stage of the war, or that its effects would be so incalculable that neither side could be sure that it stood to gain more than lose from its use, or that it were bound to inflict ruin on any community against which it were directed and its availability to both sides could not be affected by any steps within the power of either set of belligerents. In the Second World War we may have been protected from the use of gas by doubts concerning its military effectiveness or by the difficulty of estimating its consequences; and it is hoped that fears of mutual annihilation will protect us from all-out nuclear warfare. But it has been pointed out that, even if the rationality of all interested parties is assumed, the development of antimissile systems or weapons completely destructive of second-strike capacity, might, at any time, undermine the effectiveness of this deterrent factor. The second answer to the effectiveness of fear of reprisals is that—as I have already remarked—hatred is a very powerful solvent of fear. In the Hungarian rising of 1956 men and women were seen to attack Soviet tanks with their naked fists. Is it to be doubted that they would have used nuclear weapons had they been able to do so even if they had known that reprisals were certain and would be completely annihilating? Thirdly, in major wars defeat is represented as absolutely ruinous in its consequences. Hence, in the final stages of a conflict the party close to defeat will see itself as having nothing further to lose, and therefore as having no reason to abstain from any injury it still has in its power to inflict on the enemy. Hitler's free use of his missiles when he had obviously lost the war is an excellent illustration of the nihilistic despair we have so much reason to fear.

I gin to be aweary of the sun,
And wish the estate o' the world were now undone,

expresses the authentic voice of the defeated tyrant.

Is the destructiveness of warfare likely to be limited by the renunciation of certain weapons by one or other set of belligerents? I shall restrict myself to two comments on this possibility as I shall have occasion to return to it further on in this chapter. To begin with, since defeat is very probable if one denies oneself the use of any effective weapon or technique employed by the enemy, no one so burdened with scruple as to be unwilling to imitate the enemy without limit would ever have recourse to war. Consequently, the importance of this factor is confined to those situations in which both sides are rigidly scrupulous in the manner of waging war, those in which the relatively scrupulous side has weapons at its disposal not available to the enemy and refuses to use them, and those in which weapons used by the enemy are judged to be of little military value. There may have been cases in which one side has refrained from using weapons employed by the enemy because its circumstances were such that their use would have been valueless. But there seems to be little evidence of cases in which both sides have been rigidly scrupulous in the conduct of warfare or in which one or other has foregone the use of effective weapons not available to the enemy; and it is only in these sorts of cases that the limiting factor under examination has much importance. Again, war represents the triumph of that morality which holds that how well you can afford to treat an opponent depends on how well he is prepared to treat you. Consequently, if you suppose that he would use any weapon whatsoever to injure or destroy you, you will deny yourself no available means of injuring or destroying him.

Summing up, then, it seems clear that the destructiveness of war, at least in the case of hostilities between groups of major powers, is not significantly limited by any of the factors which normally check the disruptiveness of conflict. It follows that, under present conditions of warfare, unless one side is able quickly and with little loss to itself to inflict an unexpected and crushing defeat upon the other, the damage which it must do to all the communities involved is absolutely enormous. But such a defeat is so improbable that it can be disregarded. Indeed, current policies of deterrence presuppose its impossibility. Consequently, it is almost certain that, in the event of another major war, the logic of unrestricted violence will manifest itself to the full.

The moral relevance of this conclusion will be much greater on some systems of values than on others. But there is at least one sort of relevance which it must have on any, namely, that which stems from its bearing on the rationality of such a total conflict. I shall restrict myself to this aspect of the question, and my brief remarks will look forward to possible future wars rather than backward towards the terrible but far less deadly contests of the recent past.

War, being undesirable in itself, can only be rational on at least four conditions: (1) that the outcome for the two sides is different, one being able to do things or make decisions which the other is unable to do or make; (2) that the powers conferred by victory could not be attained without resort to war; (3) that these powers are sufficient to enable the victors to realize the ends for which the war is supposed to have been fought, the ends including such positive objectives as the preservation of a certain way of life as well as the negative aims associated with enmity; and (4) that the victors retain the will to use these powers to achieve their positive ends. The second condition will be questioned in later chapters where I shall argue for the feasibility of nonviolent systems of defence. The first condition remains unfulfilled if neither side survives the conflict, or if there is no balance of military success, or if that balance is so small that it does not appreciably affect the consequences of the war. Weapons have been predicted that would make mutual annihilation inevitable. But even now it is most improbable that either side could emerge from a nuclear struggle with an appreciable balance of advantage. However, the nonfulfillment of the third condition is still more certain. Who, for example, can suppose that it would be satisfied after either of the two kinds of nuclear conflict envisaged by Richard Fryklund in his book, *A Hundred Million Lives,* in one of which America would have 150 million dead while in the other it would have 110 million dead? Such losses imply psychological, social, and material damage on a scale that would make democratic goals completely irrelevant to the shattered society which would emerge from the struggle. If Beveridge is right when he says, "if full employment is not won and kept, no liberties are secure, for to many they will not seem worth while," [1] how much attachment to liberal values is to be expected in a world that has sustained the shock of nuclear conflict? Is it not obvious that only a ruthless and authoritarian regime would be able to cope with the resulting chaos? And if one counters this argument by saying that such a form of rule need not persist, cannot one say at least as much of the social order which might result from a refusal to make war? [2] As Hannah Arendt has pointed out,

---

[1] *Full Employment in a Free Society* (2nd ed. 1960), p. 258.
[2] This point is made in a telling way by Herbert Butterfield in his *International Conflict in the Twentieth Century* (1960), p. 95.

to sound off with a cheerful "give me liberty or give me death" sort of argument in the face of the unprecedented and inconceivable potential destruction in nuclear warfare is not even hollow; it is downright ridiculous. Indeed it seems so obvious that it is a very different thing to risk one's life for the life and freedom of one's country and one's posterity from risking the very existence of the human species for the same purpose that it is difficult not to suspect the defenders of the "better dead than red" or "better death than slavery" slogans of bad faith.[3]

As for the last of these four conditions for the rationality of war, namely, the victors' continued determination to realize their positive aims, it is notorious that it often remained unfulfilled even in prenuclear times. The essential points were made in an early book of Bertrand Russell's:

> As the effort of will grows greater and more difficult through war weariness, the vital force of the nations will be more and more weakened. When at last peace comes, it is to be feared that no stimulus will be adequate to rouse men to action. After the fierce tension of combat, nothing will seem important; a weak and relaxed dissipation will succeed the terrible and unnatural concentration.[4]

WAR AS MORALLY EROSIVE

The crisis of war often creates those conditions of heightened social cohesion which enable men and women to make personal sacrifices of a different order from those normally to be expected from them. Even the most sharply delimited egos tend to blur at their edges in some wartime situations, releasing their possessors from the thraldom of calculating selfishness. The result is that, in romantic and blinkered quarters, war has sometimes enjoyed a high moral reputation. And it is true that men have often shown immense fortitude and loving concern for one another in combat situations. But this sum of moral grandeur, much depleted as it must be when the total of self-sacrifice and boldness that is of biological rather than of moral significance is subtracted from it, has to be balanced against the processes of moral erosion which are set in motion by the outbreak of any major war. I now wish to say a little about one of these processes.

---

[3] *On Revolution* (1964), pp. 3–4.
[4] *Justice in Wartime* (1916), pp. 14–15.

Each military enterprise involves actions which are morally significant (or are usually regarded as such) in other ways than their alleged conduciveness to certain ends. For example, it probably requires the taking of human life on an enormous scale; it is likely to inflict immense suffering on neutrals as well as on belligerents; it may necessitate the dissemination of lying propaganda; it is possible that it involves the breaking of treaties, the betrayal of allies, and the violation of neutral frontiers. These are, in the relevant sense, the means it uses to prosecute the war. In the past the initial selection of means was seldom governed exclusively by military considerations. In the early stages of a war at least, some concern has usually been shown for the customary rules of decent and civilized behaviour, especially that part of these rules which is embodied in international law.

Part of this concern is probably attributable to prudence. Thus, if certain actions are normally regarded as specially evil it is prudent to avoid the reputation of having committed them; and even in wartime, when lies gain wider currency than in times of peace, calumny is apt to be less blackening than truthful report. But although such prudential considerations can be stretched to explain many policies of clemency, forbearance, and apparent good faith, their elasticity seems insufficient to account for every apparent manifestation of moral scrupulousness. For example, one weapon is sometimes preferred to another because it is less lethal or more discriminating, and treaties are honoured and neutral frontiers are respected where this does not involve grave sacrifices; and it would be unduly cynical to deny that these self-imposed restraints are partly moral in character.[5]

But this initial position is not enduring. Hatred, bitterness, and fear—all of which steadily increase throughout the period of hostilities—produce tremendous temptations to set aside these self-denying ordinances.[6] And these temptations are aggravated by the systematic representation of the enemy as even more vicious than he is. So one is pushed along the broad road that leads to mutual destruction, reprisals being followed by counterreprisals of ever greater bloodiness, the whole process being a terrifying illustration of the self-validating power of that fear and hatred which transmutes enemies who are much like ourselves into absolute monsters. Again, savagery can be resorted to as a means of intimidating the enemy. Ruthlessness can also add to the effectiveness of a surprise

---

[5] But these restraints are less marked than in earlier times. See, e.g., Bertrand de Jouvenel's verdict on the morality of the twentieth century, *The Pure Theory of Politics* (Yale, 1963), p. 180.

[6] A convincing testimony to this view is to be found in Albert Camus's collected wartime essays, *Resistance, Rebellion and Death* (1964), pp. 44–45.

assault, as instanced by the Japanese attack on Pearl Harbor. And finally, any scruple is necessarily cramping from a military standpoint. As wars develop and military considerations become increasingly paramount even in the eyes of politicians, anything which places one at the slightest military disadvantage is bound to be set aside.

Thus, quite inevitably, each war traces a path of moral descent. Initially there is a tendency to speak of some courses of action as "unthinkable," as not allowable in any circumstances whatsoever. But these harsh proscriptions are soon replaced by gentler pieties, regrets or indignation being expressed at having been forced, as a matter of sheer military necessity, into abominations first perpetrated by the enemy. Later still bare malevolence is allowed to overrule military effectiveness and there is much talk about the need to punish the enemy—as the Allies claimed to do when they continued the blockade of Germany for several months after the Armistice of 1918. As for the rule that the introduction of new horrors should be left to the other side, it later suffices to claim that the enemy would have used the novel techniques or weapons if he had been the first to think of them. And so one moves inexorably from genuine indignation over the criminal destruction of Rotterdam and Coventry to acceptance of the far more abominable obliteration of Hiroshima and Nagasaki, eventually experiencing "the ultimate horror that there was no horror." [7]

This is a fearful descent. But it can scarcely be described as astonishing in view of its inevitability. For the pressures of war are such that it is as strictly predictable as anything in human life. To enter a war is to ensure that it will take place. Consequently, any prospective combatant who fails to come to moral terms with it, for example by denying its inevitability or by continuing to justify wars in a way that demands moral discrimination in the choice of means, is radically dishonest.

The question whether the advent of nuclear weapons has affected this moral descent turns upon whether a major future war would first be fought with conventional weapons. If it would be fought with such weapons the descent remains predictable; if, on the other hand, it would be fought from the outset with nuclear weapons one would begin where one used to end—at the foot of the descent.

Thus, although we ordinarily condemn the doctrine that the end justifies the means, the practice of war not only accords, but must accord, with that doctrine. It seems to follow that we should either cease to condemn it or withdraw our conditional acceptance of war itself.

---

[7] Quoted from the Quaker pamphlet, *Speak Truth to Power* (1954), p. 9.

WAR AS A VIOLATION OF THE PRINCIPLE
OF RESPECT FOR PERSONS

The most fundamental of the moral problems connected with large-scale human conflict are most easily brought into view through a consideration of the need to preserve a basic tension: that involved in standing true to what one believes to be right at the same time as one continues to act in ways that preserve and reflect a consciousness that one's moral assessment of the situation may be mistaken. This tension imposes such strains, especially when the recognition of moral fallibility is not entertained simply as a possibility but as something which must find practical expression, that it is usual to retreat from it, either by adopting an attitude of indifference and taking shelter in cynicism and ineffectuality, or, alternatively, by embracing that intense partisanship which divides the world into blacks and whites and pursues irreversible policies of violence with every appearance of moral assurance. There is always a minority which chooses the former alternative. Some conscientious objectors to war belong to this minority. They are deficient in conviction, not courage. But the vast majority of men and women can usually be prevailed upon to participate in policies, which, both because of what they involve in themselves and of the reactions which they produce in opponents, are calculated to destroy the tension to which I refer.

It is worth pausing for a moment to consider three of the many processes whereby the last shreds of doubt as to the justice of their cause are removed from people's minds once war has begun. First, few can accept the suffering which war necessitates—for others if not always for oneself—unless they have a deep conviction that great issues are at stake. Mere self-interest is not enough to sustain them; they must feel that their own side stands for justice, freedom, and decency while the enemy represents the forces of evil in the world. Secondly, this sense of high moral purpose, so essential if the greatest sacrifices are to be made, is perpetually threatened in a war by the moral descent which I have already described. As one moves from retaliation to the seizing of the initiative, introducing new weapons of superior destructiveness or using them with less and less discrimination, it is easy to become oppressed with a sense of moral nullity; and so one clings still more tightly to the great positive ends which are supposed to cancel this appearance of moral collapse. Thus, the more terrible the acts to which one has been driven in pursuit of military success the more assured one must be of the justice of one's cause. Finally, the enemy's ruthless response to one's military effort, represented by one's own propaganda as even more vicious than it is, serves to confirm the belief that he is devoid of moral sense. "The only good German is a dead German"—it is only the unsophisticated who make such pronouncements, but convictions of the sort which they express are activated in the minds of most belligerents each time a fresh disaster overtakes their forces. After all, wars are not won by those who see all that lies within the view of a retrospective eye; they are won by those who see what reinforces the determination to prosecute them to the bitter end.

A simple illustration of these processes must suffice. Prior to the outbreak of war it was often said that Hitler's case against the Treaty of Versailles was not without merit. But once hostilities had commenced Nazi efforts to undo the work of that treaty were condemned with absolute assurance. Yet it is surely obvious that if earlier doubts as to the justice of Versailles were reasonable, their reasonableness was not affected by the dismemberment of Czechoslovakia and Poland. But who, in 1940, could have been found to defend those doubts? The view which then prevailed was that Germany had been treated with fatal generosity.

However, it is less the failure to maintain the tension in question than the consequences of losing it which deserve our attention. Even in peacetime these consequences are probable if international fear and suspicion are running high; in wartime they must be regarded as inevitable. To lose sight of the possibility that the enemy is partially in the right makes it easy to represent him as wholly evil, and this in its turn prepares the way for the belief that he is quite irreclaimable. But once take the enemy to be irreclaimable and one is on the point of denying that he is really human. And, in fact, it is a commonplace of war to utter such a denial, declaring that he is a mad dog, a hyena, a jap-rat, or whatever, something which should be got rid of with as little compunction as accompanies the despatch of an insect. But this, within our own scheme of values is the final abomination, namely, a denial of the respect due to all human persons as such, regardless of their shortcomings.[8]

In time of war it can be vitally important not to see the enemy as a mixed assortment of ordinary human beings. It is for this reason that, even in peacetime, scenes from everyday life in potentially hostile countries are seldom televised. In a few moments they can undo the work of years, seriously undermining the monstrous misconceptions that politicians and publicists have been labouring to impress upon the popular mind.

---

[8] For a full discussion of the principle involved see W. G. Maclagan's two articles entitled "Respect for Persons," *Philosophy,* 1960.

It may be contended that in time of war it is excusable to deny to the enemy the respect which is due to persons. After all, insofar as this is the principle which underlies our faith in democracy its future influence in human affairs is dependent upon the survival of those who value it. In my view, such an answer represents the extreme of self-deception. But it also seriously underrates the extent to which war encourages us to violate this basic principle and to degrade human beings to the status of tools and chattels. For this tendency is so strong that it shows itself in relation to one's own nationals as well as in relation to the enemy. Thus, in the First World War there were times when the loss of a horse was deemed of greater importance than the loss of a man. Again, in a radio talk during the Second World War Sir Philip Joubert discoursed at length about the relative value, in terms of man-hours of production, of aeroplanes and those who fly them, adding that when aeroplanes are wrecked they can be partially salvaged whereas a dead airman must be written off altogether.[9] Sir Philip Joubert betrayed no feeling of awkwardness in making such a comparison and his hearers do not seem to have protested against it. But what would be the response to an economist who argued against the introduction of new safety devices in the mines on the ground that they cost more than the total value of the lives which they would save? That industrialists, public health authorities, cabinet ministers, often make calculations of this general kind I have no doubt whatsoever. But they are only dropped into the ear of the general public in time of war. For it is widely appreciated that the world of war is a world of exclusively technical problems in which there is no room for such refinements as the distinction between persons and things.

In the first part of the above critique I question the cogency of the utilitarian justification of war as the lesser of two evils. And in the second and third parts I suggest that war becomes still more difficult to defend once one abandons a purely utilitarian standpoint. But I have purposely left the critique in an inconclusive form, omitting to assemble the separate arguments in a manner that would lend support to explicitly pacifist conclusions. For it has not been my intention to argue that war cannot function as an acceptable instrument of any moral purpose under present-day conditions. My aim throughout has been the more modest one of activating the doubts which most of us feel when faced with its full tally of evil consequences and implications. Thus, the critique is intended to

---

[9] The Nazis had a greater talent for this kind of thinking as the salvage operations in the death camps makes clear. Since logic is on their side we must question their premises if we reject their conclusions.

justify the search for a substitute, not to vindicate those who would renounce war regardless of whether any substitute can be found.

It is also intended to bring out the respects in which any satisfactory
alternative must show itself to be superior to war. There are quite a
number of these and they could be classified in different ways. Those
which I most wish to stress are the following: placing limits on the destructiveness of conflict; preserving the scruples of its users with regard to
the selection of means; maintaining the basic tension between the conviction that one's cause is just and awareness of one's own fallibility; and
allowing its users to demonstrate their moral respect for their opponents
(as well as for themselves).

2
WAR AS A MEANS FOR ACHIEVING SOCIAL JUSTICE

Introduction

The preceding two selections seem to support the view that war can only be justified when it is fought in the cause of justice. Their thrust, however, is that most wars are likely to be morally unjustifiable, since even if the causes are just, the peculiar character of "modern" or "total" war is that it cannot be fought in a morally acceptable way. New weapons and strategies often ignore the distinction between soldier and civilian and entail costs that could rarely be offset by the values to be gained in warfare.

Many argue that guerrilla war represents an exception to this position. It largely escapes the attention of the two previous authors, and in this they are typical of contemporary writers on the morality of war. Yet guerrilla fighters and leaders claim to be fighting for social reform, and since they are primitively armed, guerrilla war cannot be condemned with modern war simply because of the destructiveness of new weapons technology. On the other hand, the nature of a guerrilla struggle as a

"people's war" makes it difficult to distinguish between the fighters themselves and civilians who ought to be seen as innocent bystanders. Because the next thirty years are likely to witness widespread guerrilla
fighting in the world's poor regions, the subject merits close attention.

The selections that follow pose questions about the morality of "peoples' wars" that are usually overlooked and suggest a causal model of
guerrilla struggle that links it with social injustice and severe disparities
in the distribution of economic goods.

The first selection is an excerpt from Ernesto "Che" Guevara's book,
Guerrilla Warfare, the Cuban revolutionary leader's guide to starting
guerrilla movements throughout Latin America. Although much of the
book is highly practical and detailed, the excerpt below is theoretical. It
sets out Che's view of guerrilla war as war for social reform that must
be supported by the masses if it is to be successful. For Che, the main
justification for guerrilla war is intolerable oppression by an established
government. As civil war, its immediate aim is a change of government
leading to a transformation of social structure. While Che agrees that
guerrilla war should be employed increasingly as an instrument of change
by the world's dispossessed, he differs from other theorists of guerrilla
struggle, such as Lin Piao, in his contention that guerrilla war can
succeed even if it is not part of a coordinated world revolution.

Vladimir Dedijer, who was himself a partisan fighter in Yugoslavia,
generalizes from several instances of guerrilla warfare in Europe, Latin
America, and Afro-Asia in an essay that reinforces many of Che's impressions. Since 1945, Dedijer claims, most guerrilla fighting has taken
place in poor, agricultural regions of the world. It has been the form
of peasant revolutions everywhere and must be understood in a social
context of low living standards, agrarian life-styles, and primitive technology. The guerrilla warrior is basically a social reformer; while the
guerrilla army itself may be small relative to the total population and
to the government's own armed forces, public support for the guerrilla
movement is generally widespread. For guerrilla wars to become more
than minor instances of political violence, the masses must become involved in some aspect of a revolutionary movement and provide active
support for the revolutionary army. Hence, a guerrilla struggle can be
mounted only when a large proportion of the population wants a radical
change in the conditions of economic and social life.

Strategically, Dedijer claims that the unorthodox tactics of guerrilla
warriors make them virtually immune to conventional armed attack.
They move by sabotage of the local government and interference with
transportation and communication more than by armed maneuvers

against an opposing force, and if they succeed because of popular support, conventional armed opposition is likely only to drive more people into the guerrilla camp. Dedijer concludes in words prophetic of the American tragedy in Vietnam:

> To sum up, guerrilla warfare is likely to remain militarily viable, whatever weapons are used to combat it, unless those weapons are so morally indefensible or indiscriminately destructive that the user forfeits all his political purposes. . . . In this sense, it represents the eternal truth that you cannot destroy a political belief without killing, one by one, all the people who possess it.

Counterinsurgency warfare, which attempts to frustrate guerrilla struggles, seems to be justifiable only rarely, since to succeed it would have to resort to indiscriminate destruction of soldiers and civilians alike. Thus many following the claims of Dedijer and Guevara view guerrilla fighters as usually justified in their fight and counterinsurgency soldiers as unjustified. But there is another side to this issue, which is touched on in Potter's lecture in section 1. That is the question whether guerrilla warriors themselves should bear the blame for using tactics that destroy the distinction between soldier and civilian. Guerrilla partisans like Guevara and Dedijer tend to assume that the noble purpose of some guerrillas gives them a license to break the moral rules of war, for example, by knifing school teachers or local magistrates or by burrowing under civilian villages for refuge. This claim deserves careful thought rather than blind, sometimes romantic, acceptance.

The final selection in this section, from Kenneth W. Grundy's book *Guerrilla Struggle in Africa,* attempts to explain guerrilla warfare as a reaction to "systemic frustration," or a condition in which the majority of people in a given population believe that they cannot win the social and economic rewards they think they deserve within the established political system. Grundy argues that guerrilla struggle is a kind of "political violence," and thus is more analogous to civil insurrections or ghetto riots than to international war. His analytical model of guerrilla struggles is based on a model of political violence proposed by the political scientist Ted Gurr in *Why Men Rebel.* The key feature of this model violence is the guerrillas' reliance on "perceived relative deprivation" as the principal cause of violence. Gurr defines relative deprivation as

> actors' perception of discrepancy between their value expectations and their value capabilities. Value expectations are the goods and conditions of life to which people believe they are rightfully entitled. Value capa-

bilities are the goods and conditions they think they are capable of getting and keeping [within the political structure which then exists.] [1]

According to this account, guerrilla war is to be understood as a natural outgrowth of severely oppressive social and economic conditions that fail to change as rapidly as the expectations of those who are subject to them. In applying this concept to contemporary Africa, Grundy suggests that the potential for guerrilla warfare is increasing with the disparity between rich and poor, and argues that it is to the underlying economic and political questions that those concerned with controlling war should direct their attention.

Grundy's study has several implications regarding the morality of guerrilla war. It supports the claims of Dedijer and Guevara that guerrilla struggle is often a reaction against social injustice, but it also underscores the anarchic character and unmanageability of guerrilla fighting. Despite the moralism of Dedijer and Guevara, the moral status of guerrilla war remains at least open to question depending on the situation in which it occurs.

SUGGESTIONS FOR FURTHER READING

Harry Eckstein, ed., *Internal War: Problems and Approaches*. New York: Free Press, 1964.

Franz Fanon, *The Wretched of the Earth*. New York: Grove Press, 1963.

John Gerassi, ed., *Venceremos! The Speeches and Writings of Che Guevara*. New York: Macmillan, 1968.

Vo Nguyen Giap, *People's War, People's Army*. Hanoi: Foreign Languages Publishing House, 1961.

Ted Robert Gurr, *Why Men Rebel*. Princeton: Princeton University Press, 1970.

H. L. Nieburg, *Political Violence*. New York: St. Martin's Press, 1969.

Franklin Mark Osanka, ed., *Modern Guerrilla Warfare: Fighting Communist Movements, 1941–1961*. New York: Free Press, 1962.

John S. Pustay, *Counterinsurgency Warfare*. New York: Free Press, 1965.

Paul Ramsey, *The Just War*. New York: Scribner's, 1968.

Eric Wolf, *Peasant Wars in the Twentieth Century*. New York: Harper and Row, 1970.

[1] Ted Robert Gurr, *Why Men Rebel* (Princeton, N.J.: Princeton University Press, 1970), p. 24.

Guerrilla Warfare

CHE GUEVARA

The armed victory of the Cuban people over the Batista dictatorship was not only the triumph of heroism as reported by the newspapers of the world; it also forced a change in the old dogmas concerning the conduct of the popular masses of Latin America. It showed plainly the capacity of the people to free themselves by means of guerrilla warfare from a government that oppresses them.

We consider that the Cuban Revolution contributed three fundamental lessons to the conduct of revolutionary movements in America. They are:

1. Popular forces can win a war against the army.
2. It is not necessary to wait until all conditions for making revolution exist; the insurrection can create them.
3. In underdeveloped America the countryside is the basic area for armed fighting.

Of these three propositions the first two contradict the defeatist attitude of revolutionaries or pseudo-revolutionaries who remain inactive and take refuge in the pretext that against a professional army nothing

From *Guerrilla Warfare,* by Che Guevara (New York: Monthly Review Press, 1961), pp. 15–20. Copyright © 1968 by Monthly Review Press, Inc. Reprinted by permission. Footnotes have been omitted. Ernesto "Che" Guevara was a leader of the Cuban revolution and spokesman for guerrilla causes throughout Latin America.

can be done, who sit down to wait until in some mechanical way all necessary objective and subjective conditions are given without working to accelerate them. As these problems were formerly a subject of discussion in Cuba, until facts settled the question, they are probably still much discussed in America.

Naturally, it is not to be thought that all conditions for revolution are going to be created through the impulse given to them by guerrilla activity. It must always be kept in mind that there is a necessary minimum without which the establishment and consolidation of the first center is not practicable. People must see clearly the futility of maintaining the fight for social goals within the framework of civil debate. When the forces of oppression come to maintain themselves in power against established law, peace is considered already broken.

In these conditions popular discontent expresses itself in more active forms. An attitude of resistance finally crystallizes in an outbreak of fighting, provoked initially by the conduct of the authorities.

Where a government has come into power through some form of popular vote, fraudulent or not, and maintains at least an appearance of constitutional legality, the guerrilla outbreak cannot be promoted, since the possibilities of peaceful struggle have not yet been exhausted.

The third proposition is a fundamental of strategy. It ought to be noted by those who maintain dogmatically that the struggle of the masses is centered in city movements, entirely forgetting the immense participation of the country people in the life of all the underdeveloped parts of America. Of course the struggles of the city masses of organized workers should not be underrated; but their real possibilities of engaging in armed struggle must be carefully analyzed where the guarantees which customarily adorn our constitutions are suspended or ignored. In these conditions the illegal workers' movements face enormous dangers. They must function secretly without arms. The situation in the open country is not so difficult. There, in places beyond the reach of the repressive forces, the inhabitants can be supported by the armed guerrillas.

We will later make a careful analysis of these three conclusions that stand out in the Cuban revolutionary experience. We emphasize them now at the beginning of this work as our fundamental contribution.

Guerrilla warfare, the basis of the struggle of a people to redeem itself, has diverse characteristics, different facets, even though the essential will for liberation remains the same. It is obvious—and writers on the theme have said it many times—that war responds to a certain series of scientific laws; whoever ignores them will go down to defeat. Guerrilla warfare as a phase of war must be ruled by all of these; but besides, because of its special aspects, a series of corollary laws must also be recognized in order to carry it forward. Though geographical and social conditions in each country determine the mode and particular forms that guerrilla warfare will take, there are general laws that hold for all fighting of this type.

Our task at the moment is to find the basic principles of this kind of fighting and the rules to be followed by peoples seeking liberation; to develop theory from facts; to generalize and give structure to our experience for the profit of others.

Let us first consider the question: who are the combatants in guerrilla warfare? On one side we have a group composed of the oppressor and his agents, the professional army, well armed and disciplined, in many cases receiving foreign help as well as the help of the bureaucracy in the employ of the oppressor. On the other side are the people of the nation or region involved. It is important to emphasize that guerrilla warfare is a war of the masses, a war of the people. The guerrilla band is an armed nucleus, the fighting vanguard of the people. It draws its great force from the mass of the people themselves. The guerrilla band is not to be considered inferior to the army against which it fights simply because it is inferior in fire power. Guerrilla warfare is used by the side which is supported by a majority but which possesses a much smaller number of arms for use in defense against oppression.

The guerrilla fighter needs full help from the people of the area. This is an indispensable condition. This is clearly seen by considering the case of bandit gangs that operate in a region. They have all the characteristics of a guerrilla army, homogeneity, respect for the leader, valor, knowledge of the ground, and, often, even good understanding of the tactics to be employed. The only thing missing is support of the people; and, inevitably, these gangs are captured and exterminated by the public force.

Analyzing the mode of operation of the guerrilla band, seeing its form of struggle and understanding its base in the masses, we can answer the question: why does the guerrilla fighter fight? We must come to the inevitable conclusion that the guerrilla fighter is a social reformer, that he takes up arms responding to the angry protest of the people against their oppressors, and that he fights in order to change the social system that keeps all his unarmed brothers in ignominy and misery. He launches himself against the conditions of the reigning instituitons at a particular moment and dedicates himself with all the vigor that circumstances permit to breaking the mold of these institutions.

When we analyze more fully the tactic of guerrilla warfare, we will see that the guerrilla fighter needs to have a good knowledge of the surrounding countryside, the paths of entry and escape, the possibilities of speedy maneuver, good hiding places; naturally also, he must count on the support of the people. All this indicates that the guerrilla fighter will carry out his action in wild places of small population. Since in these places the struggle of the people for reforms is aimed primarily and almost exclusively at changing the social form of land ownership, the guerrilla fighter is above all an agrarian revolutionary. He interprets the desires of the great peasant mass to be owners of land, owners of their means of production, of their animals, of all that which they have long yearned to call their own, of that which constitutes their life and will also serve as their cemetery.

It should be noted that in current interpretations there are two different types of guerrilla warfare, one of which—a struggle complementing great regular armies such as was the case of the Ukrainian fighters in the Soviet Union—does not enter into this analysis. We are interested in the other type, the case of an armed group engaged in struggle against the constituted power, whether colonial or not, which establishes itself as the only base and which builds itself up in rural areas. In all such cases, whatever the ideological aims that may inspire the fight, the economic aim is determined by the aspiration toward ownership of land.

The China of Mao begins as an outbreak of worker groups in the South, which is defeated and almost annihilated. It succeeds in establishing itself and begins its advance only when, after the long march from Yenan, it takes up its base in rural territories and makes agrarian reform its fundamental goal. The struggle of Ho Chi Minh is based in the rice-growing peasants, who are oppressed by the French colonial yoke; with this force it is going forward to the defeat of the colonists. In both cases there is a framework of patriotic war against the Japanese invader, but the economic basis of a fight for the land has not disappeared. In the case of Algeria, the grand idea of Arab nationalism has its economic counterpart in the fact that nearly all of the arable land of Algeria is utilized by a million French settlers. In some countries, such as Puerto Rico, where the special conditions of the island have not permitted a guerrilla outbreak, the nationalist spirit, deeply wounded by the discrimination that is daily practiced, has as its basis the aspiration of the peasants (even though many of them are already a proletariat) to recover the land that the Yankee invader seized from them. This same central idea, though in different forms, inspired the small farmers, peasants, and slaves of the eastern estates of Cuba to close ranks and defend together the right to possess land during the thirty-year war of liberation.

Taking account of the possibilities of development of guerrilla warfare, which is transformed with the increase in the operating potential of the guerrilla band into a war of positions, this type of warfare, despite its special character, is to be considered as an embryo, a prelude, of the other. The possibilities of growth of the guerrilla band and of changes in the mode of fight until conventional warfare is reached, are as great as the possibilities of defeating the enemy in each of the different battles, combats, or skirmishes that take place. Therefore, the fundamental principle is that no battle, combat, or skirmish is to be fought unless it will be won. There is a malevolent definition that says: "The guerrilla fighter is the Jesuit of warfare." By this is indicated a quality of secretiveness, of treachery, of surprise that is obviously an essential element of guerrilla warfare. It is a special kind of Jesuitism, naturally prompted by circumstances, which necessitates acting at certain moments in ways different from the romantic and sporting conceptions with which we are taught to believe war is fought.

War is always a struggle in which each contender tries to annihilate the other. Besides using force, they will have recourse to all possible tricks and stratagems in order to achieve the goal. Military strategy and tactics are a representation by analysis of the objectives of the groups and of the means of achieving these objectives. These means contemplate taking advantage of all the weak points of the enemy. The fighting action of each individual platoon in a large army in a war of positions will present the same characteristics as those of the guerrilla band. It uses secretiveness, treachery, and surprise; and when these are not present, it is because vigilance on the other side prevents surprise. But since the guerrilla band is a division unto itself, and since there are large zones of territory not controlled by the enemy, it is always possible to carry out guerrilla attacks in such a way as to assure surprise; and it is the duty of the guerrilla fighter to do so.

"Hit and run" some call this scornfully, and this is accurate. Hit and run, wait, lie in ambush, again hit and run, and thus repeatedly, without giving any rest to the enemy. There is in all this, it would appear, a negative quality, an attitude of retreat, of avoiding frontal fights. However, this is consequent upon the general strategy of guerrilla warfare, which is the same in its ultimate end as of any warfare: to win, to annihilate the enemy.

Thus it is clear that guerrilla warfare is a phase that does not afford in itself opportunities to arrive at complete victory. It is one of the initial phases of warfare and will develop continuously until the guerrilla army in its steady growth acquires the characteristics of a regular army. At that moment it will be ready to deal final blows to the enemy and to achieve victory. Triumph will always be the produce of a regular army, even though its origins are in a guerrilla army.

Just as the general of a division in a modern war does not have to die in front of his soliders, the guerrilla fighter, who is general of himself, need not die in every battle. He is ready to give his life, but the positive quality of this guerrilla warfare is precisely that each one of the guerrilla fighters is ready to die, not to defend an ideal, but rather to convert it into reality. This is the basis, the essence of guerrilla fighting. Miraculously, a small band of men, the armed vanguard of the great popular force that supports them, goes beyond the immediate tactical objective, goes on decisively to achieve an ideal, to establish a new society, to break the old molds of the outdated, and to achieve, finally, the social justice for which they fight.

Considered thus, all these disparaged qualities acquire a true nobility, the nobility of the end at which they aim; and it becomes clear that we are not speaking of distorted means of reaching an end. This fighting attitude, this attitude of not being dismayed at any time, this inflexibility when confronting the great problems in the final objective is also the nobility of the guerrilla fighter.

Guerrilla Warfare:
The Poor Man's Power

VLADIMIR DEDIJER

Among people in the industrially advanced countries fears about future wars tend to focus on nuclear weapons carried by long-range missiles, on other possible methods of mass destruction, and on the dangers of open conflict between major powers such as the United States and the Soviet Union, or others. But to be concerned only with the threat of worldwide thermonuclear war is to ignore the character of actual warfare since 1945. Guerrilla wars have been in progress, more or less continuously, in one part of the world or another, but always in economically underdeveloped countries. We can see such wars continuing today and, looking at the world of the future, one can only predict a series of guerrilla wars arising from the grave social unrest that is latent in large regions of the earth.

It is a potent form of warfare available to the most technically backward populations and scarcely susceptible at all to control by international treaty or other disarmament measures. If the nuclear stalemate continues between the major powers, guerrilla warfare will persist as the principal military factor of our time. As we have seen in the recent past, major powers may be drawn into antiguerrilla operations; in turn

From *Unless Peace Comes,* edited by by Nigel Calder (New York: Viking Press, 1968), pp. 18–29. Reprinted by permission of Grossman Publishers. Dedijer, a historian, was a senior officer in Tito's guerrilla army in Yugoslavia during World War II.

there may be intervention on behalf of the guerrillas so that, superficially, the struggle may come to resemble a conventional war. There is an ever-present risk that what begins as a revolutionary civil war may grow and grow until major powers are in open conflict. With a view both to avoiding errors in response to guerrilla outbreaks and, above all, to dispel conditions in which such outbreaks are likely to occur, it is essential to understand the character and motives of guerrilla warfare. Only on that basis, too, is it possible to approach the question of how and where guerrilla warfare may be waged in the future.

GUERRILLA WARS OF THE RECENT PAST

The distinction between guerrilla warfare and other military and paramilitary activities they may resemble is best illustrated from experiences in occupied Europe during World War II. Then, we witnessed various forms of resistance against German rule, but not all of them could be described as guerrilla warfare. In each occupied country the resistance movement had its own special style and waged war in its own way. Some of these actions assumed the character of national wars continued after military defeat, with the sole purpose of ending the German rule. Such was the case particularly in industrialized countries with good national and social cohesion (Norway, Denmark, the Netherlands, Belgium, and France). There was little or no purpose beyond the defeat of the Germans; no major change in the social patterns of these countries followed the end of German occupation. The forms of resistance in these countries could not be identified with the classical concept of guerrilla warfare, as I interpret it or as it will figure in the world of the future. To be sure, techniques used by these movements had much in common with those of guerrilla warfare: the use of irregular troops; reliance on elusiveness, knowledge of the local terrain, and sympathy from a large section of the civilian population; sabotage and ambush; capture of arms and supplies from the enemy. But both the motives and organization of these resistance activities lacked the political and revolutionary character of guerrilla warfare.

Consider now the economically underdeveloped parts of Europe during World War II. In these countries, particularly those of southern Europe, there were preexisting social and political conflicts when the Germans or Italians occupied them. Here the resistance assumed much more clearly political forms, and in Yugoslavia, Albania, and Greece a species of guerrilla warfare appeared. Because these countries were economically backward there was little or no working class in the historical sense of the term; the guerrilla movements found their social basis in the peasantry, by far the most numerous part of the populations.

Guerrilla warfare in these countries was not exclusively military in purpose, in the technical sense of the defeat of the German occupying forces. It was also aimed at the destruction of preexisting institutions, either domestic or foreign in origin, that represented barriers to social emancipation within the countries. The guerrilla fighter was thus, basically, a social reformer. In the very process of fighting, new institutions were created, particularly the new type of army, molded from the guerrilla units with an eye to its social and political character as well as to the special strategy and tactics of guerrilla warfare.

The nature of the guerrilla war depended as much upon circumstance as upon ideology. Although the Communist Party took the leading role in Yugoslavia, for example, the warfare there was quite different from the operations of the partisans in the occupied parts of the Soviet Union. Soviet resistance behind the German lines was the strongest in occupied Europe, both in terms of the number of partisans and in the style of the military operations, but the Soviet partisans were an auxiliary arm of the Red Army, centrally directed, with the particular task of harassing the rear of the German army and its lines of communication, in concert with the operations of the regular army and with specific tactical aims. By contrast, the guerrilla army in Yugoslavia was self-created and had no regular army on which to depend. It was a new kind of army, springing out of a revolutionary situation in occupied Yugoslavia. New civil organs of power were formed, together with the new army.

The strength of the guerrilla movements in Yugoslavia, Albania, and Greece, compared with those of other economically underdeveloped countries of occupied Europe, needs some explanation. Spontaneous resistance by the population at large is of primary importance because, without it, organized resistance cannot prosper. But spontaneous resistance is not sufficient; only when backed with ideology and organization did it bear fruit. But the guerrilla ideology had to match the mood of the majority of the population, typically in the national aim of eliminating not only German rule but also all foreign influences and the social structures linked to them. It also had to be an ideology matching the facts of life. Resistance movements survived when there was no discrepancy between ethical principles and real life; otherwise they were subject to internal crisis.

With the origins of guerrilla warfare lying in the spontaneous resistance and social discontents of the general population, on whom it depends for active support, it follows that measures of intimidation or reprisal by the opposing regular forces have the opposite effect to what is intended by them. In Europe, when political and organizational factors favored the guerrilla movement, reprisals by the Germans lead, not to secure rule over masses, but, on the contrary, to even more determined revolt than before, with more of the population joining the guerrillas. As a general principle in guerrilla warfare, manpower is fundamental to victory, and is to be valued above control of territory. A guerrilla war is essentially a psychological and political war. The decisive role of morale in warfare is nowhere so obvious as in a guerrilla movement, which is usually confronted by strong enemy forces equipped with powerful weapons and having total command of the air.

But a guerrilla war is not a closed system, immune to other world events. Comparison of the outcome for the Yugoslav and Greek movements shows the influence of the Soviet Union, the United Kingdom, and the United States, which had carried the main burden in the war against Germany. After 1941 the Adriatic region was not regarded by the Allies, or the Germans for that matter, as a major theater of war. The guerrilla warfare sprang up before any direct aid was delivered by the Allies; when aid came, it was of political importance but only secondarily significant from a military point of view. Yet the eventual success of the movements was settled by secret agreements between the Soviet Union, the United Kingdom, and the United States, concerning the division of influence in liberated Europe. Greece was put firmly in the Western sphere of influence, and the Soviet Union refused to intervene when British troops crushed the Greek resistance movement in December 1944; the social revolution for which the guerrillas had fought did not occur. Similar motives led Moscow to send instructions to Palmiro Togliatti that the Italian partisans were not to occupy the factories of Turin and Milan, at the end of the war. Yusoslavia, on the other hand, was "fifty-fifty" in relation to the Eastern and Western spheres of influence, and no doubt this fact was of great importance in allowing the final political success of the Yugoslav guerrilla war.

Since 1945 guerrilla warfare has exhibited almost all the features I have ascribed to it in the narrow European context. It has occurred in the economically underdeveloped countries of Africa and Southeast Asia and in Cuba, all inhabited by peasant masses. It has been nationalist in spirit, directed against colonial rule or domestic governments dominated by foreign influences. The conditions for success are still the same: for example, the guerrilla movement cannot thrive in a countryside that does not give them active support. In Malaya most of the guerrillas were Chinese and represented a minority of the local population; they were defeated. In post-1945 guerrilla movements, as in Eu-

rope, severe retaliatory measures by the opposing forces have strengthened rather than weakened the guerrillas.

Successful guerrilla warfare is essentially an art of the undogmatic
and the original-minded social reformer. The political springs of guerrilla
warfare have changed since 1945; Communists have not the special
place they had in the European guerrilla wars. In Cuba guerrilla warfare against the former regime was started against the wishes of the
Cuban Communist Party. During the Algerian war, the French Communist Party took no strong action in support of the Algerian guerrillas,
even though it was backed by one-fifth of the French electorate and
could have called general strikes or sought to subvert French troops in
Algeria. The party's behavior was similar during the French army's
struggle with the guerrillas in Indo-China.

It would indeed be rash to generalize about the political or geopoliti-
cal connotations of guerrilla movements, or seek to apply some conspiratorial theory of history to them. Despite many similarities of conditions
and governing principles, the movements in Cuba, Algeria, and Vietnam have differed markedly in their historical, social, and international
traits. The relations or conflicts between guerrilla movements and great
powers are, as in the case of Europe, very important but not necessarily
decisive. In particular, material aid from outside is not vital for guerrillas who are accustomed to seizing their arms from the enemy and otherwise living a very simple life. (For the same reasons, any policy of
bombing supposed "lines of communication" is likely to be futile.)

On the other hand, the established rule and institutions against which
guerrilla warfare is directed are characteristically dependent on foreign
support—political, financial, material, and often military, too. Without
such support the war could not continue because if, as we have defined
it, a guerrilla movement matches the political wishes of the general
populations, the existing government could not survive; in other words,
the event would be a brief revolution rather than a protracted guerrilla
war. There are now few nations on earth in which some great power
does not have an interest in maintaining the existing regime, for the
principle of "spheres of influence" now extends far from the Elbe and
Adriatic. Therefore, in many countries, one would predict that attempts
at social revolution would lead to long-drawn-out guerrilla wars.

THE FOCI OF REVOLUTION

Reformist revolutions do not occur in countries with broadly contented
populations, such as the industrialized "welfare states." Standards of
living of the industrially advanced countries are rising continuously.

These countries have good reason to feel materially contented, though perhaps their consciences should be uneasy. With one-sixth of the world's population they dispose of three-quarters of the world's wealth, as measured by gross income. The gap is widening between the developed and underdeveloped countries.

In many underdeveloped countries, in Latin America, Southeast Asia, and parts of Africa, the social tensions associated with economic backwardness are potentially explosive. Not only is the theoretical average income very low by the standards of the industrially advanced countries, but great inequalities may exist in the distribution of that income because of the social and economic structures of the nations concerned. These structures may also be a positive impediment to increase in national wealth, because the strata of society that, by virtue of conservative patriarchal, tribal, and feudal relations, controls the surplus wealth is not prepared to invest it productively in modern ways. Just as the gap between rich and poor nations is widening, so are the richer sectors of some underdeveloped countries becoming richer while the poor grow poorer. These sources of strain are compounded with the effects of the population explosion, and the outlook for the world's poor is indeed bitter. Populations will tend to grow most rapidly in the very countries where the people are poorest; in the underdeveloped regions as a whole, the rate of growth is expected to be twice as great as in the industrialized countries.

The statistics of world poverty and exploding populations, and grim evidence at times of crisis and famine of the human realities that underlie the statistics, have long been available to the great powers. Yet they have failed to agree on a common plan for massive aid without political "strings," which would accelerate development and release hundreds of millions of people from the tightening grip of despair. Relatively little aid is available from truly "neutral" sources such as the United Nations. Aid given bilaterally, even with subjectively pure and humane motives, will tend to be seen as politically motivated by dissident elements within the receiving country—as a foreign influence of the very kind that bolsters the existing regime, the kind that nationalist guerrilla wars are fought to end. Similarly, investments of foreign capital, useful though they may be in strictly economic terms, may well become a focus for nationalist and revolutionary discontent, especially if the profits are exported and if the investors form a political alliance with the regime. Many commentators treat multilateral (United Nations) and bilateral aid as though they were merely interchangeable sources of funds for economic development, without appreciating the great subjective differences, from the viewpoint of a nationalist rebel. In short, economic aid with conscious or unconscious political connotations, just as much as military and political assistance, may reinforce rather than diminish the unrest in the poor countries of the world, even though massive economic aid is the only way of removing the long-term economic causes of the unrest.

Unless there is a fresh, concerted approach to world development, by the powerful and rich countries of East and West, neither the scale nor the manner of economic assistance is likely to prevent violent outbreaks of guerrilla-style warfare in country after country, as poverty and exploitation become worse than the peasantry will tolerate. I have already mentioned Latin America, Southeast Asia, and parts of Africa as the principal regions where such wars must be expected. Today, the population of Latin America is about 200 million; by the year 2000, it will be about 500 million, unless famine supervenes. It is simply not credible that such growth can occur without major social changes in the countries of Latin America. If those changes are not brought about voluntarily by the ruling strata, popular revolutions will occur. As it is unlikely that they will be allowed to take their course swiftly and without foreign intervention, long and terrible guerrilla wars will ensue.

GUERRILLA WARFARE AND NEW WEAPONS

A general feature of guerrilla warfare is as plain in Vietnam in the 1960s as it was in Algeria in the 1950s or Yugoslavia in the 1940s. It is that technical superiority in arms and logistic support possessed by the forces opposing the guerrillas is quite unimportant in determining the outcome of the war. A second general feature is that military commanders tend to be blind to the true character of a guerrilla movement that they are fighting, and that they make the same political, psychological, and tactical mistakes over and over again. This is not the place to discuss guerrilla strategy and tactics in general, but something should be said about their relation to the fearsome new weapons that military science and technology are making available to regular forces.

From a military point of view the art of guerrilla warfare is largely a matter of improvisation and opportunism. As I have mentioned, greater importance attaches to conserving manpower than to holding ground. With this principle in mind, the guerrilla is always ready, if need be, to run away and hide. Consequently, when regular ground or air forces attack with powerful modern weapons, the guerrilla makes it his business not to be present. It is possible that areas of open country which are regularly patrolled on the ground or surveyed from the air will be entirely denied to him, unless he moves in the guise of a civilian. The use of chemical agents to defoliate trees may rob the guerrilla of cover in some places. A massive sweep through a particular area by the regular forces may force him out of it, temporarily. The important point is that, unless the regular forces are prepared to lay waste to the entire country, with nuclear weapons, for example (which cannot correspond with any rational political goal), there will always be somewhere for the guerrilla to conceal himself from attack by modern weapons systems. From his hiding place he can emerge at a moment of his own choosing to attack the enemy at a vulnerable point. The only strategy open to the regular forces is to attempt to eliminate the guerrillas, one by one, in infantry engagements over a huge area and a long period of time. The war becomes uncontrollably large and costly in lives and materials for the regular forces.

If the guerrilla movement (by our earlier definition) is supported by a large section of the population, it has a reservoir of manpower on which to draw. Clumsy, destructive, and impatient action by the regular forces will always tend to drive civilians into the guerrilla camps. A characteristic of advanced and powerful weapons systems by land and air seems to be that, despite the allegedly "sophisticated" electronic systems for fire control, the impression at the target is of clumsiness and purposeless destruction. For this reason advanced weapons systems may be much more of a liability than an asset in antiguerrilla warfare. And even if some highly lethal new weapon, such as a nerve gas or an infectious microorganism, were used effectively against the guerrillas, that local military victory of the regular forces would be bought at a price of moral catastrophe that would make political victory utterly impossible.

A secondary consideration about the use of advanced or novel weapons against guerrillas is that, as the guerrillas rely largely upon captured arms, these weapons, too, are quite likely to fall into their hands and be turned upon the original owners.

To sum up, guerrilla warfare is likely to remain militarily viable, whatever weapons are used to combat it, unless those weapons are so morally indefensible or indiscriminately destructive that the user forfeits all his political purposes. The well-organized guerrilla movement in a country of reasonable size, based on popular support, is indestructible except by enormously costly and protracted infantry warfare which is almost beyond the resources of even the biggest nations. In this sense, it represents the eternal truth that you cannot destroy a political belief without killing, one by one, all the people who possess it. That is something that no scientific advances in weaponry can alter, even though they make the killing easier to accomplish.

The Causes of Political Violence

KENNETH W. GRUNDY

AN ABBREVIATED MODEL OF POLITICAL VIOLENCE

Not all violence is politically motivated. Nor is all violence necessarily important to the political system. Likewise, all political violence cannot be termed guerrilla warfare. Guerrilla warfare is a specific form of political violence characterized by a high degree of organization, political involvement, dedication, focus, and fairly explicit goals. Nevertheless, it is a form of political violence and for guerrilla warfare to be perceived as a viable policy alternative by political dissidents, certain conditions associated with the broader generic category of political violence must prevail. It becomes necessary, then, to sketch a simplified and abbreviated model of political violence that will be applicable to our discussion of guerrilla warfare in Africa.

Perhaps the term "model" is a little formalistic here, as it implies a more technical meaning than is intended. "Formulations" might be more in order, since what follows is a loose, suggestive set of conceptualizations. But for my basic purpose—that of outlining a set of interrelated

From *Guerrilla Struggle in Africa: An Analysis and Preview,* by Kenneth W. Grundy (New York: Grossman Publishers, 1971), pp. 7–26. Copyright © 1971 by World Law Fund. Reprinted by permission of Grossman Publishers. Grundy, a political scientist and specialist on current African affairs, teaches at Case Western Reserve University.

and interacting variables—it is best, probably, to persevere with the term "model," since it conveys with more precision what I am attempting to accomplish. To the specialist this brief model will appear to be inadequate. Certainly there are numerous variables that have some effect on political violence and that have been excluded here, but to include all variables that have some effect on the system would be to create a model so complex as to be useless for our purposes.[1]

Political violence, the dependent variable, is here taken to mean physical attacks upon persons or property associated with the political or civil order.[2] To be sure, it is equally important to recognize that regime violence (i.e., attacks by or sanctioned by the established order on various elements of the population) is a form of political violence, but for our purposes antisystemic violence is the phenomenon we are chiefly concerned with. Regime violence is an important factor affecting the total magnitude of antisystemic political violence and will be treated shortly rather than be included in this particular definition. When men become frustrated in the pursuit of their goals, they experience a state of mind known as anger and manifested as aggressive behavior. Although such aggression may be internalized (i.e., directed against self) or externalized, it is the externalized version that we seek to understand. Naturally, the extent and nature of frustration varies, and with it aggressive behavior varies. What we are concerned with here are the conditions by which aggression may take violent forms aimed at the established political order. Frustration with the established order is the independent variable and will be dealt with in more detail in a subsequent section of this chapter. Suffice to say at this point that such systemic frustration occurs when persons feel that things they value are threatened by the sociopolitical system. The crucial consideration here is the matter of *perception* rather than the actual cause of the frustration itself. By and large, the major form that systemic frustration takes in Africa is that perceived as denying the attainment of values which the frustrated individual does not possess, but which he has been conditioned to desire and believes that he can attain. Occasionally, individuals perceive that the political system is seeking to take away something they value and already possess, but the expression of political violence in this form is usually associated with the coup d'état (military or by some

---

[1] For the reader who desires a more complete and rigorous product, consult Ted Robert Gurr, *Why Men Rebel* (Princeton, N.J.: Princeton University Press, 1970).

[2] I am indebted to my colleague, Professor Don R. Bowen, for conversations relevant to these issues and to his unpublished paper, "A Model of Civil Violence," as a basis for the following discussion.

élite group) or with primordial turmoil. Though the latter variety (primordial turmoil) may find expression in some form of guerrilla warfare, the likelihood of its success is limited given the narrow base of its appeal.

But seeking to isolate the conditions that frustrate men is not, in itself, explanatory. We know that men are often frustrated, at least to some degree. We know as well that large numbers of persons may be frustrated and discontented, but may not engage in violent, antisystemic behavior. It becomes necessary to locate additional determinants that serve to increase or decrease the likelihood of violent behavior. Six intervening variables come to mind: (1) the force capabilities of both the regime and the dissidents; (2) the legitimacy of both the regime and those who seek to replace the regime; (3) the norms relating to violence in a system; (4) the factors external to the domestic political system in question; (5) the ideology of the potential dissidents; and (6) the leadership available to the contestants. Each will be dealt with separately.

Severe disparities in the distribution of the means of coercion, particularly if they favor the established order, tend to minimize the likelihood of political violence. If the dissidents possess an overwhelming preponderance of force, it is likely that a single act, usually in the form of a coup, will be adequate to topple the regime. In either case, the total magnitude of political violence will probably be low. More frequently, when systemic frustration is acute, the capability levels of the contending forces are likely to be more symmetrical; in that event, the extent of political violence is likely to be high, and its form will resemble internal war, as opposed to anomic or disorganized turmoil. Such a result precipitates further systemic frustration, and the familiar cycle continues. The Debray thesis of guerrilla warfare is based on the explicit technique of launching military action so that the act of warfare will serve as a catalyst to instigate further frustration and facilitate mobilization of popular discontent.

A legitimate regime is one whose subjects accept its right to rule. When a government enjoys this quality of rightful rule, its goals and policies are generally regarded as proper. The value of legitimacy is that such a regime need not maintain itself primarily by force. Thus, if a regime is perceived to be legitimate, the level of political violence is low, at least among that segment of the population so recognizing legitimacy. It should be clear, however, that two additional features of the quality of legitimacy bear mention. One is that legitimacy is divisible: some segments of society may regard the regime as legitimate at the same time that other segments are convinced of the absence of its right to rule. A fruitful and common avenue for the analysis of political violence is to explore the nature and depth of the divided indicators of legitimacy.[3] A second aspect of legitimacy refers to its temporal quality. The distribution of the perceptions, as well as the intensity of the feelings, can decline or increase with time. Repeated acts (or failures to act) that outrage a society's sense of right may forfeit or bring legitimacy into question. If legitimacy is withheld as an outcome of increasing systemic frustration, political violence grows and the regime must find alternative sources of support. The reaction is often a spread of regime violence and an augmentation of force capabilities on both sides. Both the regime and the potential dissidents at this point are caught up in the problem of establishing their claims to rightful rule. Attempts at coercive social control by the regime (and challengers, on occasion) may occur when it perceives that its support is diminishing. Depending on how the established order employs force, the result may be a widening of feelings of systemic frustration or the establishment of an artificial and ominous calm. Securing the data for assessing the various levels of perceived legitimacy is, at this point, nearly impossible.

A third intervening variable refers to the ways in which the various societies and segments of societies view violence as a political means. Various cultures possess structures of norms governing the use of violence. These may not necessarily be explicit, but they can be studied. A culture may, rather than sanction violent behavior, provide alternate channels to vent anger and frustration—channels which represent no challenge to the established system. Even within a given culture various subgroups may be sanctioned to behave differently with regard to violence. The societal norms affecting violence and the provision of approved, substitute outlets for aggressive feelings deeply affect the magnitude of political violence. These elements must, if at all possible, be explored with regard to various African cultures.

External factors can take numerous forms. The initial spark for the political unrest can originate outside the target system. Direct military and economic aid and assistance to either the dissidents or the regime or both can serve to affect the duration and intensity of political violence, and of course, the ultimate outcome of the contest. We have been told countless times of the importance of an accessible sanctuary for guerrilla forces. Unrest abroad likewise has a demonstration effect on both parties. Ideas and examples know no formal political boundaries. . . .

Ideology is a vital ingredient in any form of revolutionary behavior.

---

[3] See my paper, "Segmented Instability: An Exploration of the Problems of Comparative Analysis," delivered at the Annual Meeting of the Southern Political Science Association, Gatlinburg, Tennessee, November 10–12, 1966 (mimeo.).

Ordinary citizens whose anger and aggression stem from systemic frustration are often perplexed and even fatalistic about their emotions and the future. If they react violently, it is usually without direction or manifest purpose. The result is a series of spontaneous and disorganized acts. So, while systemic frustration is the raw material out of which revolution or internal war is manufactured, other elements must be added to the productive mix. A revolutionary ideology can perform at least four services for the disaffected population. First and most importantly, an ideology contains a set of transcendental objectives with which its adherents can agree and toward which they can labor. Second, it provides a set of images by which the real world can be interpreted. As such a system of knowledge and communication, ideology provides its adherents with an analytical prism through which they see the world and with a set of unified thought patterns that enables them to communicate with one another easily. Particularly useful for revolutionary purposes is the third possible function of ideology as an action strategy and a set of general guidelines for revolutionary behavior. Fourth, ideology serves to condone and justify violent behavior that otherwise would be rejected by traditional belief systems. Thus, ideology is a system of higher rationalization that legitimizes the behavior of its proponents and supplies a symbol of continuity with fallen leaders of the past.[4] An ideology becomes a necessary ingredient to revolutionary behavior since it galvanizes support in the individual's mind and among the committed, explains to them the cause of their frustration, focuses grievances on a single target, and convinces the faithful that change is possible, and that fatalism must be abandoned and replaced with positive action of their own making.

For these views to be translated into revolution, leaders are necessary. Not only must such leaders be dedicated and immersed in their revolutionary ideology, but they must be capable of applying it to concrete problems of policy and be imbued with the leadership skills necessary to appraise the political situation accurately and to organize and direct the movement. Without leadership, revolutionary frustrations will probably be dissipated in disoriented, sporadic, and, from the viewpoint of the established order, controllable turmoil.

---

[4] These ideas have been drawn from the excellent discussion of the variegated functions of Marxism-Leninism for Soviet foreign policy found in Vernon V. Aspaturian, "Soviet Foreign Policy," and in Roy C. Macridis (ed.), *Foreign Policy in World Politics,* 3rd ed. (Englewood Cliffs, N.J.: Prentice-Hall, 1967), pp. 65–72. See esp. the map on p. 22.

THE FOCUS OF SYSTEMIC FRUSTRATION

It now becomes necessary to apply to sections of this model data relevant to the African experience.[5] Let's first look at the independent variable, systemic frustration, to see if we can isolate, at least for analytical purposes, the conditions by which people become frustrated. We said earlier that systemic frustration arises out of feelings that people are being denied or deprived of values they regard as important. Thus we must discuss not only the objective environment, but also the psychological environment that leads to systemic frustration. What we are really concerned with is the relationship between the two environments. Since there is little data available to us regarding the psychological environment among Africans, certain inferences must be drawn on the basis of our knowledge of the objective conditions in which people function. We shall have to concentrate on the objective environment here. To be sure, the correlations between environments are not perfect. Frustration is a perceptual condition that does not always accompany actual relative deprivation. This is why the presence or absence of the intervening variables discussed above becomes so important.

There are four major sets of conditions that seem to lead directly to systemic frustration in Africa. They are: (1) the generally low level of productivity and the existence of wide inequities in the distribution of the economic values of a society; (2) the inability and unwillingness (in some cases) of the established order to cope with fundamental grievances; (3) the lack or deliberate closure of channels for the legitimate expression of discontent and for the peaceful realization of fundamental societal change; and (4) the set of frustrations related to the heterogeneity of the population. Usually systemic frustration that leads to violent behavior cannot be traced to any single condition described above, but, rather, to an often complex intermix difficult to sort out in any generalizable sense.

Relative Economic Deprivation   The relatively low level of economic productivity in Africa does not need documentation. The overall material standards of living are low by whatever criteria one wishes to apply. Within Africa there are immense disparities from state to state,

---

[5] A good, brief, generalized treatment of political conflict in Africa is Aristide R. Zolberg's "The Structure of Political Conflict in the New States of Tropical Africa," *American Political Science Review,* 62, No. 1 (March 1968), 70–87. Governmental efforts to overcome conflict patterns are treated in Zolberg's *Creating Political Order: The Party-States of West Africa* (Chicago: Rand McNally, 1966).

as we can clearly see in Table 1, which shows the average per capita incomes in African states. But data of this sort is incomplete in regard to our specific interest in political violence.

A more revealing picture can be gleaned by the realization that economic development in Africa usually radiates outward from isolated pockets, or islands, of economic activity . . . .[6] These urban and industrial-mining concentrations that propel economic growth also symptomize the tremendous inequities inherent in the uneven development of retarded and fundamentally capitalistic economies, particularly those based upon external investment or expatriate skills.

Within a given territory there are profound regional differences in the level of economic activity. Actually, it is necessary to develop this argument a step farther to trace the patterns of wealth distribution. These regional stratifications may coincide with known socioeconomic cleavages. The most obvious cleavage is between African and non-African employees in societies with racial heterogeneity. The wage levels that obtain in independent Zambia, for example, are illustrated in Table 2.

This data could be further broken down by age group, region, and ethnic group to lay bare some staggering disparities.[7] In territories where ethnic identities had been eroding, the uneven nature of economic growth has reintroduced stratification based upon primordial considerations.[8] In contrast, there are countries where divisions are growing up across traditional sociocultural lines, creating what amounts to class cleavages, unencumbered by deep ethnic, racial, linguistic, or subethnic concerns. We should not exclude the very real existence of what Mazrui calls the "trans-class man," the person who feels compelled to belong to more than one class in a situation of great structural fluidity.[9] By far the more common pattern in Africa has been ethnic and regional stratification reinforced by uneven economic development and reward. In

---

[6] This argument is carefully developed in L. P. Green and T. J. D. Fair, *Development in Africa: A Study in Regional Analysis with Special Reference to Southern Africa* (Johannesburg: Witwatersrand University Press, 1962).

[7] For detailed discussions of the resultant patterns of life, see Hortense Powdermaker, *Copper Town: Changing Africa* (New York and Evanston, Ill.: Harper and Row, 1962), esp. pp. 69–147; J. Clyde Mitchell and A. L. Epstein, "Occupational Prestige and Social Status Among Urban Africans in Northern Rhodesia," *Africa*, 29, No. 1 (January 1959), 22–40; James R. Scarritt and John L. Hatter, *Racial and Ethnic Conflict in Zambia*, Studies in Race and Nations, 2, No. 2 (Denver: Center on International Race Relations, 1970).

[8] Professor Ali A. Mazrui has discussed and labelled this problem in "Violent Contiguity and the Politics of Retribalization in Africa," *Journal of International Affairs*, 23, No. 1 (1969), 89–105.

[9] See Ali A. Mazrui, "Political Superannuation and the Trans-class Man," paper presented to the Seventh World Congress of the International Political Science Association, Brussels, September 18–23, 1967 (mimeo.).

TABLE 1

Estimated Per Capita Gross National Income, 1963–1967
(At Market Prices, $US)

Rank	Country	Year	GNI/capita
1	Libya	1967	$ 883
2	Republic of South Africa	1967	618
3	Gabon	1966	392
4	Zambia	1967	298
5	Ivory Coast	1966	256
6	Ghana	1967	252
7	Algeria	1963	245
8	Rhodesia	1967	233
9	Senegal	1966	227
10	Liberia	1966	210
11	Tunisia	1967	208
12	Morocco	1967	191
13	United Arab Republic	1966	189
14	Congo (Brazzaville)	1963	188
15	Swaziland	1966	178
16	Sierra Leone	1963	128
17	Cameroon	1963	120
18	Kenya	1967	117
19	Madagascar	1967	116
20	Central African Republic	1963	113
21	Congo (Kinshasa)	1966	108
22	Mauritania	1963	107
23	Sudan	1963	104
24	Guinea	1963	99
25	Botswana	1966	96
26	Uganda	1967	95
27	Lesotho	1966	88
28	Togo	1963	86
29–30	Gambia	1963	81
29–30	Niger	1963	81
31	Nigeria	1966	77
32–33	Dahomey	1963	75
32–33	Mali	1963	75
34	Portuguese African Territories	1963	71
35–36	Somalia	1963	69
35–36	Tanzania	1967	69
37	Chad	1963	66
38	Ethiopia	1966	64
39	Malawi	1967	51
40	Upper Volta	1966	49
41–42	Burundi	1963	40
41–42	Rwanda	1963	40
	Total, Africa	1963	140
	United States	1967	4,037
	Europe	1967	1,760

Source: United Nations, Statistical Office, Department of Economic
and Social Affairs, *Statistical Yearbook, 1968* (New York: United
Nations, 1969), Table 191.

TABLE 2
Average Annual Earnings of Employees, by Industry,
Zambia, 1966 (In Pounds)

	African			Others		
	Overall	Gov't	Private	Overall	Gov't	Private
Agriculture	88	134	71	1,548	2,148	1,172
Mining	443	—	443	3,521	—	3,521
Manufacturing	228	254	226	1,756	1,651	1,761
Construction	184	165	192	1,528	1,528	1,925
Electricity, water, and sanitary services	193	179	210	2,557	2,186	2,693
Commerce	241	263	238	1,425	1,546	1,421
Transport and communications	306	271	394	2,262	2,363	1,919
Services (excluding domestic)	223	233	181	1,431	1,605	1,053
All employees	254	214	271	2,194	1,854	2,305

Source: Data abstracted from: Republic of Zambia, Central Statistical Office, *Statistical Year-Book, 1967* (Lusaka: Government Printer, 1967), pp. 40–41.
Note: Estimates are based on earnings in the first quarter, 1966.

territories like Rhodesia, Portuguese Africa, and the Republic of South Africa, these sorts of divisions are not simply the fortuitous results of the supply and demand character of the labor market. (See Table 3 for comparable data on Rhodesia.) Rather, they have been strengthened and maintained by legislation, trade union structure, and immigration patterns, as well as by the social mores of the dominant segment of society.

Similar artificial supports for inordinate economic disparities prevail in parts of Black Africa as well.[10] The concept of relative deprivation demands further exploration here. Crawford Young deals in detail with the application of this concept to political unrest in the Congo.[11] He posits that the widespread sense of deprivation that existed in the Congo could be measured along three dimensions: in temporal space, in vertical social space between strata, and in horizontal communal space between ethnic groupings. As he sees it, the temporal dimension has two aspects, "the immediate recollection of a more ordered and materially prosperous life situation, and a utopian vision of future well-being

[10] See esp. René Dumont, *False Start in Africa* (New York: Praeger, 1966), pp. 78–97, *et passim,* who maintains this view with emotional as well as experiential conviction; P. C. Lloyd, *Africa in Social Change* (Baltimore: Penguin Books, 1967), esp. pp. 304–320; and P. C. Lloyd (ed.), *The New Élites of Tropical Africa* (London: Oxford University Press, 1966).

[11] The following analysis is drawn from Crawford Young, "Rebellion and the Congo," in Robert I. Rotberg and Ali A. Mazrui (eds.), *Protest and Power in Black Africa* (New York: Oxford University Press, 1970), pp. 969–1011.

TABLE 3

Average Annual Earnings of Employees, by Industry,
Rhodesia, 1969 (in $ Rhodesian)

Industry	Africans	Others*
Agriculture	147	2,857
Mining and quarrying	322	4,224
Manufacturing	476	3,332
Building and construction	371	3,193
Electricity and water	408	3,672
Distribution	436	2,534
Banking, insurance and finance	656	3,110
Transport and communication	638	3,394
Government administration	408	3,082
Education	544	2,700
Health	564	2,314
Private domestic services	244	1,000
Other services	390	2,243
Total	296	2,980

Source: Data abstracted from Rhodesia, Ministry of Finance, *Economic Survey of Rhodesia, 1970* (Salisbury: Government Printer, April 1970), pp. 24–25.
* Includes European, Asian and Colored Persons.

briefly generated by the explosion of terminal colonial nationalism." Thus, the promises of nationalist politicians and the generally optimistic attitudes preceding independence, and also a relative decline in living conditions for large segments of the population, served to accentuate discontent.

The social stratification dimension stems from a rapid growth in income disparities and from the disparities in access to material rewards. Those individuals able to assume occupational roles vacated by expatriates enjoyed tremendous status mobility and rewards therefrom, but only some 10,000 positions were thus available, mostly filled by clerks and military noncommissioned officers. In addition, further concentration of inflated reward positions accrued to certain political appointments and commercial entrepreneurs.

Certain obvious conclusions can be drawn from this presentation. As Young observed:

The rapid polarization of the socio-economic strata was rendered dramatic in its impact by the frequently conspicuous display of new wealth. The opulent life style of the colonial establishment served as a

reference point for the administrative bourgeoisie. . . . A rough estimate of those benefitting materially from independence might total
150,000. Awareness of the new gap between the political-administrative
class and laborers, unemployed, and peasantry was general by 1962.[12]

TABLE 4
Rise in Salaries by Social Categories, Congo, 1960–1965

Category	Nominal	Real
Civil Servants		
Auxiliaries (messengers, etc.)	498	102
Clerks	678–1073	139–219
Bureau chiefs	241	49
Permanent secretaries	153	31
Military		
Privates	414	85
Sergeants	571	117
Teachers		
Teachers	333	68
Primary teachers without degree	566	116
Private sector		
Legal minimum (bachelor)	306	63
Legal minimum (married, 3 children)	255	52

Source: Reproduced from Young, "Rebellion in the Congo," p.
979.
Note: Indexes as of December 31, 1965 has as their base June 30,
1960 = 100.

These general conditions were compounded by factors such as a
massive rise in unemployment, the growth of female militancy based on
obstructed mobility, the development in the provinces of an enormous
growth in the lower ranks of the public works system (an illusive form
of employment since it was often accompanied by pay arrearages, often
up to two years), and the presence of unemployed school leavers in
increasing numbers, with their attendant crushed dreams and their
determination to do something about their future.

The third dimension of felt relative deprivation—ethnic and regional
disparities—cuts horizontally across Congolese society. As Young puts
it: ". . . the cognitive map through which groups evaluated the distribution of social and material rewards gave a prominent place to the ethnic

---

[12] *Ibid.,* pp. 979–980.

landscape." [13] Each group, the beneficiaries of independence and those who suffered by it, maintained linkages based upon ethnicity. At the regional and local levels, as well as at the national level, movements for change and patterns of relative deprivation became identified with particular ethnic groups, or segments thereof, and these designations became increasingly self-reinforcing. Even among groups who shared the same socioeconomic grievances, divisions would occur. Economic deprivation, therefore, was not the sole determinant of support for revolutionary change. Although, in the Congolese case, most revolutionaries sprung from economically disadvantaged groups, all deprived groups did not rally to the revolutionary banner. Frequently, local animosities and traditional cleavages were simply reexpressed in socioeconomic terms. In broad terms, there was an overall division between the nodes of intense economic activity (Kinshasa/Lower Congo and Katanga Copperbelt) and the "interior," according to the pattern illustrated by Green and Fair. The tridimensional nature of relative deprivation outlined by Young helps clarify the further questions of who supported the movements and why. In terms of the model . . . , systemic frustration was widespread throughout the Congo, but the expression it took was differentiated from region to region. This extensive illustration from the Congo experience is used because the Congo has undergone virtually every variety of political violence. It is, in some respects, a microcosm and caricature of Black Africa itself. Such an analysis might be applicable to other territories in Africa where political violence has surfaced or is just beneath the surface—the Sudan, Chad, the Cameroons, Nigeria, and others.

Governmental Ineptitude　　There are at least three facets of this issue that demand inclusion here: (1) inability on the part of the governments to satisfy expectations that they have encouraged; (2) corruption; and (3) low regime force levels. In one respect, African governments have to withstand the convergence of several forces that seem to have reached their prime in the mid-twentieth century. One is that with independence has come the departure of a fairly substantial segment of the colonial expatriate civil service. Some regimes have been able to make the transition with no really appreciable decline in the quality and efficiency of the services provided. Others, such as the Congo, have suffered tremendously by the precipitous flight of thousands of skilled governmental employees. Unfortunately, however, with the general decline in qualified personnel has come an increasing demand that existing government

---

[13] *Ibid.,* p. 983.

services not only be improved and expanded, but that the government provide new services as well as move into functions heretofore fulfilled by private groups. In Guinea this led to a virtual standstill in the export-import services and wholesale commercial enterprise when the government decided prematurely to establish government-managed commercial services.[14] Governmental inefficiency is not necessarily a continent-wide phenomenon. It can be isolated, sometimes by service, sometimes by country, sometimes by region or locale. But where it occurs, it contributes to frustration. Occasionally the politicians are themselves responsible for intensifying these frustrations, since they have promised, or appeared to promise, immediate material benefits to those who supported their claims to govern. Not infrequently, the politicians had no intention of attempting to satisfy high expectations. Nevertheless, the goverment is commonly regarded as responsible for general economic growth. Frustrations that result are often oriented toward the established regime.

The matter of corruption in Africa is a difficult issue to deal with. Most definitions of corruption are culture-bound, particularly as they apply to non-Western countries. By tying corruption to a clear-cut standard, it may be possible to determine a useful definition. Corruption, then, can mean the violation of the letter or spirit of a law by a public official acting for the purpose of private gain. In short, it involves the misuse of authority for considerations of private gain. There is no need to discuss the causes or possible benefits in political or developmental terms. Our primary interest is to sketch the costs of corruption in terms of the growth of systemic frustration. To the ordinary citizen, who neither pockets corrupt money nor can afford to pay it, corruption appears to institutionalize unfairness. His mistrust of government grows as governmental corruption grows, since, ultimately, little is accomplished without a bribe.[15] This in turn leads to a decline in regime legitimacy, as well as to an economic drain as the costs of doing business and administration increase. At the very least, corruption further distorts the already inequitable distribution of national wealth. In societies where resources are scarce, corruption tends to feed upon itself, forcing other public officials, out of self-defense, to indulge. Since there are built-in limitations on the base to which corruption can expand, the final by-product will be widespread growth of disaffection and frustration.

Not only may the civil service pool of talent be shallow with an ac-

---

[14] S. Amin, *Trois expériences africaines de développement* (Paris: Presses Universitaires de France, 1965).

[15] A vibrant portrait of such attitudes is painted in Chinua Achebe's cogent novel, *A Man of the People* (London: Heinemann, 1966).

companying decline in the extent and quality of public service, but the police and military services of a new regime may fail to perform adequate services for either the people or the regime itself. These forces may be unable to provide protection for the citizens or may, even more negatively, be unable to maintain domestic order; indeed, may even contribute to political violence. Military and police forces in Africa have so far been employed primarily for purposes of maintaining internal order. But Black Africa's level of military preparedness is low, in absolute as well as relative terms. The ratio of military to civilian population is about 1:1131 compared to 15:1000 for the United States and 10:1000 for the United Kingdom and the Middle East.[16]

This overall low force level becomes more significant when one considers the additional problems of logistics in underdeveloped countries, and the fact that the indices of instability are high in these states, thereby necessitating a more efficient coercive arm of the regime. What prevails is a modified variation of Boulding's "loss of strength gradient" in which a government's power declines with distance from the capital city.[17] As if these rather straightforward problems were not enough, Africa's militaries must overcome a deep-seated popular fear and distrust of them that dates back many decades.[18] Since independence they have done little to erase this stigma. Attempted coups, mutinies, disorderly attacks upon citizens, the experiences of the Congo and Nigeria, stunning defeats at the hands of small mercenary units, the periodic demands for expanded budgets and privileges, all contribute to reinforcing a negative image. Reputations for ruthlessness are not always associated with a distinction for efficiency. So, a low level of efficiency does not discourage violent expression of systemic frustration.

Channels for the Expression of Discontent   It is assumed that in any society where resources are scarce, where regime legitimacy is widely questioned, where both economic development or lack of it unleash forces that lead to high levels of discontent, and where socioeconomic transition is destabilizing, systemic frustration is likely to be high. Thus it becomes all the more necessary that the established regime institute

---

[16] Calculations based on figures for January 1966 drawn from David Wood, *Armed Forces of African States,* Adelphi Papers No. 27 (London: Institute for Strategic Studies, April 1966), p. 28. Comparative data for other regions from I. William Zartman, *International Relations in the New Africa* (Englewood Cliffs, N.J.: Prentice-Hall, 1966), p. 90.

[17] Kenneth E. Boulding, *Conflict and Defense: A General Theory* (New York: Harper & Bros., 1960), pp. 227–248, 260–262, and 268–269.

[18] For more detail on this point, see Kenneth W. Grundy, *Conflicting Images of the Military in Africa* (Nairobi: East African Publishing House, 1968).

procedures and techniques for dealing with expected grievances or, at least, create the appearances of concern and reformist activity. It must, in short, establish and keep open the various channels for the legitimate expression of discontent and the peaceful settlement of societal grievances. It would be naive to expect that grievances will not arise, and blind to think that real complaints can be socialized away by education and indoctrination. Most regimes have created grievance procedures (either by law or in extralegal practice), but usually the range of complaint has certain vaguely defined limits. When the regime feels endangered, it may react by attempting to shut off any kind of expression of discontent. But an unwillingness to resolve legitimate grievances does not result in their disappearance. Frustrated people may, as a consequence, revert to more violent and better organized forms of expression.

Heterogeneity of the Population   Many aspects of cultural heterogeneity have already been discussed in reference to other aspects of political violence. Actually this is desirable, for it illustrates two points that should be deeply etched in this analysis. First, it indicates the ubiquity of this issue of cultural heterogeneity, not only in spatial and temporal terms, but in its tendency to insinuate itself into virtually all political issues. Hardly a major political event occurs without someone explaining it in terms of the primordial communities that exist in the society in question. Second, it illustrates the constant interaction of variables and, perhaps more importantly for analytical purposes, the difficulty of formulating discrete variables, clearly distinguishable from one another.

The presence of several distinct cultural communities within a single polity in itself poses no insuperable problems for orderly rule. It is the combination of cultural heterogeneity with other issues common in new states that leads to systemic frustration and hence to violent behavior. Thus, when the distribution of economic values, or values relating to political authority, status, and reward are at issue, or when the central government insists on breaking down existing relationships and instituting new, more integrated ones, or simply when frustrations arise when old patterns of life are changed or threatened by socioeconomic change, then the ethnic or subnational focus is often regarded as relevant for the expression of conflicting positions.[19] Despite their ostensible ubiquity and persistence, ethnic factors are not necessarily constant and unassail-

---

[19] See Clifford Geertz, "The Integrative Revolution: Primordial Sentiment and Civil Politics in the New States," in Geertz (ed.), *Old Societies and New States* (New York: Free Press, 1963), pp. 105–157; Lloyd, *Africa in Social Change*, pp. 288–303.

able.[20] They have, though, an uncanny habit of reappearing, even among population segments frequently and erroneously regarded as having transcended primordial attachments. It becomes necessary to distinguish between ethnicity as a way of life and ethnicity as loyalty to an ethnic group. Thus we should not prematurely regard Africa's nationalist leaders as being "detribalized." They are "detribalized" in the sense that they have abandoned a traditional way of life. But, as Professor Mazrui maintains, "this erosion of traditionality did not necessarily entail the diminution of ethnicity." [21] The sentiments and emotions associated with ethnic identification serve to inflate the importance of cultural distinctions and, when they surface, to make the politico-economic conflict that emerges more profound and bitter. Thus, ethnic issues are often, though not the fundamental cause of conflict, the structural lines on which the struggle is organized and expressed. Income distinctions can be superimposed upon ethnic labels and thereby obfuscate the initial cause of the conflict.[22] It is not always easy, therefore, to discern the root cause of violent behavior by the context in which it is expressed and the form it takes.

Table 5 attempts to depict in graphic form the model outlined thus far.

POLITICAL VIOLENCE IN AFRICA

Before moving into a discussion of guerrilla warfare in Africa, a few general words about political violence in Africa are in order. By this point it should be evident that political violence can be categorized in a number of ways, depending on the criteria employed.[23] We are interested

---

[20] See the excellent paper by Nelson Kasfir, "The Decline of Cultural Subnationalism in Uganda," in V. A. Olorunsola (ed.), *Cultural Nationalism in Africa* (forthcoming); and also Robert H. Bates, "Approaches to the Study of Ethnicity," (unpublished paper, mimeo., 30 pp.), which tests various explanations of ethnicity with data from a copper town in Zambia.

[21] See Mazrui, "Violent Contiguity," 93. Professor Mazrui prefers the term tribalism to ethnicity. See also Robert Melson and Howard Wolpe, "Modernization and the Politics of Communalism: A Theoretical Perspective," *American Political Science Review,* 64, No. 4 (December 1970), 1112–1130.

[22] See, for example, Richard L. Sklar, "Political Science and National Integration—A Radical Approach," *Journal of Modern African Studies,* 5, No. 1 (May 1967), 1–11.

[23] Two useful examinations of approaches to typologies can be found in Victor T. LeVine, "The Course of Political Violence," in William H. Lewis (ed.), *French-Speaking Africa: The Search for Identity* (New York: Walker & Co., 1965), pp. 58–79; and Harry Eckstein, "Toward the Theoretical Study of Internal War," in Eckstein (ed.), *Internal War: Problems and Approaches* (New York: Free Press, 1964), pp. 1–32.

TABLE 5
An Abbreviated Model of Political Violence—Variables

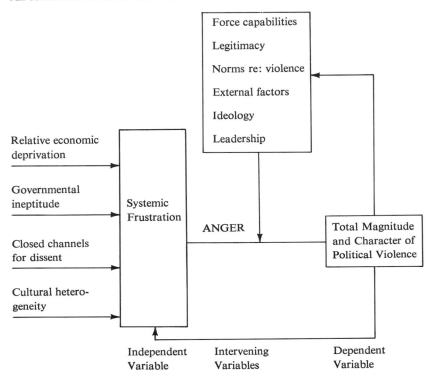

primarily in intrastate (domestic) violence of political importance which is antiregime in purpose. By and large, the violence guerrilla warfare exemplifies would fall within this concern. Although it obviously has interstate ramifications and it is likely that external events contribute to sustaining guerrilla efforts (and to sustaining the regime as well), guerrilla warfare is primarily a form of internal, or civil, war. Any typology of political violence, then, that would cover adequately the sorts of phenomena discussed in the first two sections of this chapter must include, at least, dimensions based on spatial, effectual, structural, and goal considerations. Along the various continua that might be constructed, these varieties of political violence may be found: demonstration, riot, strike, turmoil, partisan conflict, communal warfare, mutiny, assassination, and coup. Stated briefly the problem is this: there is a tremendous variety of classificatory schemes and a diversity of approaches. These analytical and conceptual challenges grow out of the scope and universality of political violence.

Moreover, the magnitude of political violence in Africa is relatively high, as demonstrated by the large number of refugees fleeing unrest or the threat of violence in its various forms, and the magnitude of acts of political violence quantifiable despite the data limitations noted earlier. Although many of the causes of guerrilla warfare are the same as for political violence in general, it becomes necessary to delimit the phenomenon—guerrilla warfare—so that our analysis can proceed unencumbered by extraneous data.

From one perspective, guerrilla warfare is a form of *political* and *military* warfare in which relatively small units try to isolate even smaller units of the enemy and, in a quick engagement, defeat or inflict losses upon them and then disperse before larger units with superior fire power and superior technology can be brought to bear against the guerrillas. The guerrilla forces attempt to maintain the initiative and to engage the enemy only when the guerrillas are prepared for the confrontation. In such operations a premium is placed on speed, mobility, organization, planning, initiative, surprise, and intelligence. As Samuel Huntington says, "Guerrilla warfare is a form of warfare by which the strategically weaker side assumes the tactical offensive in selected forms, times and places." [24] But this definition is only a part of a definition. It is inadequate for it omits at least two additional crucial dimensions of guerrilla warfare. First of all, it places too much emphasis on tactical military considerations. To be sure, in all types of war, tactics of this sort can be employed, but the philosophy of guerrilla warfare sees in this sort of encounter not simply tactical advantage, but strategical advantages as well. Thus, the whole rationale of those who utilize guerrilla warfare (as opposed to guerrilla operations) is the steady physical and psychological deterioration of a numerically and materially superior enemy by a series of numerous small encounters, until such time that the guerrilla forces decide to escalate or raise the level of warfare to more conventional proportions. Second, by being overly concerned with military considerations, there is a temptation to overlook the fundamentally political component of a guerrilla strategy. Not only does the choice of a guerrilla strategy enable an ostensibly inferior military force to defeat an ostensibly superior enemy, but, just as importantly, there are political ramifications of this strategy. The successful employment of guerrilla

---

[24] Samuel P. Huntington, "Guerrilla Warfare in Theory and Policy," in Franklin Mark Osanka (ed.), *Modern Guerrilla Warfare: Fighting Communist Movements, 1941–1961* (New York: Free Press, 1962), p. xvi.

warfare is ideally accompanied by a high level of political as well as military organization, involving large numbers of people, concerned with political mobilization, participation, and indoctrination. Not only does guerrilla warfare provide a materially weaker movement the chance for military success, but it also contains the organizational wherewithal to structure a governmental apparatus once victory in the field is assured. Indeed, under the ideal theoretical model, the two components—military and political organization—function simultaneously and in concert and frequently involve the same persons. These considerations shall be dealt with in some detail later. Thus, though it is perhaps neat to categorize *forms* of warfare on the basis of military criteria, as does Huntington, it is rather misleading in the case of guerrilla warfare.[25]

---

[25] *Ibid.,* pp. xv–xxii.

3

WAR AND DETERRENCE AS INSTRUMENTS OF DIPLOMACY

Introduction

In the years since Hiroshima, the war system has evolved into a far more subtle and complex phenomena than in previous history. A century ago, Clausewitz explained that war was simply an extension of diplomacy by other methods; war was then a straightforward instrument of coercion used by one nation against another. At the international system level, war has been regarded, at least since the Peace of Westphalia (1648), as the principal means of deciding conflicts among nations over boundaries, access to resources, etc. Because the potential costs of total war in the atomic age are so great, war is no longer allowed such an unambiguous status among the various modes of international interaction. Even military men now justify preparations for war as ways of keeping peace.

Thomas Schelling, a leading strategic theorist, explains the new situation in the selection reprinted here. The "power to hurt," he claims, has replaced the capacity to win battles as the main value to be sought in national military preparations. The contemporary war system, unlike the war systems of previous historical periods, is based largely on threats and counterthreats. The system succeeds when the threat of war alone is sufficient to coerce another nation to act in a certain way. It fails when war actually occurs. Thus, large-scale conventional war, and certainly nuclear war as well, might be seen as the result of a miscalculation by one of the members of the system. War would then be superficially similar to a car accident: it cannot be predicted and it represents a threat to life that all try to avoid, yet it happens with regularity in a system where each nation, like each driver, sets its own course.

Many, following Schelling, would even argue that there is no "war system" at all; in fact, there is a war prevention system based on a balance of military power. Reality seems more complicated, however. Clearly, it is true that the *threat* of military force is used by nations to influence or control the behavior of other nations. And it is also clear that the logic of nuclear deterrence seems to have worked to prevent nuclear war. But within this framework there is room for a wide range of small wars in which violence is still used as a means of coercion. One study counted over two hundred instances of international war since World War Two! It should be asked whether the image of a war-preventing threat system truly represents the functions of military power, or whether this power serves a variety of sometimes conflicting purposes, some of which can only be served by resort to war itself.

The answer to this question is obscured by much contemporary literature on deterrence, defense, and strategic theory, as some of the selections in this section indicate. The reason for this is that the existing literature has been written for a number of purposes, only one of which is to serve the needs of dispassionate academic inquiry. Other purposes are to help define immediate national policy choices—for example, should we rely on missile defense or do we need a large army?—and to justify the continued growth of a sprawling military establishment. It is often forgotten that the military-industrial complex (discussed more fully in section 7) includes a large number of researchers and theorists both inside and outside of colleges. One must read strategic literature with care to separate the facts about the role of the military in keeping peace from self-serving fiction.

An example of how strategic theory can be used to obscure the political realities of armament and war planning can be found in the following article by Robert S. McNamara. This essay, extracted from his book *The Essence of Security,* is a straightforward account of the theory of nuclear deterrence. It explains how sufficient nuclear armaments in the United States can deter first use of nuclear weapons by the Soviet Union, and vice versa. This is a complicated logic, but important in reaching an understanding of the nuclear threat. McNamara's account, however, was originally delivered as a speech when the author was secretary of defense and was attempting to build public support for defense budget increases. This may explain why his account of deterrence theory seems incomplete by comparison with the more sophisticated essay by Schelling. He points out that the logic of deterrence—that is, the belief that the superpowers can dissuade each other from nuclear attack by maintaining an adequate capacity to respond in kind—is only part of a larger logic. We accumulate military power, not only to deter, but also to threaten; we use our "power to hurt," not only to prevent the Soviets from attacking the United States, but also to influence their behavior as well as the behavior of other powers. The Soviets tend to manipulate international behavior using their own military power in the same way. Thus, weapons systems are systems of international coercion at the same time that they are instruments of deterrence. While they provide nuclear stability among superpowers, they lend themselves to destabilizing uses in international diplomatic interaction.

The logic of nuclear deterrence and the "power to hurt" raises several crucial questions only touched on in the preceding readings on morality and war. Is it moral, for example, to threaten nuclear devastation if it is immoral actually to carry out the threat (thus breaking the rule against indiscriminate killing of civilians)? Is deterrence justifiable because it *prevents* nuclear war? To answer this question one would have to make a judgment about whether the Soviets, for example, would actually attack with nuclear weapons if they were not opposed by the American nuclear arsenal. Another important question is whether there is a difference between using military power to deter and using it to coerce. In the first instance, power is clearly used defensively. In the second instance, however, the "power to hurt" is used to influence behavior, possibly aggressively. This new fact of military power suggests that moral judgments about its possible uses are becoming even more imperative.

The chapter by Henry Kissinger was originally written long before its author assumed his current (1972) position in the Nixon administration, and hence is not as obviously a political argument as McNamara's. It carries through the claim that only adequate military preparedness for a wide variety of possible conflict situations will help keep world peace. Kissinger is specifically concerned with limited wars, that is, wars in which both sides tacitly limit the scope of the conflict, abstain from using nuclear weapons, and have in mind clear and limited military and political objectives. He distinguishes four types of limited wars, including counterinsurgency warfare, which, he argues, American armies should be prepared to fight. Kissinger believes that limited war is essentially a political act, and justifies his argument for all forms of limited war with reference to what he perceives as the American need to oppose the threat of Soviet expansionism. Clearly, he is most worried about manifestations of "communist expansionism" in Vietnam-type guerrilla wars. If America is not prepared to fight, Kissinger says, Russian armies could overrun Eastern and Central Europe as well as parts of the Near and Middle East. Since such a turn of events would seriously jeopardize American interests, we must be prepared to fight in order to deter Soviet expansionist impulses.

Kissinger's position is a further illustration of the preeminent role that Schelling attributes to the "power to hurt" in contemporary military strategy. Preparing for war is seen as a way of influencing the adversary's behavior and hence of preventing war itself from breaking out. The success of such a strategy, Kissinger says, depends on the United States' actually being willing and able to fight limited wars, if necessary, to safeguard our interests.

An evaluation of this position should include a judgment about whether such wars could be justified with regard to the traditional moral criteria for just wars (see section 1). Equally important, it should also examine the underlying assumptions about the structure of world politics and the nature of the Soviet threat. According to all that we know about Soviet intentions, is it realistic to assume (a) that they spearhead an international communist expansionist conspiracy, and (b) that only American armies are holding them back?

The articles in this section all address these key questions: What is the role of war in modern diplomacy? Can war or its threat be morally justified as an instrument of coercive diplomacy? What kinds of total and limited wars are possible, likely, or significant in defense planning? What legitimate ends can be served by American military power, and how much armed might do we need to advance these purposes?

Finally, the overriding question is whether the prevailing system of deterrence and threat guarantees a just and stable peace. If not, then it is important to explore possibilities for changing or modifying the war system to reduce the threat of war and provide nonviolent mechanisms of change.

SUGGESTIONS FOR FURTHER READING

War in the International System

Raymond Aron, *Peace and War: A Theory of International Relations*. Garden City, N.Y.: Doubleday, 1965.

Richard A. Falk, *This Endangered Planet*. New York: Random House, 1971.

Stanley Hoffmann, *The State of War*. New York: Praeger, 1965.

Klaus Knorr, *On the Uses of Military Power in the Nuclear Age*. Princeton: Princeton University Press, 1966.

Robert E. Osgood and Robert W. Tucker, *Force, Order and Justice*. Baltimore: Johns Hopkins Press, 1966.

Anatol Rapoport, *Strategy and Conscience*. New York: Harper and Row, 1966.

Kenneth N. Waltz, *Man, the State, and War*. New York: Columbia University Press, 1959.

Quincy Wright, *A Study of War*, 2 vols. Chicago: University of Chicago Press, 2d. ed., 1965.

American Defense Policy

Richard J. Barnet, *Intervention and Revolution*. New York: World Publishing Company, 1968.

————, *Roots of War*. New York: Atheneum, 1972.

Morton H. Halperin, *Limited War in the Nuclear Age*. New York: Wiley, 1963.

Stanley Hoffmann, *Gulliver's Troubles, or the Setting of American Foreign Policy*. New York: McGraw-Hill, 1968.

Herman Kahn, *On Thermonuclear War*. Princeton: Princeton University Press, 1960.

Gabriel Kolko, *The Roots of American Foreign Policy*. Boston: Beacon Press, 1968.

Glenn H. Snyder, *Deterrence and Defense: Toward a Theory of National Security*. Princeton: Princeton University Press, 1961.

William A. Williams, *The Roots of the Modern American Empire*. New York: Random House, 1969.

The Diplomacy of Violence

THOMAS C. SCHELLING

The usual distinction between diplomacy and force is not merely in the instruments, words or bullets, but in the relation between adversaries —in the interplay of motives and the role of communication, understandings, compromise, and restraint. Diplomacy is bargaining; it seeks outcomes that, though not ideal for either party, are better for both than some of the alternatives. In diplomacy each party somewhat controls what the other wants, and can get more by compromise, exchange, or collaboration than by taking things in his own hands and ignoring the other's wishes. The bargaining can be polite or rude, entail threats as well as offers, assume a status quo or ignore all rights and privileges, and assume mistrust rather than trust. But whether polite or impolite, constructive or aggressive, respectful or vicious, whether it occurs among friends or antagonists, and whether or not there is a basis for trust and goodwill, there must be some common interest, if only in the avoidance of mutual damage, and an awareness of the need to make the other party prefer an outcome acceptable to oneself.

With enough military force a country may not need to bargain. Some things a country wants it can take, and some things it has it can keep, by sheer strength, skill, and ingenuity. It can do this *forcibly,* accom-

Excerpted from *Arms and Influence,* by Thomas C. Schelling (New Haven, Conn.: Yale University Press, 1966), pp. 1–34. Copyright © 1966 by Yale University. Reprinted by permission. Schelling is regarded as one of America's leading strategic theorists. He teaches at Harvard University.

modating only to opposing strength, skill, and ingenuity and without trying to appeal to an enemy's wishes. Forcibly a country can repel and expel, penetrate and occupy, seize, exterminate, disarm and disable, confine, deny access, and directly frustrate intrusion or attack. It can, that is, if it has enough strength. "Enough" depends on how much an opponent has.

There is something else, though, that force can do. It is less military, less heroic, less impersonal, and less unilateral; it is uglier, and has received less attention in Western military strategy. In addition to seizing and holding, disarming and confining, penetrating and obstructing, and all that, military force can be used *to hurt*. In addition to taking and protecting things of value it can *destroy* value. In addition to weakening an enemy militarily it can cause an enemy plain suffering.

Pain and shock, loss and grief, privation and horror are always in some degree, sometimes in terrible degree, among the results of warfare; but in traditional military science they are incidental, they are not the object. If violence can be done incidentally, though, it can also be done purposely. The power to hurt can be counted among the most impressive attributes of military force.

Hurting, unlike forcible seizure or self-defense, is not unconcerned with the interest of others. It is measured in the suffering it can cause and the victims' motivation to avoid it. Forcible action will work against weeds or floods as well as against armies, but suffering requires a victim that can feel pain or has something to lose. To inflict suffering gains nothing and saves nothing directly; it can only make people behave to avoid it. The only purpose, unless sport or revenge, must be to influence somebody's behavior, to coerce his decision or choice. To be coercive, violence has to be anticipated. And it has to be avoidable by accommodation. The power to hurt is bargaining power. To exploit it is diplomacy—vicious diplomacy, but diplomacy.

THE CONTRAST OF BRUTE FORCE WITH COERCION

There is a difference between taking what you want and making someone give it to you, between fending off assault and making someone afraid to assault you, between holding what people are trying to take and making them afraid to take it, between losing what someone can forcibly take and giving it up to avoid risk or damage. It is the difference between defense and deterrence, between brute force and intimidation, between conquest and blackmail, between action and threats. It is the difference between the unilateral, "undiplomatic" recourse to strength, and coercive diplomacy based on the power to hurt.

The contrasts are several. The purely "military" or "undiplomatic" recourse to forcible action is concerned with enemy strength, not enemy interests; the coercive use of the power to hurt, though, is the very exploitation of enemy wants and fears. And brute strength is usually measured relative to enemy strength, the one directly opposing the other, while the power to hurt is typically not reduced by the enemy's power to hurt in return. Opposing strengths may cancel each other, pain and grief do not. The willingness to hurt, the credibility of a threat, and the ability to exploit the power to hurt will indeed depend on how much the adversary can hurt in return; but there is little or nothing about an adversary's pain or grief that directly reduces one's own. Two sides cannot both overcome each other with superior strength; they may both be able to hurt each other. With strength they can dispute objects of value; with sheer violence they can destroy them.

And brute force succeeds when it is used, whereas the power to hurt is most successful when held in reserve. It is the *threat* of damage, or of more damage to come, that can make someone yield or comply. It is *latent* violence that can influence someone's choice—violence that can still be withheld or inflicted, or that a victim believes can be withheld or inflicted. The threat of pain tries to structure someone's motives, while brute force tries to overcome his strength. Unhappily, the power to hurt is often communicated by some performance of it. Whether it is sheer terroristic violence to induce an irrational response or cool premeditated violence to persuade somebody that you mean it and may do it again, it is not the pain and damage itself but its influence on somebody's behavior that matters. It is the expectation of *more* violence that gets the wanted behavior, if the power to hurt can get it at all.

To exploit a capacity for hurting and inflicting damage one needs to know what an adversary treasures and what scares him and one needs the adversary to understand what behavior of his will cause the violence to be inflicted and what will cause it to be withheld. The victim has to know what is wanted, and he may have to be assured of what is not wanted. The pain and suffering have to appear *contingent* on his behavior; it is not alone the threat that is effective—the threat of pain or loss if he fails to comply—but the corresponding assurance, possibly an implicit one, that he can avoid the pain or loss if he does comply. The prospect of certain death may stun him, but it gives him no choice.

Coercion by threat of damage also requires that our interests and our opponent's not be absolutely opposed. If his pain were our greatest delight and our satisfaction his greatest woe, we would just proceed to hurt and to frustrate each other. It is when his pain gives us little or no satisfaction compared with what he can do for us, and the action or inaction that satisfies us costs him less than the pain we can cause, that there is room for coercion. Coercion requires finding a bargain, arranging for him to be better off doing what we want—worse off not doing what we want—when he takes the threatened penalty into account.

It is this capacity for pure damage, pure violence, that is usually associated with the most vicious labor disputes, with racial disorders, with civil uprisings and their suppression, with racketeering. It is also the power to hurt rather than brute force that we use in dealing with criminals; we hurt them afterward, or threaten to, for their misdeeds rather than protect ourselves with cordons of electric wires, masonry walls, and armed guards. Jail, of course, can be either forcible restraint or threatened privation; if the object is to keep criminals out of mischief by confinement, success is measured by how many of them are gotten behind bars, but if the object is to *threaten* privation, success will be measured by how few have to be put behind bars and success then depends on the subject's understanding of the consequences. Pure damage is what a car threatens when it tries to hog the road, or to keep its rightful share, or to go first through an intersection. A tank or a bulldozer can force its way regardless of others' wishes; the rest of us have to threaten damage, usually mutual damage, hoping the other driver values his car or his limbs enough to give way, hoping he sees us, and hoping he is in control of his own car. The threat of pure damage will not work against an unmanned vehicle.

This difference between coercion and brute force is as often in the intent as in the instrument. To hunt down Comanches and to exterminate them was brute force; to raid their villages to make them behave was coercive diplomacy, based on the power to hurt. The pain and loss to the Indians might have looked much the same one way as the other; the difference was one of purpose and effect. If Indians were killed because they were in the way, or somebody wanted their land, or the authorities despaired of making them behave and could not confine them and decided to exterminate them, that was pure unilateral force. If *some* Indians were killed to make *other* Indians behave, that was coercive violence— or intended to be, whether or not it was effective. The Germans at Verdun perceived themselves to be chewing up hundreds of thousands of French soldiers in a gruesome "meatgrinder." If the purpose was to eliminate a military obstacle—the French infantryman, viewed as a military "asset" rather than as a warm human being—the offensive at Verdun was a unilateral exercise of military force. If instead the object was to make the loss of young men—not of impersonal "effectives," but of sons, husbands, fathers, and the pride of French manhood—so anguishing as to be unendurable, to make surrender a welcome relief, and to spoil the foretaste of an Allied victory, then it was an exercise in coercion, in applied violence, intended to offer relief upon accommodation. And of course, since any use of force tends to be brutal, thoughtless, vengeful, or plain obstinate, the motives themselves can be mixed and confused. The fact that heroism and brutality can be either coercive diplomacy or a contest in pure strength does not promise that the distinction will be made, and the strategies enlightened by the distinction, every time some vicious enterprise gets launched.

The contrast between brute force and coercion is illustrated by two alternative strategies attributed to Genghis Khan. Early in his career he pursued the war creed of the Mongols: the vanquished can never be the friends of the victors, their death is necessary for the victors' safety. This was the unilateral extermination of a menace or a liability. The turning point of his career, according to Lynn Montross, came later when he discovered how to use his power to hurt for diplomatic ends. "The great Khan, who was not inhibited by the usual mercies, conceived the plan of forcing captives—women, children, aged fathers, favorite sons—to march ahead of his army as the first potential victims of resistance." Live captives have often proved more valuable than enemy dead; and the technique discovered by the Khan in his maturity remains contemporary. North Koreans and Chinese were reported to have quartered prisoners of war near strategic targets to inhibit bombing attacks by United Nations aircraft. Hostages represent the power to hurt in its purest form.

THE NUCLEAR CONTRIBUTION TO TERROR AND VIOLENCE

Man has, it is said, for the first time in history enough military power to eliminate his species from the earth, weapons against which there is no conceivable defense. War has become, it is said, so destructive and terrible that it ceases to be an instrument of national power. "For the first time in human history," says Max Lerner in a book whose title, *The Age of Overkill,* conveys the point, "men have bottled up a power . . . which they have thus far not dared to use." And Soviet military authorities, whose party dislikes having to accommodate an entire theory of history to a single technological event, have had to reexamine a set of principles that had been given the embarrassing name of "permanently operating factors" in warfare. Indeed, our era is epitomized by words like "the first time in human history," and by the abdication of what was "permanent."

For dramatic impact these statements are splendid. Some of them display a tendency, not at all necessary, to belittle the catastrophe of earlier wars. They may exaggerate the historical novelty of deterrence and the balance of terror. More important, they do not help to identify just what is new about war when so much destructive energy can be packed in warheads at a price that permits advanced countries to have them in large numbers. Nuclear warheads are incomparably more devastating than anything packaged before. What does that imply about war?

It is not true that for the first time in history man has the capability to destroy a large fraction, even the major part, of the human race. Japan was defenseless by August 1945. With a combination of bombing and blockade, eventually invasion, and if necessary the deliberate spread of disease, the United States could probably have exterminated the population of the Japanese islands without nuclear weapons. . . .

It is a grisly thing to talk about. We did not do it, and it is not imaginable that we would have done it. We had no reason; if we had had a reason, we would not have the persistence of purpose, once the fury of war had been dissipated in victory and we had taken on the task of executioner. If we and our enemies might do such a thing to each other now, and to others as well, it is not because nuclear weapons have for the first time made it feasible.

Nuclear weapons can do it quickly. . . . To compress a catastrophic war within the span of time that a man can stay awake drastically changes the politics of war, the process of decision, the possibility of central control and restraint, the motivations of people in charge, and the capacity to think and reflect while war is in progress. It *is* imaginable that we might destroy 200,000,000 Russians in a war of the present, though not 80,000,000 Japanese in a war of the past. It is not only imaginable, it is imagined. It is imaginable because it could be done "in a moment, in the twinkling of an eye, at the last trumpet."

This may be why there is so little discussion of how an all-out war might be brought to a close. People do not expect it to be "brought" to a close, but just to come to an end when everything has been spent. It is also why the idea of "limited war" has become so explicit in recent years. Earlier wars, like World Wars I and II or the Franco-Prussian War, were limited by *termination,* by an ending that occurred before the period of greatest potential violence, by negotiation that brought the *threat* of pain and privation to bear but often precluded the massive *exercise* of civilian violence. With nuclear weapons available, the restraint of violence cannot await the outcome of a contest of military strength; restraint, to occur at all, must occur during war itself.

This is a difference between nuclear weapons and bayonets. It is not in the number of people they can eventually kill but in the speed with which it can be done, in the centralization of decision, in the divorce of the war from political processes, and in computerized programs that threaten to take the war out of human hands once it begins.

That nuclear weapons make it *possible* to compress the fury of global war into a few hours does not mean that they make it *inevitable*. We have still to ask whether that is the way a major nuclear war would be fought, or ought to be fought. Nevertheless, that the whole war might go off like one big string of firecrackers makes a critical difference between our conception of nuclear war and the world wars we have experienced.

There is no guarantee, of course, that a slower war would not persist. The First World War could have stopped at any time after the Battle of the Marne. There was plenty of time to think about war aims, to consult the long-range national interest, to reflect on costs and casualties already incurred and the prospect of more to come, and to discuss terms of cessation with the enemy. The gruesome business continued as mechanically as if it had been in the hands of computers (or worse: computers might have been programmed to learn more quickly from experience). One may even suppose it would have been a blessing had all the pain and shock of the four years been compressed within four days. Still, it was terminated. And the victors had no stomach for doing then with bayonets what nuclear weapons could do to the German people today.

There is another difference. In the past it has usually been the victors who could do what they pleased to the enemy. War has often been "total war" for the loser. With deadly monotony the Persians, Greeks, or Romans "put to death all men of military age, and sold the women and children into slavery," leaving the defeated territory nothing but its name until new settlers arrived some time later. But the defeated could not do the same to their victors. The boys could be castrated and sold only after the war had been won, and only on the side that lost it. The power to hurt could be brought to bear only after military strength had achieved victory. The same sequence characterized the great wars of this century; for reasons of technology and geography, military force has usually had to penetrate, to exhaust, or to collapse opposing military force—to achieve military victory—before it could be brought to bear on the enemy nation itself. The Allies in World War I could not inflict coercive pain and suffering directly on the Germans in a decisive way until they could defeat the German army; and the Germans could not coerce the French people with bayonets unless they first beat the Allied troops that stood in their way. With two-dimensional warfare, there is a tendency for troops to confront each other, shielding their own lands while attempting to press into each other's. Small penetrations could not do major damage to the people; large penetrations were so destructive of military organization that they usually ended the military phase of the war.

Nuclear weapons make it possible to do monstrous violence to the enemy without first achieving victory. With nuclear weapons and today's means of delivery, one expects to penetrate an enemy homeland without first collapsing his military force. What nuclear weapons have done, or appear to do, is to promote this kind of warfare to first place. Nuclear weapons threaten to make war less military, and are responsible for the lowered status of "military victory" at the present time. *Victory is no longer a prerequisite for hurting the enemy.* And it is no assurance against being terribly hurt. One need not wait until he has won the war before inflicting "unendurable" damages on his enemy. One need not wait until he has lost the war. There was a time when the assurance of victory—false or genuine assurance—could make national leaders not just willing but sometimes enthusiastic about war. Not now.

Not only *can* nuclear weapons hurt the enemy before the war has been won, and perhaps hurt decisively enough to make the military engagement academic, but it is widely assumed that in a major war that is *all* they can do. Major war is often discussed as though it would be only a contest in national destruction. If this is indeed the case—if the destruction of cities and their populations has become, with nuclear weapons, the primary object in an all-out war—the sequence of war has been reversed. Instead of destroying enemy forces as a prelude to imposing one's will on the enemy nation, one would have to destroy the nation as a means or a prelude to destroying the enemy forces. If one cannot disable enemy forces without virtually destroying the country, the victor does not even have the option of sparing the conquered nation. He has already destroyed it. Even with blockade and strategic bombing it could be supposed that a country would be defeated before it was destroyed, or would elect surrender before annihilation had gone far. In the Civil War it could be hoped that the South would become too weak to fight before it became too weak to survive. For "all-out" war, nuclear weapons threaten to reverse this sequence.

So nuclear weapons do make a difference, marking an epoch in warfare. The difference is not just in the amount of destruction that can be accomplished but in the role of destruction and in the decision process. Nuclear weapons can change the speed of events; the control of events, the sequence of events, the relation of victor to vanquished, and the relation of homeland to fighting front. Deterrence rests today on the threat of pain and extinction, not just on the threat of military defeat. We may argue about the wisdom of announcing "unconditional surrender" as an aim in the last major war, but seem to expect "unconditional destruction" as a matter of course in another one.

Something like the same destruction always *could* be done. With nuclear weapons there is an expectation that it *would* be done. . . . What is new is . . . the idea that major war might be just a contest in the killing of countries, or not even a contest but just two parallel exercises in devastation.

That is the difference nuclear weapons make. At least they *may* make that difference. They also may not. If the weapons themselves are vulnerable to attack, or the machines that carry them, a successful surprise might eliminate the opponent's means of retribution. That an enormous explosion can be packaged in a single bomb does not by itself guarantee that the victor will receive deadly punishment. Two gunfighters facing each other in a Western town had an unquestioned capacity to kill one another; that did not guarantee that both would die in a gunfight—only the slower of the two. Less deadly weapons, permitting an injured one to shoot back before he died, might have been more conducive to a restraining balance of terror, or of caution. The very efficiency of nuclear weapons could make them ideal for starting war, if they can suddenly eliminate the enemy's capability to shoot back.

And there is a contrary possibility: that nuclear weapons are not vulnerable to attack and prove not to be terribly effective against each other, posing no need to shoot them quickly for fear they will be destroyed before they are launched, and with no task available but the systematic destruction of the enemy country and no necessary reason to do it fast rather than slowly. Imagine that nuclear destruction *had* to go slowly—that the bombs could be dropped only one per day. The prospect would look very different, something like the most terroristic guerrilla warfare on a massive scale. It happens that nuclear war does not have to go slowly; but it may also not have to go speedily. The mere existence of nuclear weapons does not itself determine that everything must go off in a blinding flash, any more than that it must go slowly. Nuclear weapons do not simplify things quite that much.

In recent years there has been a new emphasis on distinguishing what nuclear weapons make possible and what they make inevitable in case of war. The American government began in 1961 to emphasize that even a major nuclear war might not, and need not, be a simple contest in destructive fury. Secretary McNamara gave a controversial speech in June 1962 on the idea that "deterrence" might operate even in war itself, that belligerents might, out of self-interest, attempt to limit the war's destructiveness. Each might feel the sheer destruction of enemy people and cities would serve no decisive military purpose but that a continued *threat* to destroy them might serve a purpose. The continued threat would depend on their not being destroyed yet. Each might reciprocate the other's restraint, as in limited wars of lesser scope. Even the worst of enemies, in the interest of reciprocity, have often not mutilated prisoners of war; and citizens might deserve comparable treatment. The fury of nuclear attacks might fall mainly on each other's weapons and military forces.

"The United States has come to the conclusion," said Secretary McNamara,

> that to the extent feasible, basic military strategy in a possible general war should be approached in much the same way that more conventional military operations have been regarded in the past. That is to say, principal military objectives . . . should be the destruction of the enemy's military forces, not of his civilian population . . . giving the possible opponent the strongest imaginable incentive to refrain from striking our own cities.

This is a sensible way to think about war, if one has to think about it and of course one does. But whether the secretary's "new strategy" was sensible or not, whether enemy populations should be held hostage or instantly destroyed, whether the primary targets should be military forces or just people and their source of livelihood, this is not "much the same way that more conventional military operations have been regarded in the past." This is utterly different, and the difference deserves emphasis.

In World Wars I and II one went to work on enemy military forces, not his people, because until the enemy's military forces had been taken care of there was typically not anything decisive that one could do to the enemy nation itself. The Germans did not, in World War I, refrain from bayoneting French citizens by the millions in the hope that the Allies would abstain from shooting up the German population. They could not get at the French citizens until they had breached the Allied lines. Hitler tried to terrorize London and did not make it. The Allied air forces took the war straight to Hitler's territory, with at least some thought of doing in Germany what Sherman recognized he was doing in Georgia; but with the bombing technology of World War II one could not afford to bypass the troops and go exclusively for enemy populations —not, anyway, in Germany. With nuclear weapons one has that alternative.

To concentrate on the enemy's military installations while deliberately holding in reserve a massive capacity for destroying his cities, for exterminating his people and eliminating his society, on condition that the enemy observe similar restraint with respect to one's own society, is not the "conventional approach." In World Wars I and II the first order of business was to destroy enemy armed forces because that was the only promising way to make him surrender. To fight a purely military engagement "all-out" while holding in reserve a decisive capacity for violence, on condition the enemy do likewise, is not the way military operations have traditionally been approached. Secretary McNamara was proposing a new approach to warfare in a new era, an era in which the power to hurt is more impressive than the power to oppose.

FROM BATTLEFIELD WARFARE TO THE DIPLOMACY OF VIOLENCE

Almost one hundred years before Secretary McNamara's speech, the Declaration of St. Petersburg (the first of the great modern conferences to cope with the evils of warfare) in 1868 asserted, "The only legitimate object which states should endeavor to accomplish during war is to weaken the military forces of the enemy." And in a letter to the League of Nations in 1920, the President of the International Committee of the Red Cross wrote, "The Committee considers it very desirable that war should resume its former character, that is to say, that it should be a struggle between armies and not between populations. The civilian population must, as far as possible, remain outside the struggle and its consequences." His language is remarkably similar to Secretary McNamara's.

The International Committee was fated for disappointment, like everyone who labored in the late nineteenth century to devise rules that would make war more humane. When the Red Cross was founded in 1863, it was concerned about the disregard for noncombatants by those who made war; but in the Second World War noncombatants were deliberately chosen as targets by both Axis and Allied forces, not decisively but nevertheless deliberately. The trend has been the reverse of what the International Committee hoped for.

In the present era noncombatants appear to be not only deliberate targets but primary targets, or at least were so taken for granted until about the time of Secretary McNamara's speech. In fact, noncombatants appeared to be primary targets at both ends of the scale of warfare; thermonuclear war threatened to be a contest in the destruction of cities and populations; and, at the other end of the scale, insurgency is almost entirely terroristic. We live in an era of dirty war.

Why is this so? Is war properly a military affair among combatants, and is it a depravity peculiar to the twentieth century that we cannot keep it within decent bounds? Or is war inherently dirty, and was the Red Cross nostalgic for an artificial civilization in which war had become encrusted with etiquette—a situation to be welcomed but not expected?

To answer this question it is useful to distinguish three stages in the involvement of noncombatants—of plain people and their possessions—in the fury of war. These stages are worth distinguishing; but their sequence is merely descriptive of Western Europe during the past three hundred years, not a historical generalization. The first stage is that in which the people may get hurt by inconsiderate combatants. This is the status that people had during the period of "civilized warfare" that the International Committee had in mind.

From about 1648 to the Napoleonic era, war in much of Western Europe was something superimposed on society. It was a contest engaged in by monarchies for stakes that were measured in territories and, occasionally, money or dynastic claims. The troops were mostly mercenaries, and the motivation for war was confined to the aristocratic elite. Monarchs fought for bits of territory, but the residents of disputed terrain were more concerned with protecting their crops and their daughters from marauding troops than with whom they owed allegiance to. They were, as Quincy Wright remarked in his classic *Study of War,* little concerned that the territory in which they lived had a new sovereign. Furthermore, as far as the King of Prussia and the Emperor of Austria were concerned, the loyalty and enthusiasm of the Bohemian farmer were not decisive considerations. It is an exaggeration to refer to European war during this period as a sport of kings, but not a gross exaggeration. And the military logistics of those days confined military operations to a scale that did not require the enthusiasm of a multitude.

Hurting people was not a decisive instrument of warfare. Hurting people or destroying property only reduced the value of the things that were being fought over, to the disadvantage of both sides. Furthermore, the monarchs who conducted wars often did not want to discredit the social institutions they shared with their enemies. Bypassing an enemy monarch and taking the war straight to his people would have had revolutionary implications. Destroying the opposing monarchy was often not in the interest of either side; opposing sovereigns had much more in common with each other than with their own subjects, and to discredit the claims of a monarchy might have produced a disastrous backlash. It is not surprising—or, if it is surprising, not altogether astonishing—that on the European continent in that particular era war was fairly well confined to military activity.

One could still, in those days and in that part of the world, be concerned for the rights of noncombatants and hope to devise rules that both sides in the war might observe. The rules might well be observed because both sides had something to gain from preserving social order and not destroying the enemy. Rules might be a nuisance, but as they restricted both sides the disadvantages might cancel out.

This was changed during the Napoleonic wars. In Napoleon's France, people cared about the outcome. The nation was mobilized. The war was a national effort, not just an activity of the elite. It was both political and military genius on the part of Napoleon and his ministers that an entire nation could be mobilized for war. Propaganda became a tool of warfare, and war became vulgarized.

Many writers deplored this popularization of war, this involvement of the democratic masses. In fact, the horrors we attribute to thermonuclear war were already foreseen by many commentators, some before the First World War and more after it; but the new "weapon" to which these terrors were ascribed was people, millions of people, passionately engaged in national wars, spending themselves in a quest for total victory and desperate to avoid total defeat. Today we are impressed that a small number of highly trained pilots can carry enough energy to blast and burn tens of millions of people and the buildings they live in; two or three generations ago there was concern that tens of millions of people using bayonets and barbed wire, machine guns and shrapnel, could create the same kind of destruction and disorder.

That was the second stage in the relation of people to war, the second in Europe since the middle of the seventeenth century. In the first stage people had been neutral but their welfare might be disregarded; in the second stage people were involved because it was *their* war. Some fought, some produced materials of war, some produced food, and some took care of children; but they were all part of a war-making nation. When Hitler attacked Poland in 1939, the Poles had reason to care about the outcome. When Churchill said the British would fight on the beaches, he spoke for the British and not for a mercenary army. The war was about something that mattered. If people would rather fight a dirty war than lose a clean one, the war will be between nations and not just between governments. If people have an influence on whether the war is continued or on the terms of a truce, making the war hurt people serves a purpose. It is a dirty purpose, but war itself is often about something dirty. The Poles and the Norwegians, the Russians and the British, had reason to believe that if they lost the war the consequences would be dirty. This is so evident in modern civil wars—civil wars that involve popular feelings—that we expect them to be bloody and violent. To hope that they would be fought cleanly with no violence to people would be a little like hoping for a clean race riot.

There is another way to put it that helps to bring out the sequence of events. If a modern war were a clean one, the violence would not be ruled out but merely saved for the postwar period. Once the army has been defeated in the clean war, the victorious enemy can be as brutally coercive as he wishes. A clean war would determine which side gets to use its power to hurt coercively after victory, and it is likely to be worth some violence to avoid being the loser.

"Surrender" is the process following military hostilities in which the power to hurt is brought to bear. If surrender negotiations are successful and not followed by overt violence, it is because the capacity to inflict pain and damage was successfully used in the bargaining process. On the losing side, prospective pain and damage were averted by concessions; on the winning side, the capacity for inflicting further harm was traded for concessions. The same is true in a successful kidnapping. It only reminds us that the purpose of pure pain and damage is extortion; it is *latent* violence that can be used to advantage. A well-behaved occupied country is not one in which violence plays no part; it may be one in which latent violence is used so skillfully that it need not be spent in punishment.

This brings us to the third stage in the relation of civilian violence to warfare. If the pain and damage can be inflicted during war itself, they need not wait for the surrender negotiation that succeeds a military decision. If one can coerce people and their governments while war is going on, one does not need to wait until he has achieved victory or risk losing that coercive power by spending it all in a losing war. General Sherman's march through Georgia might have made as much sense, possibly more, had the North been losing the war, just as the German buzz bombs and V-2 rockets can be thought of as coercive instruments to get the war stopped before suffering military defeat.

In the present era, since at least the major East-West powers are capable of massive civilian violence during war itself beyond anything available during the Second World War, the occasion for restraint does not await the achievement of military victory or truce. The principal restraint during the Second World War was a temporal boundary, the date of surrender. In the present era we find the violence dramatically restrained during war itself. The Korean War was furiously "all-out" in the fighting, not only on the peninsular battlefield but in the resources used by both sides. It was "all-out," though, only within some dramatic restraints: no nuclear weapons, no Russians, no Chinese territory, no Japanese territory, no bombings of ships at sea or even airfields on the United Nations side of the line. It was a contest in military strength circumscribed by the threat of unprecedented civilian violence. Korea may or may not be a good model for speculation on limited war in the age of nuclear violence, but it was dramatic evidence that the capacity for violence can be consciously restrained even under the provocation of a war that measures its military dead in tens of thousands and that fully preoccupies two of the largest countries in the world.

A consequence of this third stage is that "victory" inadequately expresses what a nation wants from its military forces. Mostly it wants, in these times, the influence that resides in latent force. It wants the bargaining power that comes from its capacity to hurt, not just the direct consequence of successful military action. Even total victory over an enemy provides at best an opportunity for unopposed violence against the enemy population. How to use that opportunity in the national interest, or in some wider interest, can be just as important as the achievement of victory itself; but traditional military science does not tell us how to use that capacity for inflicting pain. And if a nation, victor or potential loser, is going to use its capacity for pure violence to influence the enemy, there may be no need to await the achievement of total victory.

Actually, this third stage can be analyzed into two quite different variants. In one, sheer pain and damage are primary instruments of coercive warfare and may actually be applied, to intimidate or to deter. In the other, pain and destruction *in* war are expected to serve little or no purpose but *prior threats* of sheer violence, even of automatic and uncontrolled violence, are coupled to military force. The difference is in the all-or-none character of deterrence and intimidation. Two acute dilemmas arise. One is the choice of making prospective violence as frightening as possible or hedging with some capacity for reciprocated restraint. The other is the choice of making retaliation as automatic as possible or keeping deliberate control over the fateful decisions. The choices are determined partly by governments, partly by technology. Both variants are characterized by the coercive role of pain and destruction—of threatened (not inflicted) pain and destruction. But in one the threat either succeeds or fails altogether, and any ensuing violence is gratuitous; in the other, progressive pain and damage may actually be used to threaten more. The present era, for countries possessing nuclear weapons, is a complex and uncertain blend of the two.

Coercive diplomacy, based on the power to hurt, was important even in those periods of history when military force was essentially the power to take and to hold, to fend off attack and to expel invaders, and to possess territory against opposition—that is, in the era in which military force tended to pit itself against opposing force. Even then, a critical question was how much cost and pain the other side would incur for the disputed territory. The judgment that the Mexicans would concede Texas, New Mexico, and California once Mexico City was a hostage in our hands was a diplomatic judgment, not a military one. If one could not readily take the particular territory he wanted or hold it against attack, he could take something else and trade it. Judging what the enemy leaders would trade—be it a capital city or national survival—was a critical part of strategy even in the past. Now we are in an era in which the power to hurt—to inflict pain and shock and privation on a country itself, not just on its military forces—is commensurate with the power to take and to hold, perhaps more than commensurate, perhaps decisive, and it is even more necessary to think of warfare as a process of violent bargaining. This is not the first era in which live captives have been worth more than dead enemies; the power to hurt has been a bargaining advantage. But it is the first in American experience when that kind of power has been a dominant part of military relations.

The power to hurt is nothing new in warfare, but for the United States modern technology has drastically enhanced the strategic importance of pure, unconstructive, unacquisitive pain and damage, whether used against us or in our own defense. This in turn enhances the importance of war and threats of war as techniques of influence, not of destruction; of coercion and deterrence, not of conquest and defense; of bargaining and intimidation.

Quincy Wright, in his *Study of War,* devoted a couple of pages to the "nuisance value" of war, using the analogy of a bank robber with a bomb in his hand that would destroy bank and robber. Nuisance value made the threat of war, according to Wright, "an aid to the diplomacy of unscrupulous governments." Now we need a stronger term, and more pages, to do the subject justice, and need to recognize that even scrupulous governments often have little else to rely on militarily. It is extraordinary how many treatises on war and strategy have declined to recognize that the power to hurt has been, throughout history, a fundamental character of military force and fundamental to the diplomacy based on it.

War no longer looks like just a contest of strength. War and the brink of war are more a contest of nerve and risk-taking, of pain and endurance. Small wars embody the threat of a larger war; they are not just military engagements but "crisis diplomacy." The threat of war has always been somewhere underneath international diplomacy, but for Americans it is now much nearer the surface. Like the threat of a strike in industrial relations, the threat of divorce in a family dispute, or the threat of bolting the party at a political convention, the threat of violence continuously circumscribes international politics. Neither strength nor goodwill procures immunity.

Military strategy can no longer be thought of, as it could for some countries in some eras, as the science of military victory. It is now equally, if not more, the art of coercion, of intimidation and deterrence. The instruments of war are more punitive than acquisitive. Military strategy, whether we like it or not, has become the diplomacy of violence.

Mutual Deterrence

ROBERT S. McNAMARA

In a complex and uncertain world, the gravest problem that an American secretary of defense must face is that of planning, preparation, and policy against the possibility of thermonuclear war. It is a prospect that most of mankind understandably would prefer not to contemplate, for technology has now circumscribed us all with a horizon of horror that could dwarf any catastrophe that has befallen man in his more than a million years on earth.

Man has lived now for more than twenty years in what we have come to call the Atomic Age. What we sometimes overlook is that every future age of man will be an atomic age, and if man is to have a future at all, it will have to be one overshadowed with the permanent possibility of thermonuclear holocaust. About that fact there is no longer any doubt. Our freedom in this question consists only in facing the matter rationally and realistically and discussing actions to minimize the danger.

No sane citizen, political leader, or nation wants thermonuclear war. But merely not wanting it is not enough. We must understand the differences among actions which increase its risks, those which reduce them, and those which, while costly, have little influence one way or another.

From pp. 51–62 in *The Essence of Security* by Robert S. McNamara. Copyright © 1968 by Robert S. McNamara. Reprinted by permission of Harper and Row, Publishers, Inc. McNamara was secretary of defense under Presidents Kennedy and Johnson.

But there is a great difficulty in the way of constructive and profitable debate over the issues, and that is the exceptional complexity of nuclear strategy. Unless these complexities are well understood, rational discussion and decision-making are impossible.

One must begin with precise definitions. The cornerstone of our strategic policy continues to be to deter deliberate nuclear attack upon the United States or its allies. We do this by maintaining a highly reliable ability to inflict unacceptable damage upon any single aggressor or combination of aggressors at any time during the course of a strategic nuclear exchange, even after absorbing a surprise first strike. This can be defined as our *assured-destruction capability.*

It is important to understand that assured destruction is the very essence of the whole deterrence concept. We must possess an actual assured-destruction capability, and that capability also must be credible. The point is that a potential aggressor must believe that our assured-destruction capability is in fact actual, and that our will to use it in retaliation to an attack is in fact unwavering. The conclusion, then, is clear: if the United States is to deter a nuclear attack on itself or its allies, it must possess an actual and a credible assured-destruction capability.

When calculating the force required, we must be conservative in all our estimates of both a potential aggressor's capabilities and his intentions. Security depends upon assuming a worst plausible case, and having the ability to cope with it. In that eventuality we must be able to absorb the total weight of nuclear attack on our country—on our retaliatory forces, on our command and control apparatus, on our industrial capacity, on our cities, and on our population—and still be capable of damaging the aggressor to the point that his society would be simply no longer viable in twentieth-century terms. That is what deterrence of nuclear aggression means. It means the certainty of suicide to the aggressor, not merely to his military forces, but to his society as a whole.

Let us consider another term: *first-strike capability.* This is a somewhat ambiguous term, since it could mean simply the ability of one nation to attack another nation with nuclear forces first. But as it is normally used, it connotes much more: the elimination of the attacked nation's retaliatory second-strike forces. This is the sense in which it should be understood.

Clearly, first-strike capability is an important strategic concept. The United States must not and will not permit itself ever to get into a position in which another nation, or combination of nations, would possess a first-strike capability against it. Such a position not only would constitute an intolerable threat to our security, but it obviously would remove our ability to deter nuclear aggression.

We are not in that position today, and there is no foreseeable danger of our ever getting into that position. Our strategic offensive forces are immense: 1,000 Minuteman missile launchers, carefully protected belowground; 41 Polaris submarines, carrying 656 missile launchers, with the majority hidden beneath the seas at all times; and about 600 long-range bombers, approximately 40 percent of which are kept always in a high state of alert.

Our alert forces alone carry more than 2,200 weapons, each averaging more than the explosive equivalent of one megaton of TNT. Four hundred of these delivered on the Soviet Union would be sufficient to destroy over one-third of her population and one-half of her industry. All these flexible and highly reliable forces are equipped with devices that ensure their penetration of Soviet defenses.

Now what about the Soviet Union? Does it today possess a powerful nuclear arsenal? The answer is that it does. Does it possess a first-strike capability against the United States? The answer is that it does not. It cannot because we are determined to remain fully alert and we will never permit our own assured-destruction capability to drop to a point at which a Soviet first-strike capability is even remotely feasible.

Is the Soviet Union seriously attempting to acquire a first-strike capability against the United States? Although this is a question we cannot answer with absolute certainty, we believe the answer is no. In any event, the question itself is—in a sense—irrelevant; for the United States will maintain and, where necessary, strengthen its retaliatory forces so that, whatever the Soviet Union's intentions or actions, we will continue to have an assured-destruction capability vis-à-vis their society.

But there is another question that is most relevant. Does the United States, then, possess a first-strike capability against the Soviet Union? The answer is that we do not. We do not have this capability, not because we have neglected our nuclear strength; on the contrary, we have increased it to the point that we possess a clear superiority over the Soviet Union. We do not possess first-strike capability against the Soviet Union for precisely the same reason that they do not possess it against us. Quite simply, we have both built up our second-strike capability— in effect, retaliatory power—to the point that a first-strike capability on either side has become unattainable.

There is, of course, no way by which the United States could have prevented the Soviet Union from acquiring its present second-strike capability, short of a massive preemptive first strike in the 1950s. The fact is, then, that neither the Soviet Union nor the United States can attack the other without being destroyed in retaliation; nor can either of us attain a first-strike capability in the foreseeable future. Further, both the Soviet Union and the United States now possess an actual and credible second-strike capability against one another, and it is precisely this mutual capability that provides us both with the strongest possible motive to avoid a nuclear war.

The most frequent question that arises in this connection is whether or not the United States possesses nuclear superiority over the Soviet Union. The answer is that we do.

But the answer, like everything else in this matter, is technically complex. The complexity arises in part out of what measurement of superiority is most meaningful and realistic. Many commentators on the matter tend to define nuclear superiority in terms of gross megatonnage, or in terms of the number of missile launchers available. By both these standards the United States does have a substantial superiority over the Soviet Union in the weapons targeted against each other. But it is precisely these two standards of measurement that are themselves misleading. Instead, the most meaningful and realistic measurement of nuclear capability is the number of separate warheads that can be delivered accurately on individual high-priority targets with sufficient power to destroy them.

Gross megatonnage alone is an inadequate indicator of assured-destruction capability since it is unrelated to survivability, accuracy, or penetrability, and poorly related to effective elimination of multiple high-priority targets. There obviously is no advantage in overdestroying one target at the expense of leaving undamaged other targets of equal importance. Further, the number of missile launchers available is also an inadequate indicator of assured-destruction capability since many of our launchers will carry multiple warheads.

But using the realistic measurement of the number of warheads available, those which could be delivered with accuracy and effectiveness on appropriate targets in the United States or Soviet Union, the United States currently possesses a superiority over the Soviet Union of at least three or four to one. Furthermore, we will maintain superiority by these same realistic criteria for as far ahead as we can realistically plan.

One point should be made quite clear, however: our current numerical superiority over the Soviet Union in reliable, accurate, and effective warheads is both greater than we had originally planned and more than we require. In the larger equation of security our superiority is of limited significance, for even with our current superiority, or indeed with any numerical superiority realistically attainable, the blunt, inescapable fact remains that the Soviet Union, with its present forces, could still effectively destroy the United States, even after absorbing the full weight of an American first strike.

I have noted that our present superiority is greater than we had planned. How this came about is a significant illustration of the intrinsic dynamics of the nuclear arms race.

In 1961 when I became secretary of defense, the Soviet Union had a very small operational arsenal of intercontinental missiles. However, it did possess the technological and industrial capacity to enlarge that arsenal very substantially over the succeeding several years. We had no evidence that the Soviets did plan, in fact, fully to use that capability. But, as I have pointed out, a strategic planner must be conservative in his calculations; that is, he must prepare for the worst plausible case and not be content to hope and prepare merely for the most probable.

Since we could not be certain of Soviet intentions, since we could not be sure that they would not undertake a massive buildup, we had to insure against such an eventuality by undertaking a major buildup of our own Minuteman and Polaris forces. Thus, in the course of hedging against what was then only a theoretically possible Soviet buildup, we took decisions which have resulted in our current superiority in numbers of warheads and deliverable megatons. But the blunt fact remains that if we had had more accurate information about planned Soviet strategic forces, we simply would not have needed to build as large a nuclear arsenal as we have today.

Let me be absolutely clear. I am not saying that our decision in 1961 was unjustified; I am saying that it was necessitated by a lack of accurate information. Furthermore, that decision in itself, justified as it was, in the end could not possibly have left unaffected the Soviet Union's future nuclear plans.

What is essential to understand here is that the Soviet Union and the United States mutually influence one another's strategic plans. Whatever their intentions or our intentions, actions—or even realistically potential actions—on either side relating to the buildup of nuclear forces necessarily trigger reactions on the other side. It is precisely this action-reaction phenomenon that fuels an arms race.

In strategic nuclear weaponry the arms race involves a particular irony. Unlike any other era in military history, a substantial numerical superiority of weapons today does not effectively translate into political control or diplomatic leverage. While thermonuclear power is almost inconceivably awesome and represents virtually unlimited potential destructiveness, it has proven to be a limited diplomatic instrument. Its uniqueness lies in the fact that it is at the same time an all-powerful weapon and a very inadequate weapon.

The fact that the Soviet Union and the United States can mutually destroy one another regardless of who strikes first narrows the range of Soviet aggression which our nuclear forces can effectively deter. Even with our nuclear monopoly in the early postwar period, we were unable to deter the Soviet pressures against Berlin or their support of aggression in Korea. Today our nuclear superiority does not deter all forms of Soviet support of Communist insurgency in Southeast Asia. What all of this has meant is that we, and our allies as well, require substantial non-nuclear forces in order to cope with levels of aggression that massive strategic forces do not, in fact, deter.

This has been a difficult lesson both for us and for our allies to accept. There is a strong psychological tendency to regard superior nuclear forces as a simple and unfailing solution to security and an assurance of victory under any set of circumstances. What must be understood is that our nuclear strategic forces play a vital and absolutely necessary role in our security and that of our allies, but it is an intrinsically limited role. Therefore we and our allies must maintain substantial conventional forces, fully capable of dealing with a wide spectrum of lesser forms of political and military aggression. This is a level of aggression against which the use of strategic nuclear forces would not be to our advantage, and thus a level of aggression which these strategic nuclear forces by themselves cannot effectively deter. One cannot fashion a credible deterrent out of an incredible action. Thus security for the United States and its allies can only arise from the possession of a range of graduated deterrents, each of them fully credible in its own context.

In recent years the Soviets have substantially increased their offensive forces. We have been watching and evaluating this very carefully, of course; clearly the Soviet buildup is in part a reaction to our own buildup since the beginning of the 1960s. Soviet strategic planners undoubtedly reasoned that if our buildup were to continue at its accelerated pace, we might conceivably reach in time a credible first-strike capability against the Soviet Union.

That was not, in fact, our intention. Our goal was to ensure that they, with their theoretical capacity to reach such a first-strike capability, would not outdistance us. But they could not read our intentions with any greater accuracy than we could read theirs. The result has been that we have both built up our forces to a point that far exceeds a credible second-strike capability against the forces we each started with. In doing so neither of us has reached a first-strike capability. And the realities of the situation being what they are—whatever we believe their intentions to be, and whatever they believe our intentions to be—each of us can deny the other a first-strike capability in the foreseeable future.

How can we be so confident that this is the case? How can we be so certain that the Soviets cannot gradually outdistance us, either by some dramatic technological breakthrough or simply through our imperceptibly lagging behind, for whatever reason; reluctance to spend the requisite funds, distraction with military problems elsewhere, faulty intelligence, or simple negligence and naivete? All of these reasons and others have been suggested by some commentators in this country who fear that we are, in fact, falling behind to a dangerous degree.

The answer is simple and straightforward. We are not going to permit the Soviets to outdistance us, because to do so would be to jeopardize our very viability as a nation. No president, no secretary of defense, no Congress of the United States of whatever political persuasion is going to permit this nation to take that risk. We do not want a nuclear arms race with the Soviet Union, primarily because the action-reaction phenomenon makes it foolish and futile. But if the only way to prevent the Soviet Union from obtaining first-strike capability over us is to engage in such a race, the United States possesses in ample abundance the resources, the technology, and the will to run faster in that race for whatever distance is required.

What we would much prefer to do is to come to a realistic and reasonably riskless agreement with the Soviet Union which effectively prevents such an arms race. We both have strategic nuclear arsenals greatly in excess of a credible assured-destruction capability. These arsenals have reached that point of excess in each case for precisely the same reason: we each have reacted to the other's buildup with very conservative calculations. We have, that is, each built a greater arsenal than either of us needed for a second-strike capability, simply because both wanted to be able to cope with the worst plausible case.

Since we each now possess a deterrent in excess of our individual needs, both of our nations would benefit from a properly safeguarded agreement first to limit and later to reduce both our offensive and defensive strategic nuclear forces. We believe such an agreement is fully feasible since it is clearly in the interests of both our nations. But formal agreement or not, we can be sure that neither the Soviets nor we are going to risk the other's obtaining a first-strike capability. On the contrary, we can be sure that we are both going to maintain a maximum effort to preserve an assured-destruction capability.

The Problems of Limited War

HENRY A. KISSINGER

Perhaps the basic problem of strategy in the nuclear age is how to establish a relationship between a policy of deterrence and a strategy for fighting a war in case deterrence fails.

Given the power of modern weapons, a nation that relies on all-out war as its chief deterrent imposes a fearful psychological handicap on itself. The most agonizing decision a statesman can face is whether or not to unleash all-out war; all pressures will make for hesitation, short of a direct attack threatening the national existence. And he will be confirmed in his hesitations by the conviction that, so long as his retaliatory force remains intact, no shift in the territorial balance is of decisive significance. Thus both the horror and the power of modern weapons tend to paralyze action: the former because it will make few issues seem worth contending for; the latter because it causes many disputes to seem irrelevant to the overall strategic equation. The psychological equation, therefore, will almost inevitably operate against the side which can extricate itself from a situation *only* by the threat of all-out war. Who can be certain that, faced with the catastrophe of

From *Nuclear Weapons and Foreign Policy,* by Henry A. Kissinger (New York: W. W. Norton and Company, Inc., 1969), pp. 114–129 and 139–144. Copyright © 1957, 1958 by Council on Foreign Relations, Inc.; copyright © 1969 by W. W. Norton and Company, Inc. Reprinted by permission of W. W. Norton and Company. Kissinger, formerly of Harvard University, is now special assistant to the president for national security affairs.

all-out war, even Europe, long the keystone of our security, will seem worth the price?

As the power of modern weapons grows, the threat of all-out war loses its credibility and therefore its political effectiveness. Our capacity for massive retaliation did not avert the Korean war, the loss of northern Indo-China, the Soviet-Egyptian arms deal, or the Suez crisis. Moreover, whatever the credibility of our threat of all-out war, it is clear that all-out thermonuclear war does not represent a strategic option for our allies. Thus a psychological gap is created by the conviction of our allies that they have nothing to gain from massive retaliation and by the belief of the Soviet leaders that they have nothing to fear from our threat of it.

This gap may actually encourage the Soviet leaders to engage in aggression. The destructiveness of nuclear weapons having made it unlikely that any responsible statesman will lightly unleash a general war, one of the gravest dangers of all-out war lies in miscalculation. This is the only war which is within our power to avoid, assuming we leave no doubt concerning our capabilities and our determination. But even this "avoidable" war may break out if the other side becomes convinced that we cannot interfere locally and that our threats of all-out war are bluff. If that should happen, the Soviet bloc may then decide, as its nuclear arsenal grows, to absorb the peripheral areas of Eurasia by means short of all-out war and to confront us with the choice of yielding or facing the destruction of American cities. And because the Sino-Soviet leaders may well be mistaken in their assessment of our reaction to such a contingency, the reliance on "massive retaliation" may bring about the total war it seeks to prevent. . . .

What strategic doctrine is most likely to enable us to avoid the dilemma of having to make a choice between all-out war and a gradual loss of positions, between Armageddon and defeat without war? Is limited war a conceivable instrument of policy in the nuclear period? Here we must analyze precisely what is meant by limited war.

It is a historical accident reflecting the nature of our foreign involvements that we should have come to consider limited war an abberation from the "pure" case and that we have paid little attention to its strategic opportunities. In a sense this is due, too, to the manner in which we have legitimized the limited wars which we *have* fought. Every war in which we have been engaged in the Western Hemisphere was a limited war, in the sense that it did not involve a mobilization of all our material resources. But since we generally justified them as expeditions, punitive or otherwise, they rarely entered our national consciousness as part of the phenomenon of limited war.

The debate which has raged since Korea on the subject of limited war has tended to confuse the issues because it has not sufficiently distinguished between the various forms of limited war. Some wars are inherently limited because of the disparity in power between the protagonists. A war between the United States and Nicaragua would not require more than a fraction of our strength whatever the objectives we set ourselves. Such a war would be all-out in relation to Nicaragua, but limited with respect to us. Another variation of this form of limited war occurs when the stronger power is restrained from exerting its full potential by moral, political, or strategic considerations. This was the case in the Korean war, in which the Chinese probably made the maximum military effort of which they were capable while we, for a variety of reasons, limited our commitments. Still another kind of limited war is one between major powers in which the difficulty of supply prevents one side from making a total effort. An example of this is the Russo-Japanese war of 1905 in which the Russian commitment was limited to the forces that could be supplied over a single-track railway. Finally there may occur limited wars between major powers which are kept from spreading by a tacit agreement between the contestants and not by difficulties of technology or of logistics.

If one inquires which of these types of limited war are possible in the present situation, four broad categories can be distinguished. The first includes wars between secondary powers, such as between Israel and Egypt or between India and Pakistan, whether or not they involve the danger of the major powers joining in. The second type consists of wars involving either the Western powers or the Soviet bloc against powers which are clearly outmatched and under circumstances in which outside intervention is not likely. Examples of this would be Soviet intervention in the satellites, or United States military action in the Western Hemisphere. A third category are conflicts which begin as struggles between a major and a minor power but which may evolve the prospect of spreading as in the case of a Chinese move against South Vietnam or the Anglo-French "police action" against Egypt. Finally, there is the problem of limited war which begins explicitly as a war between the major powers. This is obviously the most explosive situation. If a war between major powers can be kept limited, it is clear that the first three situations would also stand a good chance of being kept from expanding.

A limited war is fought for specific political objectives which, by their very existence, tend to establish a relationship between the force employed and the goal to be attained. It reflects an attempt to *affect* the opponent's will, not to *crush* it, to make the conditions to be imposed seem more attractive than continued resistance, to strive for specific goals and not for complete annihilation.

Limited war presents the military with particular difficulties. An all-out war is relatively simple to plan because its limits are set by military considerations and even by military capacity. The targets for an all-out war are fixed, and the force requirements are determined by the need to assemble overwhelming power. The characteristic of a limited war, on the other hand, is the existence of ground rules which define the relationship of military to political objectives. Planning becomes much more conjectural, much more subtle, and much more indeterminate, if only because a war against a major enemy can be kept limited only if both parties so desire, and this desire in itself tends to introduce a factor which is outside the control of planning officers. Since the military can never be certain how many forces the opponent will in fact commit to the struggle and since they feel obliged to guard against every contingency, they will devise plans for limited war which insensibly approach the level of all-out conflict.

From a purely military point of view they are right, for limited war is essentially a political act. Its distinguishing feature is that it has no "purely" military solution. The political leadership must, for this reason, assume the responsibility for defining the framework within which the military are to develop their plans and capabilities. To demand of the military that they set their own limits is to set in motion a vicious circle. The more the military plan on the basis of crushing the enemy even in a limited area, the more the political leadership will recoil before the risks of taking *any* military action. The more limited war is conceived as a "small" all-out war, the more it will produce inhibitions similar to those generated by the concept of massive retaliation. The prerequisite for a policy of limited war is to reintroduce the political element into our concept of warfare and to discard the notion that policy ends when war begins or that war can have goals distinct from those of national policy.

It is often argued that since limited wars offer no inherent guarantee against their expansion, they may gradually merge into all-out war. On purely logical grounds, the argument is unassailable. But it assumes that the major protagonists will be looking for an excuse to expand the war whereas in reality both sides will probably grasp at every excuse, however illogical, to keep a thermonuclear holocaust from occurring. [That], in fact, [is] what happened in the Korean war, at a time when the weapons technology was much less horrendous. We refused to retaliate against the Manchurian air bases from which enemy planes were attacking our forces. And the Chinese made no effort to interfere with our aircraft carriers, or with our bases in Japan, or even to launch an attack against our only two big supply ports, Pusan and Inchon.

These limitations were not brought about by logic or agreement but by a mutual reluctance to expand the conflict. It is clear that war cannot be limited unless both sides wish to keep it limited. The argument in favor of the possibility of limited war is that both sides have a common and overwhelming interest in preventing it from spreading. The fear that an all-out thermonuclear war might lead to the disintegration of the social structure offers an opportunity to set limits to both war and diplomacy.

The conduct of limited war has two prerequisites: a doctrine and a capability. So long as we consider limited war as an aberration from the "pure" case of all-out war we will not be ready to grasp its opportunities, and we will conduct the wars we do fight hesitantly and ambiguously, oscillating between the twin temptations to expand them (that is, to bring them closer to our notion of what war should be like), or to end them at the first enemy overture.

A doctrine for limited war will have to discard any illusions about what can be achieved by means of it. Limited war is not a cheaper substitute for massive retaliation. On the contrary, it must be based on the awareness that with the end of our atomic monopoly it is no longer possible to impose unconditional surrender at an acceptable cost.

The purpose of limited war is to inflict losses or to pose risks for the enemy out of proportion to the objectives under dispute. The more moderate the objective, the less violent the war is likely to be. This does not mean that military operations cannot go beyond the territory or the objective in dispute; indeed, one way of increasing the enemy's willingness to settle is to deprive him of something he can regain only by making peace. But the result of a limited war cannot depend on military considerations alone; it reflects an ability to harmonize political and military objectives. An attempt to reduce the enemy to impotence would surely lead to all-out war.

Nevertheless, a strategic doctrine which renounces the imposition of unconditional surrender should not be confused with the acceptance of a stalemate. The notion that there is no middle ground between unconditional surrender and the *status quo ante* is much too mechanical. To be sure, a restoration of the *status quo ante* is often the simplest solution, but it is not the only possible one. The argument that neither side will accept a defeat, however limited, without utilizing every weapon in its arsenal is contradicted both by psychology and by experience. There would seem to be no sense in seeking to escape a limited defeat through bringing on the cataclysm of an all-out war, particularly if all-out war threatens a calamity far transcending the penalties of losing a limited war. It simply does not follow that because one side stands to lose from a limited war, it could gain from an all-out war. On the contrary, both sides face the same dilemma: that the power of modern weapons has made all-out war useless as an instrument of policy, except for acts of desperation.

The West has accepted several contractions of its sphere without resorting to all-out war. If the military position of the Soviet leadership became untenable and it were offered face-saving alternatives short of surrender, it too might accept local withdrawals without resorting to all-out war. Even if limited war offered no more than the possibility of local stalemates, it would represent a strategic improvement, for our current problem is our inability to defend major areas except by the threat of a thermonuclear holocaust which we should make every effort to avoid.

The development of a wide spectrum of capabilities would be of no crucial importance even shou'd it be assumed that any war between us and the U.S.S.R. or China will inevitably be all-out. For, unless the exchange of nuclear and thermonuclear blows leads to the social collapse of both contenders—a distinct possibility—the side which has in being superior forces for other forms of conflict may win out in the end. If the Red Army, for example, should succeed in overrunning Eurasia during or after an exchange of all-out blows, we would probably not have sufficient resources remaining to undertake a reconquest. As stock-piles of the largest modern weapons are exhausted or delivery vehicles are used up, an increasing premium is placed on a diversified military capability and not only vis-à-vis the enemy but toward hitherto secondary powers as well. In the absence of forces for other forms of conflict, all-out war may merely pave the way for the dominance of the world by states whose social structure and forces-in-being have remained more or less intact during the struggle-to-death of the superstates.

There exist three reasons then for developing a strategy of limited war. First, limited war represents the only means for preventing the Soviet bloc, at an acceptable cost, from overrunning the peripheral areas of Eurasia. Second, a wide range of military capabilities may spell the difference between defeat and victory even in an all-out war. Finally, the intermediate applications of our power offer the best chance to bring about strategic changes favorable to our side.

For while a balance can be maintained along existing lines on the Eurasian continent, it will always be tenuous. So long as Soviet armies are poised on the Elbe, Western Europe will be insecure. So long as Chinese might presses upon free Asia, the uncommitted powers will seek safety in neutralism. The United States faces the task not only of stemming the Soviet expansion, but also of reducing Soviet pressures and demonstrating the limitations of Soviet power and skills. The resolution of the free world, now assailed by a sense of its impotence, will improve to the extent that it realizes that the Soviet bloc, behind its facade of monolithic power, also shrinks from certain consequences. When we have achieved this capability and this understanding, we may be in a position to reduce the Soviet sphere. . . .

Whatever the theoretical advantages of limited war, is it practical? Does not a policy of limited war run up against the geographic reality that the Soviet bloc possesses interior lines of communication and may therefore be able to assemble a superior force at any given point along its periphery? Can we afford a policy of limited war or will it not overstrain our resources just as surely as would all-out war? Does not the concern with local resistance mistake the real security problem which, in major areas, is political instability and a standard of living considered oppressively low by the majority of the population?

Admittedly, we alone cannot possibly defend the Soviet periphery by local actions and the present period of revolutionary change will not be managed solely by reliance on a military doctrine. Our task also includes strengthening the will to resist among the peoples threatened by Communist expansionism. In the underdeveloped third of the world this means pursuing a variety of measures: a political program to gain the confidence of local populations and to remove the stigma of colonialism from us, together with a degree of economic assistance which will help bring about political stability. But such programs, although essential, will in the end be ineffective unless we improve our capacity for local defense. We have a weakness for considering problems as "primarily" economic or "primarily" military rather than as total situations in which political, economic, and military considerations merge, which is the way the Soviet leadership regards policy.

Thus one of the conditions of political stability is our capacity to react to local aggression at the place of its occurrence. Few leaders of threatened countries will wish to rely for protection on our strategic superiority in an all-out war. Victory in a general war will mean little to a country which meanwhile has undergone the moral and physical ravages of Soviet occupation.

Can the non-Soviet countries of Eurasia be defended, assuming the willingness of the threatened countries to resist and an ability on our part to help them? In support of a negative answer such factors are cited as the "unlimited" Soviet manpower and the vast distances of the threatened areas from the centers of our strength. Absolute numbers are important, but only the part of them that can be utilized effectively is strategically significant. The value of Sino-Soviet manpower is limited by the capacity of the Soviet bloc to equip and train it, and its effectiveness is reduced by the power of modern weapons and by difficulties of communications and supply.

The particular danger zone for limited wars is the arc which stretches from the eastern border of Turkey around the periphery of Eurasia. Within that area the Indian subcontinent is protected by mountain barriers and by extremely difficult communications. Aggression against the Middle East would have to count on the flanking position of Turkey and, despite the Suez fiasco, Great Britain would probably join in resistance. An attack on Burma would antagonize India and would be difficult to supply, and the same would be true of the remainder of Southeast Asia. An attack in the Far East would have to take place either across water or against indigenous forces, as in Korea. Moreover, if we utilize nuclear weapons there will be an inherent upper limit to the number of troops that can be profitably employed in threatened areas. Thus if we could develop forces capable of conducting limited war and of getting into position rapidly, we should be able to defeat the Soviet Union or China in local engagements despite their interior position.

If we commit ourselves to a strategy of local defense, do we not run the risk of having our forces always at the wrong place? Cannot the Soviet bloc utilize its interior position to keep us constantly off balance? To be sure, the Soviet bloc is able to pick the initial point of attack, but the greater mobility of its interior position is illusory because of the difficulties of communication. Once the Soviet armies are committed in one area, they cannot be shifted at will against our air power or with greater speed than we can shift ours by sea or air. The Chinese Communists, for example, cannot draw us into Indo-China and then attack in Burma with the same army. They can, of course, build up two armies, but we should be able to learn of this in time and then decide to defend one or the other area, or both, depending on the strategic situation. . . .

Limited war is not simply a question of appropriate military forces and doctrines. It also places heavy demands on the discipline and subtlety of the political leadership and on the confidence of the society in it. For limited war is psychologically a much more complex problem than all-out war. In an all-out war the alternatives will be either surrender or resistance against a threat to the national existence. To be sure, psychological factors will largely determine the relative willingness to engage in an all-out war, and the side more willing to run risks may gain an important advantage in the conduct of diplomacy. However, once the decision to fight is taken, a nation's physical ability to conduct war will be the most important factor in the outcome.

In a limited war, on the other hand, the psychological equation will be of crucial importance not only with respect to the decision to enter the war but throughout the course of military operations. A limited war among major powers is kept limited by the conscious choice of the protagonists. Either side has the physical power to expand it, and, to the extent that each side is willing to increase its commitment in preference either to a stalemate or to a defeat, the war will gradually become an all-out one. The restraint which keeps a war limited is a psychological one: the consequences of a limited victory or a limited defeat or a stalemate—the three possible outcomes of a limited war—must seem preferable to the consequences of an all-out war.

In a limited war the choices are more varied than in an all-out conflict and their nature is more ambiguous. Victory offers no final solution and defeat does not carry with it the penalty of national catastrophe. As a result, the psychological correlation of forces in a limited war is not stable; it depends on a series of intangibles. The side which is more willing to risk an all-out war or can convince its opponent of its greater readiness to run that risk is in the stronger position. Even when the willingness of both sides to run risks is equal at the beginning of the war, the psychological equation will constantly be shifting, depending on the course of military operations. Because the limitation of war is brought about by the fear of unleashing a thermonuclear holocaust, the psychological equation is, paradoxically, constantly shifting *against* the side which seems to be winning. The greater the transformation it seeks, the more plausible will become the threat by its opponent of launching an all-out war. The closer defeat in the limited war brings the losing side to the consequences which it would suffer by defeat in an all-out war, the less it will feel restrained from resorting to extreme measures.

At the same time, the winning side may become increasingly reluctant to test the opponent's willingness to resort to all-out war. For while the winning side is staking its chance for obtaining a favorable transformation, the losing side is risking an adverse change of position. The better the position of the winning side, the more secure it will feel and the less it will be willing to take the risks of an all-out war. The more precarious the position of the losing side becomes, the more insecure it will feel and the more likely it is to raise its commitment toward the level of an all-out war. The prerequisite of victory in a limited war is therefore to determine under what circumstances one side may be willing to run greater risks for winning than its opponent will accept to avoid losing. A calculation of this character must pay special attention to the importance of diplomatic overtures which make clear that national survival is not at stake and that a settlement is possible on reasonable terms. Otherwise the result is almost certain to be either stalemate or all-out war.

If an opponent attaches great importance to an area in dispute— or is thought to attach great importance to it—he will have a distinct psychological advantage in a limited war. This was the case with China's role in Korea. Some areas may be thought so important to one of the contenders that they will be protected by the belief of the opponent that any attack on them will lead to a general war. Protection for these areas will be achieved less by local defense than by overall strategic balance. This has been the case up to now with Western Europe with respect to the United States, or with the satellite regions with respect to the U.S.S.R. As total war poses increasingly ominous prospects, however, the overall strategic balance will be a less and less adequate protection to threatened areas, for ever fewer regions will seem worth this price. As the implications of all-out war with modern weapons become better understood, security for many areas will increasingly depend on the capability for local action. Limited war would thereby become a test of the determination of the contenders, a gauge of the importance they attach to disputed issues. If one side attaches greater importance to an area or an issue and is willing to pay a higher price, and if it possesses a capability for waging a limited war, it may well achieve a favorable shift in the strategic equation.

The key to a successful policy of limited war is to keep the challenge to the opponent, whether diplomatic or military, below the threshold which would unleash an all-out war. The greater the risk in relation to the challenge, the less total the response is likely to be. The more the challenge approximates the risks posed by all-out war, the more difficult it will be to limit the conflict. A policy of limited war therefore presupposes three conditions: the ability to generate pressures other than the threat of all-out war; the ability to create a climate in which survival is not thought to be at stake in each issue; and the ability to keep control of public opinion in case a disagreement arises over whether national survival is at stake. The first condition depends to a considerable extent on the flexibility of our military policy; the second on the subtlety of our diplomacy; the third will reflect the courage of our leadership. . . .

But assuming that it will be possible to create a spectrum of military capabilities to meet the widest range of Soviet challenges, will our diplomacy be able to bring about a framework in which national survival is thought not to be at stake? Pressures severe enough to cause withdrawal or stalemate may, after all, seem severe enough to threaten survival, especially to a regime like that of Soviet Russia. It must be admitted that the challenge to our diplomacy is formidable. It would be hopeless except against the background of a retaliatory capability which can make the Soviet leadership recoil from the prospect of an all-out war. As long as we maintain a powerful strategic striking force, an all-out conflict is likely in only two contingencies: if the Soviets see an opportunity to achieve hegemony in Eurasia by peripheral actions which we would be unable to counter except by all-out war; or if the U.S.S.R. should misunderstand our intentions and interpret each military move on our part as a prelude to a thermonuclear holocaust.

Provided our military policy equips us with a wide spectrum of capabilities, the task of our diplomacy will be to convey to the Soviet bloc what we understand by limited war, at least to some extent. This becomes all the more important because Soviet reactions to our measures will depend less on what we intend than on what we are thought by the Soviet leaders to intend. The power and speed of modern weapons make too much obscurity dangerous. Unless there has been some degree of comprehension of the nature of limited war on both sides, it may be impossible to improvise it in the confusion of battle. Diplomacy should therefore strive to insure that the opponent obtains the information he requires to make the correct decisions. To be sure, such a course will not restrain an enemy determined on a showdown. It may, however, prevent him from stumbling into an all-out war based on miscalculation or on the misinterpretation of our intentions. . . .

Whatever aspect of our strategic problem we consider—mitigating the horrors of war, creating a spectrum of capabilities to resist likely Soviet challenges—we are brought to recognize the importance of developing a strategy which makes room for the possibility of limited war. Creating a readiness for limited war should not be considered a problem of choice but of necessity. It results from the impossibility of combining both maximum force and the maximum willingness to act. . . .

. . . The strategy outlined in this chapter will not be easy to implement. It presupposes a military capability which is truly graduated. It assumes a diplomacy which can keep each conflict from being considered the prelude to a final showdown. And it requires strong nerves. We can make a strategy of limited war stick only if we leave no doubt about our readiness and our ability to face a final showdown.

4

WAR AS AN EXPRESSION
OF HUMAN NATURE

Introduction

It is often said that war is a natural manifestation of innate human aggressiveness, or that human nature itself makes recurrent war inevitable.
This position, which many believe to have been indicated by the work of
Sigmund Freud, has received renewed support in Konrad Lorenz's celebrated book *On Aggression*. It seems to follow that efforts to prevent
war are misguided attempts to change the eternal order of nature. The
following articles deal with this claim about the anthropological and
psychological roots of war.

The simplest form of the claim that human nature itself is the cause
of war is based on the observation that group conflict seems to be a
universal characteristic of all but the most primitive of human cultures.
It is said that war is the result of the division of labor, the fragmentation
of the extended family, and the rise of communities with relatively distinct political institutions. Since these characteristics are the facts of
social life in all but primitive cultures, war is thought to be inevitable.

Margaret Mead's article is a classic refutation of this position. Mead argues that there are both primitive and advanced cultures that do not include organized war among their patterns of social behavior. She contends that war must be viewed as a social invention, much like trial by jury, brought about by a complex of innate and environmental characteristics. Thus, there is some hope that war could be replaced by other social inventions serving the same purposes when it becomes clear that war is no longer a functional mode of social behavior.

Another claim regarding the relationship of human nature and war is that, while it is clearly not true that all or most of us are so innately aggressive that war is "in our blood," *some* men are so aggressive that they will always resort to violence to achieve their objectives. War is violent behavior by organized groups of these aggressive individuals (armies) used as a means of controlling the behavior of others. Advocates of this position see war as the result of two connected factors: the innate aggressiveness of some individuals and the dynamics of group behavior. Both are part of what is thought of as "human nature."

Mead responds to this claim by distinguishing between extreme forms of interpersonal violence and group-sanctioned mass violence, or war. She argues that there are cultures in which instances of the former are commonplace, yet war as a distinct kind of group behavior is unknown. In these cultures other mechanisms are employed to resolve intergroup conflicts and to punish aggressive individual behavior. This supports her belief that a prerequisite of war is a culture possessing the *idea* of war.

Corning's paper responds to this claim more fully and summarizes a wide range of psychological and anthropological literature that has appeared since publication of Mead's famous essay. Corning outlines three major schools of thought concerning the roots of human violence. None of these, he contends, provides a sufficient account of the phenomenon of interpersonal violence, although they do indicate that aggression is a far more complex and multifaceted propensity than has conventionally been assumed. Furthermore, what is known about aggressive behaviors indicates that their relation to *group* violence is at best indirect. A variety of social and environmental factors must be present for aggressive drives to manifest themselves in war. Even when these factors are present, war can be either functional or dysfunctional in terms of evolution. If, from an evolutionary viewpoint, war is adaptive to natural or environmental pressures, it may not be undesirable. However, Corning concludes, the chances now seem to be slim that war can continue to be a functional mode of group interaction given the destructiveness of modern weapons and the kinds of conflicts that characteristically dominate international relations.

The weight of psychological and anthropological thought now indicates that any formulation of the argument that human nature makes recurrent war inevitable is bound to be misleading. Regardless of whether war is seen as a social invention or as a mode of group behavior specific to a particular evolutionary period, it remains possible that other, less violent and costly ways could be found to serve the social functions now served by war and its threat. Corning, for example, believes that we should once and for all renounce group violence for conflict resolution in favor of politics on an international scale. He further claims that there are no psychological or anthropological reasons why this should not be possible.

SUGGESTIONS FOR FURTHER READING

Leonard Berkowitz, *Aggression—A Social-Psychological Analysis.* New York: McGraw-Hill, 1962.

Leon Bramson and George Goethals, eds., *War: Studies from Psychology, Sociology and Anthropology.* New York: Basic Books, 1968.

Jerome Frank, *Sanity and Survival.* New York: Random House, 1967.

Sigmund Freud, *Civilization and Its Discontents.* New York: W. W. Norton & Co., 1961.

Konrad Lorenz, *On Aggression.* New York: Harcourt, Brace and World, 1966.

Elton H. McNeil, ed., *The Nature of Human Conflict.* Englewood Cliffs, N.J.: Prentice-Hall, 1965.

M. F. Ashley Montagu, ed., *Man and Aggression.* New York: Oxford University Press, 1968.

Warfare Is Only an Invention—
Not a Biological Necessity

MARGARET MEAD

Is war a biological necessity, a sociological inevitability or just a bad invention? Those who argue for the first view endow man with such pugnacious instincts that some outlet in aggressive behavior is necessary if man is to reach full human stature. It was this point of view which lay back of William James's famous essay, "The Moral Equivalent of War," in which he tried to retain the warlike virtues and channel them in new directions. A similar point of view has lain back of the Soviet Union's attempt to make competition between groups rather than between individuals. A basic, competitive, aggressive, warring human nature is assumed, and those who wish to outlaw war or outlaw competitiveness merely try to find new and less socially destructive ways in which these biologically given aspects of man's nature can find expression. Then there are those who take the second view: warfare is the inevitable concomitant of the development of the state, the struggle for land and natural resources of class societies springing, not from the nature of man, but from the nature of history. War is nevertheless inevitable unless we change our social system and outlaw classes, the struggle for power, and possessions; and in the event of our success warfare would disappear, as a symptom vanishes when the disease is cured.

One may hold a sort of compromise position between these two ex-

From *Asia,* vol. 40, no. 8 (August 1940), pp. 402–405. Reprinted by permission of the author. Margaret Mead, a leading anthropologist and author, is president of the American Museum of Natural History in New York.

tremes; one may claim that all aggression springs from the frustration of man's biologically determined drives and that, since all forms of culture are frustrating, it is certain each new generation will be aggressive and the aggression will find its natural and inevitable expression in race war, class war, nationalistic war, and so on. All three of these positions are very popular today among those who think seriously about the problems of war and its possible prevention, but I wish to urge another point of view, less defeatist perhaps than the first and third, and more accurate than the second: that is, that warfare, by which I mean recognized conflict between two groups *as groups,* in which each group puts an army (even if the army is only fifteen pygmies) into the field to fight and kill, if possible, some of the members of the army of the other group— that warfare of this sort is an invention like any other of the inventions in terms of which we order our lives, such as writing, marriage, cooking our food instead of eating it raw, trial by jury or burial of the dead, and so on. Some of this list any one will grant are inventions: trial by jury is confined to very limited portions of the globe; we know that there are tribes that do not bury their dead but instead expose or cremate them; and we know that only part of the human race has had the knowledge of writing as its cultural inheritance. But, whenever a way of doing things is found universally, such as the use of fire or the practice of some form of marriage, we tend to think at once that it is not an invention at all but an attribute of humanity itself. And yet even such universals as marriage and the use of fire are inventions like the rest, very basic ones, inventions which were perhaps necessary if human history was to take the turn that it has taken, but nevertheless inventions. At some point in his social development man was undoubtedly without the institution of marriage or the knowledge of the use of fire.

The case for warfare is much clearer because there are peoples even today who have no warfare. Of these the Eskimo are perhaps the most conspicuous examples, but the Lepchas of Sikkim described by Geoffrey Gorer in *Himalayan Village* are as good. Neither of these peoples understands war, not even defensive warfare. The idea of warfare is lacking, and this idea is as essential to really carrying on war as an alphabet or a syllabary is to writing. But whereas the Lepchas are a gentle, unquarrelsome people, and the advocates of other points of view might argue that they are not full human beings or that they had never been frustrated and so had no aggression to expand in warfare, the Eskimo case gives no such possibility of interpretation. The Eskimo are not a mild and meek people; many of them are turbulent and troublesome. Fights, theft of wives, murder, cannibalism, occur among them—all outbursts of passionate men goaded by desire or intolerable circumstance.

Here are men faced with hunger, men faced with loss of their wives, men faced with the threat of extermination by other men, and here are orphan children, growing up miserably with no one to care for them, mocked and neglected by those about them. The personality necessary for war, the circumstances necessary to goad men to desperation are present, but there is no war. When a traveling Eskimo entered a settlement he might have to fight the strongest man in the settlement to establish his position among them, but this was a test of strength and bravery, not war. The idea of warfare, of one *group* organizing against another *group* to maim and wound and kill them was absent. And without that idea passions might rage but there was no war.

But, it may be argued, isn't this because the Eskimo have such a low and undeveloped form of social organization? They own no land, they move from place to place, camping, it is true, season after season on the same site, but this is not something to fight for as the modern nations of the world fight for land and raw materials. They have no permanent possessions that can be looted, no towns that can be burned. They have no social classes to produce stress and strains within the society which might force it to go to war outside. Doesn't the absence of war among the Eskimo, while disproving the biological necessity of war, just go to confirm the point that it is the state of development of the society which accounts for war, and nothing else?

We find the answer among the pygmy peoples of the Andaman Islands in the Bay of Bengal. The Andamans also represent an exceedingly low level of society; they are a hunting and food-gathering people; they live in tiny hordes without any class stratification; their houses are simpler than the snow houses of the Eskimo. But they knew about warfare. The army might contain only fifteen determined pygmies marching in a straight line, but it was the real thing none the less. Tiny army met tiny army in open battle, blows were exchanged, casualties suffered, and the state of warfare could only be concluded by a peacemaking ceremony.

Similarly, among the Australian aborigines, who built no permanent dwellings but wandered from water hole to water hole over their almost desert country, warfare—and rules of "international law"—were highly developed. The student of social evolution will seek in vain for his obvious causes of war, struggle for lands, struggle for power of one group over another, expansion of population, need to divert the minds of a populace restive under tyranny, or even the ambition of a successful leader to enhance his own prestige. All are absent, but warfare as a practice remained, and men engaged in it and killed one another in the course of a war because killing is what is done in wars.

From instances like these it becomes apparent that an inquiry into the causes of war misses the fundamental point as completely as does an insistence upon the biological necessity of war. If a people have an idea of going to war and the idea that war is the way in which certain situations, defined within their society, are to be handled, they will sometimes go to war. If they are a mild and unaggressive people, like the Pueblo Indians, they may limit themselves to defensive warfare; but they will be forced to think in terms of war because there are peoples near them who have warfare as a pattern, and offensive, raiding, pillaging warfare at that. When the pattern of warfare is known, people like the Pueblo Indians will defend themselves, taking advantage of their natural defenses, the *mesa* village site, and people like the Lepchas, having no natural defenses and no idea of warfare, will merely submit to the invader. But the essential point remains the same. There is a way of behaving which is known to a given people and labeled as an appropriate form of behavior; a bold and warlike people like the Sioux or the Maori may label warfare as desirable as well as possible; a mild people like the Pueblo Indians may label warfare as undesirable; but to the minds of both peoples the possibility of warfare is present. Their thoughts, their hopes, their plans are oriented about this idea, that warfare may be selected as the way to meet some situation.

So simple peoples and civilized peoples, mild peoples and violent, assertive peoples, will all go to war if they have the invention, just as those peoples who have the custom of dueling will have duels and peoples who have the pattern of vendetta will indulge in vendetta. And, conversely, peoples who do not know of dueling will not fight duels, even though their wives are seduced and their daughters ravished; they may on occasion commit murder but they will not fight duels. Cultures which lack the idea of the vendetta will not meet every quarrel in this way. A people can use only the forms it has. So the Balinese have their special way of dealing with a quarrel between two individuals: if the two feel that the causes of quarrel are heavy they may go and register their quarrel in the temple before the gods, and, making offerings, they may swear never to have anything to do with each other again. Today they register such mutual "not-speaking" with the Dutch government officials. But in other societies, although individuals might feel as full of animosity and as unwilling to have any further contact as do the Balinese, they cannot register their quarrel with the gods and go on quietly about their business because registering quarrels with the gods is not an invention of which they know.

Yet, if it be granted that warfare is after all an invention, it may nevertheless be an invention that lends itself to certain types of personality, to the exigent needs of autocrats, to the expansionist desires of crowded peoples, to the desire for plunder and rape and loot which is engendered by a dull and frustrating life. What, then, can we say of this congruence between warfare and its uses? If it is a form which fits so well, is not this congruence the essential point? But even here the primitive material causes us to wonder, because there are tribes who go to war merely for glory, having no quarrel with the enemy, suffering from no tyrant within their boundaries, anxious neither for land nor loot nor women, but merely anxious to win prestige which within that tribe has been declared obtainable only by war and without which no young man can hope to win his sweetheart's smile of approval. But if, as was the case with the Bush Negroes of Dutch Guiana, it is artistic ability which is necessary to win a girl's approval, the same young man would have to be carving rather than going out on a war party.

In many parts of the world, war is a game in which the individual can win counters—counters which bring him prestige in the eyes of his own sex or of the opposite sex; he plays for these counters as he might, in our society, strive for a tennis championship. Warfare is a frame for such prestige-seeking merely because it calls for the display of certain skills and certain virtues; all of these skills—riding straight, shooting straight, dodging the missiles of the enemy and sending one's own straight to the mark—can be equally well exercised in some other framework, and, equally, the virtues—endurance, bravery, loyalty, steadfastness—can be displayed in other contexts. The tie-up between proving oneself a man and proving this by a success in organized killing is due to a definition which many societies have made of manliness. And often, even in those societies which counted success in warfare a proof of human worth, strange turns were given to the idea, as when the plains Indians gave their highest awards to the man who touched a live enemy rather than to the man who brought in a scalp—from a dead enemy—because the latter was less risky. Warfare is just an invention known to the majority of human societies by which they permit their young men either to accumulate prestige or avenge their honor or acquire loot or wives or slaves or sago lands or cattle or appease the blood lust of their gods or the restless souls of the recently dead. It is just an invention, older and more widespread than the jury system, but none the less an invention.

But, once we have said this, have we said anything at all? Despite a few instances, dear to the hearts of controversialists, of the loss of the useful arts, once an invention is made which proves congruent with human needs or social forms, it tends to persist. Grant that war is an invention, that it is not a biological necessity nor the outcome of certain special types of social forms, still, once the invention is made, what are we to do about it? The Indian who had been subsisting on the buffalo for generations because with his primitive weapons he could slaughter only a limited number of buffalo did not return to his primitive weapons when he saw that the white man's more efficient weapons were exterminating the buffalo. A desire for the white man's cloth may mortgage the South Sea Islander to the white man's plantation, but he does not return to making bark cloth, which would have left him free. Once an invention is known and accepted, men do not easily relinquish it. The skilled workers may smash the first steam looms which they feel are to be their undoing, but they accept them in the end, and no movement which has insisted upon the mere abandonment of usable inventions has ever had much success. Warfare is here, as part of our thought; the deeds of warriors are immortalized in the words of our poets; the toys of our children are modeled upon the weapons of the soldier; the frame of reference within which our statesmen and our diplomats work always contains war. If we know that it is not inevitable, that it is due to historical accident that warfare is one of the ways in which we think of behaving, are we given any hope by that? What hope is there of persuading nations to abandon war, nations so thoroughly imbued with the idea that resort to war is, if not actually desirable and noble, at least inevitable whenever certain defined circumstances arise?

In answer to this question I think we might turn to the history of other social inventions, and inventions which must once have seemed as firmly entrenched as warfare. Take the methods of trial which preceded the jury system: ordeal and trial by combat. Unfair, capricious, alien as they are to our feeling today, they were once the only methods open to individuals accused of some offense. The invention of trial by jury gradually replaced these methods until only witches, and finally not even witches, had to resort to the ordeal. And for a long time the jury system seemed the one best and finest method of settling legal disputes, but today new inventions, trial before judges only or before commissions, are replacing the jury system. In each case the old method was replaced by a new social invention; the ordeal did not go out because people thought it unjust or wrong, it went out because a method more congruent with the institutions and feelings of the period was invented. And, if we despair over the way in which war seems such an ingrained habit of most of the human race, we can take comfort from the fact that a poor invention will usually give place to a better invention.

For this, two conditions at least are necessary. The people must recognize the defects of the old invention, and someone must make a new one. Propaganda against warfare, documentation of its terrible cost in human suffering and social waste, these prepare the ground by teaching people to feel that warfare is a defective social institution. There is further needed a belief that social invention is possible and the invention of new methods which will render warfare as out-of-date as the tractor is making the plow, or the motor car the horse and buggy. A form of behavior becomes out-of-date only when something else takes its place, and in order to invent forms of behavior which will make war obsolete, it is a first requirement to believe that an invention is possible.

Human Violence:
Some Causes and Implications

PETER A. CORNING

> Winston could not definitely remember a time when his country
> had not been at war . . . war had literally been continuous,
> though strictly speaking it had not always been the same war.
>
> GEORGE ORWELL, *1984*

War, like poverty, seems always to be with us. And the experience of protagonist Winston Smith in Orwell's futuristic nightmare, *1984*, could be applied without too much exaggeration to almost any epoch in human history.

Indeed, the record is appalling. Since man began keeping track of such things, warfare has been virtually incessant. Wright (1962) estimated that between 1500 A.D. and 1942 there were on the average 500 armed clashes per year, while the total number of distinct, formal wars has averaged somewhat less than one a year. And those figures exclude internal wars, which have added their fair share to the toll; between 1900 and 1965, alone, there were some 350 violent revolutions, or more than five a year.

All told, Richardson (1960) has estimated that, for the 125-year period from 1820 to 1945, there were at least 59 million deaths from human violence—individual and group—while countless millions more

Prepared for the symposium, "Value and Knowledge Requirements for Peace," American Association for the Advancement of Science, 138th Annual Meeting, Philadelphia, Pennsylvania, December 1971. Partial support for the preparation of this paper was provided by NIMH training grant No. MH-11167. The author also gratefully acknowledges the support of the Institute for Behavioral Genetics, University of Colorado. Corning teaches political science at Fordham University.

have been injured and maimed at the hands of their fellow human beings.[1]

Yet we shrink from the unpleasant conclusion: Man is a violent and destructive animal. He is easily provoked to violence and very often seems to enjoy it. Not only that, but violent behavior is, in many instances, socially approved, encouraged, and rewarded.

Facing the truth about ourselves is a start. But we must also face up to the question of why man is so violence-prone. How do we explain the extreme aggressiveness of this killer ape? Clearly he is one of the more successful species (at least, as viewed from our current vantage point). Can it be that man is successful in spite of his violent ways—or perhaps because of them? And what are the mechanisms involved? Do we understand enough about the causes of human violence at this point to hope that we may ultimately be able to predict, and, if we should choose, control it?

Before human aggression became a major concern of behavioral scientists, it had long been the subject of philosophical speculation, and hypotheses about what the Christian theologians referred to as "the problem of evil" go back to the taproots of Western culture. Aristotle, for instance, took a balanced view of the subject, treating human aggressiveness as innate but controllable: "Man, when perfected, is the best of animals; but if he be isolated from law and justice he is the worst of all. . . . If he be without virtue, he is a most unholy and savage being."

However, some philosophers have taken a far more dour view. Writing in the cutthroat atmosphere of Renaissance Italy, Machiavelli argued that: "All those who have written upon civil institutions demonstrate . . . that whoever desires to found a state and give it laws, must start with assuming that all men are bad and ever ready to display their vicious nature. . . ."

Similarly, Thomas Hobbes surveyed the carnage of the English civil war of 1688 and asserted as "a general inclination of all mankind, a perpetual and restless desire for power after power that ceaseth only in death." Unless restrained by some superior authority, the natural state of man would be, according to Hobbes, a "war of every man against every man."

At the other extreme, Jean Jacques Rousseau portrayed man as being naturally innocent, a *tabula rasa* whose violent behavior was the product of sick societies. Rousseau believed it would be possible to transform

---

[1] Of course, any such reckoning of human violence should include the uncounted members of *other* species killed by *Homo sapiens*—in many cases for the "fun" of it.

man into a pacific and sociable creature if only his culture could be transformed.

In recent decades, the argument about human violence has been taken over by the behavioral scientists, and three major alternative explanations have been advanced over the years—the so-called "biological-instinctual," "social learning" (or "socio-behavioristic"), and "frustration-aggression" hypotheses.[2]

The biological-instinctual hypothesis, tracing its heritage to Freud, postulates an instinctive aggressive drive, or appetite. As Freud wrote: "A powerful measure of desire for aggression has to be reckoned as a part of man's instinctual endowment . . . *Homo homini lupus;* who has the courage to dispute it in the face of all the evidence in his own life and history?" More recently, this hypothesis has been associated with ethologist Konrad Lorenz (1966), psychiatrist Anthony Storr (1968), and others.

The social learning theory, by contrast, derives from a purely environmentalist, or behaviorist, model of man. Proceeding from the Rousseauian assumption that the human animal begins life essentially as a blank slate and is programmed almost entirely by his social environment (a viewpoint that drew support from some crude experiments with newborns in the 1920s by psychologist John B. Watson and others), behaviorists posited that the "antecedent social stimulus events" in each person's life experience serve to program a "response hierarchy" which predetermines how the individual will respond to subsequent stimuli. Violent behavior is thus a learned behavior, they postulate.

Perhaps the most exhaustively tested, if not influential, explanation of aggression—the frustration-aggression hypothesis—represents a middle-ground position. Originally put forward in 1939 by a group of Yale psychologists, the basic hypothesis, as first formulated, was very simple —in fact, too simple: "The proposition is that the occurrence of aggressive behavior always presupposes the existence of frustration and, contrariwise, that the existence of frustration always leads to some form of aggression." Frustration occurs "when a goal response suffers interference," and the existence of frustrations presupposes certain innate desires or desired goal-states (Dollard *et al.* 1939). Aggression was thus seen by the Yale group as a secondary drive that was induced by the interaction between innate primary drives and the environment.

In the years since 1939, frustration-aggression proponents have greatly modified their position in response to criticisms and fresh evidence, and

---

[2] For a detailed review of each of these theories, see Corning and Corning (1971) and sources cited therein.

their current stance is summed up by psychologist Leonard Berkowitz (1969b: 2): "Basically, I believe a frustrating event increases the probability that the thwarted organism will act aggressively soon afterward. . . ." However, in contrast with the original formulation, Berkowitz concedes that "the existence of frustration *does not* always lead to some form of aggression, and the occurrence of aggressive behavior *does not necessarily* presuppose the existence of frustration."

Of course, all of the above are explanations only of individual violence, but each has been utilized as well in attempts to explain the causes of collective violence. For instance Freud (1932) suggested that group violence derives from a simple extension of the individual "death" or "destructive" instinct. The social learning hypothesis, likewise, has been advanced by several behavioral scientists as the main cause of warfare, the basic premise being that "man's biological nature is neither good nor bad, aggressive nor submissive, warlike nor peaceful, but neutral in these respects. He is capable of developing in either direction depending on what he is compelled to learn by his environment and by his culture" (May 1943: 151; see also Montagu 1968). May cites Sparta and the Third Reich as examples of nations in which systematic education for group aggression took place, while Montagu suggests that, at the opposite pole, cultural conditioning has minimized aggressive behaviors among the Hopi and the Zuni Indians.

Frustrations, both individual and collective, have also been linked to collective violence. It has been hypothesized, for example, that the socializing process involves many personal frustrations, and that the anger created by these frustrations would most naturally be vented by acts of "simple aggression." But, since such acts are commonly forbidden and frequently punished, the individual finds it necessary to repress his anger. The anger is not, however, destroyed but remains "deeply hidden or disguised" and is readily released in adulthood through the socially approved channel of group aggression. Thus, individual frustrations may lead to collective violence through a process of displacement or projection (Durbin and Bowlby 1938; see also Tolman 1942).

More recently, political scientists have been exploring the evidence for a relationship between environmental deprivations, or "systemic frustrations," and collective violence. In one cross-national study of violence in 114 polities during the period from 1961 to 1965, outbreaks of internal group violence correlated highly with data reflecting socioeconomic deprivations (Gurr 1968).

It is certainly true that biological factors, social learning, and frustrations each constitute significant sets of variables in human aggression.[3]

---

[3] Some of the evidence is reviewed in Corning and Corning (1971).

Biological differences between the sexes, between age groups, and between individuals probably account for some of the variance in aggressive behavior. (See Appendix.) It is no coincidence that most human violence is perpetrated by young males. There is also mounting evidence that individuals with specific brain abnormalities, some of which may be genetically based, are responsible for at least some instances of pathological human violence (Mark and Ervin 1970). By the same token, social learning can facilitate or inhibit violent behaviors (in addition to defining the precise mode by which such behaviors are expressed), and environmental frustrations of various kinds can serve to trigger violence, or, more subtly, lower the threshold point at which subsequent stimuli will evoke violent responses.

Yet, at the same time, none of these global explanations has proven to be, in itself, *sufficient*. It is important to note that all three are in reality theoretical constructs. When originally put forward, they were, in effect, confessions of ignorance about what actually goes on inside the human brain, although each was based on certain biological assumptions: The bio-instinctualists posited a spontaneous aggressive drive; socio-behaviorists viewed man as a sort of behavioral sponge, with human aggressiveness being a learned drive or conditioned response; and supporters of the frustration-aggression hypothesis asserted that aggression is a biologically "preprogrammed" response to various environmental frustrations.

However, as research has progressed, it has become increasingly obvious that such monolithic theoretical constructs are no longer tenable. Advances in such fields as physiological psychology, neurophysiology, endocrinology, behavior genetics, and ethology (as well as our increasingly sophisticated understanding of the processes of biological evolution and of the evolutionary significance of behavior)[4] have forced us to recognize that a more comprehensive theoretical umbrella is required.

In the first place, we are coming to recognize that aggression, in humans and other species, is not a unitary phenomenon; there are a number of physiologically and functionally different kinds of aggression. Moyer has recently suggested that there may in fact be as many as eight different categories of aggression: Predatory, intermale, fear-induced, irritable, territorial, maternal, instrumental and sex-related (Moyer 1968a, 1968b, 1969a). Each of these categories, or classes, may be differentiated on the basis of the stimulus configurations that trigger them. The evidence points to the fact that aggressive behaviors in most species

---

[4] A review of the literature can be found in Corning and Corning (1971). Also, see Appendix.

are stimulus-bound; they are elicited only by highly specific environmental cues, or cue complexes (although there may be some overlapping, as when territorial and intermale aggression coincide).

Furthermore, there is evidence that each class of aggression may have a distinct neural and endocrine substrate. That is, the neurophysiological and biochemical mechanisms associated with each kind of aggression are inborn and the product of evolution, even if they are partially programmed by the individual's interaction with his social and ecological environment. We are coming to realize, in fact, that there must be internal correlates for every facet of aggressive behavior. The complex interaction between environmental stimulus, sensory structures, information processing, emotional affect, motor response, and even inhibitory or control mechanisms must reflect an interaction among specific internal subsystems and their linkages.

Elsewhere, the author has proposed that such a classification of aggressive behaviors should also lend itself to functional analysis. If the different forms of aggression are physiologically distinct and stimulus-bound, this is strong presumptive evidence of a "design for survival" that has been worked out by natural selection. It should thus be possible to explain the adaptive significance of the various kinds of aggressive behavior.[5]

Indeed, whenever any set of behavioral traits is observed to be widespread in nature, we are compelled to consider it from an evolutionary viewpoint, and a category of behavior as frequent throughout the living world as aggression must be the product of selection. (Natural selection works upon behavior—that is, upon the neural and endocrine substrate which makes behavior possible—just as readily as it does upon other aspects of animal morphology. In fact, behavior and morphology represent an integral unit in relation to evolution. There is thus a mutual feedback process at work between behavior and its structural basis.)

On balance, therefore, aggression must have had adaptive value for those species which today exhibit aggressive behaviors as species-specific traits. These behaviors must have been favored by natural selection to the degree that they enhanced, even if only marginally, the relative survival and reproductive chances of aggressive individuals and groups (in cases of group selection). Accordingly, to the extent that aggression was and is an adaptive trait, or set of traits, it should thus make some specific contribution to survival and reproductive success. It should in theory at least, have a quantifiable fitness value.

---

[5] See the discussion of the functions of various aggressive behaviors in Corning and Corning (1971).

This is not equivalent, however, to asserting that violent aggression is always and everywhere adaptive, or that the mere existence of any behavior represents *a priori* evidence that it is eufunctional in evolutionary terms. There are many instances of once adaptive behaviors that have become maladaptive (and violent forms of human aggression may well be one of them) as the environmental context has changed. Furthermore, adaptiveness is always situation-specific; a behavior that is adaptive in one instance may prove to be maladaptive in another.

For example, Horn (1968) has noted that the manipulation of a single parameter—the distribution of food supply—can profoundly affect the relative adaptiveness of different forms of aggression. If food is evenly distributed in a habitat, it is more advantageous for animals to pair off and defend exclusive territories. A social structure of this type helps animals to space themselves out so as to maintain a suitable balance between population and resources. On the other hand, if food supplies are concentrated and/or shifting in location, then foraging in flocks or herds, with minimal intragroup aggression, would be more adaptive. By the same token, the need for defense against predation, or for cooperation in securing prey, would reduce the relative adaptive value of aggressively competitive as against cooperative behaviors.

It must also be emphasized that there are very definite limits upon the extent to which aggressiveness may be adaptive. If violent aggression were always adaptive, one would expect it to be universal. But, in point of fact, the majority of species are nonviolent. Therefore, violent aggression is a behavioral category of only limited usefulness in relation to the total survival and reproductive problem of a species. Tinbergen (1956) has pointed out that aggression is a time- and energy-consuming activity (and sometimes injury-producing or fatal), so it is not the sort of behavior a species should engage in casually.[6]

Some experiments on maternal aggression, by myself and a colleague (Dennis St. John) at the Institute for Behavioral Genetics, represent a case in point. Female aggression in laboratory strains of the house mouse (*Mus musculus*) is directed primarily against strange male mice, not against females or mates. It is also confined to the period when females are nursing pups. (At other times, the females must be receptive to strange males, for obvious reasons.) So in the course of evolutionary history, *Mus musculus* (or its ancestor species) evolved internal mechanisms that serve to limit female attacking behaviors for the most part

---

[6] See Wilson (1971). Evidence of the potentially maladaptive consequences of aggressive behaviors in relation to other aspects of the survival problem (what is referred to in the literature as "aggressive neglect") has been reported by Nelson (1964, 1965) and Ripley (1959, 1961).

to the period when the females are caring for young. The function of this form of aggression should be self-evident, but the fitness value is easily demonstrated. If not checked, male mice will frequently attack and kill strange mouse pups.

The broadened, evolutionary approach to aggression described above can also be applied to collective violence in human (and other animal) societies.

Some insights into collective aggression as an adaptive phenomenon can be gained from ethological observations.[7] Group defense against predators is seen in many species where the individual is vulnerable but where cooperative defense or attack may be effective. Crows will "mob" a stray cat (Lorenz 1966: 26), and male baboons have been observed routing cheetahs in coordinated charges (Pfeiffer 1969; Hall and DeVore 1965).

When a baboon troop moves across the open savannah, a defensive formation is assumed in which the dominant males accompanied by females with young are clustered in the group's center.

Animals which are predators themselves are less vulnerable to attack but still find it useful to defend their home areas and hunting range from others of the same species. Thus lion prides attack any trespasser, including a strange lioness (Schenkel 1966). The spotted hyena pack enforces its territorial rights to the extent that strangers, pursuing prey into another territory, will be forced to yield up their kill to the resident pack (Cruuk 1966). Indeed, the phenomenon of in-group cohesion and out-group hostility, widely observed in human societies (Coser 1956), is common as well in the animal world (Etkin 1967: 18).

Collective aggression has served some of the same functions for human societies. A single human would be extremely vulnerable to large predators (sabre-tooth tigers or grizzly bears, for instance), but a group of humans cooperating in self-defense can usually deter a potential predator. In fact, small groups of Bushmen regularly scare off big cats and appropriate their kills for themselves.

The degree of territorial exclusivity among proto-hominid hunting bands is not known, but a survey of contemporary isolates indicates that "in all cases there is some, and in most a rather strict, definition of the band in terms of the general locality it occupies even when boundaries are not specific" (Service 1966). The need to defend the home territory by resorting to collective violence is reduced through the use of what may have been a very early instance of "foreign policy"—that is, al-

---

[7] A useful review of relevant examples is found in Ewer (1968).

liances and intermarriage. Washburn has noted that "excessive fighting over territorial borders both disturbs game and dissipates the energy of the hunters. The exchange of mates between neighboring groups helps to insure friendly relations . . . because it disperses persons with close emotional ties among many groups and over a large area" (quoted in Pfeiffer 1969: 144). Nonetheless, history is full of examples of a breakdown in the system of agreements which may lead to a situation in which the territory must be defended through violence if it is not to be lost altogether. In such cases, it is common for the possessors of a territory to fight stubbornly and suffer staggering losses if necessary.

War is obviously one way of gaining access to needed resources—and of eliminating potential threats to your own population or resources. In addition, warfare may serve, at least in primitive societies, to regulate population in relation to land and other resources, correct imbalances in sex ratios, and release tensions generated by within-group conflicts (Vayda 1968, 1970).[8] For instance, Vayda (1970) reports that the warfare system of the close-knit Maori tribes of New Zealand served the adaptive functions of distributing population and opening up fresh land for exploitation. With the coming of the European musket, however, killing became far more efficient and the human costs soon outweighed the ecological benefits.[9]

Some theorists—ranging from Herbert Spencer in the nineteenth century to, more currently, anthropologist Robert Bigelow (1969)—have gone so far as to propose that warfare may have been the principal engine of human evolution (through the mechanism of group selection in favor of the winners). Since the chances of success in war are enhanced by intelligence, cooperation, discipline, and other human characteristics besides brute aggressiveness, presumably all such war-relevant human traits would have been favored in struggles between competing groups.

The hypothesis cannot be discounted. But, unfortunately, there is no direct evidence either for or against it, and the indirect evidence is inconclusive. There are, after all, other human endeavors that could well have functioned in a similar manner—hunting, group defense against predation, and cooperative foraging for food and water being among the

---

[8] This is not to suggest that wars are necessarily desirable. There may well be alternative, less costly ways of performing the same functions (see below).

[9] European exploitation of the North American continent makes an interesting contrast, for the American cultural system permitted a far different strategy: A division of labor and specialization of function, social and political permissiveness and flexibility; maintenance of internal peace (save during the Civil War); and an organized armed force that drove out indigenous populations and acted as a shield against external threats.

more obvious examples. But it may well be that wars have in the past constituted one selecting agent among others in human evolution.

Collective aggressive action *within* a society may also be viewed as a coping or adaptive mechanism. Wallace (1956) has defined a phenomenon which he terms a "revitalization movement"—a "deliberate, organized, conscious effort by members of a society to construct a more satisfying culture." Wallace includes in his concept a great variety of social movements, including cargo cults, religious revivals, reform movements, utopian communities, revolutions, and charismatic movements. Although he does not explicitly link such behaviors to the theory of evolution (as adaptive responses), they certainly fit well into an evolutionary framework. It is obvious and has been much emphasized in the literature that revolutions and riots are destructive of life and property. Less analyzed is the possibility that some uprisings may prove adaptive for a society insofar as institutional change is desirable and alternative modes of bringing about change have been frustrated.

In sum, collective human violence is not necessarily undesirable, at least from an evolutionary viewpoint. Rather, violence may represent an adaptive response to a variety of survival problems. If, on the other hand, the costs outweigh the benefits, or if the likelihood of self-destruction exceeds the likelihood of success, then violent aggression may become a maladaptive behavior.

We must also recognize that collective violence in human societies cannot be explained in terms of simple extrapolations from individual motivation states. Organized violence also involves several elements of group dynamics and collective decision-making—causal variables that transcend either the individual or any sort of summation of numerous individual behaviors.

To be specific, instances of organized, collective human violence involve a nexus of several behavioral components that are often treated as separate in analyses of human or other animal behavior. These may include group bonding (and the phenomenon of in-group, out-group "psychological" polarizations), territoriality, interpersonal cooperative behavior and within-group altruism, leadership and leader-follower relationships, the cultural set (that is, inhibiting or facilitative norms and cultural practices), fear responses, a collective variant of male dominance competition,[10] socioeconomic and ecological circumstances, and cognitive processes (or more or less conscious and formal cost-benefit analyses by leaders and/or followers).

---

[10] For recent examples of dominance competition, one need only recall Khrushchev's boast, "We will bury you," or the Chinese taunt that the United States is a "paper tiger."

There are, in other words, many causal variables involved in collective violence. Some arise from biologically based behavioral propensities and some from the external environment (or, more precisely, from the manner in which the environment is perceived). In different instances, moreover, the relative importance of different causal variables will fluctuate; no two wars will manifest precisely the same configuration of causal variables: For instance, an incompetent leader may stumble into a war that could have been avoided; a skillful leader, seeking desperately to avoid war, may be overwhelmed by "events"; or an ambitious and highly aggressive leader may precipitate a war that is unjustifiable on any ecological ground.

This being the case, what are some of the implications? What conclusions may we draw with respect to the problem of controlling collective violence?

Clearly, if the causes of organized violence are manifold, then our efforts to control it must also be multiform, and some of the various alternative solutions put forward over the years might well be applied in concert. Behavioral scientists of the "instinctualist" persuasion have often proposed that we ritualize (or channel) our violent propensities with sports, scientific competition, or some other "moral equivalent of war." The frustration-aggression school, on the other hand, emphasizes the need to reduce socioeconomic deprivations. Reformers of this orientation often single out the maldistribution of wealth between "haves" and "have-nots" as a particular target. And those who emphasize the role of social learning in human violence would attempt a more or less drastic reform of our culture and social practices.

Then there are those who focus on what might be called the "sick leadership" hypothesis. Recently, a prominent psychologist proposed that we develop antiaggression pills (or the equivalent) and administer them to world leaders as a way of preventing wars. The assumption, presumably, was that wars are mainly caused by the irrational aggressive urges of political leaders.

Although the proposal has been widely criticized, it deserves more serious consideration, not so much because the proposal is in itself sound, but because it draws attention to a "biological" variable that is frequently overlooked in socioeconomic and political explanations of war. Males of our species are highly volatile animals. They have a low threshold of tolerance for frustration; they learn aggressive behaviors readily; and they are quick to engage themselves in intermale competition and struggles for dominance.

In the past, these qualities were doubtless adaptive in relation to the struggle for survival. But in the nuclear age the potential costs of war have far outstripped any conceivable benefits. Indeed, the benefits, if any, are problematical. Controlling the aggressive propensities of the human male is thus directly relevant to the problem of controlling organized violence. Indeed, the very limited biological and social-psychological evidence (see Appendix) suggests that, on the average, women are less competitive and violence-prone. In general, female political leaders might be less likely to go to war for "irrational" reasons—for reasons not centrally related to survival.

Of course, the genetic diversity of *Homo sapiens* insures that aggressiveness, like other personality characteristics, will vary widely within a population and among members of the same sex. Not all women are alike biologically any more than all men are alike; there are more aggressive women and less aggressive men. Furthermore, biologically based personality dispositions are modified by the cultural environment.

But more to the point, political life represents a cultural selection process which favors more competitive and aggressive (among other qualities) individuals, and this presumably holds true for women as well. Part of the solution to the problem of human violence, then, might involve changes in the ways political leaders are chosen, or at very least changes in attitudes about the kind of qualities we want our political leaders to have.

Of course, even if such remedies were practicable and could be realized expeditiously, they would by no means purge us of organized violence. Humans often go to war for "rational" reasons—in response to pressing problems of survival. Our socioeconomic, ecological, political, and "psychological" environments are a "seamless web," and we will not ultimately eliminate the causes of war until we deal also with the potentially explosive problems of overpopulation; deterioration of the environment; social, religious, and racial conflict; and, not least, mass poverty living cheek by jowl with obscene wealth.

However, we do not necessarily have to go to war to solve these problems. The alternative is politics, that uniquely human behavioral adaptation which enables man to confront and deal with his common problems. Although the term *politics* is often used today in a derogatory sense (and practiced in a narrow, partisan way), the Greeks, who invented the word, used it to refer to cybernetic functions—conflict resolution, problem-solving, decision-making and collaborative action—in relation to the needs of the community as a whole. Anything less was considered to be "pseudo-politics," in Bay's phrase (1965). At its best, therefore, politics is preeminently a nonviolent way of coping with our ongoing survival problems, and in politics lies our best hope for peace.

APPENDIX

Although relatively little research has been devoted to the biology of aggression in humans, including possible sex differences, such evidence as does exist is supported by what we know of man's evolutionary history, the observations of anthropologists and sociologists, the data relating to other species, and the data relating to other dimensions of human behavior.

First, the functional division of labor in many primates and most human societies down to the present day makes it unlikely that the neural and endocrine substrates for various personality traits would be identical for men and women; selection seems to have favored a slightly different configuration of traits in the two sexes (as it has favored a degree of dimorphism). (See Pfieffer 1969; Lee and DeVore 1968; Service 1966; Etkin 1967; Washburn and Jay 1968; Tiger 1970. For discussion of primate social life, see Eimerl and DeVore 1965; Kummer 1971.)

This is supported by the evidence, both for Americans and cross-culturally, of differences between male and female behavior in a variety of respects, including particularly aggressivity (Scott 1958; Berelson and Steiner 1967: 30–31; Kagan 1969; Feshbach 1970). The incidence of violent behavior is far higher among males, and it is statistically improbable that such differences—being virtually universal among human societies—could be mere cultural artifacts.

This would seem to be corroborated by the widely observed sex differences in aggressive behavior in other species (Collias 1944). Collias's material on animals observed in the wild is complemented by laboratory investigations (Seward 1945; Scott 1966).

In general, marked sexual differences in agonistic behavior are evident from an early age. For example, analysis of the play of young monkeys before they reach sexual maturity reveals that the juvenile male's behavior is distinctly different from the female's: "the male is more inclined to rough-and-tumble play, more aggressive and more given to threatening facial expressions" (Levine 1966).

As for direct, biological evidence, over the years a great many experiments with other animals have illuminated some of these physiological mechanisms, both general within species, between sexes, and variable among individuals. Particularly dramatic results have come from the study and manipulation of sex hormones.[11]

---

[11] This discussion is necessarily abbreviated. Some of the rich documentation of hormonal correlates of aggressive behavior are described and reviewed in McClearn (1969), Hamburg (1971), Boelkins and Heiser (1970), Moyer (1969a), Scott (1958), Levine (1966), and Conner and Levine (1969).

The presence or absence of sex hormones (androgens) appears to be a critical variable in these sexual differences in apparent aggressiveness. Castration (which involves the removal of the hormone-producing gonads) renders young males relatively mild and tractable, a phenomenon of great utility to stockmen. However, experiments with castrated mice show that normal aggressive (and sexual) behavior can be restored by the injection of the missing testosterone or other androgens (Beach 1945). Conversely, some researchers have been able to suppress at least some forms of fighting behavior in intact (uncastrated) males through the administration of estrogens (female hormones) (Suchowsky *et al.* 1969).

The hormonal *history* of an animal is, however, as important as the presence or absence of androgens during a particular match. For instance, the *age* at which castration (loss of normal male hormones) has taken place is an important factor. The earlier in life that castration occurs, the more feminized is the behavior of a genetically male animal and the less likely he is to exhibit normal behavior, even when male hormones are administered. The prenatal and immediately postnatal period is particularly critical to the normal physical development and sexual behavior of male animals. For instance, Conner and Levine (1969) found a graded behavioral response to administration of testosterone propionate (TP)—with the effects decreasing the earlier the subject mouse had been castrated. Neo-natally castrated mice showed less sensitivity to the hormone than weaning-age castrates, and weaning-age castrates than intact males. It is apparent that the action of the hormones is mediated by the brain and that, conversely, brain development is influenced by the presence or absence of the normal male hormones at an early age. Genetically male mice who were deprived of gonadal hormones during the crucial period of sex differentiation fail to develop masculinized brain responses which would allow testosterone administration in adulthood to have the usual effects (Levine 1966).

The findings on female aggressive behavior (or lack thereof) confirm this hypothesis of early sex determination by hormones. Thus *mature* female mice, even if their ovaries are removed and androgens (TP) administered, retain their characteristic reluctance to engage in fighting behaviors (Conner and Levine 1969).[12]

Quite the opposite is true, however, of female animals exposed to androgens early in development. Androgenized female mice pups engage

---

[12] The generally submissive female mouse may become a vigorous attacker of strange males in one circumstance—when she is nursing young. And we suspect that the hormonal changes associated with lactation are crucial to the expression of this behavior.

in the same rough-and-tumble play typical of male pups and also display male mounting (sexual) behavior (Levine 1966); the same is true of monkeys (Young *et al.* 1964). Edwards (1968) compared the responsiveness to testosterone (TP) of normal females with those who had been given an injection of TP at birth. This single postnatal dose, when followed by ovary removal at weaning, resulted in a markedly masculine response to TP administration during adulthood with apparently masculine fighting behavior.

Suggestive evidence also exists for *within*-sex differences. In nature, variation is the rule, and apparently normal individuals can differ somewhat in their sex hormone *levels,* with possible consequences for their relative aggressiveness. The results of a particularly careful and extensive study have been reported by Rose, Holaday and Bernstein (1971). This study is significant because it took place in a setting closer to the natural social conditions of free animals than do the usual staged encounters of individual laboratory animals. Over a period of three months, 34 adult rhesus male monkeys sharing a large compound were observed and their plasma levels of testosterone measured. The researchers correlated behavior with testosterone levels and found that those individuals with strikingly aggressive behavior were also higher than average in testosterone levels.

Furthermore, dominance rank was positively correlated with testosterone concentrations (although the most aggressive animals in the group were not always the most dominant, nor were the least aggressive necessarily lowest in dominance). While the correlation between testosterone and aggression and dominance is significant (20–25 percent of the total variance), there are obviously other factors involved as well. This study, then, illustrates two vital points: Hormonal factors are important variables in at least some forms of aggressive behaviors, but there are other variables also at work—including other morphological characteristics of the animal and, frequently, its previous experience in the environment.

The literature on hormonal correlates of aggressiveness in humans is still relatively sparce, surprisingly so in view of the strong nonhuman evidence. However, male hormones, or fluctuations in female hormone levels, are definitely implicated in female aggressivity. There are cases known where an abnormal hormonal situation has existed for a female human fetus, in which androgens were present to an unusual degree in the prenatal period. A study of 22 girls with such a history indicates that their behavior and interests, both as described by themselves and others, is distinctly tomboyish, with preferences for outdoor sports requiring much energy and vigor, rough play, and toys usually associated with the interests of boys (such as guns) (Hamburg 1971). These find-ings are consistent with those of Ehrhardt, Epstein and Money on two groups of 10 and 15 such androgenized girls (reviewed by Boelkins and Heiser 1970: 33). The adult behavior of these girls cannot now be predicted, but the strong influence of social and family values must not, of course, be discounted.

Only a small minority of violent acts are attributed to women, but these few tend to cluster during the premenstrual week, when levels of progesterone and the estrogens are at their lowest. In one study of female prisoners, 62 percent of the crimes of violence for which they were sentenced were committed during the premenstrual week (which repre-sents on average 25 percent of the monthly cycle) (Morton *et al.* 1953).

The phenomenon of premenstrual tension and irritability is also well known. In some cases where it has been more than usually troublesome, progesterone has been successfully used for relief (Moyer 1969a: 108–9; Hamburg 1971).

In the rhesus monkey group study of Rose, Holaday and Bernstein mentioned above, the five most aggressive monkeys were also those with the highest levels of plasma testosterone. A similar finding in humans is that of Rudd, Galal and Casey (1968). These British researchers were investigating the possibility of differences in urinary testosterone levels between six XY and nine XYY prisoners in a maximum security hos-pital. They did not find significant differences between the XYY and chromosomally normal males, but they did find that "almost all of these patients"—XY or XYY—"had higher excretion rates of testosterone when compared to normal, healthy men." Rudd *et al.* suggest that this interesting phenomenon may be a result of the conditions of confinement (leading, perhaps, to disruptions in diurnal rhythms), a possibility that must of course be investigated. Curiously, though, an alternative hy-pothesis is not even mentioned—that males with unusually high testos-terone levels as a result of biologically based individual differences, may be more likely to exhibit the kind of problem behaviors that lead to their eventual confinement in maximum security hospitals.

In sum, what little data we have specifically on hormonal correlates of aggressiveness in humans is consistent with the animal findings that the male hormones tend to heighten or potentiate aggressiveness while female hormones decrease the probability of aggressive behavior (with the possible exception of maternal aggression). Besides the gross hor-monal differences between sexes, there is suggestive evidence that *in-dividual* differences in the *levels* of certain hormones may also contribute to individual behavioral differences. A series of hormonal assays recently completed for "normal" human children (Hamburg 1971) showed both sex differences and wide individual differences in prepubertal children in blood plasma levels of testosterone. Moreover, between the ages of 10 and 15, testosterone levels in boys increase dramatically, as much as tenfold.

There are also the limited data relating to the genetics of aggression and the more extensive data relating to the genetics of other "normal" personality traits. These data provide some direct, and much indirect, evidence for the hypothesis that a substantial proportion of the observed variance in aggressive behavior—both between individuals of the same sex and between sexes—has a biological basis.

The major portion of research on the heritability of aggressivity has been done on the laboratory rodents—mice and rats. And in these species, the heritability is rather high (although not inalterable by training). An excellent review of the current status of research in this area is provided by Gerald E. McClearn of the Institute for Behavioral Genetics in a report to the National Commission on the Causes and Prevention of Violence (McClearn 1969; see also Lagerspetz 1969, and Scott 1966), so the discussion here will be abbreviated.

Two general approaches are involved. In one, inbred strains, which are genetically homogenous (theoretically 98 percent homozygous at all gene loci), were compared with each other, and consistent strain differences in aggressive behavior emerged. To minimize variations due to environmental differences, experiments were performed in which newborn pups were transferred from their own natural mother to a foster mother of another strain, with no resulting alteration of the pups' characteristic strain behavior (McClearn 1969).

A second approach to the genetics of aggressivity is that pursued by Lagerspetz (1964, 1969). Using genetically heterogeneous mice, Lagerspetz tested and selected those exhibiting the highest and lowest aggressiveness. For more than seven generations, each type was selectively bred, and the "high" and "low" lines diverged in their behavior as would be expected if the genes are deeply involved. Foster mothering between the high and low lines was also utilized to confirm the degree of heritability (Lagerspetz and Wuorinen 1965). Selective breeding has also been used successfully to demonstrate the heritability of aggressiveness in dogs (Scott 1958) and leghorn chickens (Guhl et al. 1960).

Aggressivity is not, however, as simple a trait even in mice as was at first supposed. When researchers began getting contradictory strain performances in various experiments, their experimental procedures had to be examined more closely. It was found that differences in the testing situation could alter the relative fighting performances of different strains (or genotypes). For example, under conditions of high illumination, BALB/c (albino) mice lost approximately 90 percent of their bouts with C57BL (pigmented) mice. But when the degree of illumination was lowered, the albinos came into their own and won about 60 percent of the bouts (Klein, Howard and DeFries 1970). Other differences in the contest situation also affected the relative performances of these two strains. C57BL/10 mice made more strong attacks against a dangled (immobilized) mouse (Bauer 1956) but when pairs of the two strains were left together overnight, the BALB/c's killed their C57 opponents in 8 out of 10 cases (Fredericson and Birnbaum 1954). Another apparent inconsistency was noted by Ginsburg and Allee (1942), who found that the most docile strain in combat with other mice was, however, the most vicious in relation to its human caretakers.

These results indicate that different kinds of aggression with somewhat distinct genetic bases are being tested under different situations (and, in the case of the albino disadvantage under high illumination, demonstrates that different genotypes may have different optimum environments). Nonetheless, genetically based strain differences do emerge, although the rankings of different strains may vary according to the testing situation. Thus, McClearn summarizes: "These observations provide conclusive evidence that individual differences in aggressiveness within a number of species are influenced by genetic factors."

The evidence for the heritability of aggressivity in man is still fragmentary. A test of verbal aggressivity in approximately 200 sets of teen-aged twins by Vandenberg yielded a heritability estimate for boys of .76 based on within-pair correlations, and .65 based on within-pair variances (Vandenberg, personal communication). In contrast, there was no statistically significant heritability estimate obtainable from the scores of the girls. However, no attempt was made to correlate such paper-and-pencil test scores with behavioral performance, so the results must be considered no more than suggestive.

A considerable amount of indirect evidence exists, however, in the relatively high heritability estimates that have been obtained over the years for a variety of other human personality traits—such as introversion and extroversion, activity levels, need for achievement, etc. (Parsons 1967; Vandenberg 1967; Lerner 1968).

Lately a gross chromosomal abnormality, commonly referred to as the XYY syndrome, has received a great deal of publicity in connection with crimes of violence, and this has been put forward by some behavioral scientists as possible further evidence of genetic involvement in aggressive behaviors. However, experts in attendance at a recent conference of the Center for Studies of Crime and Delinquency (NIMH) were divided concerning the conclusions that can be drawn on the basis of present evidence, with one group refusing to generalize about the behavioral correlates of the extra Y chromosome, and another suggesting that "on the basis of our present knowledge they [infants with the XYY chromosome complement] would appear to have an increased risk of developing socially maladaptive and deviant patterns of behavior" (Shah 1970: 15).

It is also known that natural selection favors, at least in some instances, more aggressive animals. Many examples have been documented in nature (see Lorenz 1966; Etkin 1967) showing that superiority in aggressive encounters can enhance an individual's reproductive efficacy. In a recent study involving elephant seals, Le Boeuf (1970) found that the dominant males, after a series of bloody battles to establish and defend their rank in the social hierarchy, win almost exclusive breeding privileges with the females. In one large harem (200–300 females), five bulls (or four percent of the males) engaged in 85 percent of the copulations. In some smaller harems (perhaps 50 females), the alpha (or top-ranking) male alone does virtually all of the breeding.

Similarly, in a study of inbred mice at the Institute for Behavioral Genetics (DeFries and McClearn 1970), it was found that the dominant males in triad situations (three connected cages containing various combinations of male and female mice) fathered 92 percent of the litters.

As for humans, a number of primitive societies today practice polygamy, with fertility differentials favoring the socially dominant, and Mayr (1970) has proposed that such a system was common in early hominid evolution. If so, Mayr hypothesizes, this could account for the extraordinarily rapid evolution of human intelligence. Of course, to the extent that social dominance correlated with aggressivity, it too would have been favored in human evolution. On the other hand, there is good reason to believe that many other attributes would also have been favored—leadership abilities, cooperativeness, problem-solving capacities, hunting skills, and so forth.

BIBLIOGRAPHY

Bauer, F. J. 1956. "Genetic and experiential factors affecting social reactions in male mice." *Journal of Comparative and Physiological Psychology*, 49, 359–64.

Bay, C. 1965. "Politics and pseudopolitics: A critical evaluation of some behavioral literature." *American Political Science Review,* 59, no. 1 (March, 1965), 39–51.

Beach, F. A. 1945. "Bisexual mating behavior in the male rat: Effects of castration and hormone administration." *Physiological Zoology,* 18, 390+.

Berelson, B., and Steiner, G. A. 1967. *Human Behavior.* New York: Harcourt, Brace & World.

Berkowitz, L. (ed.). 1969a. *Roots of Aggression; a re-examination of the frustration-aggression hypothesis.* New York: Atherton Press.

———. 1969b. "The frustration-aggression hypothesis revisited." In Berkowitz (ed.), *Roots of Aggression,* 1–28.

Bigelow, R. 1969. *The Dawn Warriors.* Boston: Atlantic-Little, Brown.

Boelkins, R. C., and Heiser, J. F. 1970. "Biological bases of aggression." In Daniels, Gilula and Ochberg (eds.), *Violence and the Struggle for Existence,* 15–52.

Bramson, L., and Goethals, G. W. (eds.). 1968. *War: Studies from Psychology, Sociology, Anthropology.* Revised edition. New York: Basic Books.

Carthy, J. D., and Ebling, F. J. (eds.). 1964. *The Natural History of Aggression.* New York: Academic Press.

Clemente, C. D., and Lindsley, C. B. (eds.). 1967. *Aggression and Defense: Neural Mechanisms and Social Patterns* (Brain Function, Vol. 5). UCLA Forum Med. Sci. No. 7. Los Angeles: University of California Press.

Collias, N. E. 1944. "Aggressive behavior among vertebrate animals." *Physiological Zoology,* 17, 83+.

Conner, R. L., and Levine, S. 1969. "Hormonal influences on aggressive behaviour." In Garattini and Sigg (eds.), *Aggressive Behavior,* 150–63.

Corning, P. A. 1971. "The biological bases of behavior and some implications for political science." *World Politics,* 23, no. 3 (April, 1971), 321–70.

———, and Corning, Constance H. 1971. "An evolutionary-adaptive theory of aggression." American Political Science Association meeting, Chicago, September 1971.

Coser, L. A. 1956. *The Functions of Social Conflict.* New York: Free Press, Macmillan.

Cruuk, H. 1966. "Clan-system and feeding habits of spotted hyaenas (*Crocuta crocuta Erxleben*)." *Nature,* 209, 1257–8.

Daniels, D. N., Gilula, M. F., and Ochberg, F. M. (eds.). 1970. *Violence and the Struggle for Existence.* Boston: Little, Brown.

DeFries, J. C., and McClearn, G. E. 1970. "Social dominance and Darwinian fitness in the laboratory mouse." *American Naturalist,* 104, no. 938 (July–August), 408–11.

DeVore, I. (ed.). 1965. *Primate Behavior.* New York: Holt, Rinehart & Winston.

Dollard, J., Doob, L. W., Miller, N. E., Mowrer, O. H., and Sears, R. R. 1939. *Frustration and Aggression.* New Haven: Yale University Press.

Durbin, E. F. M., and Bowlby, J. 1938. "Personal aggressiveness and war." Reprinted in Bramson and Goethals, *War,* 81–103.

Edwards, D. A. 1968. "Mice: Fighting by neonatally androgenized females." *Science,* 161 (September 6, 1968), 1027–8.

Eimerl, S., and DeVore, I. 1965. *The Primates.* New York: Life Books.

Eisenberg, J. F., and Dillon, W. (eds.). 1971. *Man and Beast: Comparative Social Behavior.* Washington, D.C.: Smithsonian Institution Press.

Etkin, W. 1967. *Social Behavior from Fish to Man.* Chicago: University of Chicago Press.

Ewer, R. F. 1968. *Ethology of Mammals.* New York: Plenum Press.

Feshbach, S. 1970. "Aggression." In P. H. Mussen (ed.), *Carmichael's Manual of Child Psychology.* 3d ed. New York: John Wiley & Sons, 1, 159–259.

Fredericson, E., and Birnbaum, E. A. 1954. "Competitive behavior between mice with different hereditary backgrounds." *The Journal of Genetic Psychology,* 85, 271–80.

Freedman, D. G. 1967. "A biological view of man's social behavior." In Etkin, *Social Behavior from Fish to Man,* 152–88.

Freud, S. 1932. "Why War?" Reprinted in Bramson and Goethals, *War,* 71–80.

Fried, M., Harris, M., and Murphy, R. (eds.). 1968. *War: The Anthropology of Armed Conflict and Aggression.* Garden City, N.Y.: The Natural History Press.

Garattini, S., and Sigg, E. B. (eds.). 1969. *Aggressive Behavior* (Proceedings of the International Symposium on the Biology of Aggressive Behavior, held at the Instituto di Richerche Farmacologiche "Mario Negri," Milan, May 2–4, 1968). New York: John Wiley.

Ginsburg, B., and Allee, W. C. 1942. "Some effects of conditioning on social dominance and subordination in inbred strains of mice." *Physiological Zoology,* 15, no. 4 (October, 1942), 485–505.

Guhl, A. M., Craig, J. V., and Meuller, C. D. 1960. "Selective breeding for aggressiveness in chickens. *Poultry Science,* 39, 970–80.

Gurr, T. R. 1968. "A causal model of civil strife: A comparative analysis using new indices." *The American Political Science Review,* 62, no. 4 (December, 1968), 1104–24.

Hall, K. R. L., and DeVore, I. 1965. "Baboon social behavior." In DeVore (ed.), *Primate Behavior,* 53–110.

Hamburg, D. A. 1971. "Recent research on hormonal regulation of aggressive behavior." *International Social Science Journal,* 23, no. 1, 36–47.

Hebb, D. O., and Thompson, W. R. 1968. "The social significance of animal studies." In Lindzey and Aronson, *Handbook of Social Psychology,* 2, 729–74.

Hinde, R. A. 1971. "The nature and control of aggressive behavior." *International Social Science Journal,* 23, no. 1 (1971), 48–52.

Horn, H. S. 1968. "The adaptive significance of colonial nesting in the brewer's blackbird (Euphagus cyanocephalus)." *Ecology,* 49, 682–94.

Kagan, J. 1969. "Check One: Male, Female." *Psychology Today,* 39–41.

Klein, T. W., Howard, J., and DeFries, J. C. 1970. "Agonistic behavior in mice: Strain differences as a function of test illumination." *Psychonomic Science,* 19, no. 3, 177–8.

Kummer, H. 1971. *Primate Societies.* Chicago: Aldine-Atherton.

Lagerspetz, K. M. 1964. *Studies on the Aggressive Behavior of Mice.* Helsinki: Suomalainen Tiedeakatemia.

————, and Wuorinen, K. 1965. "A cross-fostering experiment with mice selectively bred for aggressiveness and non-aggressiveness." *Rep. Psychol. Inst. Univ. Turku,* 17, 1.

————. 1969. "Aggression and aggressiveness in laboratory mice." Garattini and Sigg (eds.), *Aggressive Behavior,* 77–85.

Leakey, L. S. B. 1967. "Development of aggression as a factor in early human and pre-human evolution." In Clemente and Lindsley (eds.), *Aggression and Defense,* 1–33 (with discussion).

Le Boeuf, B. J. 1970. "The Aggression of the Breeding Bulls." *Natural History,* 43, no. 10 (February, 1971), 82–94.

Lee, R. B., and DeVore, I. (eds.). 1968. *Man the Hunter.* Chicago: Aldine.

Lerner, I. M. 1968. *Heredity, Evolution and Society.* San Francisco: W. H. Freeman & Co.

Levine, S. 1966. "Sex differences in the brain." *Scientific American* (April, 1966), 84. Reprinted in McGaugh et al. (eds.), *Psychobiology.*

Levy, J. V., and King, J. A. 1953. "The effects of testosterone propionate on fighting behaviour in young male C57BL/10 mice." *Anatomical Record,* 117, 562–3.

————. 1954. "The effects of testosterone propionate on fighting behaviour in C57BL/10 young female mice." *Proceedings of the West Virginia Academy of Sciences,* 26, 14.

Lorenz, K. 1966. *On Aggression.* New York: Harcourt, Brace & World.

McClearn, G. E. 1969. *Biological Bases of Social Behavior with Specific Reference to Violent Behavior* (A Staff Report to the Commission on the Causes and Prevention of Violence). *Crimes of Violence,* vol. 13. Washington, D.C.: Government Printing Office, 979–1016.

McGaugh, J. L., Weinberger, N. M., and Whalen, R. E. (eds.). 1966. *Psychobiology: The Biological Bases of Behavior.* San Francisco: W. H. Freeman & Co.

Mark, V. H., and Ervin, F. R. 1970. *Violence and the Brain.* New York: Harper & Row.

May, M. A. 1943. "War, peace, and social learning." Reprinted in Bramson and Goethals, *War,* 151–8.

Mayr, E. 1970. *Population, Species, and Evolution* (An abridgment of *Animal Species and Evolution*). Cambridge, Mass.: Harvard University Press.

Montagu, M. F. Ashley (ed.). 1968. *Man and Aggression*. New York: Oxford University Press.

Morton, J. H., *et al.* 1953. "A clinical study of premenstrual tension." *American Journal of Obstetrics and Gynecology*, 65, 1182–91.

Moyer, K. E. 1968a. "Kinds of aggression and their physiological basis." *Communications in Behavioral Biology*, Part A, 2, no. 2 (August, 1968), 65–87.

————. 1968b. "A preliminary physiological model of aggressive behavior." (Paper presented at the AAAS Symposium on Fighting and Defeat, December 28, 1968.) Carnegie-Mellon University, Report no. 68–32.

————. 1969a. "Internal impulses to aggression." *Transactions of the New York Academy of Sciences*, Series II, vol. 31, no. 2 (February, 1969), 104–14.

————. 1969b. "The physiology of aggression and implications for aggression control." (Paper presented at a symposium on Aggressive Behavior at The City University of New York, June 6, 1969.)

Nelson, J. B. 1964. "Factors influencing clutch-size and chick growth in the North Atlantic gannet, *Sula bassana*." *Ibis*, 106, 63–77.

————. 1965. "The behaviour of the gannet." *British Birds*, 58, 233–88.

Parsons, P. A. 1967. *The Genetic Analysis of Behavior*. London: Methuen.

Pfeiffer, J. 1969. *The Emergence of Man*. New York: Harper & Row.

Price, W. H., and Whatmore, P. B. 1967. "Behavior disorders and the pattern of crime among XYY males identified at a maximum security hospital." *British Medical Journal*, 1, 533+.

Richardson, L. 1960. *Statistics of Deadly Quarrels*. Pittsburgh: Boxwood Press.

Ripley, S. D. 1959. "Competition between sunbird and honeyeater species in the Moluccan Islands." *American Naturalist*, 93, 127–32.

————. 1961. "Aggressive neglect as a factor in interspecific competition in birds." *Auk*, 78, 366–71.

Rose, R. M., Holaday, J. W., and Bernstein, I. S. 1971. "Plasma testosterone, dominance rank and aggressive behaviour in male rhesus monkeys." *Nature*, 231 (June 11, 1971), 366–8.

Rudd, B. T., Galal, O. M., and Casey, M. D. 1968. "Testosterone excretion rates in normal males and males with an XYY component." *Journal of Medical Genetics*, 5, 286–8.

Schenkel, R. 1966. "Play, exploration and territoriality in the wild lion." *Symp. Zool. Soc. London*, 18, 11–22.

Scott, J. P. 1958. *Aggression*. Chicago: University of Chicago Press.

————. 1966. "Agnostic behavior of mice and rats: A review." *American Zoologist*, 7, 683+.

————, and Eleftheriou, B. E. (eds.). 1969. *The Physiology of Fighting and Defeat*. Chicago: University of Chicago Press.

Service, E. R. 1966. *The Hunters*. Englewood Cliffs, N.J.: Prentice-Hall.

Seward, J. P. 1945. "Aggressive behavior in the rat: 1. General characteristics, age and sex differences." *Journal of Comparative Psychology,* 38, 175+.

Shah, S. A. 1970. *Report on the XYY Chromosomal Abnormality.* Washington, D.C.: Government Printing Office.

Storr, A. 1968. *Human Aggression.* New York: Atheneum.

Suchowsky, G. K., Pegrassi, L., and Bonsignori, A. 1969. "The effect of steroids on aggressive behaviour in isolated male mice." In Garattini and Sigg (eds.), *Aggressive Behavior,* 164+.

Tiger, L. 1969. *Men in Groups.* New York: Random House.

————. 1970. "The possible biological origins of sexual discrimination." *Impact of Science on Society,* 20, no. 1 (1970), 29–44.

Tinbergen, N. 1956. "On the functions of territory in gulls." *Ibis,* 98, 401–11.

————. 1968. "On war and peace in animals and man." *Science,* 160 (June 28, 1968), 1411–18.

Tolman, E. C. 1942. "Drives toward war." Reprinted in Bramson and Goethals, *War,* 159–76.

Tolman, J., and King, J. A. 1956. "The effects of testosterone propionate on aggression in male and female C57BL/10 mice." *British Journal of Animal Behaviour,* 4, 147–9.

Vandenberg, S. G. 1967. "Hereditary factors in normal personality traits (as measured by inventories)," in *Recent Advances in Biological Psychiatry,* 9. New York: Plenum Press, 65–104.

Vayda, A. P. 1968. "Hypotheses about functions of war." In *War: The Anthropology of Armed Conflict and Aggression,* edited by Fried, Harris and Murphy. Garden City, N.Y.: Natural History Press, 85–91.

————. 1970. "Maoris and muskets in New Zealand: Disruption of a war system." (Mimeographed.)

Wallace, A. F. C. 1956. "Revitalization movements." *American Anthropologist,* 58, no. 2 (April, 1956), 264–81.

Washburn, S. L., and DeVore, I. 1966. "The social life of baboons." In McGaugh *et al.* (eds.), *Psychobiology,* 10–19.

————, and Hamburg, D. A. 1968. "Aggressive behavior in old world monkeys and apes." In Jay (ed.), *Primates: Studies in Adaptation and Variability.*

————, and Jay, P. C. (eds.). 1968. *Perspectives on Human Evolution.* New York: Holt, Rinehart & Winston.

————, and Lancaster, C. S. 1968. "The evolution of hunting." In Lee and DeVore (eds.), *Man the Hunter,* 293–303.

Wilson, E. O. 1971. "Competitive and aggressive behavior." In Eisenberg and Dillon (eds.), *Man and Beast,* 183–217.

Wright, Q. 1962. *A Study of War* (1942). 2d ed. Chicago: University of Chicago Press.

Wynne-Edwards, V. C. 1962. *Animal Dispersion in Relation to Social Behavior.* Edinburgh: Oliver & Boyd.

Young, W. C., Goy, R., and Phoenix, C. 1964. "Hormones and sexual behavior." *Science,* 143, 212+.

Part TWO

BUILDING A
WORLD PEACE SYSTEM:
APPROACHES TO CHANGE

5
WORLD GOVERNMENT

Introduction

What would be necessary to change to a more peaceful world? The rest of this book is an attempt to provide a variety of answers to this question. In this section, we consider proposals for achieving world peace through world law and world government. These are among the most radical of suggestions for change because they envision a fundamental restructuring of the international system. Less radical proposals for reform of the war system are considered in sections 6–8, together with several perspectives on the relationships between changes in the way nations interact, changes in national (particularly American) defense policies, and changes in individual behavior. If one believes that people should work toward achieving a more peaceful world, all of these levels of change—international, national, and individual—must be considered.

The first selection in this section is both an introduction to the concept of a world order model and a basic case for world government. Reardon and Mendlovitz describe five "models" of world order, all of which represent aspects of the present world order system. In their view, none of these provide adequate mechanisms for resolving conflicts without resort to war, since all rely for stability on the existence of nuclear and conventional military deterrence, which is subject to accident and manipulation by national leaders. Furthermore, the authors claim the existing system of world order does not satisfy minimal criteria for achieving worldwide economic welfare or social justice, which they believe are necessary parts of any desirable world order system for two reasons: (1) they are required by a sense of justice, and (2) their attainment would significantly reduce the probability of international war, since one major cause of war is perceived social injustice.

As alternatives, the authors suggest two world order models for the future that could shape political action aimed at building a peaceful world during the next twenty years. The first—which they dismiss because it relies on war as a means for achieving global change—they call "protracted conflict II." It could more simply be called the "world revolution" or "Chinese Communist" model. It postulates a world revolution of poor, agrarian peoples against the rich, industrial nations, following the examples of recent peasant revolutions in Latin America and Asia. This model finds expression in the writings of Mao Tse-Tung, Lin Piao, Fidel Castro, and Che Guevara.

The other model they suggest is a model of limited world government, based on proposals advanced by Grenville Clark and Louis B. Sohn in *World Peace Through World Law* (Cambridge: Harvard University Press, 1958; rev'd, 1966). Reardon and Mendlovitz argue that such a world order model would be desirable, because it would reduce the likelihood of international violence and at the same time provide international mechanisms for promoting a more equitable distribution of the world's economic wealth. They argue that a contractual change— probably through negotiated treaty—to a world government could be achieved since the Clark-Sohn proposals provide two fundamental trade-offs: (1) they replace national security systems based on deterrence with a world security system based on general and complete disarmament and enforced by an armed world peacekeeping force under the command of the world government; (2) at the same time, they presumably eliminate the major cause of guerrilla war by replacing a system in which poor people must resort to guerrilla war to achieve social justice with a world authority capable of reallocating and equalizing the distribution of world wealth. Reardon and Mendlovitz portray this model as feasible because it offers something for everyone.

The next selection is excerpted from the introduction to the Clark-Sohn plan itself. It provides a general outline of their proposal, presented in the form of a suggested revision of the United Nations Charter.

It makes representation in the U.N. universal and makes voting in the General Assembly roughly proportional to each nation's population. It also includes plans for general and complete disarmament coupled with creation of a U.N. peace force under the indirect command of an executive council without veto, to replace the present Security Council. Finally, Clark and Sohn propose creation of a U.N. judicial system to resolve international conflicts, and a world development authority to channel aid funds from rich to poor nations.

It is important to note that while the Clark-Sohn plan does provide a world authority capable of controlling international conflicts, it is an extremely limited form of government. In fact, it might be more accurate to call their world organization a "federation of nations," since representation in their General Assembly would initially be by national appointment rather than by popular vote, and nations would remain relatively free from U.N. control for all matters not directly related to disarmament and war prevention. Clark and Sohn deliberately limited legal authority of their revised U.N. to the war prevention area because they thought that national governments might be more inclined to accept their proposal if it was carefully organized to be a minimal threat against national sovereignty. It is this feature of the plan, however, that leads many to argue that it would not work even if it were adopted, since national governments would still compete for advantage in the international system, possibly in harmful and even violent ways. Although other, more far-reaching plans for a genuine world government (rather than for a limited world federation) are available, it might be asked whether national loyalties are still so strong that any world government is impossible to achieve.

The concluding selection in this section, by Inis Claude, suggests several major criticisms of world government thinking. After arguing that war is not as imminent a threat as many advocates of radical world system change suggest, Claude asserts that world government would probably not work, even if it could be achieved in the not-too-distant future, which he doubts. He claims that most world government proposals are based on a primitive theory of government holding that a government's legitimacy is primarily established by its possession of a monopoly of force. In fact, Claude says, governments rule by virtue of a complex combination of shared social and political norms and expectations and established patterns of intergroup bargaining, with force always in the background. Claude also believes that proposals, like Clark and Sohn's, that envision a world federation of states underestimate the problem of coercing states that violate world laws, largely because they fail to make a clear distinction between coercing states and coercing individuals.

This failure reflects the larger theoretical problem of confusing the nation-state with a hypothetical world-state. While nations are composed of individuals and groups of individuals, a world-state would be composed of nation-states as well, adding an extra layer of organizational complexity that world government theorists often do not take into account. The most serious result of this is that civil war under a world government—that is, war between member states—still seems to Claude to be very much a possibility, since the world government, in his estimation, would not be capable of enforcing its decisions against states determined to fight for their own self-interests.

While Claude's case against world government seems strong, two points should be noted. First, as Claude himself admits, his arguments have not so much invalidated the world government idea as shown that conventional defenses of the idea are inadequate. Secondly, he has merely assumed without argument that world government is unlikely to be taken seriously by many national governments in today's world. He has not faced the question of whether a broadly based movement for world order change—with roots in many nations dedicated to programs of domestic reform—might make world government less unlikely in the middle-range future.

Beyond these questions, a more general question about proposals for world law and world government is whether and to what extent they respond to the real causes of war. The Clark-Sohn proposal, for example, is based on a diagnosis of war that links it with the structure of the international system itself. They and other world government partisans believe that war is an inevitable occurrence in a heavily armed, unorganized system of competing nation-states. On the other hand, some, like McNamara and Kissinger (in section 3), argue that war can be prevented without changing the structure of the international system, if statesmen can learn how to manipulate military power safely. A third possibility is that the existing system can be improved to provide mechanisms for dealing with conflicts before they escalate into wars. Several such proposals for reform of the state system are presented in section 6.

SUGGESTIONS FOR FURTHER READING

Elizabeth Mann Borgese, *Constitution for the World*. Santa Barbara, Calif.: Center for the Study of Democratic Institutions, 1965.

Inis L. Claude, Jr., *Swords Into Plowshares*. New York: Random House, 1956.

Richard A. Falk, *This Endangered Planet*. New York: Random House, 1971.

Richard A. Falk and Saul H. Mendlovitz, eds., *The Strategy of World Order,* vol. 1, *Toward a Theory of War Prevention,* New York: World Law Fund, 1966.

Elizabeth Jay Hollins, ed., *Peace Is Possible.* New York: Grossman, 1966.

Marion H. McVitty, *Preface to Disarmament.* Washington, D.C.: Public Affairs Press, 1970.

Emory Reves, *The Anatomy of Peace.* New York: Viking Press, 1946.

W. Warren Wagar, *Building the City of Man.* New York: Grossman, 1971.

World Law and Models of World Order

BETTY REARDON and SAUL H. MENDLOVITZ

Since World War II scholars and statesmen have projected a number of models or images of the international system that they believe are most likely to provide the greatest degree of order in the world community between now and the year 2000. In the three decades remaining in this century, the search for a viable system of world order will assume greater urgency than ever before. The destructive capability of nuclear weapons, the number of nations actually or potentially possessing them, and the dangerous tensions arising from the disparity of wealth and resources in today's world combine to create hazards unprecedented in human history. If man is to master his own military technology and at the same time deal with the problems of world economic welfare, he will have to make a sustained and vigorous effort—not to ensure "peace," if peace is understood to mean a kind of universal harmony—but to build an enforceable system for drastically minimizing the likelihood of international violence.

This essay is written in the hope of encouraging responsible academic inquiry into the problems of world order and world law. The essay be-

From *International Dimensions in the Social Studies,* ed., James M. Becker and Howard D. Mehlinger (38th Yearbook, National Council of the Social Studies; Washington, 1968), pp. 160–70. Reprinted by permission of the authors. Betty Reardon, a historian, is director of the School Program of the World Law Fund in New York. Mendlovitz is professor of international law at Rutgers University Law School and director of the World Order Models Project.

gins by describing and evaluating five of the most widely discussed contemporary models of world order, each of which purports to depict the future evolution of the international system. This is followed by a discussion of two additional models of world order, one of which, in the view of the authors, comes much closer than any of the others to satisfying the conditions of a true system of world order.

Projected models of international stability, it should be noted, have been made in two ways. Scholars have said, "This is the way, in fact, the world *will* be"—a prognostication; or, "This is the way the world *ought* to be"—a preferential statement. The following questions should therefore be asked in reviewing models of world order: How would I *like* the world to be in the year 2000? How do I think the world really *will* be in the year 2000? And most significantly, how can the gap be spanned between the way I would like the world to be and the way it is likely to be?

The five images or models of world order that are currently used quite widely either for prognostication or preferential purposes are the following:

1. THE UNITED NATIONS MODEL is based on the notion that the five big states that emerged victorious from World War II and became permanent members of the Security Council have the primary responsibility for maintaining the peace and security of the international community. They are organized into a formal authority structure in such a fashion that the big five must agree unanimously in determining whether there is a threat to peace, a breach of the peace, or an act of aggression. And if they agree that such an event has taken place, then with the vote of any other two nonpermanent members, these seven states can invoke a whole set of sanctioning processes or even call upon the rest of the international community to use force.

This particular model of world order, it is well to remember, is quite an advance over the League of Nations model, in which initiating collective security processes required the unanimity of all member states. Placing the primary responsibility upon five member states plus two auxiliary nations represents a high mark of supranational authority. The development of world community policing in cases of threats to the peace, breaches of the peace, and acts of aggression implies a rejection of the notion that any one state should be allowed to circumscribe world community action and acceptance of the idea that only a few states should have the power to prevent—or initiate—collective security actions. The United Nations model, incidentally, is of more than historical importance. The arguments that are now taking place on the east side of New York in the various committees dealing with peacekeeping operations are in fact arguments concerning the extent to which the Security Council should once again reemerge as the voice of the world community and the viable unit of world community review and control of the use of force in international society.

2. "PROTRACTED CONFLICT" is a second model of world order, which emerged chronologically about 16 to 18 months after the establishment of the United Nations. It is frequently referred to as the "cold war." In this model there are two major superpowers dominating the world community. These major superpowers—the United States and the Soviet Union—actually control the destiny of mankind because they have enormous military and economic capacity and can between them determine the course of world events. Furthermore, these two superpowers are locked in deadly ideological struggle in which one side must win and the other side must lose. What keeps peace and prevents war in this system is described as "stable deterrence" or "mutual deterrence." According to this notion, there now exists such a high level of technology in thermonuclear weapons and delivery system capacities that both sides now have the ability to annihilate one another, even after a first strike. Peace is therefore maintained in the system by mutual deterrence, or the fear of mutual suicide.

This system has a low threshold for violence; that is, while it may be suited for preventing large-scale nuclear war, it is not well adapted for averting local civil wars throughout the world or small-scale wars in which big powers are not directly involved. The model suggests that if the big powers are directly involved, there will be a series of tacit understandings or mutual agreements of a formal or an informal sort that will keep the stakes from escalating to a point where thermonuclear and atomic weapons will be used. It is asserted that over the long run—a hundred or two hundred years—one side or the other will be debilitated, lose its moral fibre, or experience a failure of leadership, and at that point the opposing state will win, leading to the emergence of a system of world order. In the meantime a kind of rudimentary world order is maintained by a system in which the two big powers determine the basic constitutional rules.

3. A THIRD SIGNIFICANT MODEL IS "REGIONALISM." The theoreticians of this model contend that it has now become increasingly apparent that no nation-state is capable of handling by itself the two major dimensions of international relations: security (territorial integrity and political independence) and economic development. No state that wants to achieve the necessary level of political and military security and economic development can depend solely upon its own resources.

The people who support this argument say that the next step in the development of world community is the coalescing of a set of supranational units. In their view, there will probably emerge in the world from five to fifteen regional supranational units that will handle the issues of political and military security and economic development. Thus for example, the Common Market will become a United Europe; the Organization of African Unity will form a continental state; Latin America will emerge into a supranational unit; and India, China, and other large states will become actors in the new international system. Peace will be maintained in this system, it is alleged, by continuous conferences either in the U.N. or in some new forum. In addition, the threat of mutual annihilation will act as an added stimulus to keeping the peace: for it is believed that each of the supranational units will have thermonuclear capacity and delivery systems, and, therefore, the system of mutual deterrence that has arisen under the bipolar or protracted conflict model will also be in effect in the regional system.

This regional model parallels the balance of power system extant in Europe during the period from 1814 to 1915. The system comprised a number of European states that had reached a fundamental agreement on the rules of the power game. These rules assumed that while nations competed with one another for power, wealth, and aggrandizement, each state has a vested interest in the system insofar as it had limited ambitions for territorial expansion, or, conversely, insofar as it opposed the expansion of other states. If any state, either by an alliance or by individual military decisions, threatened to overstep the bounds of the system, a new alliance would emerge and would bring into effect a new balance of power to prevent any single state from dominating the system. The new regionalism postulates that the supranational units or actors will evolve a similar system for maintaining the peace: a balance of power with mutual deterrence through fear of thermonuclear weapons.

4. "POLYCENTRISM" IS A FOURTH MODEL, which is sometimes labeled "nationalism rampant." Nationalism as a major force is comparatively new in the history of man and is likely to see its apotheosis over the next 150 years. Well over 65 new states have been created since 1945, and the process of creating states is not yet completed. For the next century or even the next two centuries, people's lives, their personal identities, their personality development, their sense of loyalty, and their sense of kinship with secondary groupings will probably be shaped by the nation-state. According to this model, mankind is less likely to find himself involved in a series of supranational regional units than to be living in an international system comprising 140 to 200 sovereign states.

Peace will be maintained in this system by a very complex balance of power. Given the fact that instantaneous, worldwide communication networks are rapidly becoming a reality, and granting the possibility of fast movement of men, arms, and equipment, it is most likely that by the year 1990 men and equipment will be able to be dispatched anywhere in the world within two hours. A system of this kind will produce very rapid shifting of alliances in order to meet what may look like a threat to the peace or a threat to the security, political independence, or territorial integrity of any one state.

5. THE FIFTH MODEL, "CONDOMINIUM," is in fact a reversal of protracted conflict. The theory contends that the United States and the Soviet Union have finally come to realize that they have a common interest in preserving world order. It is to their mutual advantage first, that they do not destroy each other, and second, that they maintain their respective control of various parts of the world.

This kind of common interest is evolving slowly, but it must be pursued through tacit understanding: not too much progress can be made in a formal way because there are large groups in each society that resist any kind of formal agreement between the Soviet Union and the United States—in fact, that perceive such action as anathema. Nevertheless, given the fact that these two powers have so many common interests, a system is likely to emerge over the next 20 years by which the two states will control the destiny of earth, in regard to political and military security as well as economic development.

Furthermore, so the argument goes, both the United States and the U.S.S.R. enjoy such a high level of industrial, technological, and military development that even if all the other nations of the world were to combine their military power and pool their economic resources, they could never catch up with the superpowers. The two big states will recognize that their advantage lies in maintaining this technological superiority and will guard against any risks, military or otherwise, that might jeopardize their position. Under such a system of condominium the big two will keep the peace by policing the rest of the world.

It is quite clear that each of these five models corresponds with reality to some extent, and in a few cases the "reality quotient" is extremely high. In fact, present world politics can be analyzed to illustrate that virtually any one of these models is the operative system and has already been attained. All five, moreover, have some mechanism for maintaining peace, at least in the sense of averting nuclear calamity if not in the sense of bringing about a cessation of all kinds of international violence. On the other hand, none of them embodies any positive values beyond the minimal one of human survival. All of them are implicitly based on the dangerous assumption that it is impossible to achieve world consensus about world authority structures, much less the principles or values to be comprehended in such a supranational system. None of them—not even the United Nations model—deals competently with the issues of economic development and social justice, which, in their own way, are potentially just as "explosive" as nuclear armaments themselves.

But what is perhaps the most serious shortcoming of all, none of the five models discussed above takes into account the possibility of further proliferation of nuclear weapons, breakthroughs in military technology, or additional deterioration of world political stability. None of them, in other words, provides adequately for the specific eventualities most likely to threaten the peace of the next three decades. If, for example, there should be, as seems quite possible, an acclerated proliferation of atomic weapons, models like protracted conflict, regionalism, condominium, and particularly polycentrism will immediately become dangerously anachronistic. For if a number of states eventually come to possess their own nuclear arsenals, the world will probably revert to an "autarchic" system, in which each state plays "univeto" over the life and death of mankind.

It is remarkable, in a way, that men have refrained from using atomic or thermonuclear weapons since 1945. There are five states that now have such weapons; and it must be admitted that the elites of these nations, no matter what their other failings may be, have not only exercised remarkable restraint with regard to the use of nuclear weapons, but have also shown little tendency to spread these weapons to other nations by sharing information or selling armaments. But how long will that situation continue? How long will the elites of the world demonstrate that kind of responsibility? It would take only one or two politically unstable leaders in positions of responsibility to upset the precarious balance of world peace. One need only visualize a second Hitler —this time armed with nuclear weapons—to realize the shocking inadequacies of the present system of voluntary restraint.

Furthermore, if there is a technological breakthrough that goes beyond atomic or thermonuclear weapons, making possible first strike destruction of defense systems—and making impossible any retaliation against the assailant—then a new competitive military race will be virtually certain to occur. In such a situation, states must constantly engage in costly research and development in military technology simply in order to keep up with other nations. In an arms race, moreover, the weapons themselves become an independent variable with little relationship to a war-prevention system; indeed, their very existence constitutes a threat to the system. In addition, there is little reason to believe that over the long run political stability will prevail among the world's nations or within any supranational system that may come into existence.

Given the obvious imperfections of the present structure of international relations, as well as the shortcomings of all of the five models of world order discussed above, it becomes clear that alternative systems for the control of international violence need to be developed and implemented. The search for an adequate model of world order involves a twofold procedure: first, the projection of a carefully described system of international relations (or a model of world order) that seems capable of preventing organized international violence, together with an analysis of the present system of international relations, insofar as it relates to this problem; and second, a description, in as great detail as possible, of the transition: that is, how the present system is likely to and/or can best be metamorphosed into the projected image or model. These two steps—the projection of a model of world order and the statement of transition from the present system to that model—may be termed the use of relevant utopias.

Two such utopias, with varying degrees of relevance, will be presented here. The first, to be mentioned only briefly, might be labeled "protracted conflict II." This model, which comes mainly from the rhetoric of the Chinese Communist, Lin Piao, divides the world into the industrial states of the northern hemisphere and the rural-agrarian states of the southern hemisphere and Asia. The conflict between these two giant divisions will ultimately, by an inevitable historical process, be resolved in favor of the rural-agrarian states and former colonies, which are already in the process of casting off the yoke of colonialism state by state. China is the prototype of such a revolution, which, when completed, will see the union of these rural-agrarian states into a common front united against the industrial states, forcing upon them a world order of fraternity and socialism. If violence becomes necessary to realize this vision, it is a regrettable but nonetheless useful tool for achieving the desired goal of world order.

Although this model might be said to have the merit of identifying a powerful schismatic force in the modern world—the tension between the industrial and nonindustrial nations—any potential usefulness it might possess is negated by a few readily detectable flaws. Aside from the fact that the mode of transition appears extremely perilous, an imposed system would doubtless bear the seeds of its own destruction. Nor are all nations likely to accept a single interpretation of "fraternity and socialism."

There is, however, a second projected international system that merits more serious consideration. The proponents of this model do not contend that its implementation is imminent, but they do believe that it constitutes a relevant utopia—a model, in other words, that squarely confronts the conditions most likely to threaten peace in the next 30 years. The ultimate goal of this model is the creation and preservation of world order, that is, an international system so revised as to prohibit nation-states from employing organized violence against each other, either in the pursuit of national goals or in the redress of national harms. Such a system requires the establishment of a world authority equipped with legislative bodies for making laws against international violence and, in addition, agencies to enforce these laws, keep the peace, and resolve conflicts. "World law" is a shorthand term describing such an authority and related institutions; and hence this model of world order is termed the "world law model."

Before proceeding further, it might be worthwhile to point out that international violence has not been entirely devoid of beneficial functions in past history, a fact of which even advocates of world law ought to be aware. It cannot be denied, for example, that a great deal has been done to better the human condition through the use of organized violence: tyrannies have been overthrown, slaves freed, and economic and political rights won by wars and violent revolutions. The world law model does not—indeed, could not—direct itself toward the total elimination of all forms of violence. In a nuclear age, however, violence that goes beyond certain circumscribed boundaries is potentially the trigger for a nuclear catastrophe. If the next century is to be free of the threat of annihilation, therefore, exploration of alternatives to violence must be undertaken without further hesitation.

The world law model proceeds from the following basic assumption: no person, much less a society, is likely to give up his own sense of helping himself with regard to questions of security in the absence of some substitute for self-help. Or to put it another way, no political elite would be advised to engage in any kind of disarmament, be it unilateral or complete and general, unless there were some assurance of another security system to protect its political independence and its territorial integrity.

World law thus ties together two very important notions: disarmament and a collective security system. It argues that the present system of international relations as well as the other models discussed above are based on unilateral decision-making sanctioned by armaments, and maintains that this situation results in a spiraling arms race that may very well set off a cataclysmic war. The world law model therefore posits the need for complete and general disarmament of all states in the world down to the level of police forces, and proposes the establishment of a transnational police force that can maintain the territorial integrity and political independence of each state.

The world law model further asserts that if war is to be prevented, then there must be some place where states can bring their grievances for adjudication, settlement, or third-party review. Within any national society it would be unthinkable for conflicts arising over property damage, broken contracts, or physical assaults to be settled only by self-help. Yet this is in many ways the international system that is in effect today, and it almost inevitably leads to the use of violence as a means of redressing legitimate grievances. The world law model suggests, therefore, that a warless system of international relations requires an institution with compulsory jurisdiction over grievances and claims of states.

Furthermore, if there is to be a war-prevention system based on complete and general disarmament, a transnational police force, and third-party settlement, there must also be a set of rules by which disarmament is imposed and the police force invoked. A world legislative authority is therefore needed to determine how those rules will be set up and executed.

There is one final element in a world law model that seems most crucial for the achievement of economic welfare and social justice—a world development authority based on the desirability of a more equitable system of distribution of the earth's material goods. If an international system permits two-thirds of the world to live in conditions that Americans or citizens of any other affluent nation would find intolerable, it is unreasonable to expect two-thirds of the world to display any enthusiasm for or commitment to the system. The nations of the world are presently spending between $135 and $165 billion a year on arms. Just one-third of that invested in a world development authority would, over a period of several years, save $100 billion now being channeled into resources that can be used for nothing but the destruction of other human beings, their institutions, and property.

In the view of the authors, this scheme or something like it offers the best hope for a viable and reasonably just system of world order. The world law model is admittedly utopian. But is it any less utopian than hoping to achieve world order through a series of evolutionary, small-term, incremental kinds of agreements, one-step advances, or accommodations when in the meanwhile man is likely to blow himself up along the way? The crucial question is: How can such a utopia be translated into reality?

It is here that scholars and educators have a real contribution to make; for it is up to the academic community to refine the tools of science and education and develop them into an integrated methodology for approaching the problem of world order. Responsible research can help enlarge the relevance of the world law model or other models of world order, making certain that they meet and satisfy the conditions imposed by reality. Most important, scholarly research can help identify the processes by which the present system of international relations can be transformed to the projected model. It is doubtful that even the most successful and coordinated efforts will bring about that universal brotherhood known as "peace." But the effort to create a workable system of world order may help achieve a more immediate and pressing goal: assuring the survival of human society. In this critical endeavor world law may come to be seen less as a utopia than as a necessity.

Introduction to World Peace
Through World Law

GRENVILLE CLARK

This [article] sets forth [the outline of a] plan for the maintenance of world peace in the form of a proposed revision of the United Nations Charter. The purpose is to contribute material for the worldwide discussions which must precede the adoption of universal and complete disarmament and the establishment of truly effective institutions for the prevention of war. . . .

The fundamental premise . . . is identical with the pronouncement of the President of the United States on October 31, 1956: "There can be no peace without law." In this context the word "law" necessarily implies the law of a world authority, *i.e.* law which would be uniformly applicable to all nations and all individuals in the world and which would definitely forbid violence or the threat of it as a means for dealing with any international dispute. This world law must also be law in the sense of law which is capable of enforcement, as distinguished from a mere set of exhortations or injunctions which it is desirable to observe but for the enforcement of which there is no effective machinery.

The proposition "no peace without law" also embodies the concep-

Excerpts from *World Peace Through World Law,* by Grenville Clark and Louis B. Sohn (2d ed., revised; Cambridge: Harvard University Press, 1960). Revised and updated in 1966 by Elizabeth Jay Hollins for inclusion in *Peace Is Possible: A Reader for Laymen* (New York: Grossman, 1966). Reprinted by permission of Elizabeth Jay Hollins and Harvard University Press. Grenville Clark, who died in 1967, was a leading lawyer and counselor to several presidents. In his later years he was prominent in the movement for world federalism.

tion that peace cannot be ensured by a continued arms race, nor by an indefinite "balance of terror," nor by diplomatic maneuver, but only by universal and complete national disarmament together with the establishment of institutions corresponding in the world field to those which maintain law and order within local communities and nations.

A prime motive for this [work] is that the world is far more likely to make progress toward genuine peace, as distinguished from a precarious armed truce, when a *detailed* plan adequate to the purpose is available, so that the structure and functions of the requisite world institutions may be fully discussed on a worldwide basis. Consequently, this [article] comprises a set of definite and interrelated proposals to carry out complete and universal disarmament and to strengthen the United Nations through the establishment of such legislative, executive and judicial institutions as are necessary to maintain world order.

UNDERLYING PRINCIPLES

The following are the basic principles by which Professor Sohn and I have been governed.

First: It is futile to expect genuine peace until there is put into effect an effective system of *enforceable* world law in the limited field of war prevention. This implies: (a) the complete disarmament, under effective controls, of each and every nation, and (b) the simultaneous adoption on a worldwide basis of the measures and institutions which the experience of centuries has shown to be essential for the maintenance of law and order, namely, clearly stated law against violence, courts to interpret and apply that law, and police to enforce it. All else, we conceive, depends upon the acceptance of this approach.

Second: The world law against international violence must be explicitly stated in constitutional and statutory form. It must, under appropriate penalties, forbid the use of force by any nation against any other for any cause whatever, save only in self-defense; and must be applicable to all individuals as well as to all nations.

Third: World judicial tribunals to interpret and apply the world law against international violence must be established and maintained, and also organs of mediation and conciliation—so as to substitute peaceful means of adjudication and adjustment in place of violence, or the threat of it, as the means for dealing with all international disputes.

Fourth: A permanent world police force must be created and maintained which, while safeguarded with utmost care against misuse, would be fully adequate to forestall or suppress any violation of the world law against international violence.

Fifth: The complete disarmament of all the nations (rather than the mere "reduction" or "limitation" of armaments) is essential for any solid and lasting peace, this disarmament to be accomplished in a simultaneous and proportionate manner by carefully verified stages and subject to a well-organized system of inspection. It is now generally accepted that disarmament must be universal and enforceable. That it must also be complete is no less necessary, since: (a) in the nuclear age no mere reduction in the new means of mass destruction could be effective to remove fear and tension; and (b) if any substantial national armaments were to remain, even if only 10 percent of the armaments of 1960, it would be impracticable to maintain a sufficiently strong world police force to deal with any possible aggression or revolt against the authority of the world organization. We should face the fact that until there is *complete* disarmament of every nation without exception there can be no assurance of genuine peace.

Sixth: Effective world machinery must be created to mitigate the vast disparities in the economic condition of various regions of the world, the continuance of which tends to instability and conflict.

The following supplementary principles have also guided us:

Active participation in the world peace authority must be universal, or virtually so; and although a few nations may be permitted to decline active membership, any such nonmember nations must be equally bound by the obligation to abolish their armed forces and to abide by all the laws and regulations of the world organization with relation to the prevention of war. It follows that ratification of the constitutional document creating the world peace organization (whether in the form of a revised United Nations Charter or otherwise) must be by a preponderant majority of all the nations and people of the world.

The world law, in the limited field of war prevention to which it would be restricted, should apply to all individual persons in the world as well as to all the nations—to the end that in case of violations by individuals without the support of their governments, the world law could be invoked directly against them without the necessity of indicting a whole nation or group of nations.

The basic rights and duties of all nations in respect of the maintenance of peace should be clearly defined not in laws enacted by a world legislature but in the constitutional document itself. That document should also carefully set forth not only the structure but also the most important powers of the various world institutions established or authorized by it; and the constitutional document should also define the limits of those powers and provide specific safeguards to guarantee the observance of those limits and the protection of individual rights against abuse of power. By this method of "constitutional legislation" the nations and peoples would know in advance within close limits what obligations they would assume by acceptance of the new world system, and only a restricted field of discretion would be left to the legislative branch of the world authority.

The powers of the world organization should be restricted to matters directly related to the maintenance of peace. All other powers should be reserved to the nations and their peoples. This definition and reservation of powers is advisable not only to avoid opposition based upon fear of possible interference in the domestic affairs of the nations, but also because it is wise for this generation to limit itself to the single task of preventing international violence or the threat of it. If we can accomplish that, we should feel satisfied and could well leave to later generations any enlargement of the powers of the world organization that they might find desirable.

While any plan to prevent war through total disarmament and the substitution of world law for international violence must be fully adequate to the end in view, it must also be *acceptable* to this generation. To propose a plan lacking in the basic essentials for the prevention of war would be futile. On the other hand, a plan which, however ideal in conception, is so far ahead of the times as to raise insuperable opposition would be equally futile. Therefore, we have tried hard to strike a sound balance by setting forth a plan which, while really adequate to prevent war, would, at the same time, be so carefully safeguarded that it *ought* to be acceptable to all nations.

It is not out of the question to carry out universal and complete disarmament and to establish the necessary new world institutions through an entirely new world authority, but it seems more normal and sensible to make the necessary revisions of the present United Nations Charter.

MAIN FEATURES OF THE WHOLE PLAN

In harmony with these underlying principles, the most important specific features of the proposed Charter revision may be summarized as follows:

1. *Membership.* The plan contemplates that virtually the whole world shall accept permanent membership before the revised Charter comes into effect—the conception being that so drastic a change in the world's

political structure should, in order to endure, be founded upon unanimous or nearly unanimous approval.

The assurance of assent by a great preponderance of the nations and peoples of the world would be accomplished by the revised Articles 3 and 110 providing: (a) that every independent state in the world shall be eligible for membership and may join at will; (b) that the revised Charter shall come into force only when ratified by five-sixths of all the nations of the world, the ratifying nations to have a combined population of at least five-sixths of the total world population and to include all the twelve nations which then have the largest populations. The assurance of permanent membership would be provided by the revised Article 6 whereby no nation, once having ratified the revised Charter, could either withdraw or be expelled.

The practical result would be that the plan would not even become operative until active and permanent support had been pledged by a great majority of all the nations, including as the twelve largest nations Brazil, France, the Federal Republic of Germany, India, Indonesia, Italy, Japan, Pakistan, the People's Republic of China, the United Kingdom, the U.S.A., and the U.S.S.R. . . .

2. *The General Assembly.* A radical revision is proposed as to the powers, composition and method of voting of the General Assembly. . . .

The plan calls for imposing the final responsibility for the enforcement of the disarmament process and the maintenance of peace upon the General Assembly itself, and gives the Assembly adequate powers to this end. These powers would, however, be strictly limited to matters directly related to the maintenance of peace. They would *not* include such matters as regulation of international trade, immigration, and the like, or any right to interfere in the domestic affairs of the nations, save as expressly authorized by the revised Charter in order to enforce disarmament or to prevent international violence where a situation which ordinarily might be deemed "domestic" has actually developed into a serious threat to world peace. . . .

As above mentioned, the principle is followed that all the *main features* of the whole plan shall be included in the revised Charter itself as "constitutional legislation," having in mind that the nations will be more likely to accept the plan if all its principal provisions are clearly set forth in the constitutional document itself. The effect would be to bind the nations in advance not only to all the fundamentals but also to many important details, and thus to leave for the General Assembly a more limited legislative scope than might be supposed.

Since, however, the General Assembly, even with elaborate "constitutional legislation," would need to have some definite legislative powers, the plan calls for a revision of the system of representation in the Assembly. For it cannot be expected that the larger nations would consent to give the Assembly even very limited *legislative* powers under the present system whereby Albania, Costa Rica, Iceland, Liberia, etc., have an equal vote with the United States, the Soviet Union, India, the United Kingdom, etc.

The purpose is, by abolishing the present system of one vote for each member Nation, to substitute a more equitable system, and thus to make the nations more willing to confer upon the General Assembly the limited yet considerably increased powers that it would need.

The proposed plan of representation takes account of relative populations but is qualified by the important provisions that no nation, however large, shall have more than thirty Representatives and that even the smallest nation shall have one Representative. The upper limit of thirty would be imposed partly because weighted representation is not likely to be accepted by the smaller nations unless the differences in representation between the majority of the nations and the largest nations are kept within moderate limits, and also because without some such limitation, the General Assembly would be of so unwieldy a size as to be unable to transact business. At the other extreme the purpose is to ensure that even the very small nations shall have some voice.

The proposed formula* divides the 99 nations, generally recognized in early 1960, as independent states or likely soon to be so recognized, into six categories according to relative populations, with representation as follows:

The 4 largest nations .... 30 Representatives each	......	120
The 8 next largest nations .... 15 Representatives each	......	120
The 20 next largest nations .... 6 Representatives each	......	120
The 30 next largest nations .... 4 Representatives each	......	120
The 34 next largest nations .... 2 Representatives each	......	68
The 3 smallest nations ...... 1 Representative each	......	3
99 nations		551 Representatives

* Because in 1966 the number of independent nation-states had risen to 129, the authors' revised formula for representation is as follows:

The 4 largest nations .... 30 Representatives each	......	120
The 10 next largest nations ...... 12 Representatives each	......	120
The 15 next largest nations ...... 8 Representatives each	......	120
The 20 next largest nations ...... 6 Representatives each	......	120
The 30 next largest nations ...... 4 Representatives each	......	120
The 40 next largest nations ...... 3 Representatives each	......	120
The 10 smallest nations .... 1 Representative each	......	10
129 nations		730 Representatives

As to the method of selection of the Representatives, it is proposed that a system of full popular election shall be gradually introduced. This would be done under a three-stage plan providing: (a) that in the first stage all the Representatives would be chosen by the respective national legislatures of the member Nations; (b) that in the second stage at least half the Representatives would be chosen by popular vote of those persons qualified to vote for the most numerous branch of the national legislature; and (c) that in the third stage all the Representatives would be chosen by the same sort of popular vote. . . .

With regard to the terms of service of the Representatives, it is proposed that they shall serve for four years. . . .

With relation to the powers of the revised General Assembly, a clear distinction would be made between legislative powers and powers of recommendation. The *legislative* powers would be strictly limited to matters directly related to the maintenance of peace, whereas the extensive powers of mere recommendation now possessed by the Assembly would be retained and even broadened. To this end, the Assembly's legislative authority would, as above mentioned, exclude any regulation of international trade, immigration and the like and any right to interfere in the domestic affairs of the nations, save only as strictly necessary for the enforcement of disarmament or, in exceptional circumstances, for the prevention of international violence.

On the other hand, as distinguished from the power to legislate, the General Assembly would have the right to make nonbinding recommendations on any subject which it deemed relevant to the maintenance of peace and the welfare of the world's people.

3. *The Executive Council.* It is proposed to abolish the present Security Council and to substitute for it an Executive Council, composed of seventeen Representatives elected by the General Assembly itself. This new and highly important organ would not only be chosen by the Assembly, but would also be responsible to and removable by the Assembly; and the Council would serve for the same four-year terms as the Representatives in the Assembly.

Special provision would be made for representation of the larger nations, whereby the four largest nations (China, India, the U.S.A. and the U.S.S.R.) would each be entitled at all times to have one of its Representatives on the Council; and four of the eight next largest nations (Brazil, France, West Germany, Indonesia, Italy, Japan, Pakistan and the United Kingdom) would in rotation also be entitled to representation, with the proviso that two of these four shall always be from nations in Europe and the other two from nations outside Europe. The remaining nine members would be chosen by the Assembly from the Representatives of all the other member Nations and the non-self-governing and trust territories under a formula designed to provide fair representation for all the main regions of the world and to ensure that every member Nation, without exception, shall in due course have a Representative on this all-important Council.

In contrast to the voting procedure of the present Security Council, whereby any one of the five nations entitled to "permanent" membership has a veto power in all nonprocedural matters, the decisions of the new Executive Council on "important" matters (as defined in paragraph 2 of revised Article 27) would be by a vote of twelve of the seventeen Representatives composing it, with the proviso that this majority shall include a majority of the eight members of the Council from the twelve member Nations entitled to fifteen or more Representatives in the Assembly and a majority of the nine other members of the Council. All other decisions would be by a vote of any twelve members of the Council.

The Executive Council would constitute the *executive arm* of the strengthened United Nations, holding much the same relation to the General Assembly as that of the British Cabinet to the House of Commons. Subject to its responsibility to the Assembly, the new Council would have broad powers to supervise and direct the disarmament process and other aspects of the whole system for the maintenance of peace provided for in the revised Charter. . . .

4. *Economic and Social Council, Trusteeship Council.* These two Councils would be continued, but with a somewhat different composition than under the present Charter designed to provide a better-balanced representation on these Councils. . . .

Like the Executive Council these two other Councils would be directly responsible to the Assembly. Their responsibilities would be enlarged; and their usefulness would be enhanced by reason of the greatly increased funds which would be available to them under the proposed new revenue system.

5. *The Disarmament Process.* The proposal includes a highly developed and detailed plan for general and complete disarmament, to be carried out under adequate inspection by every nation in the world without exception step by step over a six-year period.

During the first year after the coming into force of the plan, an Inspection Service would be organized and would conduct an arms census whereby every nation would supply a complete list of its armed forces, armaments and armament production facilities, but without being required to disclose the location of certain secret installations. In each six-month period thereafter 10 percent of any and all military organizations would be disbanded, and 10 percent of all armaments and armament-making facilities would be destroyed or converted to other uses. The result would be that at the end of the five-year actual disarmament period (six years after the coming into force of the plan) no nation would possess any *military* forces whatever and the only military force in the world would be the United Nations Peace Force.

This complete elimination of all national *military* forces would, however, be without prejudice to the retention by every nation of such lightly armed internal police forces as are needed for internal order only—subject to careful restrictions as to the maximum size of such police forces relative to population and as to the character of the weapons permitted to them. . . .

During each of the ten periods of six months, every nation would give the Inspection Service advance notice of the specific military units, armaments, armament facilities, and excess internal police forces which it proposes to eliminate in that period, in order to comply with the 10 percent reduction requirement. When these proposals have been checked and found adequate, the proposed reductions would take place under the direct supervision of the Inspection Service. During each six-month period the Inspection Service would also conduct a thorough inspection of a region, chosen by a decision of the Inspection Service, comprising one-tenth of the territory of each nation, in order to verify the accuracy of the initial arms census (which, for each nation, would contain a separate inventory for each of ten substantially equal regions into which the nation would be divided). The purpose and effect would be, therefore, that after five years all national military strength (and all internal police forces in excess of the prescribed limits) would have been eliminated, and the original arms census would have been completely verified.

This step-by-step reduction would provide every nation with an effective safeguard against cheating by others, since each stage would have to be completed by *all* nations before *any* nation could be called upon to begin the next stage. Provision would be made for delaying the whole process (by one or more postponements in no case exceeding six months) until any noncomplying nation was brought into line.

A portion of the eliminated national armaments would be turned over to the United Nations Peace Force, which would be built up to its full strength during the same period as that of the disarmament process. Another portion, consisting of all the nuclear weapons which have not been destroyed, all nuclear materials contained in destroyed nuclear weapons, and all nuclear materials from which nuclear weapons could be made, would be turned over to a civilian agency, to be known as the United Nations Nuclear Energy Authority. In both cases, fair compensation would be paid. All the rest of the eliminated national armaments would simply be destroyed. . . .

The disarmament plan also includes provision for a United Nations Nuclear Energy Authority with dual functions: (a) to assist the Inspection Service in guarding against possible diversion of nuclear materials to any war-making purpose, and (b) to promote the worldwide use of nuclear materials and processes for peaceful purposes. To these ends, the Nuclear Energy Authority would have wide powers to acquire by purchase at a fair price all nuclear materials in the world, with the obligation to have them put to use at fair rentals for peaceful purposes in all parts of the world under arrangements that would apportion the materials fairly and safeguard them against seizure. It is contemplated that this new Authority, having wider scope and membership than the International Atomic Energy Agency established in 1956, would take over the personnel and functions of that Agency. . . .

A new feature of the disarmament plan, made necessary by the recent penetration of outer space and its potentialities for the future, is a proposed United Nations Outer Space Agency. The broad objectives sought are: (a) to ensure that outer space is used only for peaceful purposes, and (b) to promote its exploration and use for the common benefit of all the people of this earth, rather than for the benefit of any nation or any part of mankind. . . .

6. *A World Police Force.* The plan is framed upon the assumption that not even the most solemn agreement and not even the most thorough inspection system, or both together, can be *fully* relied upon to ensure that every nation will always carry out and maintain complete disarmament and refrain from violence under all circumstances. Moreover, it must be recognized that even with the complete elimination of all *military* forces there would necessarily remain substantial, although strictly limited and lightly armed, internal police forces and that these police forces, supplemented by civilians armed with sporting rifles and fowling pieces, might conceivably constitute a serious threat to a neighboring country in the absence of a well-disciplined and heavily armed world police.

In short, our conception is that if police forces are necessary to maintain law and order even within a mature community or nation, similar forces will be required to guarantee the carrying out and maintenance of complete disarmament by each and every nation and to deter or suppress any attempted international violence. In consequence, detailed constitutional provision is made for a world police, to be organized and maintained by the strengthened United Nations and to be called the "United Nations Peace Force." This world police force would be the only *military* force permitted anywhere in the world after the process of national disarmament has been completed. It would be built up during the above-described "actual disarmament stage," so that as the last national military unit is disbanded the organization of the Peace Force would simultaneously be completed. . . .

. . . This Peace Force would consist of two components—a standing component and a Peace Force Reserve—both of which would, save in the most extreme emergency, be composed solely of volunteers.

The standing component would be a full-time force of professionals with a strength of between 200,000 and 600,000 [1966 figures: 200,-000 to 400,000] as determined from year to year by the General Assembly. The proposed term of service for its enlisted personnel would be not less than four or more than eight years, as determined by the General Assembly, with provision for the reenlistment of a limited number of especially well-qualified personnel.

In respect of the composition of the standing component, assurance would be provided through various specific limitations in Annex II that it would be recruited mainly, although not exclusively, from the smaller nations. . . .

The units of the standing component would be stationed throughout the world in such a way that there would be no undue concentration in any particular nation or region, and, on the other hand, so as to facilitate prompt action for the maintenance of peace if and when required. . . .

As distinguished from the active or standing component, the Peace Force Reserve would have no organized units whatever, but would consist only of individuals partially trained and subject to call for service with the standing component in case of need. It would have a strength of between 600,000 and 1,200,000 [1966 figures: 300,000 to 600,000] as determined by the General Assembly. Its members would be recruited subject to careful provisions as to geographical distribution identical with those applicable to the standing component. . . .

It is contemplated that the United Nations Peace Force shall be regularly provided with the most modern weapons and equipment, except that its possession or use of biological, chemical, or any other weapons adaptable to mass destruction, other than nuclear weapons, would be forbidden, special provision being made, as hereafter mentioned, for the use of nuclear weapons in extreme circumstances. . . .

With regard to the use of nuclear weapons by the Peace Force, the solution proposed is that neither component shall normally be equipped with any kind of nuclear weapons, but that some such weapons shall be held in reserve in the custody of a civilian agency for use only under the most careful precautions. This agency would be the Nuclear Energy Authority which would be authorized to release any nuclear weapons for possible use by the Peace Force only by order of the General Assembly itself, and then only if the Assembly has declared that nuclear weapons (which might have been clandestinely hidden or clandestinely produced) have actually been used against some nation or against the United Nations, or that such use is imminently threatened. . . .

It is also realized that it can be persuasively argued that nuclear weapons should not be even potentially available to the Peace Force. On balance, however, it is believed wise to make it *possible* for the Peace Force to use nuclear weapons in extreme circumstances provided that, as called for by the above-described proposals, such possible use is safeguarded with the utmost care.

The immediate direction of the Peace Force would be entrusted to a committee of five persons—to be called the Military Staff Committee— all of whom would have to be nationals of the smaller nations, *i.e.* of those nations entitled to less than fifteen Representatives in the General Assembly. Beyond this safeguard, however, the Military Staff Committee would always be under the close control of civilian authority, *i.e.* of the Executive Council. Still further, the General Assembly, through its Standing Committee on the Peace Enforcement Agencies, would exercise a general supervision over the work of the Military Staff Committee and over the Executive Council itself in respect of the organization and all the activities of the Peace Force. In short, the plan includes the utmost precautions for the subordination of the military direction of the Peace Force under all circumstances to civilian authority as represented by the Executive Council and the General Assembly. . . .

Even with these elaborate safeguards, it is realized that the danger of possible misuse of the Peace Force cannot be *wholly* eliminated any more than every *conceivable* danger of violation of the disarmament process can be eliminated. However, in order to achieve complete national disarmament and genuine peace, *some* risks must be taken. What we have attempted is to reduce these to the very minimum. On the one hand we have sought to provide for a world police so strong as to be capable of preserving peace in any foreseeable contingency. On the other hand, we propose such careful checks and limitations that there would be every possible assurance that the power of this world police would not be misused. . . .

. . . In these circumstances it seems perfectly clear that in order to provide the necessary assurance to obtain general assent to universal and complete disarmament, it will be essential to provide a world police of such strength and armament as to be able *quickly* and *certainly* to prevent or suppress *any* international violence. We firmly believe that on no cheaper terms can universal and complete disarmament be achieved, while it is equally clear that without total disarmament, genuine peace is unattainable. We submit, in short, that a strong and well-armed police force is part of the indispensable price of peace and that the sooner the world faces up to this conclusion the better it will be for all peoples.

7. *The Judicial and Conciliation System.* In accordance with the conception that the *abolition* of national armaments is indispensable to genuine peace, and that if such armaments are abolished other means must be simultaneously provided for the adjudication or settlement of international disputes and for "peaceful change," provision is made for a world system of conciliation and adjudication.

In proposing such a system, recognition is given to the existence of two main categories of international disputes, namely: (1) those disputes which are capable of adjudication through the application of legal principles, and (2) the equally or more important category of disputes which cannot be satisfactorily settled on the basis of applicable legal principles.

With respect to those international disputes which are susceptible of settlement upon legal principles, it is proposed to empower the General Assembly to *direct* the submission of any such dispute to the International Court of Justice whenever the Assembly finds that its continuance is likely to endanger international peace. In case of such submission, the Court would have compulsory jurisdiction to decide the case, even if one of the parties should refuse to come before the Court.

The International Court of Justice would also be given authority to decide questions relating to the interpretation of the revised Charter; and to decide disputes involving the constitutionality of laws enacted thereunder. Compulsory jurisdiction would also be conferred upon the Court in certain other respects as, for example, any dispute relating to the interpretation of treaties or other international agreements, or as to the validity of any such treaty or agreement alleged to conflict with the revised Charter. . . .

With regard to the other main category of international disputes, *i.e.* those inevitable disputes which are not of an exclusively legal nature, it is proposed to establish a new tribunal of the highest possible prestige, to be known as the World Equity Tribunal. To this end it is proposed that the Tribunal shall be composed of fifteen persons elected by the

General Assembly pursuant to safeguards and an elaborate procedure designed to ensure the choice of individuals whose reputation, experience, and character would furnish the best assurance of impartiality and breadth of view. . . .

In ordinary circumstances this World Equity Tribunal could not make binding decisions, as distinguished from recommendations, except with the consent of the parties. But provision is made that if the General Assembly votes by a large special majority, *i.e.* by a three-fourths majority of all the Representatives then in office (including two-thirds of all the Representatives from the twelve largest nations), that the carrying out of the Tribunal's recommendations is essential for the preservation of peace, the recommendations of the Tribunal shall become enforceable by the same means as a judgment of the International Court of Justice.

The purpose of this important departure is to supplement other methods for settling *nonlegal* international disputes (such as negotiation, conciliation, and agreed arbitration) by providing an impartial world agency of so high a stature that, under exceptional conditions involving world peace, its recommendations may be given the force of law.

Through the adoption of these proposals in respect of both legal and nonlegal international disputes, world institutions would at last exist whereby *any* nation could be compelled to submit *any* dispute dangerous to peace for a final and peaceful settlement; and the world would no longer be helpless, for lack of adequate machinery, to deal by peaceful means with any and all dangerous disputes between nations.

In order to provide means for the trial of individuals accused of violating the disarmament provisions of the revised Charter or of other offenses against the Charter or laws enacted by the General Assembly, and to provide safeguards against possible abuse of power by any organ or official of the United Nations, provision is also made for regional United Nations courts, inferior to the International Court of Justice, and for the review by the International Court of decisions of these regional courts. . . .

In addition to these judicial agencies, it is proposed to establish a World Conciliation Board which could be voluntarily availed of by the nations, or to which the General Assembly could refer any international dispute or situation likely to threaten peace. The functions of this new Board would be strictly confined to mediation and conciliation; and, if it failed to bring the disputing nations to a voluntary settlement, resort could be had to the International Court of Justice or the World Equity Tribunal, as might be most suitable in view of the nature of the issues involved.

In order to achieve genuine peace we must have more than total and universal disarmament and more than an effective world police. We must also have world tribunals to which the nations can resort with confidence for the adjustment or decision of their disputes and which, subject to careful safeguards, will have clearly defined authority to deal with any dispute which is dangerous to peace even if a nation does not wish to submit to the jurisdiction of the appropriate tribunal.

8. *Enforcement and Penalties.* The plan envisages a variety of enforcement measures, including the prosecution in United Nations regional courts of individuals responsible for a violation of the disarmament provisions.

In order to aid the Inspection Service in the detection and prosecution of any such violators, it is proposed to have a civil police force of the United Nations with a strength not exceeding 10,000. This force would be under the general direction of an Attorney General of the United Nations, to be appointed by the Executive Council subject to confirmation by the General Assembly. . . .

In case of a serious violation of the revised Charter or any law or regulation enacted thereunder for which a national government is found to be directly or indirectly responsible, the General Assembly could order economic sanctions against the nation concerned. In extreme cases the Assembly (or the Executive Council in an emergency and subject to immediate review by the Assembly) would also have authority to order the United Nations Peace Force into action. Any such enforcement action would correspond to the above-mentioned action available for the enforcement of judgments of the International Court of Justice or of the recommendations of the World Equity Tribunal for the settlement of a dispute when the General Assembly has decided that a continuance of the dispute would be a "serious danger" to peace.

9. *World Development.* The plan further provides (revised Articles 7 and 59 and Annex IV) for the establishment of a World Development Authority, whose function would be to assist in the economic and social development of the underdeveloped areas of the world, primarily through grants-in-aid and interest-free loans. This Authority would be under the direction of a World Development Commission of five members to be chosen with due regard to geographical distribution by the Economic and Social Council, subject to confirmation by the General Assembly.

The World Development Commission would be under the general supervision of the Economic and Social Council which would have power to define broad objectives and priorities. Since that Council would be composed of twenty-four Representatives, of whom twelve would come from the member Nations having the highest gross national products and twelve from among the Representatives of the other member Nations selected with due regard to geographical distribution, there would thus be reasonable assurance that account would be taken both of the views of those nations contributing large shares of United Nations revenue, and also of the nations most in need of the Authority's assistance.

This proposed World Development Authority could, if the General Assembly so decided, have very large sums at its disposal, since the Authority's funds would be allocated to it by the Assembly out of the general revenues of the United Nations. With the large resources which the Assembly could and should provide, the World Development Authority would have the means to aid the underdeveloped areas of the world to the extent necessary to remove the danger to world stability and peace caused by the immense economic disparity between those areas and the industrialized regions of the world.

While universal, enforceable, and complete disarmament, together with adequate institutions and methods for the peaceful settlement of disputes, are certainly indispensable, no solid and stable peace can be assured by these means alone. There is also required a more positive approach through the amelioration of the worst economic ills of mankind. To this end, the new World Development Authority, together with the Nuclear Energy Authority, would serve as important arms of the strengthened United Nations.

10. *A United Nations Revenue System.* It would obviously be futile to establish the proposed new world institutions called for by the plan (including the United Nations Peace Force, the Inspection Service, the World Development Authority, the Nuclear Energy Authority, the Outer Space Agency, the World Equity Tribunal and the World Conciliation Board) unless a well-planned system is provided for their sufficient and reliable financial support. . . .

The United Nations Peace Force, with an assumed strength for its standing component of, say, 400,000 (midway between the proposed constitutional maximum of 600,000 and minimum of 200,000) and with an assumed strength for the Peace Force Reserve of, say, 900,000 (midway between the proposed constitutional maximum of 1,200,000 and minimum of 600,000) would alone require some $9 billion annually. The minimum annual amount required for the General Assembly and Executive Council, the judicial system, the Secretariat, the Inspection Service, the Nuclear Energy Authority, the Outer Space Agency and the other organs and agencies other than the World Development Authority may be estimated at $2 billion. To this should be added a large amount on the order of $25 billion which should be annually appropriated by the General Assembly for the proposed World Development Authority in order to make a real impression on the vast problem of mitigating the worst economic disparities between nations and regions. . . .

It is apparent, therefore, that the reasonable expenses of a world authority adequately equipped to deter or suppress any international violence, to administer a comprehensive system for the peaceful settlement of all disputes between nations and *also* to do something substantial for the economic betterment of the underdeveloped parts of the world, could easily run to $36 billion per annum. And while this amount would be less than one half the 1960–61 budget of a single nation—the United States—it would, nevertheless, be so large a sum that reliance for supplying it should not be placed on a system of yearly contributions by the separate governments of nearly one hundred nations. . . .

A chief feature of this system would be that each member Nation would assign in advance to the United Nations all or part of certain taxes designated by it and assessed under its national laws. Each nation would undertake the entire administrative function of collecting the taxes thus assigned to the United Nations, these taxes to be paid directly to a fiscal office of the United Nations in each member Nation. In this way it would be unnecessary to create any considerable United Nations bureaucracy for this purpose. . . .

The General Assembly would adopt the annual United Nations budget covering all its activities, and would determine the amounts to be supplied by the taxpayers of each member Nation for that budget. These amounts would be allotted on the basis of each member Nation's estimated proportion of the estimated gross world product in that year subject to a uniform "per capita deduction" of not less than 50 or more than 90 percent of the estimated average per capita product of the ten member Nations having the lowest per capita national products, as determined by the Assembly. A further provision would limit the amount to be supplied by the people of any member Nation in any one year to a sum not exceeding 2½ percent of that nation's estimated national product. . . .

11. *Privileges and Immunities.* Annex VI relates to the privileges and immunities of the United Nations itself and of the greatly expanded personnel (including the United Nations Peace Force) which, under the revised Charter, would be in the service of the United Nations.

For the successful operation of an effective world organization to maintain peace, a body of genuinely international servants of high morale is clearly essential. To this end, it seems advisable to provide constitutionally and in some detail not only as to the privileges and immunities of the United Nations as an organization, but also as to the rights and privileges of all United Nations personnel and the limitations thereon.

12. *Bill of Rights.* Annex VII contains a proposed Bill of Rights having a two-fold purpose: (a) to emphasize the limited scope of the strengthened United Nations by an explicit reservation to the member Nations and their peoples of all powers not delegated by express language or clear implication; and (b) to guarantee that the strengthened United Nations shall not in any manner violate certain basic rights of the individual, that is to say of any person in the world.

The reason for the former is to make doubly sure that the authority of the United Nations shall not be enlarged by indirection, but shall be confined within the limits set forth in the revised Charter.

The latter set of provisions would not extend to any attempted protection of the individual against the action of his own government. It may be argued that the time has come for a world organization to guarantee to every person in the world and against any authority whatever a few fundamental rights—such as exemption from slavery, freedom from torture, and the right to be heard before criminal condemnation. We have not, however, thought it wise to attempt so vast a departure; and the proposed guarantees relate solely to possible infringements by the United Nations itself. Against such violations it does seem advisable and proper to have the explicit assurances which would be provided by Annex VII.

The assurances thus provided would include: guarantees, in considerable detail, of the right of fair trial for any person accused of a violation of the revised Charter or of any law or regulation enacted thereunder; a guarantee against double jeopardy, *i.e.* against being tried twice for the same alleged offense against the United Nations; and also a prohibition against any *ex post facto* law of the United Nations, *i.e.* against any law making criminal an act which was not criminal at the time the act occurred.

Provisions would also be included against excessive bail and any cruel or unusual punishment, including excessive fines; and the death penalty would be specifically prohibited. . . .

Unreasonable searches and seizures would also be forbidden, subject to the proviso that this prohibition shall not prejudice searches and seizures clearly necessary or advisable for the enforcement of total disarmament.

Finally, it would be provided that the United Nations shall not restrict or interfere with freedom of conscience or religion; freedom of speech, press, or expression in any other form; freedom of association and assembly; or freedom of petition. . . .

13. *Ratification.* The proposed requirements for ratification of the

revised Charter are: (a) that ratification shall be by five-sixths of the world's nations, including all the twelve largest nations, the aggregate of the populations of the ratifying nations to equal at least five-sixths of the total world population; and (b) that each nation's ratification shall be by its own constitutional processes. . . .

14. *Amendment.* The proposed requirements concerning the procedure for amendments to the revised Charter are almost as strict as those provided for its ratification. Any future amendments would be submitted for ratification when adopted by a vote of two-thirds of all the Representatives in the General Assembly, whether or not present or voting, or by a two-thirds vote of a General Conference held for that purpose. In order for an amendment to come into effect, ratification by four-fifths of the member Nations would be required, including three-fourths of the twelve member Nations entitled to fifteen or more Representatives in the Assembly. . . .

15. *Continued Organs and Agencies.* It should be emphasized that far from impairing the existing organs and agencies of the United Nations, which despite all obstacles have accomplished important results, the intention is not only to preserve but also to strengthen them. Thus the General Assembly would have much greater scope through having the final responsibility for the maintenance of peace, through the new system of representation and voting, and through the new, although limited, power to legislate.

The Security Council would, indeed, be abolished, but would be replaced by the veto-less Executive Council, chosen by and responsible to the General Assembly. The Economic and Social Council and the Trusteeship Council would be continued, with important changes as to their composition and functions, and with much stronger financial support under the new revenue system. The International Court of Justice would be continued with greatly enlarged jurisdiction and greater authority. And as to various other organs, and such agencies as the Food and Agricultural Organization (FAO), the United Nations Educational, Scientific and Cultural Organization (UNESCO), the International Labor Organization (ILO) and the World Health Organization (WHO), the revision would not only provide for their continuance but would also give opportunity for the enlargement of their activities and usefulness.

The intention is not to dispense with anything which has proved useful, but rather to revise, supplement, and strengthen the existing structure so that the United Nations will be fully and unquestionably equipped to accomplish its basic purpose—the maintenance of international peace. . . .

THE PRACTICAL PROSPECTS

What are the practical prospects for the realization of genuine peace, through universal and complete disarmament and enforceable world law, not in some indefinite future but, let us say, by 1980?

The question is crucial because the achievement of genuine peace will largely depend upon the persistent effort of many people and, unfortunately, only a small fraction of the human race seems capable of working persistently for a purpose, however desirable, that appears far off and uncertain. On the other hand, if convinced that the goal is attainable within a reasonably short time, they will work for it in greater numbers and with greater zeal, and by this very fact make it the more realizable.

I take a hopeful view on the question and will, in fact, venture a reasoned prediction as follows: (a) that by 1980 a comprehensive plan for total and universal disarmament and for the necessary world institutions to make, interpret and enforce world law in the field of war prevention will have been officially formulated and will have been submitted to all the nations for approval; and (b) that within four to six years thereafter (by, say, 1985) such a plan will have been ratified by all or nearly all the nations, including all the major Powers, and will have come into force. . . .

The most important single adverse factor I suppose to be the reluctance of the average person to make any drastic change in his traditional form of behavior. As experience shows, he will, of course, try hard to save himself from destruction when he is not only in actual and imminent danger but also comprehends that danger. Short of these circumstances, however, his tendency is to procrastinate and hold to his old ways, often until it is too late.

This deep-seated trait of human nature is very evident at the beginning of the 1960s as a grave obstacle to genuine peace. This is so because nothing is more certain than that under the conditions of our nuclear age the realization of genuine peace will require a truly revolutionary change in human thinking and behavior—a change so drastic that human nature almost automatically resists it, no matter how clear the necessity may appear. As the historian, Arnold Toynbee, has put it, "we shall have a hard struggle with ourselves to save ourselves from ourselves."

For many centuries the units into which mankind has combined—family, tribe, town, city, national state—have been accustomed to assert or defend their interests, real or supposed, by violence or the threat of it—culminating during our "advanced" twentieth century in the two greatest wars in history and, by 1960, in the maintenance of the most elaborate and destructive armed forces that the world has ever possessed. And yet, no matter how obvious it may be that, in order to achieve genuine peace, these forces must be abolished, along with the whole ancient method of international violence, it is foolish to ignore the strongly adverse influence of these habits and traditions and of certain special influences and vested interests created by them.

Of these special influences and interests, by far the most formidable, I judge, is that of the military profession which, in many nations, has sufficient influence to force their governments to resist rather than to aid the cause of total disarmament and the establishment of the world institutions that are essential to the settlement of all international disputes by peaceful means. Unfortunate as it may be, it is necessary to accept the fact that, as of 1960, there is throughout most of the world what has been aptly called a "vested interest in armament" on the part of the military profession, which is a constant and powerful influence adverse to the new conceptions which can alone suffice to achieve genuine peace.

In appraising the weight of this pervading military influence, it is necessary to recognize its good faith in most cases. The typical professional soldier, sailor, airman, or missileman does not deprecate or oppose disarmament because he is any less humane or less civilized than the average civilian. He does so because his training and environment have irrevocably *conditioned* him to assume that his profession is indispensable. In consequence, it is simply too much to expect that the military professions as a whole will do otherwise than oppose or at least "drag their feet" in respect of all proposals for total disarmament and all that this implies. It follows that there will be no solution for the problem of world peace until the "vested interest in armament" of the military profession everywhere is firmly overruled.

A less important yet significant adverse "vested interest" is that of traditional diplomacy. It must be remembered that for centuries a principal occupation of the professional diplomat has been to deal in "power politics," that is to say, in the making of alliances or in seeking to undermine counteralliances or in veiled or open threats of force as a means of advancing the real or supposed interests of his particular country. These habits of thought are almost as difficult to shake off as those of the professional military man; and, consequently, those who seek peace through total disarmament and enforceable world law will do well to discount the almost certain resistance of the "professionals" in many foreign offices in all parts of the world.

Another "vested interest" sometimes mentioned as an important obstacle to disarmament and peace is the presumed interest of many millions of armament workers in a continuance of their jobs and the corresponding interest of proprietors in their profits from armament contracts. But while the problem of readjustment to nonarmament work is certainly one that will call for attention and planning, this should not be regarded as a serious difficulty. What is often overlooked is that the process of disarmament would necessarily be a gradual one. At the outset there would almost surely be an interval of several years between the formulation of a comprehensive disarmament agreement and its coming into force through ratification by the respective nations, and this interval would serve as a warning period in which to plan for and partially carry out the shift of workers and materials to nonmilitary purposes. There would then undoubtedly follow a considerably longer period for the carrying out, stage by stage, of the process of actual disarmament, during which the conversion of the armament plants would be completed. Remembering also the immense tax burden which would be lessened year by year and the release of manpower and materials for such purposes as roads, hospitals, schools, urban renewal, and other pressing needs even in the most prosperous nations, it seems clear that this particular obstacle to disarmament and peace will prove to be a minor one.

Far more serious is the factor of mutual fears and recriminations which as of 1960 so poison the East-West atmosphere as to bring under suspicion in the West almost any proposal coming from the East and correspondingly in the East almost any proposal proceeding from the West. This state of affairs is unfortunately deeply rooted on both sides. It has been built up over a long period "conditions" the thinking of millions of people—East and West—who on other subjects are capable of unbiased judgment. There is little use in seeking to assess the blame which both sides must share, and we must accept this mutually poisoned atmosphere as a fact of life which cannot be got rid of for a long time. This mutual fear and suspicion is indeed a most formidable barrier to peace and we should recognize that success in the accomplishment of total disarmament and the establishment of enforceable world law will not be because this barrier will soon disappear but because it will be pushed aside under the pressure of necessity.

Apart from the just-mentioned deeply rooted obstacles, there are several others which are only less important because they are likely to be more transitory. These include the exclusion of mainland China from world councils, a lack of sufficient understanding as to the necessity for complete, rather than partial, disarmament and a similar lack of understanding of the necessity for a comprehensive and interrelated plan rather than a piecemeal approach.

Taking together all the adverse factors—especially the strong tendency to resist any drastic change, the certain opposition of the military profession and of traditional diplomacy, and the mutual fears and suspicions between East and West—we have a truly formidable group of obstacles. What are the *favorable* factors which are capable of offsetting or overcoming them?

Of these favorable factors the most important single one seems very clearly to be the *steadily increasing risk* of world catastrophe resulting from a continuance of the arms race and a continuing lack of effective world machinery to settle international disputes by peaceful means.

In specifying the increasing risk of world disaster, it is realized that the likelihood of all-out nuclear war may not increase at all and may even diminish during the 1960s because of a greater mutual understanding of its destructive consequences. But more than offsetting this factor is, I believe, the rapidly mounting potentialities of destruction if a large-scale nuclear war should, nevertheless, occur. For while it may be true that the chances of an all-out nuclear war may not increase during the 1960s, it is a certainty that the potential damage from such a war, if it should occur, will steadily increase from year to year. It follows that, taking the two factors together, the real risk will, in the absence of universal and complete disarmament under effective world law, be a steadily mounting one. A greater comprehension of this fact will be, I judge, the major influence in bringing about the formulation and acceptance of an agreement for total disarmament under enforceable world law. . . .

Next in importance to the risk of appalling disaster from the increasing destructiveness of modern weapons and the increasing popular pressure on the governments to remove this risk is, I believe, an increasing impatience with the vast economic waste and burden of the arms race. In terms of money this burden as of 1960 amounts to not less than $100 billion per annum, while in terms of human energy it means the full-time employment in the armed forces of some 15 million men and of not less than 30 million civilians in the manufacture of arms and other military activities—or a total of at least 45 million persons.

In the United States the resulting cost of about $46 billion per annum in 1960–61 absorbs more than half of the total Federal budget and about 9 percent of the gross national product, while in the Soviet Union the proportion of the national product devoted to military purposes is even higher. In many other nations the cost, although proportionately smaller, is nevertheless a heavy drain on their economies which prevents or handicaps the carrying out of many badly needed improvements. Even in so affluent a country as the United States, the vast military expenditure holds back such urgent needs as the improvement of education and of medical care for lower-income people, urban renewal, and the conservation of natural resources; and in nations less economically fortunate, like India, the adverse effects of military expenditure are naturally much greater. As the years have passed, there has been a growing consciousness that the existence of these burdens is incompatible with economic and social reforms urgently demanded by the peoples of many nations. In the 1960s, this consciousness will almost certainly become a more powerful force in favor of total disarmament.

Another helpful development should be a clearer realization from year to year that it is impossible to arrive at any important political settlements in the absence of an agreement for comprehensive disarmament. There has been much ill-considered talk to the effect that the settlement of various difficult political problems—such as the problem of Berlin and German reunification, the problem of Soviet dominance in Eastern Europe, the questions of Korean and Vietnam reunification, and the Quemoy-Matsu situation—must precede, or at least be simultaneous with, any comprehensive disarmament. The common sense of the matter is, however, that *in an armed world* it is most improbable that any of these difficult East-West issues can be settled—for the simple reason that it is virtually impossible to settle any hard controversy between opponents of equal strength and pride when the opposing parties are armed to the teeth and, therefore, bitterly suspicious of each other. All experience shows that before such opponents can settle any important issue, they must first agree to dispense with violence and cease their mutual threats and insults.

It has taken a long time to grasp this simple truth as applied to the crucial disputes between East and West; but in the 1960s it will become more and more apparent to most reasonable men and women that an agreement for universal and complete disarmament must be reached *before* these thorny East-West issues can be resolved.

Another favorable factor will be the almost certain abandonment during the 1960 decade of the exclusion of mainland China from the United Nations and from normal relations with the United States and many other nations. The bankruptcy of this policy, which has so greatly prejudiced adequate negotiations for peace, has long been apparent and it is hardly conceivable that it can much longer survive. When China, with its more than one-fifth of all the people of the earth, is admitted to full participation in world councils, an important barrier to the formulation of a comprehensive plan for peace will have been removed.

Still another encouraging sign is the increasing knowledge of the *ways and means* whereby genuine peace can be achieved. The persistent and rising *desire* since the end of World War II for the abolition of war has unfortunately been accompanied by considerable defeatism as to the feasibility of accomplishing this result. This defeatism has, however, been largely caused by an exaggerated view of the difficulty of the problem which has been due in turn to a lack of sufficient study and discussion of the concrete problems that are involved, *i.e.* the various interrelated questions as to the nature and form of the world institutions requisite for world order. At the start of the 1960s we can discern a marked change in this respect, in that a beginning has at last been made in a closer study of the specific problems—not only by private persons but even by public officials. There is a definite relation between the development of this study and progress toward the desired goal. This is true because the problems involved are by no means insoluble, and as more and more people begin to apprehend how these problems can be dealt with, the spirit of defeatism will naturally lessen and the better will be the prospect for the acceptance of an adequate plan for peace.

An important result of the more intense study just mentioned will inevitably be a more general understanding that *total, rather than partial,* disarmament will alone meet the situation. In 1960 it is almost universally recognized that, in order to induce acceptance of any important disarmament, a well-organized inspection system is essential, while only a minority as yet seems to understand that *complete* disarmament is equally indispensable. For this proposition there are three main reasons: (a) because experience has shown that it is virtually impossible to agree upon any plan of any consequence for merely partial disarmament, since one nation or another is almost certain to claim, and with some justification, that the particular proposed reduction would put it at a disadvantage; (b) because even if agreed upon any merely partial disarmament would not fulfill the purpose, since in the nuclear age the retention of even a small fraction of the armed forces of 1960 would be enough to keep in existence many pernicious fears and tensions between the nations; and (c) because, although an effective world police force is clearly indispensable as a condition for disarmament, there is a distinct practical limit upon the size and expense of such a force, so that if even as much as 10 percent of the national armed forces of 1960 were retained, it would be impossible to maintain a world police of sufficient strength to ensure its capacity to deter or suppress any possible international violence. As the disarmament negotiations of the 1960s develop, it can safely be predicted that the validity of these reasons will be more and more recognized. And when it is generally accepted that total, rather than partial, disarmament is no less necessary than an effective inspection system, a long step forward will have been taken.

Along with a clearer understanding that nothing less than the abolition of all national armaments will suffice, there is badly needed a clearer realization of the necessity for a comprehensive rather than any piecemeal or partial plan. No intelligent person sets out to build an adequate house without a plan providing for all the elements necessary to make the structure fulfill its purpose. He knows from the start that foundation, sidewalls, floors and roof must all be provided and that they must be so fitted together that, with each performing its necessary function, the house will stand. It is deplorable, therefore, that even in 1960 only a small minority seems to realize that the necessity for a complete *initial* plan applies also to the structure of peace; and that, if the structure is to stand, all the basic organs necessary for the maintenance of peace must be included in that plan. A more general realization of this truth will almost certainly come in the 1960s and will be a powerful force for world order. . . .

What the whole question comes down to in last analysis is whether the human race will show enough intelligence to enable it to make the required adjustment to the nuclear age. In 1960 the issue as to the future of mankind is whether the human race is sufficiently *resourceful* to formulate and accept world institutions which will once and for all abolish war and utilize the great new discoveries of science for peaceful uses alone. This issue will, however, depend not upon any *inherent* lack of intelligence but upon whether sufficient *effort* is made to make effective use of our present fund of intelligence. If the peoples are so apathetic as to permit the domination of military and old-style diplomatic thinking, they can expect nothing better than an indefinite continuance of the arms race and ultimate disaster. On the other hand, if the peoples make an even reasonable effort to comprehend the danger and the available means to remove it, it lies within their power to solve the problem and to institute an age of genuine peace under world law. . . .

World Government

INIS L. CLAUDE, JR.

In general, the theory of world government envisages the erection of authoritative and powerful central institutions for the management of relationships among states, specifically for the purpose of preventing international war. This positive task is typically taken to require the endowment of those institutions with legal authority to establish and apply whatever rules may be needed for this purpose, and with the coercive capacity to enforce the rules. Thus, it is conceived as creating "an effective system of *enforceable* world law in the limited field of war prevention." On the negative side, the world government project involves the reduction of the legal competence and the military capability of states to the point of making them subject to effective war-preventing control. As Norman Cousins has put it, "the answer must lie in the establishment of an authority which takes away from nations, summarily and completely, not only the machinery of battle that can wage war, but the machinery of decision that can start a war."

This, in short, is a program for the centralization of power and policy in those areas deemed relevant to the maintenance of international peace and order. The centralization of power involves the disarmament of states and the creation of an international enforcement agency; the centralization of policy is expressed in the diminution of the sovereign

From *Power and International Relations,* by Inis L. Claude, Jr. (New York: Random House, 1962), pp. 206–278 (with excisions). Reprinted by permission of Random House, Inc. Claude, an international relations specialist and author of several books on the subject, teaches at the University of Virginia.

authority of states in the international sphere, and a corresponding assignment of legal authority to central organs of the community. Federalism, the brand of government which is almost invariably contemplated in discussions of this conceptual scheme, expresses both the positive and the negative aspects of the matter. It suggests the creation of a superior agency, supreme over the constituent units of the community within its delimited zone of competence, and the reduction of sovereign states to the status of nonsovereign members of a federal system within that same zone. Federalism symbolizes functionally limited centralization, but centralization nonetheless, within the affected sphere. Rule of law and disarmament are key themes in world government thought—the former standing for the development of central authority in the system of international relations, and the latter for the elimination of the capacity of states to challenge that authority. . . .

I do not propose to deal extensively with the question of the *feasibility* of world government in the present era, or in the foreseeable future. This abstention is in part a reflection of my conviction that the answer is almost self-evidently negative; if I must plead guilty to dismissing this question summarily, I do so in the belief that there is little point in laboring the obvious. Suffice it to say that I see no realistic prospect of the establishment of a system of world government as a means for attempting to cope with the critical dangers of world politics in our time. Moreover, it appears that few advocates of world government are genuinely convinced of the attainability of their ideal, at least in the short run. Clark and Sohn take "a hopeful view" and "venture a reasoned prediction" that such a system will be in operation by 1975, but their analysis of the prospects is characterized by a sober appraisal of possibilities, not a sanguine assertion of probabilities. . . .

This points to the primary reason for my refraining from detailed examination of the issue of feasibility: The major significance of the concept of world government lies in its widespread acceptance as the theoretically correct solution to the problem of the management of power. Gerhart Niemeyer expressed a view which enjoys considerable popularity among scholars when he wrote that "While the only certain guarantee against further international wars is the formation of a world state, global unity is not feasible at the present time." Morgenthau, who is of course best known as a balance of power theorist, concludes "that the argument of the advocates of the world state is unanswerable: There can be no permanent international peace without a state coextensive with the confines of the political world."

The advocacy of world government has made a great impact on contemporary thinking about international relations, not because the claim of practical attainability has been taken seriously, but because the claim that it expresses a theoretically valid approach to world order has been acknowledged by numerous statesmen and scholars who are not in any sense committed to the organized movement for promoting world government. Hence, it is the latter claim that deserves careful examination.

APPRAISAL OF THE CASE FOR WORLD GOVERNMENT

Much of the literature pertaining to world government exhibits the qualities usually associated with impassioned advocacy. Typically, the major themes are as follows: The world is in a state of anarchy, which makes war inescapable; the elimination of war has become a dire necessity; this goal cannot be reliably achieved by any means other than world government; the establishment of this fundamentally new system is the necessary and probably sufficient means to world order. If the assurance of a peaceful order *with* world government is less than total, the hope for such an order *without* world government is virtually nil. Thus, world government is presented as a system—the uniquely promising system—for the management of power in international relations. . . .

However reached, the conclusion that peace is impossible without world government is a generalization that is not wholly warranted by the available evidence. The international picture is not in fact marked by such a constant and universal "war of every state against every other state" as one might be led to expect by the colorful and extravagantly Hobbesian language employed by some commentators on world politics. The record of international relations is sorry enough, and the present situation dangerous enough, without the unrealistic embroidery of "realistic" analyses which take the image of an international "jungle" too literally. In sober fact, most states coexist in reasonable harmony with most other states, most of the time; the exceptions to this passable state of affairs are vitally important, but they are exceptions nonetheless. Most obviously, states which are widely separated, not involved in intimate interrelationships and not engaged competitively in the pursuit of interests far beyond their own territories, are unlikely to find themselves in strenuous conflict with each other in a world without government. The history of relations between Peru and Belgium, or Cuba and New Zealand, would presumably make rather dull reading; within such combinations as these, the incidence of war, not the maintenance of peace, would require special explanation. In such cases, it is not to be assumed that hostilities will occur unless prevented by the subjection of the states to a common government, but that peace will prevail in the absence of exceptional disruptive factors. More importantly, one should note that settled and highly reliable relationships of a peaceful nature exist in many instances between states that are not significantly isolated from each other. One might consider the relationships between Canada and the United States, or the United States and Britain, or Britain and Belgium. Within these pairs, we find situations of "peace without government," relationships marked by expectations of nonviolence substantially higher than might be found within many national states.

As a British statesman described Anglo-American relations in 1935:

> War between us is, we hope, unthinkable. . . . I can say with confidence, after a Cabinet experience of more than a quarter of a century, that such a possibility has never entered into Great Britain's consideration of her requirements for defense and has never influenced the strength of the forces maintained by her, whether on land or sea.

In the case of Norway and Sweden, Karl W. Deutsch has observed that peaceful relations between them have been more stable during the recent era of their sovereign separateness than in the earlier period of their linkage under a common government. Moreover, Deutsch and his collaborators in an analysis of a number of historical security-communities—groupings within which dependable expectations of nonviolence are to be found—concluded that the record of those characterized by the retention of political pluralism was generally more favorable than that of those which achieved amalgamation; in short, peace without government tended to be more secure in these cases than peace with government.

These observations are not intended to suggest the general conclusion that anarchy is more productive of peace and order than is government. The fact that happy relationships sometimes develop between independent states does not overshadow the facts that the expectation of war somewhere within the system is endemic in the multistate pattern, that all members of the system are presently endangered by the possibilities of disorder inherent in the international situation, and that no reliable means of controlling or eliminating those possibilities has yet been devised. Proponents of the "no peace without government" line will properly point out that the instances of the formation of pluralistic security-communities are regrettably exceptional, and that we have no evidence that the process by which, say, Anglo-American relationships became dependably peaceful can be put into operation on a universal scale—or even on a Soviet-American scale. Quite so; but it might be retorted that the evidence for the peacekeeping efficacy of government is similarly limited. The point is simply that peace without government is a phenomenon which occurs with sufficient frequency to destroy the basis for the dogmatic assertion that human relationships cannot conceivably be ordered except by government. "Never" does not have to be invalidated by "Always"; "Sometimes" will suffice. . . .

Government, of course, is not a mere abstract concept, a hypothetical system the merits of which are to be determined by logical derivation from its definition. It is a social institution with which mankind has had considerable experience; it has a long and extensive record of performance, available for examination and evaluation. Advocates of world government are, naturally, aware of this fact, and they do not by any means base their case entirely upon the demonstration that an institution which is by definition capable of keeping order must be judged suitable for that task. In many instances, the argument is explicitly grounded upon a favorable appraisal of the record of government as an order-keeping institution within national societies, followed by the assumption or reasoned contention that government would—or, more modestly, might—function equally well within a globally organized society. In some cases, reference is made to the record of government in general; thus, "An area of government is an area of peace. You are familiar with the keeping of peace in the areas of your city, your state and your nation. A world government is obviously the path to world peace—if government is somehow possible over so great an area." . . .

Citation of the record of government within national societies as the basis for assurance that a world government could be relied upon to maintain global peace and order is a very dangerous expedient. Aside from the obvious point that macro-government would not necessarily function as effectively as micro-government, the hard fact is that the record does not support the generalization that the establishment of government, within a social unit of whatever dimensions, infallibly brings about a highly dependable state of peace and order.

The ominous phrase *civil war* serves as only the most dramatic symbol of the fallibility of government as an instrument of social order. The student of history and contemporary world politics will discover numerous manifestations of the incapacity of government to guarantee peace; outcroppings of uncontrolled violence are a familiar phenomenon in human societies equipped with governmental mechanisms. Government, indeed, has a very mixed and spotty record in this respect. The glorification of government as a near-panacea for the ill of social disorder may come easily to Americans, whose civil war has faded into a romantic historical memory and who are citizens of one of that small band of happy countries in which domestic order has become a normal and highly dependable expectation. It is likely to seem much less plausible to the unfortunately numerous "peoples whose country is the frequent scene of revolution and domestic violence or suffers the cruel terrors of tyranny; to them 'civil society,' or 'order under government,' if it is experienced at all, possesses most of the objectionable features we attribute to international anarchy." The Latin American region is a notable example of an area in which government has worked badly as an order-keeping institution: "In many Latin-American countries military rebellion is a recognized mode of carrying on political conflict." In Bolivia, for instance, it has been estimated that 178 "revolutions or violent, illegal changes of regime" occurred between 1825 and 1952.

Given the elementary facts about the record of government, historical and contemporary, it becomes impossible to conceive how Emery Reves could assert that the establishment of "a superior system of law" has produced, "in all cases and at all times," the elimination of the use of violence among previously discordant groups. It becomes difficult, moreover, to understand the general tendency of champions of world government to minimize the significance of the civil war problem even when they concede its existence. . . .

. . . while civil war is not inherent in an abstract definition of the governed state, or in an idealized image of the state, it is clearly inherent in the actual operating experience of real states. The historical slate cannot be wiped clear of civil wars by the simple device of asserting that, according to one's definition of the state, they should not have occurred. The judgment that civil wars are relatively improbable is subject to serious challenge. As Philip C. Jessup has observed, "Civil war, revolution, mob violence are more frequent manifestations of man's unruly and still savage will than are wars between states." Moreover, such civil wars as those which have occurred in Spain and China certainly deserve a place in any list of the most significant events in world affairs of the last generation.

At the present time, the list of states that an informed student could describe as virtually immune from the threat of large-scale domestic violence is certainly shorter than the list of those in which such disorder must be ranked as an easily conceivable or highly probable occurrence. Moreover, a world government might have a relatively high susceptibility to organized revolt, since it would encompass previously independent states that would undoubtedly retain a considerable capacity to function as bases and organizing centers for dissident movements.

This analysis should not be taken as inviting the conclusion that government is a device of negligible importance in the human quest for social order. Clearly, this is not the case. But, equally, the tactic of creating a government is not tantamount to the waving of a magic wand which dispels the problem of disorderliness. Peace without government is, despite dogmatic denials, sometimes possible; war with government is, despite doctrinaire assurances, always possible. Wars sometimes occur in the absence of government, in the exercise of the freedom from higher social discipline which prevails in that situation. Wars also occur in the presence of government, in protest against and defiance of the central control which is attempted. In short, the concept of world government deserves not to be seized upon as the one and only solution, the obviously effective solution, to the problem of the management of power in international relations, but to be treated as a theoretical approach promising enough to warrant careful consideration.

THE CONCEPT OF THE MONOPOLY OF POWER

I have identified world government as that theoretical approach to the ordering of international relations which goes farthest in the direction of centralizing the possession of power and the direction of policy. In sharpest contrast to the notion of *balance* of power, world government thought tends to postulate a *monopoly* of power, or a condition approximating that extreme of centralization. As Harold D. Lasswell put it: "The prerequisite of a stable order in the world is a universal body of symbols and practices sustaining an elite which propagates itself by peaceful methods and wields a monopoly of coercion which it is rarely necessary to apply to the uttermost." Similarly, Pope Pius XII is said to have looked forward to the creation of "a constituted international authority possessing a monopoly of the use of armed force in international affairs," as a solution to the problem of war. . . .

Thus, we find champions of world government postulating a concentration of power which will serve for all practical peacekeeping purposes as a monopoly of power, and doing this on the assumption that such a quasi-monopoly is the key to the effectiveness of government on any level: This is the indispensable characteristic of a national government, and it must be reproduced at the level of the global society. Indeed, this assumption seems frequently to be made by persons who are not necessarily associated with the advocacy of world government. Commentators on the United Nations often link a discussion of that organization's incapacity to order and compel with a reminder that it is not, of course, a government, in such a manner as to invite the inference—and perhaps to betray the assumption—that if the United Nations were a world government, it would, of course, be capable of operating coercively to whatever degree circumstances might require. William R. Frye, noting that, during the Suez crisis of 1956, many people wondered why Secretary General Hammarskjold could not "simply tell Nasser to go jump in the Suez Canal," patiently explained that "The difficulty was that the UN is not a world government." This explanation suggests the belief that, if the United Nations were endowed with the essential characteristics of a government, its head would presumably have the capacity to deal in this remarkably summary fashion with the leader of one of the constituent units of the world state. Government, then, whether national or global, is deemed to involve something resembling a monopoly of power. . . .

What, then, is to be made of the proposition that the state has a monopoly of power? The concept clearly has its uses in the realm of legal theory. It points to the basic principle that the state has the authority to qualify private violence as illegal, and to claim legitimacy for its own resorts to force; the state is legally competent to assign acts of coercion to the categories of crime and punishment. This is obviously a matter of considerable importance, but it should be evident that the possession of such theoretical competence by a state, whether national or universal, is not equivalent to a solution of the problem of maintaining order; it leaves open the question of the capacity of the state to give practical effect to its will. In most of its versions, the concept does not neglect this aspect of the problem. Monopoly of legitimate authority is customarily tied in with monopoly, literal or virtual, of the physical capacity to coerce. Indeed, one of the significant merits of the notion of monopoly of power is that it serves to symbolize the essential role of physical compulsion in the ordering of society; it focuses attention upon the coercive aspect of the state's operations, countering any temptation to assume naively that governments acting as the instruments of states need only be equipped with authority on paper or that they can rely exclusively upon the efficacy of the powers of influence and persuasion. The concept emphasizes the point that force must always be in the background and may on occasion have to be moved to the foreground.

The difficulty is that the concept of the state's monopoly of power—which, in practice, must mean a monopoly by the government which at any given time functions as custodian of the state's affairs—tends to be taken too literally. The assumption that the state possesses, by definition, a monopoly of power may lead to the assumption that actual states, in fact, find themselves in that situation; the assumption that this monopoly is the key to the effectiveness of the state as an order-keeping institution may lead to an exaggerated notion of the degree to which actual states can and do rely upon coercion, and thus to a distorted understanding of the basis for a hypothetical world state.

The notion that a state is an entity which is inherently capable of realizing the ideal of maintaining its authority, if necessary by exercising "the power to coerce the opponents of the government, to break their wills, to compel them to submission," is one which cannot survive exposure to the facts of life—unless one is prepared drastically to reduce the commonly accepted roster of states, and to hold in constant suspense the question of the genuine statehood of most entities which claim that status. In addition to full-fledged civil wars, the ills which plague so-called states include an interesting variety of riots, rebellions, and coups d'etat. According to one account, at least seventy coups occurred in Latin American states during the decade, 1945–1954; eighteen of these successfully toppled governments in eleven of the twenty states; only two of the states were immune from attempts to overthrow their governments; and each of four states experienced more than five such efforts. . . . The same sort of record could be cited and the same sort of prediction could be made for many other states, in all parts of the world.

The realist will not respond, I suggest, that these so-called states are not states at all, since they are demonstrably unable or doubtfully able to exercise a monopoly of power within their territories. It would seem much more to the point to take the evidence as indicating that many states are not in fact characterized by a monopoly of power, and to challenge the doctrinaire generalization which carries the contrary implication. Violent upheavals, directed against the authority of established governments, may or may not be suppressed and punished. The outcome is, of course, a significant matter, but the crucial fact is that such upheavals can take place at all; these phenomena indicate that the states in which they occur do not possess a literal or virtual monopoly of the instruments of coercion, and when they are successful they prove that the government concerned was actually inferior in power to its enemies (although, in some instances, external power may have reinforced the strength of domestic dissidents). The inescapable conclusion is that the creation of a state, equipped with governmental apparatus, is *not* to be regarded as a step which automatically involves the centralization of power to such a degree that disorder is effectively prevented or subjected to control. . . .

Even though a government may be, at a given time, the exclusive owner and operator of organized armed forces within a society, this does not necessarily mean that it will be able to cope handily with any conflicts that might arise. The armed forces may withdraw their support, turning their attention from service of the state to mastery of the state; the military *coup,* in which the organized forces or portions thereof destroy and replace the regime to whose service they are theoretically committed, is one of the most familiar phenomena of political history. In short, it may be said, with apologies to Robert Frost, that the government which possesses a monopoly of power may someday find itself possessed by that which it no longer possesses.

Moreover, in a case of deep conflict within the civilian body of a society, organized forces of rebellion may be built up while the organized forces of the state may break down; these are likely to appear as two aspects of the same process. The military power of the state should not be conceived as an abstract quantity. It is, ultimately, a matter of human loyalties; the state's power to engage in coercive action is dependent upon its capacity to enlist and maintain the support of men who wield weapons. In the nature of the case, that power is at its maximum when it is turned outward, and at its minimum when it is turned inward. One ought not to expect an army to display the same solidarity in conducting a civil war as in an international war, for it must be remembered that the men who constitute the armed forces of a state are members of the society, not fighting machines unconditionally at the disposal of the government of the day. Any significant split in the society is likely to be reflected in the armed forces; as L. H. Jenks has pointed out, "Most successful revolutions during the past century have been tolerated or even actively supported by important sections of the armed forces." The dissolution of the armed power of the state tends to accompany the dissolution of the political consensus—and to contribute to the improvisation of organized forces directed against the state or the governing regime.

It might be recalled that, in the American Civil War, approximately one-third of the officers of the United States Army joined the forces of the Confederacy. These included 182 general officers, among them Robert E. Lee, the man who might have commanded the Federal forces but who took the rebel command instead. The American loyalty pattern has changed considerably in the past century, but it is still a reasonable hunch that a Texan in the American forces who is certainly available to bomb Moscow is probably not available to bomb Houston.

It cannot be lightly assumed that the armed power which a government has at its disposal for domestic purposes is identical with that which it commands for foreign purposes; the usability of that power within the state is highly conditional. This is not to suggest that a successful revolution within, say, the Soviet Union, can be readily conceived.

It is to suggest that one should be skeptical of the generalization that the state, by its very nature, is reliably equipped to maintain peace and order within its boundaries.

Indeed, it would be difficult to sustain the argument that every state, or the typical state, represents an attempt at the achievement of a high degree of centralization of effective coercive capacity. The founding fathers of the United States, whose handiwork is so often cited by advocates of world government, gave little evidence of intending to vest a monopoly of power in the Federal Government. Rather, they stressed a division of powers, a separation of powers, a system of checks and balances—elements of a design for limited government. It may be pointed out that these constitutional principles pertain to political and legal components of power, rather than to power conceived narrowly as physical force. However, explicit references in the United States Constitution to the matter of military power for domestic use prescribe a pattern of divided authority and responsibility, involving both federal and state governments.

True, states are forbidden, without the consent of Congress, to "keep troops or ships of war in time of peace," or to "engage in war, unless actually invaded or in such imminent danger as will not admit of delay," and the United States is given a mandate to guarantee the maintenance in every state of "a republican form of government" and to protect the states against invasion or, by their request, against domestic violence.

Nevertheless, it must be noted that the Constitution assigns to the states a major share in the control of the militia except when it is called into federal service, including the right to appoint officers and conduct training, and that the Second Amendment makes the forthright pronouncement that "A well-regulated militia being necessary to the security of a free State, the right of the people to keep and bear arms shall not be infringed." This segment of the bill of rights has been described as "a resounding statement of the sentiment that the states ought to have significant and traditional governing functions of which they cannot be deprived by the national government." The militia—explicitly described as "the militia of the several States"—seems to have been conceived by the founding fathers as "the central defensive force for the new nation"; moreover, the Militia Act of 1792, designed to implement the basic constitutional provisions, "allowed state legislatures to organize the militia largely in their own fashion."

Riker argues:

> The framers of the Constitution and the Second Amendment clearly intended that the states be the managers of the militia. If, as was then

true, the militia was the chief, and indeed the only, military force, then the states would also be the managers of national military policy.

In the War of 1812, the militia constituted 88 percent of the total American force, and at the start of the Spanish-American War, the National Guard (the rechristened militia) numbered 100,000 as against the Regular Army of 28,000. As recently as the administration of Woodrow Wilson, the Secretary of War complained that the United States was "in the position that we have always been in since the institution of the Government—to rely upon the States doing this for the Nation—a situation in which the Nation is relying upon a military force that it does not raise, that it does not officer, that it does not train, and that it does not control."

Clearly, the modern National Guard is neither so independent of federal control nor so significant a segment of American armed strength as it was in the nineteenth century. It can still be described, however, as "A half-national, half-state force, financially supported largely by the nation, supervised and inspected by the Regular Army, but yet commanded by the chief executives of the states." At a minimum, it remains the symbol of the traditional American resistance to the concept of the extreme centralization of power; in 1957, the Governor of Alabama argued the case for safeguarding the National Guard against "a Federal clique of brass and bureaucrats seeking complete control of all military forces in our country."

The conclusion is inescapable that the framers of the American Constitution did not undertake to create a design for a monopoly of power, or a monopoly of organized force. The United States was indubitably a state in 1805, although its army of 2,576 hardly qualified as an instrument capable of coercing any dissident movement that might arise within its territories; it was a state in 1860, although it maintained a Regular Army of 16,367 men which was obviously incapable of exercising coercive control over 31 million people scattered across three million square miles. For many years after the establishment of the federal union, "Americans continued to rely on their militia—and hence on member-state forces—for their defense, and the federal government long remained both unable and unwilling to coerce any member state, even on several critical occasions." In the crisis of the Civil War, the ultimate victory of the federal government proved not that it maintained a monopoly of power, but only that it had been able, when put to the severest test, to muster somewhat more power and loyalty than the states of the Confederacy.

In the final analysis, the proposition that the concentration of all or most of the coercive capability of a society in an authoritative central institution is the solution to the problem of disorder which has been adopted and proved effective on the national level appears most dubious. This is an exceedingly weak foundation for the thesis that a governmental monopoly of power should be created, or could be achieved, or would prove effective, on the global level.

INDIVIDUALS AND GROUPS AS THE OBJECTS OF CONSTRAINT

The difficulty of contemplating a governmental monopoly of power, or, what comes to the same thing, a concentration of organized power adequate to enforce order in all circumstances, is minimized when one conceives society as a collection of individual atoms, and associates dissidence and disorderliness with individual behavior. It is probably difficult for anyone, even a person addicted to the glib repetition of the axiom that the state is all-powerful within its territory, to imagine that governments in general can handle revolutionary violence and threats of civil war as a cat toys with a mouse; this might be true of the Soviet government, but one can hardly believe that it holds for the government of Indonesia, or Guatemala, or Iran, or France. It requires no straining of the imagination, however, to conceive that governments in general may be able to enforce their will upon individual citizens. There is nothing flagrantly improbable in the picture of government, the massive order-keeping apparatus of society, majestically and overpoweringly confronting the single, isolated lawbreaker. The modern version of the miserable miscreant trembling before the throne is a plausible image in almost any state, no matter how weak and unstable its government may be. This is, indeed, the image typically suggested by champions of world government —which may go far toward explaining the fact that they are seldom troubled by the suspicion that the monopoly of power may be a mirage.

A major theme in the theory of world government is the subjection of the individual to the disciplinary authority and power of a central regime, insofar as this may be essential to the preservation of world order. The organization of United World Federalists included in its platform, adopted in 1948, the principle that "World law should be enforceable directly upon individuals." As Vernon Nash expressed it, "All law in a disarmed society must be applicable to, and enforced upon, individuals." . . .

The distinguished work of Grenville Clark and Louis B. Sohn in this field is, on the face of it, free from confusion and indecisiveness in regard to the question of the objects of legal regulation. These scholars make the straightforward assertion that world law must be "uniformly applicable to all nations and all individuals," and they provide for "enforcement measures against individuals, organizations and nations." They do not regard the notion of coercing states as a theoretical embarrassment, something which has to be admitted but cannot be accepted. They propose means for bringing world law to bear upon individuals, and tackle with equal seriousness the task of providing for enforcement against states.

Even in this case, however, one finds more than an inkling of the world government theorist's distaste for and uneasiness about the task of dealing with the national state. This appears, first of all, in the statement that "It is reasonable to assume that in most instances the government of a nation in whose territory a violation [of the disarmament regulations] occurs would not be involved in it and that such violations could be adequately dealt with by prompt action against the individuals responsible for them." One must ask whether it *is* reasonable to assume that the phenomenon of rearmament in a disarmed world would more probably be an expression of individual criminality than of governmental policy. In my judgment, the reverse seems infinitely more likely. The authors' assumption, running against the evidence that governments regard themselves as the guardians of national security and the instruments of national ambitions, and against the probability that they would continue so to regard themselves even after entering into disarmament arrangements, is suggestive of a reluctance to face the issue, a wistfulness which expresses itself in the slender hope that the state will kindly go away and leave the field to world government and individuals. Clark and Sohn have provided boldly for an international mechanism to control states, but at this point they appear excessively eager to believe that it may prove superfluous. The urge to define the problem in terms of coercing individuals seems irresistible.

Clark and Sohn also betray a basically negative attitude toward the state in their detailed provisions for world governmental institutions. They acknowledge that the central task is to deal with national governments; they cast their proposals in the form of a revised Charter of the United Nations, and do not notably alter the provisions of the original document in this basic respect. The new United Nations is to regulate the relationships of states, to assist in the settlement of disputes, to promote international cooperation, and to check the illegitimate ambitions of states. Moreover, the revised organization is expected to address itself to states, to consider issues brought by them, and to rely upon their cooperation and assistance in the performance of its functions. The fundamental conception of the United Nations as "a center for harmonizing the actions of nations" is explicitly retained in the Clark-Sohn draft.

Curiously, however, the institutional system which is thus to concern itself with governments is to have virtually nothing to do with them. The central organ, the General Assembly, is, after a transitional period, to be composed of individuals elected by popular vote and expected to function independently, without instructions from governments. Members of the other major organs are to be chosen by the Assembly from among the representatives which compose it. At no point in the machinery of the system is provision made for governments of the states constituting the organization to be represented by spokesmen authorized to state their policies and positions, present their complaints, negotiate agreements, or accept commitments. Member governments are apparently expected to bring issues to the organization and otherwise to participate in its processes, without being officially represented in it; ironically, the only governments granted the right to be represented by persons chosen and instructed by themselves are those of states which reject membership in the organization. Governments of member states are even deprived of the function of participating in the negotiation of the constitutions of specialized agencies which they are expected to ratify.

The bias of Clark and Sohn against admitting the role of national governments is reflected in the proposed arrangements for financing the world organization, which actually envisage budgetary support by governments—assessments are to be made on a national basis, and governments are to collect and pay revenue to the United Nations—but which camouflage this dependence behind a screen of taxation levied against individuals.

The authors display further hopefulness about the withdrawal of governments into insignificance in their assumption that representatives of countries will in fact remain uncontaminated by any trace of obligation to follow the instructions of their governments. This would appear most improbable, for governments deprived of any formal status in the system would surely be impelled to grasp the means at hand for making their voices heard in some fashion. Nevertheless, Clark and Sohn make it plain that they take it seriously when they provide that the General Assembly may, by a no-confidence vote, discharge the members of its Standing Committees, the Executive Council, the Economic and Social Council, or the Trusteeship Council, subject in each case to the rule that the Assembly must reconstitute these bodies by electing representatives from the same delegations as those who were turned out of office. Clearly, this rule makes sense only if it be assumed that the representatives from a given state do not function as spokesmen for governmental policy; otherwise, the substitution of one representative for another of the same delegation could not be expected to alter the situation.

This analysis suggests that Clark and Sohn, despite their frank recognition of the necessity for control over states as well as individuals, share in some degree the tendency of most other proponents of world government to shy away from the problem of grappling with the reality of states. It can be argued, of course, that the Clark-Sohn proposals merely reflect their federalistic quality in providing for the demotion of states to a subordinate role; the federal system of the United States also tends to brush constituent states aside, giving their governments slight opportunity for official participation in the processes of the federal government. However, it must be noted that the American system does not purport to focus on the management of interstate relationships to anything like the same degree as the system advocated by Clark and Sohn; the central difficulty in the latter case is that the scheme promises to deal with states while excluding them from effective participation. Moreover, it might be contended that the lack of provision for official involvement of state governments in the central machinery is a significant defect of the American federal system. Given this lack, the United States has been forced to the unsatisfactory expedient of improvising informal devices for promoting coordination among the state governments, which bear important responsibilities within the system.

The establishment of world government will not in itself produce a magical transformation, rendering states insignificant and making it possible to define the problem of world order in terms which exclude the necessity of coping with the potential disorderliness of states. A proposal to create a world federal system may be taken as a plan to eliminate the multistate system, but it does not involve the elimination of the states; by the same token, it does not abolish the task of preventing states from serving as the focal points of disruptive movements. As advocates of world government might be informed by adherents of a certain other ideological creed, the withering away of the state is not lightly to be presumed.

THE ANALOGY OF NATIONAL STATE
AND WORLD STATE

The theory of world government is essentially analogical; it proposes to reproduce the national state on an international scale, and it looks to the operation of government as an instrument of order within national society for clues as to the means by which global order might be achieved. This clearly means that the preliminary problem for the designer of global institutions and processes is to develop an understanding of national institutions and processes. How does government function within the national state? How then might government function within the world state?

It should be acknowledged that government might not function in the same manner, or with the same degree of success, in the larger as in the smaller setting, and that devices and techniques quite different from those normally associated with government might be found appropriate for international order-keeping. Champions of world government frequently seem too much concerned about the persuasiveness of advocacy to make these acknowledgments. Such dogmatic assurance that effective global institutions can be simply defined as national government writ large is as regrettable in intellectual terms as it may be satisfying in emotional terms, and one might reasonably ask for less dedication and more qualification. However, it must be stressed that this sort of ideological exuberance is not inherent in the position itself. One can legitimately ask what can be learned from national governmental experience that *might* usefully be adopted or adapted for the purpose of building a system of world order, without indulging in the illusion that the national and international problems are perfectly comparable or that solutions are perfectly transferable from the one level to the other. Indeed, I should argue that one *must* do so, for we are not so well supplied with promising ideas for solving the problem of war that we can afford to neglect the possibility that decisively valuable insights might be gained in this way. Whatever its defects, the world government school of thought has to its credit the achievement of directing attention to this important question. . . .

Leaving aside the writings of staunch advocates of world government, we find that scholars and statesmen who invoke the analogy of domestic government when considering international problems tend overwhelmingly to envisage it in terms of suppressing individual violence. Thus John Foster Dulles, discussing the prevention of international aggression, said:

> [It] involves an effort, within the society of nations, to apply the principle used to deter violence within a community. There, laws are adopted which define crimes and their punishment. A police force is established, and a judicial system. Thus there is created a powerful deterrent to crimes of violence. This principle of deterrence does not operate 100 percent even in the best ordered communities. But the principle is conceded to be effective, and it can usefully be extended into the society of nations.

While he was Vice President of the United States, Richard M. Nixon asserted that "More and more the leaders of the West have come to the conclusion that the rule of law must somehow be established to provide a way of settling disputes among nations as it does among individuals." Numerous scholars have agreed, implicitly or explicitly, that the possibility of duplicating the domestic government's relationship to the individual citizen is the issue that must be raised when one considers the problem of achieving international order. . . .

It is strange that those who have been most devoted to the idea that the solution of the problem of relations among states is to be found in the creation of a global version of the national state have displayed so little interest in the peace-among-groups aspect of domestic government. It would seem to be almost self-evident that national societies are most comparable to the international society when they are viewed as pluralistic rather than atomistic communities, and that the problem of civil war is the closest domestic analogue of the problem of international war. If one is concerned about preventing an aggressive state from disrupting world peace, it would be more natural, I suggest, to turn one's thoughts to the prevention of large-scale rebellion against the public order in a federal system than to the prevention of armed robbery in a well-governed city. How, then, is one to explain the concentration of attention upon the analogy of domestic government as a regulator of individual behavior?

To some degree, this peculiar focus appears to be the product of an utterly unsophisticated conception of government. In schoolboyish fashion, one sees government as a legislature, a code of law, a policeman, a judge, and a jail; those who misbehave are arrested and punished. The social discipline of government is located essentially at the end of the night stick wielded by the cop on the corner. If this works in Kalamazoo, why should it not work on a worldwide scale, with a global cop intimidating potential criminals everywhere, or controlling states assimilated to the position of individual offenders in Kalamazoo?

This explanation ought not to be pushed too far. Many prominent advocates of world government are thoroughly cognizant of the complexity of the modern governmental process; they are men whose image of government takes in the intricacies of public affairs in Washington as well as the simplicities of the street-corner situation in Kalamazoo. How is it that men such as these consider the problem of world government as if it were a large-scale reproduction of the problem of domestic law-enforcement against individuals?

A clue may perhaps be found in the intimate association between the idea of world government and the fashionable theme of a world rule of law. *Law* is a key word in the vocabulary of world government. One reacts against anarchy—disorder, insecurity, violence, injustice visited by the strong upon the weak. In contrast, one postulates law—the symbol of the happy opposites to those distasteful and dangerous evils. Law suggests properly constituted authority and effectively implemented control; it symbolizes the supreme will of the community, the will to maintain justice and public order. This abstract concept is all too readily transformed, by worshipful contemplation, from one of the devices by which societies seek to order internal relationships, into a symbolic key to the good society. As this transformation takes place, law becomes a magic word for those who advocate world government and those who share with them the ideological bond of dedication to the rule of law—not necessarily in the sense that they expect it to produce magical effects upon the world, but at least in the sense that it works its magic upon them. Most significantly, it leads them to forget about *politics,* to play down the role of the political process in the management of human affairs, and to imagine that somehow *law,* in all its purity, can displace the soiled devices of politics.

Inexorably, the emphasis upon law which is characteristic of advocates of world government carries with it a tendency to focus upon the relationship of individuals to government; thinking in legal terms, one visualizes the individual apprehended by the police and brought before the judge. The rejection, or the brushing aside, of politics involves the neglect of the pluralistic aspect of the state, for the political process is preeminently concerned with the ordering of relationships among the groups which constitute a society. In short, it would appear to be the legal orientation of world government theory which produces its characteristic bias against treating government as an instrument for dealing with groups.

The effect of the *rule of law* stress in discouraging attention to politics, with its pluralistic implications, is illustrated by the contention of Clark and Sohn that the representatives constituting the General Assembly of their projected world organization would, after a transitional period of voting largely along national lines, "more and more tend to vote in accordance with their individual judgment as to the best interests of all the people of the world, as in the case of national parliaments where the interests of the whole nation are usually regarded as of no less importance than the interests of a particular section or group." One cannot deny that legislators sometimes exercise individual judgment or that they sometimes show great devotion to the general interest, but one would expect commentary on this subject to reflect awareness of the phenomenon of political parties. . . .

The political process by which governments attempt to manage the relationships of segments of society with each other and with the society as a whole, with all the pulling and hauling, haggling and cajoling that it involves, is not so neat and orderly, so dignified and awe-inspiring, as the law-enforcement process by which they assert authority over individuals. But it is a vitally important aspect of the role of government, and the one which bears the closest relation to the problem of establishing order in international affairs. It is ironical that those who have done most to stimulate consideration of the possible applicability of the lessons of domestic governmental experience to the problem of world order have been so enamored of the concept of law that they have neglected and discouraged consideration of the most relevant aspect of that experience.

Politics never enjoys as good a press as law, and is unlikely to inspire such ideological lyricism as has been devoted to the rule of law. Law is the poetry of government; politics is its prose. When scholars and statesmen turn from ringing affirmation to serious analysis, they customarily suggest the conclusion, implicitly or explicitly, that a successful political process, rather than effective legal process, is the dominant feature of government at its best. . . .

. . . Harry S Truman has been quoted as saying that "the principal power that the President has is to bring people in and try to persuade them to do what they ought to do without persuasion. That's what I spend most of my time doing. That's what the powers of the President amount to." It is notable that government is pictured in all these statements not as a machine for imposing law upon individuals, but as a center for the operation of a process of political accommodation within a pluralistic society.

Looking specifically at the United States, I suggest that the tributes which are regularly paid to the "rule of law" should more realistically be paid to the "rule of politics." In a society of contending groups, law is *not* the only effective way of preventing violence, or even the most important method; instead, politics is the device which has proved most useful. The American Civil War was the result of a failure of political adjustment among sectional forces, not of a breakdown of law enforcement against individuals. As Dean Acheson explains this tragedy, it occurred because the basic conflicts in American society came to exceed "the power of politicians and statesmen to channel [them] into peaceful accommodation and eventual resolution." The legal process, as exemplified in the Supreme Court's *Dred Scott* decision, contributed to the ultimate failure of politicians' efforts to avert the conflict. . . .

Emphasis upon the political accommodation aspect of the role of government should not be permitted to obscure the obvious facts that governments *do* deal with individuals and enforce law upon them, and that governments rely in some degree upon command and coercion in their dealings with groups. In the broadest sense, governmental restraint of isolated or random individuals is a method of coping with the problem of *crime,* and as such is not particularly relevant to the problem of *civil war.* The distinction between individual lawlessness and individual leadership of group dissidence is a crucial one for government; nothing is more likely to promote disorder than to treat leaders of organized political protest as if their activities were merely criminal. To some degree, however, governmental action against individuals does relate to the problem of keeping groups under control. Insofar as government can pull the individual out of his group and deal with him by legal process, without inciting the group to rebellion, we have evidence that the group is not a solid bloc, divorced from the social consensus and unamenable to the process of political adjustment; we have here a symptom of adjustment potential. Governments may succeed in controlling groups by threatening or undertaking legal action against their leaders or segments of their membership, on occasions when vital group interests are not involved. This is to say that the susceptibility of significant groups to control by the governmental device of law enforced against individuals is a function of the solidarity and self-consciousness of the groups, and of their conviction regarding the importance of a given issue for specific group interests. The estimate of the limits of tolerance of a particular group with respect to a particular issue is a determination which requires great political sensitivity. . . .

One of the lessons of governmental experience is that coercion can seldom be usefully invoked against significant collectivities which exhibit a determination to defend their interests, as they conceive them, against the public authority. The order-keeping function of government is not fulfilled by the winning of a civil war, but by its prevention. If groups cannot be coerced without the disruption of the order which government exists to maintain, it does not follow that the alternative tactic of coercing individuals should be adopted. What follows is rather that the difficult task of ordering group relationships by political means should be attempted.

Clearly, governments are not always able to carry out this task; the incidence of civil wars and analogous disorders testifies to this fact. The establishment of government does not automatically create a social situation in which group conflicts are subject to political accommodation, nor does it necessarily carry with it the development of the institutions and techniques best suited to the exploitation of such adjustment potential as the society may exhibit. But if government does not make order through political adjustment easy or certain, neither does it provide a substitute. Governments maintain social order by presiding over a successful political process, or not at all.

To some degree, this general conception of the operation of government may seem inapplicable to modern totalitarian governments. It is true that totalitarian regimes undertake to atomize their societies, breaking down the collectivities which are deemed likely to challenge the monolithic quality of the state, and to fasten a tyranny of coercion upon their peoples. In some instances, they have succeeded to a degree which is appalling to men who value human freedom, but the evidence suggests that they have never wholly succeeded in this infamous enterprise. Moreover, such regimes are not wholly reliant upon this technique; some trace of political methods of managing social forces always remains in their operations. In any case, advocates of world government are not motivated by the hope of reproducing the totalitarian pattern on a global scale. It would indeed be ironical if men passionately devoted to the rule of law should define their ideal pattern of order-keeping as one which is realized only, or best, in totalitarian systems. The sort of national government which champions of world government propose to emulate is best exemplified by liberal regimes which depend primarily upon processes of political adjustment for maintaining social order.

I would conclude that theorists of world government are not mistaken in their insistence that one should look to domestic governmental experience for clues as to the most promising means for achieving world order, but that they tend to misread the lessons of that experience. In some instances, they treat the domestic problem of crime prevention as comparable to the international problem of war, and draw from national experience the conclusion that the central function of a world government would be to maintain order by enforcing legal restrictions upon individual behavior. In other instances, they note the domestic problem of coping with dissident groups, acknowledge its comparability to the problem of dealing with aggressive states, and suggest that the governmental pattern requires that a central authority be equipped with adequate military force to coerce any possible rebellion within the larger society.

In contrast, I would argue that the prevention of civil war is the function of national government most relevant to the problem of ordering international relations, that governments cannot and do not perform this function by relying primarily upon either police action against individuals or military action against significant segments of their societies, and that governments succeed in this vitally important task only when they are able to operate an effective system of political accommodation.

As Gerhart Niemeyer has said:

> If we wish to draw a comparison between the order within the nations and order among nations, war should be compared not with crime but with revolution. Grave civil strife is not avoided by police and courts, but through adjustments between classes by disposing of their differences and grievances before they lead to high emotional tension and open violence. Such a moment calls for the statesman, not the judge or sheriff; it is the statesman alone who, through foresight and political acumen, can prevent such a situation from arising, and thereby preserve domestic peace through continuous adjustment, compensation, conciliation and balance. Legal machinery helps to preserve the stability thus attained, but it does not in itself constitute the main condition of social peace.
>
> The prevention of war, like the prevention of revolution within the state, does not depend on legal procedures, but on the art of adjustment.

This conception treats government not as a monopoly of power which effectuates a rule of law, but as the focal point of a political process. If the history of national government tells us anything about the problem of achieving international order, it seems to me to be this: There is no substitute for political adjustment as a means of managing relationships among the units which constitute complex human societies, and there is no magic formula for producing either the kind of society which lends itself to ordering in this manner or the kind of institutional system which can effectively preside over the process of adjustment.

I do not contend that this analysis demonstrates the invalidity of the concept, or that it disproves the desirability of a system of world government. It does, I think, call into question the assumption that the task of devising an adequate theoretical scheme for world order has been completed—that we know the answer to the problem, and now face only the issue of whether, and how, the answer can be translated from theory into reality. To say that the institution of government in international affairs would transform that realm from a world of politics into a world of law seems to me to deny the lessons of experience with governed national societies, and to lead to false expectations regarding the means by which relations among states may be regulated. To say that the management of power in international relations cannot be achieved except by concentrating an effective monopoly of power in a central agency, which thus becomes capable of maintaining order by the threat of bringing overwhelming coercion to bear against any and all dissident elements, seems to me to misstate the position which governments occupy in national societies and to overstate both the requirements and the possibilities of the centralization of coercive capacity in the global society. To say that governments succeed, if they do and when they do, in maintaining order by sensitive and skillful operation of the mechanisms of political adjustment seems to me to be correct—but it does not point the way to a revolutionary new system of international relations, or promise a dramatic escape from the perils of international conflict. The idealized concept of government which advocates of world government expound exists primarily in their own minds; few actual governments are very government-like in their terms. The more mundane version of government which I have described is not wholly missing even in the international sphere; in my terms, the United Nations is not entirely "un-government-like." Government, defined in terms of the function of promoting order through political management of intergroup relations, is a matter of degree. Looking at it in this way, we can say that British society enjoys a high degree of government, that Indonesian society suffers from having achieved only a precarious minimum of government, and that the international society is in dire peril because of the manifest inadequacy of the level of government which it has thus far reached.

In the final analysis, it appears that the theory of world government does not *answer* the question of how the world can be saved from catastrophic international conflict. Rather, it helps us to *restate* the question: How can the world achieve the degree of assurance that intergroup conflicts will be resolved or contained by political rather than violent means that has been achieved in the most effectively governed states? This is a valuable and provocative restatement of the question —but it ought not to be mistaken for a definitive answer. . . .

The theory of world government makes its contribution, in part, by its uncompromising insistence upon the incompatibility of the urge for untrammeled national freedom in international relations and the urge for a dependable system of order. The history of international affairs is characterized by states' simultaneous groping for law and clinging to sovereignty; advocates of world government have most pointedly stressed the necessity for resolving the inconsistencies between these efforts. While they may have stated the range of alternatives with undue restrictiveness, ignoring or denying the possibility of finding a middle ground, they have nevertheless stimulated a confrontation of the necessity for choice which was long overdue. Moreover, the theory of world government has the merit of infusing the quest for world order with an innovating spirit, an openness to new ideas that challenge conventional modes of thought and established conceptions of the limits of possibility. This, along with the incentive provided for reinterpreting the implications of mankind's long experience in seeking order within societies of restricted scope, may well be the primary contribution of world government thought.

6

REFORMING THE STATE SYSTEM

Introduction

If the world law model of world order is seen as a proposal for a *radical* change in the structure of the international system, then the several less ambitious proposals presented here can be regarded as system *reform*. Functionalism, regionalism, U.N. peacekeeping, and arms control all represent approaches at the international system level to the problem of achieving a more peaceful world order, although of course any of these changes would have to find acceptance first at the level of national governments. These reformist world order proposals conflict with each other in regard to their assumptions about how the international system works, how it should work, and how it is most likely to change in the next ten to thirty years. But in many ways, they are complementary, both with each other and with more radical and longer-range proposals for world government or global integration. It is important to evaluate them, because many immediate policy choices—such as whether an America concerned with building a lasting peace system should support regional security alliances—depend on one's image of a preferable world order.

Furthermore, these reformist proposals might be regarded as potential elements of a strategy of world order change linking a long-range global future with immediate first steps.

The first selection, by David Mitrany, argues that functional solutions to European problems are preferable to federal ones. The argument can quite easily be expanded to the global level as Mitrany himself did in his famous study, *A Working Peace System* (London: Royal Institute of International Affairs, 1943). The "functionalists" hold that since nations are unlikely to give up their sovereignty to a world problem-solving authority, each problem should be attacked by a specific international body with just enough authority to deal with the problem. A "functional" organization thus has only one function, which is clearly defined in advance, as in the cases of the World Meteorological Organization, the Inter-American Development Bank, and the General Agreement on Tariffs and Trade. The nations that are parties to these organizations give them operating authority commensurate with the requirements of their specific functions. No functionalist agency would ever be perceived as a threat to any nation's sovereignty, because the organization could only be formed after there was a clear consensus that the problem at hand needed international attention. Thus, functionalists argue that functional solutions are far more likely to be acceptable to governments than federal solutions.

Mitrany argues for a world order composed of a network of functional units, each with its own limited jurisdiction, authority, and membership. He argues that such a model for solving problems would have several advantages in addition to its greater acceptability to national governments. It would, for example, allow a body of international common law to grow in every area of functional cooperation. It would lead to a corps of international civil servants for whom loyalty to functional agencies would replace loyalty to national government bureaucracies. And it would promote the formation of international customs, habits, procedures, and values, which are important components of an integrated world community. Functionalism, then, is not only a way of responding to problems that demand transnational solutions, but also a way of building world community. Those who believe that world community must precede world government could regard the functionalist model of world order as a crucial part of the change process. On the other hand, since a functionalist world order would have no central capacity for management or coercion, it might be asked whether the really divisive world problems—those that are most likely to cause wars—would be any less troublesome than they are today. It might also be asked whether these problems and other threats to human survival, such as the threat of ecological collapse, are so interrelated that we need some central co-ordination in managing them.

Another approach to reform of the international system is that of the regionalists. They are more concerned than the functionalists with problems of security, but less concerned with achieving eventual global integration. The excerpt by Bruce Russett is an analysis of the prospects for regionalism as a means of reducing the probability of wars and of facilitating trade and commerce. Existing forms of regional organization fall into two major categories: those concerned primarily with regional security, such as NATO or the OAS, and those concerned with economic and cultural integration, such as the European Common Market. A regionalist world order would be composed of a small number of regions organized for one or both purposes, with or without some sort of overarching world political structure.

Russett's remarks are from the concluding chapter of a study of the growth and functions of regional organizations in the international system. In summarizing his findings, he indicates that modest growth has taken place in both universal, or global, and regional organization, but the latter have been growing at a much more rapid rate. Furthermore, the number of transactions—diplomatic, political, and economic,— *within* regions have far outstripped those between regions. However, Russett observes a leveling off of these trends and does not expect significant further growth of regionalization in the near future.

Russett also provides a helpful comparison of regional and global integration as strategies of world change. Regional organization has the positive value of substantially reducing the probability of conflict within regions, while promoting social and economic integration within them. It is unclear whether a continuation of the regionalist trend would promote conflict between regions, and whether the lack of global cultural integration would lead to ideological and cultural polarization. Russett acknowledges the values of functional "cross-cutting solidarities that bind," and indicates that regional integration without such a level of global integration is a choice against these ties. Yet, in a world not ready for significant further steps toward an overarching world government, the promotion of regional integration might be regarded as a first step toward reducing the probability of war and encouraging cross-national political and economic ties.

Both functionalists and regionalists proceed from the belief that world authority structures like the U.N. are, at least for the moment, unlikely to be prominent in any further reform of the structure of the international system. Others believe, however, that with sufficient popular pressure, major governments can be induced to give greater support to proposals to revise the U.N. so that it will be better able both to prevent war and to help solve other global problems. One such proposal calls for creation of a permanent U.N. peacekeeping force. It was recently advanced by a policy panel of the U.N. Association of the United States and is included below.

It suggests some concrete steps toward a permanent peacekeeping force which will act as a buffer in big-power conflicts and prevent conflicts between smaller powers—Israel and Egypt, for example—from escalating into tests of superpower strength. Advocates of U.N. peacekeeping argue that such a force could be created now without other significant changes in the world order system; that it could be financed through voluntary contributions from U.N. member states; and that, joined with improved U.N. machinery for conciliation and mediation, peacekeeping could provide an important new method of coping with threats to world peace.

In the case of the Middle East, this would seem to be clearly in the interest of the superpowers, since it would provide an answer to domestic political pressures moving them toward intervention. In other cases, like Vietnam, the potential superpower support for peacekeeping is less clear. It might be asked if the U.N. could intervene in a conflict where one superpower has already established a military presence and believes that it could benefit from military success. There is also the question of the political uses to which a peacekeeping force would be put. Could it, for example, intervene legally under the Charter in an internal, civil, or guerrilla war? Would third world nations regard it as an agency of repression by rich, industrial nations? Would peacekeeping have to be joined with disarmament plans in order to win broadbased support?

The last selection included here might appear to be the most conventional perspective on system reform. At the same time, its analysis of the political meaning of arms control is quite radical. Herbert York suggests a variety of "next steps" toward disarmament that should follow the Strategic Arms Limitation agreements of spring 1972. In charting a path toward general and complete disarmament, York is in the mainstream of international reformers concerned with the war problem. War prevention is best and most simply achieved, they believe, by eliminating the armaments and military systems that make war possible. York argues that United States policy should be directed toward achieving additional agreements on disarmament as soon as practical after the SALT agreement is approved, even if this means substantial changes in the military and defense policies of the United States. His article lists several features that should characterize these post-SALT agreements if they are to mark a real change in the structure of the world order system.

These recommendations are based on the perception that the SALT agreements, in themselves, do not represent a step toward disarmament or a reduction of the role of the military in U.S. or Soviet decision making. Instead, by creating the impression that a step toward disarmament has been taken, arms control agreements free the military to press for increased expenditures for arms not covered in the arms limitation treaty. The SALT agreement, he says, is a "minor, palliative measure" that must not be allowed to stand in the way of more far-reaching moves toward a disarmed world.

Nevertheless, compared with the other world order models represented in this and the previous section, York's preferred world future is marked by modest expectations. He imagines a world in which the big powers have disarmed substantially, having begun with offensive nuclear weapons systems involving such especially dangerous features as multiple warheads; computer-operated targeting; and rapid, automatic launching. While his dream is of general and complete disarmament, he sees a definite value in merely reducing the level of nuclear threat. Of course, this design for minimizing the probability of nuclear war, leaves several problems to be dealt with. For example, some argue that the nuclear balance is a stabilizing and restraining influence on big power behavior and question whether without it there would be less to lose if local wars were to escalate. Might not the big powers be more inclined to intervene in small wars after nuclear disarmament? Another problem is the acquisition of nuclear weapons by the middle-range powers. Some ask how disarmed superpowers would respond to the nuclear threats of Egypt, for example, or China. Finally, there is the problem of securing agreement to a disarmament treaty by many middle-range powers without more adequate provisions for peaceful settlement of disputes, as might be accomplished through a combination of U.N. peacekeeping and mediation activities.

None of these proposals could be realized without the active support of most of the world's major governments. This support does not exist at present although a combination of changed world political conditions and popular pressure could probably induce some governments to press more strongly for reform of the international system. Yet it is often also observed that significant steps toward a more peaceful world could result from a decision by major governments to support existing international organizations more wholeheartedly. The U.N. Charter, for example, excerpts from which are included below, already authorizes the world organization to take a peacemaking role in all violent international disputes. It could do so if major governments accorded it greater moral and financial support.

The fact that these governments have thus far failed even to support existing international conflict-resolving procedures carries our inquiry a step beyond the level of world system change to the level of changing national foreign and defense policies. Why have major powers, particularly the United States, not always acted to support the cause of world peace? How can they be influenced to do so? The remaining sections will address these questions.

SUGGESTIONS FOR FURTHER READING

Lincoln P. Bloomfield, *The Power to Keep Peace: Today and in a World Without War*. Berkeley, Calif.: World Without War Council, 1971.

Inis L. Claude, Jr., *Power and International Relations*. New York: Random House, 1962.

Karl W. Deutsch, *et al., Political Community and the North Atlantic Area*. Princeton: Princeton University Press, 1957.

Ernst B. Haas, *Beyond the Nation-State: Functionalism and International Organization*. Stanford: Stanford University Press, 1968.

Marion H. McVitty, *Preface to Disarmament*. Washington, D.C.: Public Affairs Press, 1970.

David Mitrany, *A Working Peace System*. London: Royal Institute of International Affairs, 1943; reprinted Chicago: Quadrangle Press, 1966.

Joseph S. Nye, ed., *International Regionalism*. Boston: Little, Brown, 1968.

————, *Peace in Parts: Integration and Conflict in Regional Organizations*. Boston: Little, Brown, 1971.

The United Nations: The Next Twenty-Five Years. Twentieth Report of the Commission to Study the Organization of Peace. Dobbs Ferry, N.Y.: Oceana Publications, 1970.

The Functional Alternative

DAVID MITRANY

That people should turn to federalism as a form of multinational association is not unnatural: it seems the only available formula, because
our political thinking has been so long rooted in the notion that every
authority must be linked to a given territory.[1] For the rest, it is plain
that European federalism has been a blend of myth and some very mixed
sentiments.[2] That is proved in another way by the readiness of moderate
"Europeans" for something more flexible. "The majority of us do not

Excerpted from "The Prospect of Integration: Federal or Functional?" by David
Mitrany, *Journal of Common Market Studies* 4 (December 1965), pp. 134–145.
Reprinted by permission of the author. David Mitrany was an early advocate of
functionalism. His functionalist classic, *A Working Peace System*, was first published in England in 1943. He now lives in Oxford.

[1] This came out partly in the criticism of M. J. Petot, that the experience of the
European communities shows the unreality of the "functionalist" thesis that starting from small, autonomous specialized authorities one could build a complete
state! A "complete state" and its introverted nature happens to be the very idea
which functionalism seeks to overcome internationally. "Des Communautés Euro-
péens à la Fédération," *Revue Générale de Droit International Public*, 1960, vol.
64 (2).

[2] "The fallacy starts when it is believed that the motives for political integration are as rational as those for economic integration." The first are "mainly
mythical, which does not deprive them of a certain driving force. But this force
is soon spent when it clashes with the deeper and older myths and loyalties of
the national states." J. L. Heldring in special issue of *Internationale Spectator,*
April 8, 1965, p. 544.

regard the unification of Europe with the emotions of people acquiring a new fatherland," writes Prof. Samkalden; there is a need for "a diversity of new organizations for specific needs and interests," and a "plurality" of them is already available in which the value of the European communities, "but also their necessary limitation, find clear expression." [3]

"New and original phenomena" demand as at other crossroads in history suitable changes in the government of societies, and three such phenomena may be singled out as governing the present problem of international peace and development. (1) The new scientific inventions and discoveries have raised political, social and moral issues which can be dealt with only on their own global scale. Not one of them is peculiar to Europe; in the nuclear field all that Western Europe can do is to add its own pile of nuclear bombs, but not to halt their fearful menace. (2) At the same time we face the contrary prospect of twice the number of independent states entitled by their sovereign status to follow their own will, and many tempted by a revolutionary mood to do so. (3) The third factor, cutting across the other two and confusing their relation, is the trend to neomercantilist "planning." It has injected the political element into well-nigh all the manifold international activities and relations which formerly grew freely across most frontiers. That is the given equation. The key we have to find is how in these conditions "to harmonize the actions" economic and social, in the words of the UN Charter, "in the attainment of common ends." To have lasting effect the solution must be global. In theory it could be done through a world state or federation, but even if desirable such a monstrous construction could hardly come about except through conquest. Or it can be done by making use of the present social and scientific opportunities to link together particular activities and interests, one at a time, according to need and acceptability, giving each a joint authority and policy limited to that activity alone. That is the functional way.

Let it be said at once that there is nothing new in that. It has been the natural mode of Western international relations, some public and many private, before the two World Wars, but since then we have moved backwards from the liberal nineteenth century. "Before 1914 world integration was proceeding steadily by means of firm treaties and relationships, open-door arrangements and so on. In addition, a great number of pre-1914 agreements created what might be termed 'abstract regions' through multilateral contracts under the authority of international law." [4]

---

[3] *Ibid.*, pp. 641–642.
[4] Adolf Drucker, in *Regionalism and World Organization*, Washington, D.C.,

Now, as in former autocratic times, economic, social, and even cultural relations have fallen under the control of the state—"the State has almost become an organization for the prevention of free international intercourse and the growth of a normal human society." Fichte's eighteenth-century academic aberration, *Der Geschlossene Handelstaat,* is looming before us as a twentieth-century contingent reality. The trend is general, varying only in manner and degree, and informed with a ruthless pragmatism which permits any government in the name of its "plan" to change policy and practice abruptly without regard to the effect on the interests and plans of other peoples and the hurt to international goodwill. As their problems are more acute and their ways less staid the new undeveloped states are especially apt to resort to such planned licence; and as at the same time they are now protected by the incipient collective system of the UN, they can indulge—as no Great Power would have dared in the days of so-called "international anarchy"—in what is also a new phenomenon and can only be described as "total sovereignty."

That is the new world which somehow has to be brought back into working relationships, to open up a prospect and provide the elements for international government. We do not know what kind of international government will work. But we do know that as government is only a framework which enables a social community to live its life well, international government can have little sense or body without a living international community. One new phenomenon at least opens up a positive and remarkable prospect in that direction. As was said before, the immediate impact of planning, with its spreading concern for social welfare and rights, is nationalistic. But in its "external aspect one central characteristic is that it is *universal.* I believe this to be a novel, a unique historical situation. In the traditional category of 'human rights' there have always been differences from place to place in attitude, conception and practice. But now, whatever their constitutional form or cultural tradition, *all* countries have adopted the philosophy and claims of social security; and hence, inevitably, also similar machinery of administrative practice and controls." [5] If this reading be correct, two practical factors are already at work, and on a world scale, to which strands of functional cooperation could be made fast. One is the indispensable factor of a common outlook and purpose, which in this case puts into strong relief an evident identity of everyday social aims and policy. The other is the use-

---

1944, p. 102. One should note the erudite work of Professor Francois Perroux, who uses the conception of *éspaces économique* freed from the "servitudes of localization." See, e.g., *L'Europe sans Rivages,* Paris, 1954.

[5] David Mitrany, "Comment" in the Human Rights Section, 6th IPSA World Conference, Geneva, September, 1964.

ful factor of close similarity of ways and means. Administrative law is implicitly "functional" law, and so is administrative practice. Every functional link helps to build up a common legal order—as the ILO well exemplifies—specific but also concrete and cumulative, one which does not stay aloof in the atmosphere of diplomatic and juridical pacts but which enters everywhere into the daily life of the peoples themselves.

Two general considerations may be cited in support of this thesis. A general wish for a collective security system was natural after the shock of two World Wars and of the atom bomb; but new and remarkable were the first signs "of a sense of world community, of international responsibility for local conditions everywhere. The idea of the welfare state, new as it is even in our own countries, is already broadening into a sentiment for a welfare world." [6] The substantial and manifold efforts and contributions generally known as "technical assistance" are tangible proof of that; not as in the past occasional charity in some emergency, but a continuous programme of aid now accepted almost as a responsibility by the richer countries. On the other side, the new states, politically tangled up in aggressively "uncommitted" groups and leagues, have shown themselves eager to join the UN's special agencies and other such bodies "because the balance of considerations is in favour of such participation," and they have come to look upon it "as an international asset and a strengthening of their position in the world." In spite of their extreme sensitiveness the new states have shown little mistrust of such bodies, "even where the activities of the international organization within the State's territory is concerned." [7]

Considerations such as these show why one can find both opportunity and promise in working arrangements as a way of building up an international community. But it also is a natural, not a contrived idea pressed into an existing political mould. Generically speaking it represents a general turn grown out of the living complexities of twentieth-century society. Both devolution and integration tend to go that way, within states as between states. Socialist theory had contemplated some form of centralized control (state socialism or syndicalism or guild socialism) for economic sectors taken over from capitalist enterprise, but when it came to "nationalization" Labour turned instead to the nonpolitical device of autonomous boards and authorities. That has become the normal way for activities which are altogether new—aviation, atomic energy, and so on. The use made of it in existing federations is of special

---

[6] David Mitrany, "International Co-operation in Action," *Associations,* September, 1959.

[7] Benjamin Akzin, "New States and International Organizations," UNESCO, Paris, 1955, pp. 170–172.

relevance here. In America, in spite of an old and hard-set regionalism, departments of state (war, agriculture, the Federal Reserve Board, etc.) make use in their administration of functional regions ("single-purpose areas") which vary freely from service to service and seldom coincide with State lines. And so do the hundred or so executive agencies which have come into being especially since the New Deal—which itself was "not fashioned theoretically out of economic or social creeds" but was the wholly pragmatic response to the "felt necessities" of a pressing situation. The clearest evidence can be found in the great experiment of the TVA.

Because its own task could not be performed unless allowed to cut across the sovereign jurisdiction of seven of the United States, the TVA offers a good prototype for possible interstate arrangements. But for this reason it is as well to deal first with a general point raised in this connection. To the argument that even in established federations reforming activities have often had to be diverted into functional bypaths, instead of moving along the direct formal way of constitutional amendment, it has often been retorted that functional experiments have been possible and effective in America precisely because they worked within a federal system.[8] It is a plausible point, but fortunately one to which one can get closer from concrete experience. For the past century-and-a-half a growing number of international unions and services have worked well without reference to political supervision or protection. More specifically, in North America, and apart from the wartime combined boards with Canada, the U.S. since then has become a party to substantial joint activities with neighbouring states—the Alcan Highway (a likely model for an eventual Channel tunnel), the St. Lawrence Waterway, the Rio Grande project with Mexico—all of them without any offence to or intrusion by the three federal constitutions.

On the other side, as mentioned before, there are a great many cases where a federal constitution has stood in the way of internal functional developments. The TVA indeed itself provides a complete answer. In the face of a pressing social need for such river control repeated efforts by several presidents since the beginning of the century went astray, until the calamity of the great depression gave Franklin Roosevelt a chance to push through the bill which created the autonomous Authority. It was all done by May 1933, within a few weeks of his taking office; but then the TVA had to fight off forty-one legal suits over a period of five years and on a variety of constitutional objections before it was allowed

[8] See, e.g., Andrea Chitti-Batelli, "Functional Federalism," *Common Cause*, April, 1950, and David Mitrany's reply, November, 1950.

to settle down to the great work. "The TVA really introduced a new dimension into the constitutional structure of the U.S., without any change in the Constitution; but it could do so only because it was a new administrative and not a new political dimension." [9]

This is not the place to restate the political philosophy which informs the functional idea beyond saying that to prefer it to the constitutional approach is not to be timid, much less to be haphazard.[10] "It rests indeed squarely upon the most characteristic idea of the democratic-liberal philosophy, which leaves the individual free to enter into a variety of relationships—religious, political and professional, social and cultural—each of which may take him in different directions and dimensions and into different groupings, some of them of international range. Each of us is in fact a 'bundle' of functional loyalties; so that to build a world community upon such a conception is merely to extend and consolidate it also between national societies and groups." [11] The argument has grown out of a definite view of the dilemma of our time: that we can neither ignore the deep roots of nationality in the search for material efficiency, nor deny the urgent cry for social betterment for the sake of a hollow independence.

Federation was an advance on empire as a way of joining under a common government a group of separate territorial units. But federation is not only inadequate but irrelevant when the general task is not to consolidate but to loosen the hold of the territorially sovereign conception of political relations, and find a way to world peace through the revolutionary pressures of the time. Even earlier neither the British Empire nor Latin America, with their many social and historical affinities, had turned to the federal idea for political comfort. It has not served any of the postwar problems and situations. It has not proved acceptable to neighbouring groups in East Africa or the Middle East or the Caribbean in spite of pressing common needs and paucity of resources; alone the Nigerian federation survives, not too easily, in the wake of a unitary administration. It has not suggested itself as a remedy for healing the split between parts that had been formerly united. Some years ago, Mr.

---

[9] David Mitrany, *American Interpretation,* London, 1946, pp. 18–20. As against this, one must note that President Roosevelt's only "attempt at direct constitutional revision, to increase the membership of the Supreme Court from nine to fifteen, was bitterly disputed and defeated; though in effect it would have meant much less of a constitutional inroad than the experiment of the TVA and the body of new federal executive agencies." *Ibid.,* p. 22.

[10] See David Mitrany, *A Working Peace System,* 4th ed., London, 1944, and later writings. A useful chapter on international functional bodies appears in Max Sørensen, *Jus Gentium* (Danish), 1949, pp. 84–104.

[11] David Mitrany, *Associations,* 1959, p. 647.

Nehru and the Pakistani president agreed that their countries had many practical interests which could with advantage be managed in common; and now the leaders of the two parts of Ireland are working to end an old enmity by doing just that. But would either case have had a better prospect if one of the parties were to have said, "We must federate first?" Quite a number of practical activities are carried out in common by or for the British Commonwealth, but would any mere hint that they needed a political underpinning not cause at once a flight from this functional association?

When it comes to the new scientific inventions and discoveries—aviation, wireless, atomic energy, space exploration—their own technicalities defy any arrangement below the global scale. So much so that, e.g., in broadcasting, states have to respect the mutual interest even where there is no formal agreement. Flying may still claim for awhile sovereign rights in the air above a state's territory; but with satellites and space travel we have in truth reached the "no man's land of sovereignty." Nor is there any workable dividing line between military and nonmilitary usage of space: no means of self-protection is left, only all-round protection through some common authority. The programme for space exploration adopted by the General Assembly in 1962 was only a first step towards taking it out of politics; and the same intent clearly informed the Antarctica Treaty signed by twelve countries, including Soviet Russia, in 1959, which suspended all territorial claims and disputes for a period of thirty years and instead provided for scientific cooperation, and also for mutual inspection to prevent any military activities. These are, if one may be allowed the expression, not "federalizing" but "functionalizing" actions; they could never lead to any political union, let alone federation between the parties, but the Antarctica Treaty—considered as a type—which now amounts to a temporary neutralization under a joint agreement, could well lead to permanent neutralization under a joint international authority.

Before concluding, there are two points that need to be mentioned as they recur in almost every critical account of the functional approach. One is the central and difficult question of coordination. To a degree, insofar as it is raised as an abstract assumption, it expresses the difficulty which our political thinking finds to conceive of authority, as part of the tradition of sovereignty, without a territory; even the Roman Pontiff had to be allowed the Vatican territory as a base for sovereign status, though it is less than a speck on the Pontiff's vast expanse of influence and authority throughout the world. But the criticism also has a core of evident truth in the fear that a variety of autonomous organs might work at cross-purposes with each other. It is a real problem, but is it not better to wait till the need arises and experience shows what the need is? To prescribe for the sake of traditional neatness something more definite than the guidance and supervision of, e.g., the Economic and Social Council, would be to distort the whole conception from the start. To try to fit the functional bodies into a common mould would take away some of their special merits in working efficiency and flexibility of membership; while to impose upon them a "coordinating" authority, with anything like controlling status, would be to move again towards that accumulation of power at the centre which is in question here. We would be drifting back onto the political track and so miss the way to possible universality.

The second point is one of doubt, not infrequently heard: "Where will the political will for such functional union come from?" It seems a curious question. If there should be no will for working together on such lines, limited to evident self-interest, can one assume that there might be a better will for wider unlimited political integration? The question is not so much a criticism of the functional idea as a great doubt whether peaceful international cooperation is possible at all. It is perhaps an open question whether in 1945 we had been too hopeful or too form-bound in our approach. In the view of Senator J. W. Fulbright, the UN has in a manner broken down because it was based on the assumption of a unity of outlook among the Great Powers; now we had to turn to a functional approach to build up an international community, to tackle concrete problems instead of spectacular attempts at world constitution making.[12] The same question, whether they were too hopeful or too form-tied, applies to the "Europeans" who gathered at The Hague in 1948. Many of them now feel the need for "a more cautious conception of integration"; "if Europe is to pursue its fundamental goal, functional integration appears to be the only practical method of co-operation." [13] And the "fundamental goal" here means not local peace and strength, but world peace and well-being. As to this ultimate goal, in the concluding volume to the series of inquiries initiated by the Carnegie Endowment for International Peace, *The Nations and the United Nations*,[14] Prof. Robert MacIver himself concludes that the UN's main service to the cause of peace may lie not in its political activities, but in the development of the common or cooperative interests of the peoples in areas which lie outside or on the margin of the usual play of power politics.

---

[12] *Foreign Affairs,* October, 1961.
[13] Alling von Geusau, *Internationale Spectator,* April 8, 1965, p. 488.
[14] New York, 1959.

CONCLUSION

This paper has been written from the standpoint of a student of political science (with an evident international bias). It has in no way been concerned with the question whether a European union would, or would not, bring prosperity to its populations, or whether it would be a good thing or not for Britain to join it. As a student I have sought an answer to two questions: What kind of political construction was a European union likely to be, and what would be its temper—for if, as I think, function determines structure, this also means that structure must affect practice. And therefore, in the second place, what would be its relevancy to the prospects for a general international system?

Admittedly, to try to examine the "European" idea thus is like trying to hold a line on a political rainbow with its many fleeting hues—a rainbow with one horizon among those who are clear that they were not seeking "a new fatherland" and wanted Europe united that it may work the better for international union, and the opposite horizon falling in Dr. Hallstein's camp. For Dr. Hallstein is no less clear that they were after "awakening a new European patriotism"; and that—while the old nations may be left to dream their national dreams (and after dismissing any idea of supplanting the national with the supranational as "another illusion")—"perhaps it is true that only States can act politically. Then let us create the European State—or is Europe finally to abdicate?" [15]

If the aim is political union, a "United States of Europe," Dr. Hallstein's picture, with all its tactical tergiversations, is clearly nearer the mark. Both lines of inquiry have led to the same point, that by its nature and tendency a political union must be nationalistic; and that as such it must impede, and may defeat, the great historic quest for a general system of peace and development. Under the pressures of a planned and radical social transformation it is bound to shape towards a centralized system—closed, exclusive, competitive; and whatever else it may do, such a system would hardly be suited to mediate between the new ideological divisions, or temper the raw nationalism of the new states so as to steer them towards the greener pastures of a mutual international community.

More likely it is that it will cause the tentative "blocs" that have already confused policy at the UN, out of distrust of the old world, to harden into other "unions" in emulation of it. Could a European union, in the long run, benefit its own peoples if it tends in the least to split the world afresh into competing regional sovereignties? Is not breaking

---

[15] Walter Hallstein, *World Today*, January, 1965, p. 15.

through that dour barrier of sovereignty the ultimate test? In a world of a hundred and more states sovereignty can in simple fact never be dismantled through a formula but only through function, shedding national functions and pooling authority in them; unless we are to give up all purpose of wide all-round international sharing in the works of peace.

Regions and the Future
of the Global System

BRUCE M. RUSSETT

After having looked at aspects of the being and behaving of the international system, it is time to turn to questions about what it is becoming. Logically, four possibilities exist: 1) There is a continuing progression toward the integration of still larger units, and this progression will pass through a period of several large-scale regional units along with the further integration of a single worldwide system; 2) There is a progression toward the integration of still larger units, but for the foreseeable future it will involve only the integration of regional subsystems and not the entire international system;[1] 3) There is a progression toward the integration of still larger units, but it will proceed directly to the entire global system without leading to the further differentiation of regional subsystems en route; 4) No further integration at either level will occur for some time.

The evidence is sparse and sometimes contradictory, but I think that as general statements the last two possibilities are the least likely. . . .

From *International Regions and the International System,* by Bruce M. Russett (Chicago: Rand McNally, 1967), pp. 222–233. Copyright © 1967 by Rand McNally and Company. Some footnotes have been deleted and the remaining notes have been renumbered sequentially. Reprinted by permission of the publisher. Russett teaches at Yale University.

[1] This would correspond rather closely to what Southall (1953, pp. 229–63) has described as "the segmentary state," composed of highly autonomous subsystems within a larger system, with only weak central authority.

Perhaps the strongest support for the idea of progression direct to world-wide integration stems from the widespread diffusion of a potential *world culture,* of which the primary elements are Western technology and Western norms toward the use of material objects. Western technology has penetrated virtually everywhere, with some of the culturally most revolutionary instruments being modern means of communication and transportation. Nearly every country of Asia and Latin America, plus many in Africa, now has one or more television stations. Sets still are owned by only a minority, sometimes a tiny one, of the population, but in many areas receivers have been put in public places where a whole village can have access. To a very great degree these media have become carriers of Western mass culture, perhaps with local subtitles. The impending impact of communications satellites in spreading this mass culture is certain to be enormous. Among the elites, intercontinental jet transport has also had enormous influence, which may be even greater when the era of supersonic transports arrives. Largely as a result of these developments certain very basic cultural norms are widely accepted in areas where they are quite novel. The ideals of equality, national independence, and economic development are at least given lip service by the leaders of almost every country.[2] Everywhere men are coming more and more to accept the idea, previously quite specific to modern Europe, that their destinies are to a large degree controllable and can be improved by their own efforts.

In recent years, at least, the earth has become somewhat more tightly bound by *economic transactions.* Obviously the total value and volume of world commerce has expanded over the past two decades, but again we must have some benchmark against which to measure that growth. In chapter eight we have used as a measure of interdependence the ratio of trade to total product. For the entire world this relationship has changed moderately since the end of World War II. The most reliable long-term world production indices are for manufacturing production. From 1948 to 1965 world commerce grew an estimated 306 percent, as compared with an increase of manufacturing production of 259 percent. The relative growth of the former has been quite steady over the whole span. To some degree this may be attributed to recovery from the war, which disrupted trade even more than it did production. But since foreign trade continued slowly to outpace manufacturing even into the 1960s, something more permanent is probably at work.[3] The

[2] Cf. the essay by Talcott Parsons (1962).
[3] Data for recent trends in world trade and production are from United Nations (1966c, pp. vii–ix), and for previous years from Deutsch and Eckstein (1961, p.

flow of investment capital abroad has grown much faster even than trade. Benoit (1966, p. 13) estimates that the sale of goods and services produced by American-controlled companies abroad has gone up twice as fast as American exports, and now has a value about three times as great as all United States exports.

Other bits of evidence, however, are less compelling. Changes in the *relative incomes* of rich and poor nations present a very complicated pattern, but certainly not one that leads to any conclusion of a still-narrowing gap. The great difference first appeared during the nineteenth and early twentieth centuries, when the West industrialized rapidly while productivity in Asia and Africa changed hardly at all. World War II did little to change the difference between the extremes (the United States and Afro-Asia), but wartime damage in the European countries temporarily reduced the distance between them and the bottom of the scale. By the late 1950s Europe recovered from the war, and along with Japan and the communist nations of Eastern Europe showed a very rapid rate of growth in per capita income, averaging twice the rate manifested in North America. The result was a substantial reduction in income differentials among industrialized nations. Communist China also recovered and grew rapidly during this period (though not later, after the great leap forward had tripped), at a rate roughly approximating the states of Eastern Europe, so this was another instance, and one involving a quarter of the world's population, where the income gap was being narrowed. Yet China was almost the only major underdeveloped country to make such notable progress, and the other large poor states (e.g., India, Indonesia, Pakistan) began to industrialize but fell behind Europe's rate of advance, though in some cases they did keep up the pace of the United States. Measured by any of the common overall summary statistics for the entire distribution from rich to poor the degree of inequality on the globe was indeed, by the 1960s, slightly diminished. But if one looks only at the noncommunist states, and in addition excludes North America, the picture is different—of a growing gulf between Europe and the noncommunist third world.[4]

---

290). Manufacturing production probably in fact *understates* the trend, because it has grown much faster since World War II than have either mining or agriculture. These more recent data modify the conclusions of Deutsch and Eckstein, whose analysis stopped in 1959. They emphasized the low trade/production ratio of postwar years compared with that of the 1920s and even earlier, and appear not to have anticipated the continued recovery of world trade in the 1960s. At the same time, their basic conclusion is unharmed, since even the 1964 trade production ratio was well below that of the interwar years.

[4] This picture can be pieced together from a variety of sources, including Kuznets (1958), Andic and Peacock (1961), Zimmerman (1965, p. 39), and

The number of *international organizations* . . . grew, over the decade, by 52 percent (from 107 to 163). This suggests a strengthening of the institutional bonds joining the nations of the world, as new structures, to serve a variety of functions, arise to link one with another. Certainly some nations, especially those of Western Europe, were indeed enmeshed in more organizational strands than ever before. But actually the increase in the number of organizations closely paralleled the emergence of new nations, and the number of countries included in the two analyses grew at almost the same pace—48 percent (from 77 to 114).

Whatever the suggestions of a very modest growth in some of the conditions for world political integration, these same data, when examined for the growth of regional integration, give a more clearly positive answer *for certain areas.* On the side of impressions about *cultural homogeneity,* one can make a rather powerful case for an increasing similarity at least in Western Europe and in Eastern Europe. Whatever trends toward convergence may also exist, the major social and cultural fact of recent years may well be the success of the two chief centers in homogenizing their periphery. In addition, a major struggle over one other peripheral area is now underway in Southeast Asia, and the result will almost certainly be the homogenization of the area with the system of the winner.

If world trade has grown a little faster than production, intraregional *trade* has not consistently developed more rapidly than has commerce between regions. The only spectacular regional increase has been in Western Europe, where from 1953 to 1964 trade within the area grew almost 40 percent faster than did that region's trade with the entire world. Eastern Europe shows a minor (about 2 percent) relative gain in intraregional trade. Other major areas of the globe, however, exhibit a contrary trend. Slightly in Latin America, and much more in Asia, Africa, and the Middle East, worldwide trade grew faster than commerce within each of the areas—more than twice as fast in the case of Africa (United Nations, 1966a, pp. 398–405).

Among *international organizations,* by far the fastest growth has occurred in the number of regional institutions. Of the 107 intergovernmental organizations analyzed for 1951, a total of 45 could be called "regional." (They either had the name of a region in their titles, or in fact were limited in membership to a clearly identifiable and virtually contiguous geographic region.) By 1962 the figures were 163 organizations in all, of which 93 met these same regional criteria: an increment

---

Russett (1965, ch. 7). Andic and Peacock also support the earlier assertion that inequalities *between* countries are much greater than those *within* nations.

of 107 percent in the latter, but of only 13 percent in the nonregional category. . . . This applies to each of the major regions. Similarly, Robert Angell (1965), in his study which included the more than 1000 nongovernmental (private) international organizations, reported a growth of 167 percent in regional organizations over his six-year period, and an increase of only 32 percent in all other types. In both of these studies the most striking was in the EEC area (600 percent for intergovernmental organizations, 167 percent for nongovernmental organizations), but even excluding the EEC institutions the rates for other countries are also high (98 percent and 77 percent, respectively).

Of the major institutional attempts at economic regionalism over the past decade, without doubt the most successful has been the European Common Market. This coincides with the area's outstanding performance on the above criteria. Some distance behind it in impact has been the more modest, but in its way successful, Central American Common Market. COMECON too can claim limited gains in Eastern Europe. And well behind them come the European Free Trade Area (EFTA) of the peripheral seven, and the Latin American Free Trade Area (LAFTA).

The strongest argument against the conclusion that the conditions for regional integration are on the increase at the expense of worldwide integration concerns the overall correlations between studies. . . . The average correlation among all studies during the 1950s was 0.81; for the 1960s it dropped down to 0.77, a fall of four points. This is not an enormous difference—it is far less, for instance, than the average difference in correlations *within* each time period—but it still is not in the hypothesized direction. For this purpose, however, the figures . . . are deceptive, because in the 1950s many African and some Asian states were not members of the United Nations, were not independent and therefore could not be included in the international organization analysis, and in some cases did not even report their trade figures. As a result, most of the early 1950s comparisons are based primarily on countries in Europe, the Western Hemisphere, and the older Asian countries, and especially for the first two categories, this is where integration was highest anyway. But in the 1960s analysis the overall level of congruence is brought down by the addition of many new states, where the level of international integration is comparatively low. If the 1960s comparisons are recalculated to include only the same countries as were matched in the earlier years, the average correlation becomes 0.79, not enough drop from the 1950s to have much significance. Thus while in some sense the "worldwide average" potential for regional integration has declined, there has been no notable fall for those areas on which we have comparable data over the decade.

Yet this is not the same as finding that capabilities for integration in those areas have increased. For that, the best we can do is return to the evidence cited above, which is after all a more direct test than the simple presence or absence of high congruence between studies. (The latter bears more on the question of boundaries and the creation of sub-systems.) Wars have become rare in several regions. We found modest growth in capabilities in both Eastern and Western Europe, though greater in the latter. If there was some increase in ties between the two halves of Europe it was so small and started from such a low baseline as not to show up in the analyses. In the rest of the world the trends showed no clear slope either way; *possibly* there was a growth in the Arab world and in Central America, but not much in other parts of Afro-Asia or Latin America. As we have already established, the process of building regional integration is a slow one, and if we were not yet convinced the ambiguous evidence we have about just what *did* happen from the 1950s to the early 1960s should clinch the argument.

The major prediction of this section is thus for some further integration in certain regions, but not for any very great change in the number or composition of the principal coalitions operating at present in world politics. To forecast some *integration* is not to expect *unification* of the areas in question. The changes of the last five or six years, with the splits in the Atlantic Alliance and among the communist states, are probably as great as or greater than any subsequent political changes that will be witnessed during the next 15 years or so. Assuming of course that nuclear war is avoided, we probably have already passed through the most notable realignments of the postwar period, as the early bipolarity has loosened moderately but without creating a clearly multipolar or "balance of power" system.

REGIONAL INTEGRATION VS. WORLDWIDE INTEGRATION

Imagine a debate between a World Federalist and an advocate of Atlantic Union. The Federalist emphasizes the need for over-arching worldwide institutions. He knows that the world is a diverse and variegated place, but insists that only a global organization can prevent war and promote cooperative effort for the good of all mankind. The advocate of Atlantic Union may accept much of this argument as the statement of a long-term goal, but for now he dwells on the divisions and heterogeneity so manifest among nations. For the present, he says, we must take whatever islands of relative similarity we find, and integrate them as units which can solve their own internal problems and contribute to the stability of the larger international system without transforming it drastically. In the long run a world community may well be built by aggregating these units at a yet higher level of organization, in which they, not the existing nation-states, might be the basic building blocks in a global federal hierarchy.

Political events are not *determined* by the operation of background influences and aggregate events of the sort we have examined. . . . But such events do set the conditions within which statesmen must act; they close off some options and make others more feasible. An individual leader can sometimes halt or even reverse a trend which he opposes, but it is harder for him to create conditions that may be required for the achievement of his desires. President De Gaulle may be able to throw some sand in the gears of political union on the continent, but President Nasser cannot, by an act of will, produce an Arab union.[5]

If we consider the observed developments to be material for acts of creative statesmanship, some of the bases for further regional integration undoubtedly exist. Bonds linking the countries of Western Europe, Eastern Europe, and Latin America are clearly discernible, and others exist elsewhere. So far the regional subsystems of the world are far less well delineated than are the boundaries of national systems. For a nation the level of transactions, the institutional arrangements, and frequently the culture all change sharply at the political border. Neither the regional limits as defined operationally by any one criterion, nor the congruence of several different definitions, are as sharp or uniform for groups of countries. But if the path of regional integration is followed either as an intended step toward a world state or a substitute for it, the boundaries of those groups will become clearer. Their transactions with other countries within the region will grow faster than transactions with states outside the group, institutions within the group will grow even stronger and more numerous than institutions linking countries in different groups, and homogeneity within the region will increase at the cost of heterogeneity at the boundaries.

Many of the elements of such a trend are already present, but the developments of the past decade or so have been very moderate, mixed, and could be slowed or reversed. Politics is seldom so simple as the mere extrapolation of past rates and patterns of development. (Persistence forecasting is easy, but hardly the way to identify *change!*) A combination of autonomous forces and political will must be behind

---

[5] See the useful distinction by Sprout and Sprout (1965, p. 199) between the prediction of specific events and "negative prediction," or narrowing the range of possible outcomes by eliminating the most unlikely.

any continuation or quickening of the pace. Whether it can be made to move rapidly enough to solve pressing political problems in the world is a very open question.

A more serious question is whether regional integration would in fact ease or exacerbate the most dangerous political threats in world politics. Would the regional fractionation of the world improve or damage global abilities for the promotion of peaceful change? For some, the attraction of regional institution-building lies in its implication of the regional settlement of disputes, that a strengthened Organization of American States, for instance, would deal with Western Hemisphere problems without external interference. Too often in the past this scheme has been primarily a cover for great powers' spheres of influence, such as under the Monroe Doctrine or Japan's former predominance in East Asia. Those days are past and will not return. Most regional integration in the Western Hemisphere will only marginally include the United States, especially any movement that involves creating coercive institutions.

Other proponents of regional union without global integration above it seem to expect the emergence of several subsystems or superpowers in something like a balance of power system.[6] Advocacy of a "balance of power" opens up myriad questions, for it is a highly ambiguous concept that seems to mean all things to all men.[7] For many of its enthusiasts it becomes largely a nostalgic longing for a distant past that the advocates themselves could never have known first hand.

Regional integration would have the undoubted advantage of greatly reducing the risks of war within large areas of the world. From that point of view we could not but welcome it. Yet regional integration *alone* would introduce other potential threats to a stable and peaceful globe. At present the bonds among various groups of countries are too weak to permit the groupings to act in a highly unified way on very many regional or global issues. But the political integration of several large "regions," with a sharpening of the boundaries between groupings, implies a weakening of the worldwide cement that joins nations *across* regions. This would almost surely produce rigidities and heightened conflicts between groupings. The vision of a "Europe from the Atlantic to the Urals" is a distant one indeed. Regional integration along the presently indicated lines would do nothing to bridge the gaps either of the

---

[6] A notable bit of enthusiasm for this point of view is written by Masters (1966) with a more systematic theoretical statement in his earlier (1961) paper. See also the report of the Commission to Study the Organization of Peace (1953).

[7] Of many critiques of the concept, the most penetrating probably remain those of Haas (1953) and Claude (1962, ch. 2).

Cold War or between rich and poor. Much of the opposition to Atlantic Union in American intellectual circles stems from precisely this fear.[8]

If not accompanied also by stronger global ties, regional integration in itself is a choice against the cross-pressures or cross-cutting solidarities that bind, however weakly, the diverse nations from all parts of the world. The role of cross-pressures in preventing rigidity in political alignments has long been recognized as crucial. Originally the concept was applied to *sociological* cross-pressures, primarily differences in demographic attributes like the religion, occupation, or ethnic background of individuals. If groups of people as identified by one attribute, like occupation, were found to be heterogeneous by another which was also salient for them, such as religion, it was suggested that the likelihood of polarized, severe conflict between groups, such as two occupational groupings, was lower than if each group was homogeneous. Workers in one trade would be unable to present a unified front against another trade because of ties of sentiment and common interest which would make some of their number unwilling to oppose their counterparts in the other group too vigorously. Empirical studies in the United States have shown that individuals who are cross-pressured are likely to postpone making up their minds on a decision, to shift allegiance, and often to avoid taking a clear-cut position at all. It is not unreasonable to think that much the same kind of mechanisms would apply to the men in official positions in cross-pressured governments. A sharpening of regional boundaries in the world, making ties of similarity, interdependence, and institution coincide, would involve a reduction in the number of cross-pressures that currently exist in the world, and thus reduce the effectiveness of a major influence for controlling conflict between groups.

Even when considering only the groupings of a single criterion, the cross-pressure idea is still relevant. A nation with ties to two organizationally defined groupings, for instance (e.g., the United States, which belongs to many institutions in common with the Western Europeans as well as with the Latin Americans) also can serve as a useful bridge and help prevent the emergence of sharp conflicts between the two. To the extent that cleaner lines of demarcation between groups develop, these ties are lost.

To some degree the absence of sociological cross-pressures might be

---

[8] The concept of cross-pressures first gained currency in studies of voting in the United States, primarily that of Lazarsfeld, Berelson, and Gaudet (1944), and has also been given great theoretical attention by Parsons (1959, 1961a). I have applied it to international politics elsewhere (Alker and Russett, 1965, ch. 12). For a perceptive discussion of regional integration as threatening to widen interregional gaps see Yalem (1965), ch. 6, passim.

compensated by *attitude* cross-pressures, or shifting alignments of the major groupings on different issues.[9] Western Europe would have some political interests in common with Latin America, and others with Eastern Europe. But the crucial question is how long such a multibloc system would remain fluid and flexible. The mere existence of several actors of more or less equal power guarantees nothing about the ease with which coalitions would be made or broken. Building blocs might well create several units closer to an equality of economic and military power than now exist, but the coalescence of these units does imply a reduction in the number of political actors in the system, and in that sense a loss of maneuverability. The price of greater equality is the sacrifice of former opportunities for alliance formation among small powers. And one of the primary virtues of having a large number of small uncommitted states arises when that group is sufficiently incohesive that they may be split off, some aligning with one side and some with another, in patterns that change over time. But historical experience with "balance of power" systems of just four to eight roughly equal states is not altogether reassuring. If the international system becomes highly polarized between two grand coalitions as in 1914, any risk of defection by or damage to a major actor can be extremely threatening to the entire system's stability. Should a system with only a few major actors become highly polarized in the next decade or two, World War I might look like a skeet-shoot.

One wonders if the more recent counter example, the bipolar world with two great superpowers, each flanked by a retinue of much smaller states with few in between, is necessarily such an undesirable situation. It may be worse than a truly flexible and shifting multipolar system, and it certainly seemed bad in the 1950s, primarily because the risk of nuclear war appeared so great. But was the nuclear threat present because the world was bipolar, or merely because of technological developments, especially those that created deterrents which seemed for a time to be so vulnerable to surprise attack? The best-known builder of models of world politics (Kaplan, 1957, ch. 2) seems to say that the bipolar system is *inherently* unstable and tension-producing, but the evidence is not all that clear. One of his chief critics (Waltz, 1964) argues forcefully (in what he admits is perhaps a bit of nostalgia on his own part) that the bipolar system of ten years ago was really neither so unstable nor dangerous as it may have looked to those who lived in it, as compared with what may arise in a multibloc world.[10]

---

[9] Cf. Campbell et al. (1960), pp. 80–88.

[10] A "balance of power system" with a small number (but at least three) of major powers is different from the system with many independent states looked

The shift toward a modification of the bipolar conflict of the 1950s, bringing greater independence for China and for Europe, has without doubt permitted a reduction in United States-Soviet tensions. Many of the hostilities that the peoples and governments of the two great powers used to direct toward each other, however, have instead of vanishing merely been redirected toward China. For the most part this has been a consequence of China's growth in power and bellicosity, but the shift seems also to have been aided by deliberate governmental action (with some second thoughts evident in parts of the United States government as I wrote this in the late spring of 1966). Communist China is for the moment an almost ideal scapegoat. It is just big and powerful enough almost to be a credible threat to America or the Soviet Union, and visions of a billion Chinese and the "yellow horde" can be invoked. But even though the Peking regime could cause great trouble to small states around its perimeter, and a long-run world danger from China is surely no chimera, Chinese current military and economic strength is not now sufficiently great to threaten the basic sources of Russian or American power. But conscious diversion of popular hostility toward China, if indeed it is a deliberate policy of the government of either major power, carries more risks than may immediately appear from an inventory of current Chinese military hardware or a count of Chinese nuclear weapons. It is quite conceivable that the Chinese could respond to this hostility—for which, in all fairness, they can to a very large degree blame only themselves—by building the equivalent of a Doomsday machine. Such a feat is within the foreseeable capabilities of communist China, even though a sophisticated second-strike deterrent force may not be.

These comments about the dangers that remain and perhaps even are magnified as we move from a bipolar world to one with some significant second-rank powers are meant simply to emphasize the intellectual difficulties in talking too abstractly about the virtues of having more big blocs in the system. A number of other structural aspects of the system must be taken into account, and we may pertinently ask just *which* blocs are being advocated. Of the candidates for regional integration . . . the best possibility seemed to lie in Western Europe. While such a vision may not please the ex-colonial nations, and the potential of a

---

upon with favor by Deutsch and Singer (1964). It is not necessarily correct to imply, however, as Deutsch and Singer seem to do, that such a balance of power system is somewhere in between the bipolar and many-power systems in stability. For an interesting attempt to analyze these models, resulting in advocacy of a system (with the ungainly label of bi-multipolarity) containing two great powers but with the flexibility provided by a number of significant states not attached to either pole, see Rosecrance (1966).

free-floating Europe that could make some tactical arrangements with the Soviet Union ought to give Americans some pause, it is certainly the grouping that would pose the fewest threats either to American foreign policy or to the peace of the world. And from both considerations we may regret the lack of a regional unit capable of offsetting the Chinese threat. A movement toward the integration of Southeast Asia or of India and Japan would have its distinct uses, but unfortunately we found no signs pointing toward its fulfillment. With this exception, however, it is not amiss to inquire whether we would want to see the emergence of another have-not power—which like China might combine frustration with some new power, to produce dangerous aggression. Would many people, even in the underdeveloped areas, really welcome the achievement of Arab unity? It could only mean either the erasure of Israel in war, or irresistible pressures for Israeli acquisition of nuclear weapons.

Pragmatically, both the theorist and the policy-maker may favor the promotion of regional integration in some areas but not in others. Integration may in some circumstances further the solution of local conflicts, such as border disputes; in others it may relieve the threat of great power intervention or other dangers to broader peace. Many areas of Africa may well fit these descriptions. To express reservations about the wisdom of generally and indiscriminately promoting regional integration, and especially about the effort to build up aggregates that can become near-great powers, is not to be in favor of the worst aspects of Balkanization. Nor of course can we expect the political leaders of these areas always to share our doubts—their perspectives are neither those of an American State Department hand nor of a political theorist.

Nevertheless, we should retain our own perspectives and not go around the world actively fostering regional unity everywhere, but must additionally concentrate on the integration of the international system as a whole. Regional integration without concurrent pressures, and probably deliberate effort, toward integrating the entire international system would be at best a short-term and at worst a highly volatile "solution." If we take the Atlantic Unionist seriously, we must also take the World Federalist seriously. If creative statesmen choose to go down the path of regional integration they had better look far enough down that road to see the fork that will not be far ahead. The choice about what to do for *global* unity will determine whether the regional blocs will build a stable political edifice for man, or merely a shaky temple he can pull down upon his head.

These are not yet mutually exclusive roads. We must not allow the World Federalist and the Regional Unionist to polarize the debate and force us to take one of the options they offer. The world is not now ready for amalgamation in the style of the Federalist; the basic ecological underpinnings just do not exist. Maybe we will want to work in that direction in the long run. At this stage, however, a central choice of strategy is not forced upon us. The early steps toward world political unification based on amalgamating what are more or less the existing units are not so very different from the actions that should be taken for building worldwide mutual responsiveness within a pluralistic framework. We can lay a multipurpose foundation without now choosing the eventual form of the structure to be built, leaving room for the ingenuity and learning of later architects to devise a stronger habitation than we now know how to construct.

LITERATURE CITED

Alker, Hayward R., Jr., and Bruce M. Russett. *World Politics in the General Assembly.* New Haven, Conn.: Yale University Press, 1965.

Andic, Suphan, and Alan Peacock. "The International Distribution of Income, 1949 and 1957." *Journal of the Royal Statistical Society,* Series A (General), 124 (1961), 206–218.

Angell, Robert C. "Analysis of Trends in International Organizations." *Peace Research Society, Papers,* 3 (1965), 85–96.

Benoit, Emile. "Interdependence on a Small Planet." *Columbia Journal of Business,* 1 (1966), 9–18.

Campbell, Angus, Philip Converse, Warren Miller, and Donald Stokes. *The American Voter.* New York: Wiley, 1960.

Claude, Inis L. *Power and International Relations.* New York: Random House, 1962.

Commission to Study the Organization of Peace. *Regional Arrangements for Security and the United Nations.* New York: Commission to Study the Organization of Peace, 1953.

Deutsch, Karl W., and Alexander Eckstein. "National Industrialization and the Declining Share of the International Economic Sector." *World Politics,* 8 (1961), 267–299.

Haas, Ernst B. "The Balance of Power: Prescription, Concept, or Propaganda?" *World Politics,* 5 (1953), 442–477.

Kuznets, Simon. "Regional Economic Trends and Levels of Living," *in* Philip Hauser (ed.), *Population and World Politics,* Glencoe, Ill.: Free Press, 1958.

Lazarsfeld, Paul, Bernard Berelson, and Hazel Gaudet. *The People's Choice.* New York: Duel, Sloan and Pierce, 1944.

Masters, Roger D. "Goals for American Power." *Yale Review,* 55 (1966), 365–388.

Masters, Roger D. "A Multi-Bloc Model of the International System." *American Political Science Review,* 55 (1961), 780–798.

Parsons, Talcott, "Order and Continuity in the International Social System," *in* James N. Rosenau (ed.), *International Politics and Foreign Policy* New York: Free Press, 1961a.

Parsons, Talcott, "Voting and the Equilibrium of the American Political System," *in* Eugene Burdick and Arthur J. Brodbeck (eds.), *American Voting Behavior,* Glencoe, Ill.: Free Press, 1959.

Russett, Bruce M. *Trends in World Politics.* New York: Macmillan, 1965.

Southall, Aidan. *Alur Society.* Cambridge: W. Heffer & Sons, 1953.

Sprout, Harold, and Margaret Sprout. *The Ecological Perspective on Human Affairs.* Princeton, N.J.: Princeton University Press, 1965.

United Nations. *Monthly Bulletin of Statistics,* 20, 7 (July 1966).

United Nations. *Statistical Yearbook, 1965.* New York: United Nations, 1966.

Yalem, Ronald D. *Regionalism and World Order.* Washington, D.C.: Public Affairs Press, 1965.

Zimmerman, L. J. *Poor Lands, Rich Lands.* New York: Randon House, 1965.

Controlling Conflicts in the 1970's

UNA-USA POLICY PANEL

THE SHAPE OF THE FUTURE

The rising tide of expectation in the developing areas, fueled by widespread knowledge of the affluence that modern technology can provide, and frustrated by scarce capital resources and rapidly expanding populations, is certain to force recurring political instability in these areas as the pressures mount for "overnight modernization." Nationalism is on the rise, in both the developing and the developed countries, and under pressure of scarce resources and the need for internal social and political reform, there is, in many countries, a turning inward.

The difficult tasks ahead may prove too much for many of the second-generation leaders in recently decolonized areas. In some countries national unity, born of a common anticolonial stand and the excitement of creating a new nation may give way, in the face of continuing frustration, to long-standing tribal animosities and the fragmenting influence of international political involvement. The continuing difficulties in Nigeria are but one recent illustration. There will continue to be unsettled

Excerpted from *Controlling Conflicts in the 1970's,* a report of the United Nations Association of the United States of America Policy Panel on Multilateral Alternatives to Unilateral Intervention (New York: UNA-USA, 1969), pp. 12–15 and 38–51; footnotes have been renumbered sequentially. Reprinted by permission of the United Nations Association of the United States of America, from whom copies of the complete report are available.

borders—the fruit not only of colonial days but also of ancient and uncertain origins.

At a time when older leaders will be passing from the scene, these difficulties will be aggravated in some countries by the absence of any tradition of the peaceful transmission of political power. Present leadership is seventy-four years of age or older in East Germany, France, Kenya, North Vietnam, the People's Republic of China, the Republic of China, Spain, and Yugoslavia.

Our assumption must therefore be that a decade of turmoil, revolution, small wars and attempted take-overs lies ahead. The inherent impossibility of "overnight modernization" will be fertile soil for wars of liberation and the latter, while arising frequently out of genuine popular discontent, will often be stimulated by, or dabbled in by Peking, Hanoi, or Havana—and, in all probability, by the USSR despite its increasing interest in international stability.

The United States will continue to have its own interest in the promotion of "friendly governments." Thus, in the background—and frequently not too far back—will hover the basic problems inherent in the evolving superpower relationship, political and strategic, between the United States and the Soviet Union.

In the years immediately following World War II, the Soviet Union was preoccupied with internal rebuilding, with the security of its borders, and with its leadership of the international Communist movement. As its strength has grown it has greatly expanded its network of relations in the Third World and made substantial investments in the survival of many national regimes—though not necessarily in the future of particular individuals in those regimes. It is apparent that Soviet policies and programs have been based on a less than perfect political consensus in Moscow. Nevertheless, the USSR has now arrived on the Third World scene with massive economic and military assistance programs, with broad diplomatic and political support for countries and regimes, some of which are involved in actual or potential disputes with neighbors or with former metropoles, and with doctrines about the intimate connection between Socialism and "national liberation" revolutions. As we have recently seen, in some instances it has also arrived with a military presence of its own.

The political and ideological contest between the US and the USSR is being extended by technology and the speed of modern communication into polarized superpower relationships—with global implications. The development of Multiple Independently-Targetable Reentry Vehicles (MIRVs), of Anti-Ballistic Missile systems (ABMs), and of Fractional-Orbital Bombardment systems (FOBs) introduces new elements of instability into the superpower military balance. Technological advances are removing an increasing amount of secrecy from defense and security postures. By the mid-1970s development by both the United States and the Soviet Union of mobile "fast reaction forces" will have given both countries the capability of moving quickly far from their own borders to defend or reinforce what they consider to be their national interests.

While the Soviet Union must keep a back-door vigil on China, and the United States must keep the same watch out of its western window, the US-Soviet nuclear relationship will continue to be the overriding strategic consideration.

Superpower relationships are thus likely to continue to dominate the world of the 1970s with profound implications for peace and security. But the incalculable stakes in the avoidance of thermonuclear war, and the growing stakes of both superpowers in a more stable international order, will place limits on the extent to which either the Soviet Union or the United States will be willing to see small power conflicts escalate into superpower involvement.

The logic of the situation will sharply increase the need for institutional substitutes for the great power peacekeeping role of the past. There will be a need for third-party buffers, and for time-buying and face-saving devices that can keep the superpowers apart and, if they come into conflict, permit time to establish the facts and develop measures to defuse the crisis—giving them time as in the Cuban missile crisis to seek some measure, however limited, of common interest. . . .

ENLARGING UNITED NATIONS PEACEKEEPING CAPABILITIES

Efforts over the past three years to move United Nations peacekeeping into more dependable patterns have made little progress.

Ten UN member countries have earmarked approximately 11,000 men for United Nations service—a small portion of which are available on a standby basis. These military units are available to the United Nations for a very limited period, some for as little as six months. A UN force composed of such units can be stationed on the territory of a member country for as long as the host government will permit, which in effect gives the latter a veto over the composition of the force as well. In many cases the countries providing units have reserved the right to withdraw those units at any time should circumstances change.

The future of UN peacekeeping is presently being considered in a thirty-three member United Nations committee, established by the General Assembly. Thus far, it has reached no basic agreement on arrangements for future composition of forces, on guidelines for their use, or on arrangements for more secure financing. The furthest it has gone is the modest step of authorizing a Secretariat study of past UN experience with peace observation.

If the revived interest in multilateral peacekeeping is to be translated into effective United Nations capabilities, prompt and major moves will need to be made to develop United States proposals, to discuss these with the Soviet Union and other principal powers, and to determine the forum in which they should be formally considered.

There is one development in the important relationship between the two superpowers which may point the way to a new opening in the peacekeeping deadlock. This is through Article 43 [1] of the UN Charter under which member states, particularly the "Big Five," originally were to make available armed forces for Security Council collective action.

The failure of the Security Council to develop such forces, to oppose aggression and to keep the peace, was a casualty of the Cold War.

More recently both the Soviet Union and the United States have indicated a willingness to reopen negotiations under Article 43, to see if it would be possible to work out arrangements for more effective United Nations collective peacekeeping action. In July 1964 the Soviet Union suggested that such UN forces be composed of units *not* from the Permanent Members of the Security Council but rather from the middle and smaller powers. More recently Moscow has suggested that the UN Military Staff Committee, which was created for the purpose of advising the Security Council with regard to the force arrangements, should be enlarged to include not just the Permanent Members of the Council but non-Permanent Members as well.

---

[1] Article 43 of the United Nations Charter provides:

"1. All Members of the United Nations, in order to contribute to the maintenance of international peace and security, undertake to make available to the Security Council, on its call and in accordance with a special agreement or agreements, armed forces, assistance, and facilities, including rights of passage, necessary for the purpose of maintaining international peace and security.

2. Such agreement or agreements shall govern the numbers and types of forces, their degree of readiness and general location, and the nature of the facilities and assistance to be provided.

3. The agreement or agreements shall be negotiated as soon as possible on the initiative of the Security Council. They shall be concluded between the Security Council and Members or between the Security Council and groups of Members and shall be subject to ratification by the signatory states in accordance with their respective constitutional processes."

The Panel believes that these are potentially promising lines for serious exploration.

Successful UN peacekeeping depends to a substantial degree on superpower cooperation. It is increasingly unrealistic to think in terms of any major UN operation which either superpower strongly disfavors. Moreover, even if the general emphasis in the future continues to be on peacekeeping with the consent of the parties, rather than the less realistic enforcement action, the US, Soviets, and British have agreed to a new form of security assurance through the Security Council for Members that are threatened with nuclear attack after signing the Non-Proliferation Treaty. This agreement on the part of three Permanent Members of the Security Council could in itself open the way to a new set of international security considerations involving UN deterrent capabilities.

The Panel believes the time has come for a major initiative by the United States to strength the peacekeeping and crisis management capabilities of the United Nations.

The objective should be the conclusion of arrangements between the Security Council and member states under which these states make forces available to the UN on a more reliable basis and for a wider range of peacekeeping activities than is feasible under the present pattern.

The initial effort should be to reach an understanding with the Soviet Union and other key members of the Security Council on the principles that would underlie the development and use of greatly strengthened United Nations forces. This might be done within the general framework of Article 43.

One central principle, that makes such forces usable in the present international peacekeeping context, is the suggestion that the military units should come from *non-great power* countries. We interpret the Soviet proposal to this effect as a signal that they too may be willing to consider more effective UN peacekeeping capabilities.

A second principle is that the primary role of the Security Council should be emphasized. We believe the United States can accept this further emphasis on the Security Council's primary role in peacekeeping, since it reflects the reality of great power influence. Moreover, the US itself could be faced in the future with a situation in which the majority of UN Members desired a peacekeeping operation which the United States strongly opposed.

A further governing principle, however, should be the retention of the present right in any international emergency to turn to the General Assembly if action in the Council is blocked. Keeping this option open is of general importance, but it could be of particular importance if Peking ever takes China's seat in the Security Council. Under these circumstances, it might be in the interest of both the United States and the Soviet Union, as well as other UN Members, to make frequent use of the General Assembly.

If the preliminary talks we suggest prove fruitful, then we recommend more general negotiations within the framework of Article 43 with all interested UN Members.

While it would be desirable if all national units could be made available to the Council under a standard Article 43 agreement, it is unlikely that this would prove possible, or indeed that all national units would have capabilities for the variety of assignments to which the Council would, at one time or another, be directing its efforts. Some national units would be suitable only for limited observation or police-type action; others could be available for more general types of UN deployment.

A MORE CAPABLE UNITED NATIONS STANDBY FORCE

The Panel suggests that the new UN negotiations be directed to the following principal objectives:

1. The establishment of a standby United Nations peacekeeping force of 20,000 to 25,000 men, composed of land, sea, and air units from non-Permanent Members—the standby units to be supported by adequate earmarked reserves with both specially trained for UN service.[2] The standby units would represent four or five regiment/brigade task groups of approximately 5,000 men each—3,000 active ground forces with 2,000 men in air, naval, logistic, and staff support.

These standby units, which would approximate in size the UN force assembled in the Congo, should be available promptly on the UN's call and would enable the United Nations to cope with most of the crisis-type situations for which UN peacekeeping action, in the foreseeable future, is likely to be effective. The force would represent a doubling of the presently available units and would, the Panel believes, represent an appropriate and manageable next step in the development of the UN's capabilities.

In the UN operation in the Congo, one of the major problems was

---

[2] We distinguish between *standby* units from UN member governments, i.e., units such as the one infantry battalion presently maintained by Canada and available for UN service on one week's notice, and *earmarked* units which would be available on two to eight weeks notice.

the unavailability of adequate earmarked reserves and replacements. If arrangements can be made for the national contingents to be available for longer than six months, which is the period of availability of most of the present national units, a 100 percent reserve would not be necessary. In that case a 75 percent reserve of earmarked units might prove adequate.

We have suggested that not all standby or earmarked units would be suitable or available for all types of situations with which the Council would be faced. However, with 20,000 to 25,000 men on standby, and an earmarked reserve of at least 15,000 men, an overall UN capability of a trained force of 35,000 to 40,000 men would be a reasonable initial objective.

2. Arrangements between the Security Council and the countries providing the military units under which, wherever possible, the latter would be available to the Security Council for a minimum of one year's service in whatever capacity the Security Council and its executive agent, the Secretary-General, might direct.

3. UN Members not in a position to provide military units would supply bases and other facilities, including overflight privileges and prearranged rights of passage. Member countries having bases not presently used in connection with their national defense requirements could earmark certain of these bases to be made available to the Security Council as staging or storage points for future UN operations.

4. Certain member states would provide officer personnel on a more individual basis for UN fact finding and observation, and for the nucleus of elite cadres which could be of particular help in situations requiring fast UN reaction. A larger UN force would require a larger number of "support personnel" for staff, communications and security functions. This would make necessary an increase in recruiting and training of civilian personnel—including an increase in size of the UN Field Service.

5. UN Members having military assistance programs which permit assistance to countries participating in international peacekeeping under the United Nations should conclude with interested countries arrangements for the training and equipping of forces to be available to the Security Council. This might best be done on the recommendation of some appropriate UN body, or through third parties where UN peacekeeping training programs already exist. Under such arrangements it might also be possible to underwrite the training of individually recruited volunteers for UN service.

Middle powers with peacekeeping experience would be asked to give special technical training in language, civic action, communications, logistics and other peacekeeping arts, to officers and noncommissioned personnel from other countries. Training programs for middle-level officers and for civilian personnel might well be established by the United Nations.

6. The Permanent Members of the Security Council would undertake to maintain in a state of readiness and to provide logistic support for specified types of situations. One way would be to designate a specified number of types of aircraft, ships, etc. to be available on short notice if required—but not permanently tying up specific items of equipment.

THE MANAGEMENT AND CONTROL OF UN FORCES

The Secretary-General has thus far served as executive agent in the management of UN peacekeeping operations.

He derives his general responsibility from the Charter which charges him with being the "chief administrative officer of the Organization" (Article 97). But in peacekeeping operations he derives his special authority from the authorizing resolutions of the Security Council or the General Assembly.

In order to implement these resolutions charging the Secretary-General with responsibility for organizing and managing such forces, a general management system has been developed within the UN Secretariat. Under this system, first Dag Hammarskjold and subsequently U Thant have delegated much of the principal operational responsibility to one of the Under-Secretaries for Special Political Affairs. The military commander in the field reports to the Secretary-General through the Under Secretary, who in his work has had the counsel of the Secretary-General's Military Advisor and his staff.

The UN Charter, under Article 47, provides for the establishment of a Military Staff Committee "to advise and assist the Security Council on all questions relating to the Security Council's military requirements for the maintenance of international peace and security, the employment and command of forces placed at its disposal, the regulation of armaments, and possible disarmament."

The Panel believes there can be an enhanced role for the Military Staff Committee to advise the Security Council in peacekeeping operations. However, Article 47 is ambiguous as to the role of the Military Staff Committee in the management of United Nations forces once they have been activated under the Council's authority.

Sub-paragraph 3 of the Article suggests that the MSC shall be responsible "under the Security Council for the strategic direction of any armed forces placed at the disposal of the Security Council." It then goes on, however, to say that "questions relating to the command of such forces shall be worked out subsequently."

It is obvious that no Committee composed of the Chiefs of Staff of the five Permanent Members of the Security Council (or a larger group if the recent Soviet suggestion for enlarging the Committee were to be accepted) could effectively "command" UN military forces. "Strategic direction" would be workable only in the sense of the wartime combined Chiefs of Staff, or the former NATO Standing Group. We believe it important to emphasize that the Military Staff Committee's function must be purely as an advisory body to the Security Council.

The Panel believes it is crucial that a clear chain of command be retained by the United Nations in its peacekeeping operations. The Secretary-General's role as executive agent for all UN field operations must be maintained.

To reinforce the administration of peacekeeping forces, the Panel believes a Special Peacekeeping Section should be established within the UN Secretariat to assist the Secretary-General. It should be headed by an Under Secretary-General for Special Political Affairs. The Section would be composed of personnel seconded from the UN departments with specialized experience and with functions directly related to the field operation.

The tasks of the Special Peacekeeping Section would include:

(a) The administration, under the Secretary-General of field peacekeeping operations;

(b) Assistance to Member States which are providing standby or earmarked contigents;

(c) Initiation of an in-service training program;

(d) Establishment of appropriate liaison arrangements with regional organizations.

The Secretary-General and the Under Secretary-General in charge of the Special Peacekeeping Section should be aided by an Advisory Board chaired by the Secretary-General and composed of the senior Under Secretaries-General and Assistant Secretaries-General whose departments are most directly concerned with peacekeeping operations. The Military Advisor to the Secretary-General should be an ex officio member.

EFFECTIVE UNITED NATIONS
COMMUNICATIONS FACILITIES

The United Nations at the present time has a short-wave communications network with which it keeps in touch with its peacekeeping and peace observation activities. There is little comparison between this limited but still effective system and the advanced communication networks now employed by the great powers for keeping in touch with their own defense installations in various parts of the world.

Recent UN requests for funds to improve the efficiency and capability of the UN system have been refused on budgetary grounds.

There is no reason why the United Nations should be handicapped in any way by a lack of resources in this essential field. Indeed, if additional countries are to make national units available to the United Nations on a standby basis, and if proper arrangements are to be made for the use of bases, staging areas and overflights, a more capable network should have a higher priority.

The Panel believes that the member governments should make available to the United Nations the financial resources to support more effective peacekeeping communication facilities and equipment.

The Panel recommends that a United Nations Committee on Communications be established promptly to make recommendations as to the type of additional facilities required and to prepare estimates of their cost.

PEACEKEEPING, PEACEFUL SETTLEMENT,
AND PEACEFUL CHANGE

The United Nations is often brought into a dispute only after fighting has broken out. In these situations it is natural that the focus of attention should initially be on a cease-fire. The UN's record in this respect is good—witness its effective work in Indonesia, in Kashmir, and twice in the Middle East in bringing general hostilities to a close.

There is a growing conviction within the international community that UN peacekeeping efforts in any particular situation must be linked more directly with efforts at peaceful settlement of the issues underlying the dispute. Unless this is done the peacekeeping operation may cause both the UN and the parties in conflict to relax their efforts to resolve the dispute. Indeed, the incentives to settle such conflicts may be greater when fighting is still in process.

Related to the settlement of disputes is the issue of peaceful change.

Peacekeeping must not be a reason for failing to settle a dispute. Nor should it be a device for suppressing legitimate, i.e., popular, pressures for social, economic, or political change. The West has been acutely suspicious that the Communist nations cause much of the contemporary violence. On the other hand, left-of-center criticism suspects UN peacekeeping of being a cover for "capitalist antirevolutionary activities."

The purpose of UN peacekeeping is not to impose—or oppose—any ideological system. It should be to insulate the processes of internal politics from outside interference which may threaten international peace and security. In no event should it be used to freeze a situation in such a way that social and political change cannot take place. The concept of peaceful change signifies the hope that the needed economic and social changes can be brought about without violence.

The problem for the instrumentalities of international peacekeeping is to permit the necessary change, while at the same time limiting international disorder and reducing violence.

The Panel therefore recommends that:

(1) UN peacekeeping activities be linked more immediately and directly with vigorous efforts to resolve the basic issues that gave rise to the conflict;

(2) UN's peaceful settlement capabilities be strengthened by additional advance identification of individuals of exceptional talent and experience to assist the UN in its conciliation and mediation work. The UN's conflict control work has been enhanced by many men with extensive diplomatic experience. The Panel believes, however, the Organization should proceed, in advance of future crises, with the identification of additional talent and ensure that more such individuals gain experience in the work of the Organization;

(3) Such individuals, having been identified, should be brought together in occasional informal conferences with persons who have had successful UN negotiating experience, so that they may become more familiar with UN procedures and practices, and with the resources upon which they would need to draw should they at some point be asked to take on special assignments for the Secretary-General, or for one of the UN political organs;

(4) A greater effort be made to identify "justiciable" issues even in political quarrels and to encourage their adjudication by the International Court of Justice, by special chambers of the ICJ (as permitted by the Court's Statute) or by impartial arbitration.

THE FINANCING OF UN PEACEKEEPING

The legacy of debt left over from the United Nations Congo operation, exacerbated by the constitutional crisis over Article 19, has made the general question of financing UN peacekeeping a major issue clouding all discussions of strengthening UN's general capabilities. No significant progress can be expected without some mutually satisfactory answer as to how future forces are to be financed and how past debts are to be met.

Three general methods have been used by the United Nations for financing peacekeeping operations:

(1) regular or special assessments; (2) costs divided between the parties to the dispute; and (3) voluntary contributions by governments.

Regular budget assessments are suitable for only the smaller UN operations, such as those on the Kashmir cease-fire line ($1,028,100), and the UN Truce Supervisory Organization in the Middle East ($4.2 million). It was the arrearages under special assessments which precipitated the UN financial crisis of 1965. Payment by the parties to a dispute has proven workable for operations which were limited in size, cost and duration, such as those in West Irian and in Yemen. The Secretary-General's experience with the UN Cyprus Force has highlighted the inadequacies of purely voluntary financing. The Force costs about $11 million a year. The UN Cyprus account is now $14 million in debt.

Of the methods which thus far have been used by the United Nations for financing peacekeeping operations a variation of the voluntary method, apportionment by the General Assembly, is the only one likely to produce anything like the funds needed for the larger UN operations. It combines the basic principle of voluntarism with some guidelines on fair sharing, based upon ability to pay—and presents the package to the Members as a recommendation from the General Assembly. This was the method of financing UNEF in recent years. A substantial UNEF debt suggests, however, that even this method of financing is inadequate.

Each UN peacekeeping operation to date has, the Panel believes, been clearly in the United States interest. In each case, if it had been necessary for the United States to deal with the crisis through unilateral means, the costs would have been far greater.

In order to ease certain of the financial difficulties, under which the UN has labored, the Panel recommends that a United Nations Peace Fund be established primarily with voluntary governmental contributions. Funds would thus be available for the initial financing of a peacekeeping operation and to meet continuing costs. The Fund would be replenished as needed.

The Fund should be established at a level which would provide adequate funding of UN peacekeeping operations in the period between annual General Assemblies. This would suggest an initial Fund goal of $60 million. Past UN peacekeeping operations have been so clearly in the United States interest that the US should be willing to provide 50 percent of this amount. The ultimate size of the Fund would depend upon future levels of UN operations.

The establishment of the Fund should be accompanied by the setting up of a Special Finance Committee by the General Assembly, under rules permitting the Secretary-General to spend up to $10 million from the Fund for authorized peacekeeping operations but requiring that additional expenditures from the Fund would be made on the recommendation of the Special Finance Committee. The Committee might either have the same membership as the Security Council, or be composed of those countries which are Permanent Members of the Council plus other UN Members selected on the basis of past contributions to peacekeeping.

This would retain the basic Charter responsibility of the Assembly for financial matters, while at the same time making certain that these decisions are effectively shaped by, and properly coordinated with, what is likely to be the larger future role of the Security Council in decisions on the disposition and use of UN peacekeeping forces.

Estimates of the amount required to meet the Organization's peacekeeping debts range from $38 million to $60 million. The UN has received something over $23 million in pledges to a "Rescue Fund." Despite a succession of promises on the part of France and the USSR to make pledges toward this fund after the US gave in on the Article 19 deadlock, neither has done so.

If the United Nations is to make constructive moves toward a safer world through improved peacekeeping—and we strongly urge that it do so—it is essential that France and the Soviet Union do their part in making progress possible, and do so before additional delay further clouds the prospects for international peacekeeping arrangements that will benefit all.

Once this is done, the Panel believes that the United States should contribute not more than one third of the amount needed for a package settlement covering the payment of overdue UN peacekeeping assessments and the liquidation of UN debts—including the bond issue floated as one means of helping finance the Congo operation.

THE FUTURE OF REGIONAL PEACEKEEPING

There would appear to be little which the United States can do in the immediate future in moving to strengthen the direct military capability of either the Organization of American States or the Organization of African Unity. This is not to say, however, that at some point in the future, possibilities might not emerge for increasing the military capacities of at least the OAS. The United States should be alert to such possibilities, keeping in mind that the initiative should come from other members of the Organization.

In the meantime, however, the Panel believes it may be possible to enhance the capability of both the OAS and the OAU for the conciliation of difficult and pressing disputes among their Members. This could be done through strengthening the fact-finding, peace observation, and communication facilities of the two organizations. In both cases the United States could offer to make communication equipment available which would become a part of their permanent operational equipment.

The OAS could be a genuinely important instrument for crisis management in the Western hemisphere. The Panel believes its principal current need is for renewed assurance that it will have a significant role in future conflict control.

The Panel also believes we are moving into a decade likely to be characterized by a more sophisticated set of relationships than has existed in the past between regional organizations and the United Nations—with closer working relationships between the two sets of institutions.

On several recent occasions representatives of OAU, in one case four foreign ministers, were asked to represent the Organization at meetings of the Security Council when a dispute of special concern to the OAU was before the Council. There is no reason why a similiar procedure should not be followed when disputes of special concern to the OAS are before one of the United Nations political bodies. The OAS, the OAU and the Arab League all maintain accredited observers at the United Nations. As we have pointed out earlier in this report, the Dominican Republic crisis was concurrently before both the Organization of American States and the United Nations, and the UN Secretary-General at the request of the Security Council sent an observer unit which for over two years was stationed in Santo Domingo at the same time that the OAS forces were active on the island.

Chapter VIII of the Charter sets forth general relationships between the UN and regional organizations. Within this Chapter, Article 54 provides that "the Security Council shall at all times be kept fully informed of activities undertaken or in contemplation under regional arrangements or by regional agencies for the maintenance of international peace and security."

While the kind of reporting arrangement envisaged under the Charter has not developed in the manner anticipated, it would seem likely that in the future, dispute settlement in the areas in which regional organizations are concerned is likely to involve a much more differentiated and mutually reinforcing set of relationships between the global organization and the regional ones than was envisioned when the Charter was drafted.

Should a more substantial set of UN peacekeeping arrangements be developed, with a larger number of UN Members designating earmarked forces available for United Nations service, a pattern might ultimately develop in which certain of these forces were also earmarked for service with a regional organization—in case a decision was made that the dispute could better be handled on a regional basis. A reverse arrangement might be equally appropriate. A system of double earmarking has already developed on a limited basis in the European area where Holland has earmarked a force as available either to NATO or the United Nations.

The Panel believes that a system of double earmarking, while it has certain obvious limitations, is nevertheless a pattern which could over time develop to the benefit of both regional organizations and the United Nations.

A Little Arms Control Can Be a Dangerous Thing

HERBERT F. YORK

Let me briefly review, first, the facts of the arms race; second, what little has been done in the way of arms control and disarmament; third, why it is so hard to do anything about the arms race; and last, what we might expect from the Strategic Arms Limitation Talks (SALT), and what might follow SALT.

The nuclear arms race began with the Manhattan Project, which was started early in World War II in the belief that the U.S. was in a race with Germany to produce an atomic bomb. It resulted ultimately in the two atomic explosions which killed 150,000 people in Japan.

During the years immediately after World War II, the U.S. continued to produce fissile material and to fabricate bombs of more or less the same design and characteristics. By about 1950, we had accumulated a stockpile of some hundreds of bombs, each having an explosive yield equivalent to a few tens of kilotons of TNT. The total yield of this stockpile, then, contained the equivalent of some few millions of tons of chemical explosives. This was a few times the total explosive energy of all the bombs dropped on Germany during World War II.

The U.S. might have gone on slowly accumulating A-bombs except for four closely spaced events which raised new anxieties and generated new possibilities. These were the first Russian A-test in 1949, the Korean War which followed soon thereafter, the successful U.S. thermonuclear test in 1952, and the Soviet thermonuclear test in 1953. These new thermonuclear explosives were, roughly speaking, 1,000 times as powerful as the A-bombs which preceded them. Also during the early fifties,

From *War/Peace Report,* vol. 11, no. 7 (August–September 1970), pp. 3–7. Reprinted by permission of the editor. Herbert F. York is acting chancellor of the University of California at San Diego. He has served in the Defense Department and as a member of the Science Advisory Committees of presidents Eisenhower and Johnson.

we accelerated our unit production rates. The result was that by about 1960, we had thousands of bombs, many of which had tens of megatons of explosive energy each. The net result was that we could then bring about the equivalent of tens of thousands of World War IIs in a single day.

After 1960, nuclear weapons development and stockpiling continued, but such efforts were largely directed to improvements and changes in qualitative features, such as adapting these explosives to different environments and to different types of delivery systems, emphasizing special effects and improving factors such as yield to weight ratios.

Meanwhile, great changes in the mode of delivery of weapons were taking place. In 1953 the technologies of rocket propulsion, thermonuclear explosives, and guidance and control reached such a point that it was possible to begin the development of intercontinental rockets. These rockets could do more or less the same overall job as long-range aircraft, but could do it an order of magnitude faster and with greater certainty of penetrating any real or hypothetical defenses. At about the same time, the U.S. became aware of similar, and in some aspects more advanced, programs going on in the Soviet Union. As a result of the conjunction of these two events, we began those huge crash programs in missile development which dominated the technological scene in the late fifties and early sixties. Simultaneously, we initiated the Air Force's Thor, Atlas, and Titan missiles and the Army's Jupiter, and soon after we phased in the Navy's Polaris and the Air Force's Minuteman.

As we now know, the U.S. overreacted to the Soviet threat. We deployed many more rockets much faster than they did. We did so for a number of reasons: 1) the politically motivated missile gap charges of the political "outs" during the 1960 presidential campaign; 2) the genuine fears of the political "ins" promoted by "worst case analysis," and 3) the very great capacity of U.S. industry to react to a challenge of this sort when fueled by sufficient money.

By the mid-sixties, all three components of our strategic forces (bombers, ICBMs, and sub-launched missiles) each separately contained many times the amount of explosive power needed for deterrence. At that point, we leveled off our deployments. However, just as in the case of nuclear weapons, we have continued to improve qualitative features, such as accuracy, reliability, and ability to penetrate defenses. And most important, because of its future significance, we developed mechanisms making it possible for a single rocket booster to launch more than one independently targetable warhead. The name for this last development is MIRV.

MIRV-type warheads are now being deployed on both our land-based ICBMs and our sub-launched Poseidon missiles. We are outfitting each Minuteman III with three warheads, and each of the Poseidon submarine's 16 missiles with 10 or more warheads. By the time present plans are completed, the number of missile warheads will have increased from about 1,700 to approximately 7,000. Consequently, the number of gigatons (each equal to one billion tons of TNT) will decrease slightly, but the number of human lives at risk will increase substantially. The principal justification for these MIRVs is assured penetration of any hypothetical antiballistic missile. Thus, the deployment of a purely defensive weapon like the ABM is an accelerating element in the arms race. Our deployment of MIRVs is also another example of overreaction because as of now there is not much of an ABM for them to penetrate.

To summarize, in the quarter century since Hiroshima, the U.S. has moved from a technological situation in which a single bomber commander controlled the power to destroy a single medium-sized city to a situation today in which a single Poseidon submarine commander controls the power to subject more than 150 cities each to several times the destructive force unleashed on Hiroshima. Or, to put it differently, we have come from a technological situation in which a single bomber could deliver the same amount of explosive energy as 1,000 bombers carrying chemical explosive to a situation in which one single bomber can now deliver an amount of explosive energy greater than that used in all wars to date.

Throughout this whole period, the Russians have followed the same general path as the United States. They have usually been behind in the quality of strategic weapons, and until recently in the quantity of deployed weapons also. They have now surpassed the U.S. in the number of ICBMs, but remained behind in bombers and submarine launched missiles.

The arms race is only one side of the nuclear coin, though. The other side is arms control and disarmament. Sensitive and perceptive people everywhere, even before the Hiroshima explosion, realized that the nuclear arms race posed a new kind and degree of danger to the human race. Even then some saw that the day would come when the number of weapons, the power of each individual weapon, and the proliferation of control over these weapons would reach a point where man could destroy not just a few individual cities, but civilization itself, and ultimately perhaps even the entire human race.

THE BARUCH PLAN

Out of this concern came the Baruch plan, which was based on ideas developed and promoted by J. Robert Oppenheimer, David Lilienthal and others. The Baruch plan, in a nutshell, proposed to internationalize atomic energy. This would have involved giving up national sovereignty in certain vital areas, and so from the start the plan was totally unacceptable to the Soviet government then under Stalin. It did have some important support in government circles here, but I believe that had the issue come to a final showdown, the U.S., too, would have then found the plan unacceptable.

Ever since the failure of the Baruch plan, arms control efforts have focused on more modest attempts to control or stop specific weapons. Three stumbling blocks to the establishment of treaties of this type soon became evident. First, and generally speaking, the Soviet proposals involved agreements that would stop some part of the arms race at once, and leave the working out of policing and enforcement measures for later, whereas the U.S. proposed doing things in the reverse order. Second, the U.S. normally insisted on fairly large numbers of fairly extensive on-site inspections, whereas the Soviet Union nearly always rejected out of hand the idea of any at all. And third, the fact that the U.S. was then so far ahead in everything also proved to be a difficulty. Reducing arms by equal amounts would always have resulted in making our advantage even greater, and the Soviets couldn't buy that: on the other hand, reducing to equal amounts always involved greater sacrifice on the part of the U.S., and that was never politically palatable here.

Even so, some progress has been made. Considering the obstacles and the modest size of the effort, the progress has been remarkable; but compared to the great crescendo of the arms race itself, progress has hardly been noticeable. Six arms control treaties have been produced so far. The first of these was the Antarctica Treaty, signed in 1959. It forbade the militarization of Antarctica and prohibited nuclear testing there. Because Antarctica was so remote and no real vital interests were involved there, it was possible to include an inspection clause in the treaty.

But before rejoicing about this accomplishment, we should note a comment by Philip Noel-Baker, one of the great figures in the struggle for disarmament. He said, "While we were demilitarizing Antarctica, we were putting 7,000 nuclear warheads in Europe; we should have demilitarized Europe and armed Antarctica."

After the Antarctica Treaty came the Limited Test Ban Treaty in 1963, and the Latin America Denuclearization Treaty and the Outer Space Treaty in 1967. This last bars nuclear weapons testing in space or on the moon or other celestial bodies and prohibits military bases of any kind on such celestial bodies. More recently we have achieved the Nuclear Non-Proliferation Treaty and the treaty prohibiting the placing of nuclear weapons on the seabed.

It is useful to examine the Limited Test Ban Treaty more closely. It can be traced back to the Baruch plan and to some of the earliest U.N. resolutions. But public opinion also played a major role. Following the near disaster from fallout during the 1954 Pacific tests, Linus Pauling and others began to alert the scientific community and the general public to the perils of radioactive fallout. In the 1956 presidential campaign, Adlai Stevenson talked about the alarming number of babies that could develop leukemia from a teaspoon of strontium-90. Finally, in early 1958, as a direct result of growing public concern, President Eisenhower asked his Science Advisory Committee to examine the possibility of banning nuclear tests. Fortunately, the committee included at that time a number of men such as I. I. Rabi, Hans Bethe and Jerome Wiesner, who had long been concerned about the arms race problem. The committee advised that a cessation of nuclear tests would not endanger national security, that it could probably be reasonably well policed, and that it would result in a slowing of the arms race. It urged an attempt to reach an agreement with the Soviets on this matter.

By midsummer, 1958, it was possible to convene an international meeting of "experts" in matters of nuclear development, testing, and test detection in Geneva. The meeting produced enough agreement so as to lead directly to the possibility of higher level political discussions later that fall. The United States then offered a one-year moratorium on tests to begin when such political talks got under way. Serious negotiations did begin on October 31, and no further nuclear explosions took place after November 3. The most serious difficulties in these talks involved policing a ban on underground testing and on-site inspection of whatever suspicious events a seismic detection system might turn up. Finally, after talks had dragged on for more than a year, President Eisenhower announced that the U.S., having offered only a one-year moratorium in the first place, was no longer obligated to refrain from testing, but would not resume without advance notice. The next day Chairman Khrushchev announced the Soviets would not resume testing unless the West did so first. Soon after, the French began nuclear tests in the Sahara; the Soviets promptly labeled this as testing by the West and charged that connivance by the U.S. and the United Kingdom was involved. That same summer, the U-2 was shot down and the Paris summit conference collapsed. Still, neither the United States nor the Soviet Union tested any nuclear weapons. In 1961 the French continued to test, and Khrushchev commented to a U.S. emissary that *his* "scientists and military" were pressing for the test of a 100 megaton bomb.

Finally, in the fall of 1961, the Soviets suddenly began a new series of nuclear tests in the atmosphere. Two weeks later the U.S. began a series of underground tests, and six months later both the U.S. and Great Britain were testing in the atmosphere. Fallout began to accumulate in larger amounts than ever before, passions became aroused all over the world, the U.N. General Assembly pressed the nuclear powers to do something, and further conferences of experts and statesmen were held. On July 1, 1963, five years after the first serious attempt at a test moratorium, the Limited Test Ban Treaty was signed. This treaty was "limited" in that it allowed testing underground while prohibiting it elsewhere. The difficult problems of detecting, identifying, verifying, and policing underground tests had been "solved" by bypassing them. It was, of course, the hope and intention of most of those involved that this part of the problem would be intensively attacked soon after, but precious little progress has been made on this matter since that time.

In signing the Non-Proliferation Treaty in 1968, the U.S. and U.S.S.R. agreed to "pursue negotiations in good faith on effective measures relating to cessation of the nuclear arms race at an early date. . . ." But insofar as a complete ban on nuclear tests is concerned, U.S. efforts in this area have been hamstrung by a series of obstacles: exaggerated fears of possible cheating, plus exaggerated ideas of what might be learned in one or two clandestine tests of small devices, plus exaggerated fears of what new technological breakthroughs might be made with such knowledge, plus exaggerated ideas of what the political significance of such hypothetical new technology might be. The Soviets have also had their hangups, but I cannot identify them so clearly.

But what are the real results of the partial nuclear test ban? It did stop fallout, but it did not stop testing. In fact, the rate of testing has actually increased. The partial nuclear test ban has thus turned out to be not a disarmament measure, but the first environmental control measure. Worse, by eliminating fallout it eliminated public interest in the subject. Fallout produced a widespread concern in the arms race and created for a brief time, a substantial constituency vitally interested in one element of arms control. By eliminating fallout, we eliminated this constituency. By continuing and even expanding testing we have undercut any moral or political arguments we might make against testing by others.

When the army initiated steps in 1968 to put the ABM in certain suburban locations near Seattle, Chicago, and Boston, the public in those areas, including local scientists, rose up in defense of their neighborhoods. This rearousal of substantial public concern led to the almost successful effort to block the ABM, and it has been one of the important factors behind our participation in the SALT talks.

The Strategic Arms Limitation Talks, by their very name, are designed to slow down, or at best to stop, some elements of the arms race. They are not designed to roll back the arms race except perhaps in some minor ways. But the history of the last quarter century leads me to believe that if we merely limit something and do not follow through with further actions designed to really roll back the arms race, if we don't follow through with something designed to get the momentum of the whole thing reversed, then we will have accomplished very little. It's even possible, as in the case of the Limited Nuclear Test Ban, that we will have made matters worse. Palliative, partial measures may produce euphoria in the short run, but they only make things worse in the long run. When we eliminated weapons from Antarctica, we celebrated while putting more in Europe; when we prohibited tests in all environments except underground, we expanded testing there and rejoiced in the purity of the air. If we now produce a no-ABM agreement at SALT, and then do nothing more, we'll eventually have more ICBMs. If we merely freeze the number of delivery vehicles and do not follow through with something more, then we'll have MIRVs of ever-increasing multiplicity. We can be sure of the generalities even though we cannot predict all the details. Recently the U.S. and the Soviet Union took a step in the right direction when they announced an agreement to concentrate this year at the SALT talks on the limitation of the deployment of ABMs. They also agreed to coordinate any such agreement with "certain measures" to limit offensive strategic weapons. A no-ABM agreement, or a freeze in numbers, or a limit on something else could be useful if it set the stage for something more later, and if that something more actually resulted in reversing the momentum of the arms race rather than simply stopping it.

What must be the characteristics of this something more? What might be the next step following a successful arms limitation agreement?

1. Such a first post-SALT move must involve substantial disarmament. It must be enough to make it fully clear that disarmament is what's happening. It might, for example, completely eliminate one of the three components of the deterrent, and begin the reduction of one of the others.

2. It should be bilateral, but since there are many asymmetries between the U.S. and U.S.S.R., it need not involve identical steps on each side. For example, after abandoning all fixed-base missiles, the Soviets might choose to retain land-mobile missile systems which take advantage of their huge, sparsely populated regions, while we might choose to base all our mobile missiles at sea, thus taking advantage of our easier access to the ocean. Of course, at some point, China, Great Britain, and France will have to be included in an effective nuclear arms control agree-

ment. But the U.S. and the U.S.S.R. are so far ahead of the other three that for the present agreements need only be bilateral.

3. It should be obviously safe even in the event of serious cheating. In the early phases of an arms rollback, that should be easy. We now have three separate deterrent forces, each adequate by itself. If we agreed to eliminate one of them, and it later turned out that the Soviets hadn't done so, such a move on their part would still leave us with an entirely adequate deterrent. It would make us angry and the arms race would then take off in earnest, but it wouldn't leave us unsafe.

4. It should require little or no intrusive inspection. The Russians are extremely sensitive on this, and we don't like it either. This requirement presents no real problem, though. It is clear from recent arms debates that through unilateral, nonintrusive means we can observe field testing of a wide variety of strategic weapons, and we can also reliably observe the deployment of such weapons. Examples of agreements which could be monitored by unilateral means surely include cessation of MIRV development, limitation of ICBM deployment to some fixed number, and prohibition of the deployment of an extensive, credible ABM.

5. It should eliminate first those weapons requiring carefully tuned computer-generated responses, because they are the most dangerous. For example, if it should come about that the only way to protect our Minutemen from being destroyed in a preemptive attack is to arrange to launch the whole force on an electronically generated warning, then the whole force should be eliminated forthwith, and we should depend on other systems that are not so sensitive.

Let me finish by saying that whatever the next step may be, our final goal must remain the ideal of general and complete disarmament. Even if the SALT talks do succeed in stopping the arms race, and even if the talks are followed by steps for reversing the momentum of the arms race, we would still be far from that goal. I do not imagine that any rollback plan will be readily accepted by either the Russian or the American government. But I am sure that unless we resolve to make the attempt, and make it soon, our civilization is doomed.

Any reasonable extrapolation of history tells us that if we keep all those weapons around they will be used. While no one can say how to get from the present situation all the way to total nuclear disarmament, it is clear that throwing weapons away heads us in the right direction, and building more weapons, be they MIRVs, ABMs, or SS-9s, heads us in the wrong direction. We have fussed too much and too long about fine structure. We must begin to focus on direction rather than details.

Excerpts From the Charter
of the United Nations

We the peoples of the United Nations determined

to save succeeding generations from the scourge of war, which twice in our lifetime has brought untold sorrow to mankind, and

to reaffirm faith in fundamental human rights, in the dignity and worth of the human person, in the equal rights of men and women and of nations large and small, and

to establish conditions under which justice and respect for the obligations arising from treaties and other sources of international law can be maintained, and

to promote social progress and better standards of life in larger freedom,

and for these ends

to practice tolerance and live together in peace with one another as good neighbors, and

to unite our strength to maintain international peace and security, and

to ensure, by the acceptance of principles and the institution of methods, that armed force shall not be used, save in the common interest, and

to employ international machinery for the promotion of the economic and social advancement of all peoples,

have resolved to combine our efforts to accomplish these aims.

Accordingly, our respective Governments, through representatives assembled in the city of San Francisco, who have exhibited their full powers found to be in good and due form, have agreed to the present Charter of the United Nations and do hereby establish an international organization to be known as the United Nations.

Article 1   The Purposes of the United Nations are:

1. To maintain international peace and security, and to that end: to take effective collective measures for the prevention and removal of threats to the peace, and for the suppression of acts of aggression or other breaches of the peace, and to bring about by peaceful means, and in conformity with the principles of justice and international law, adjustment or settlement of international disputes or situations which might lead to a breach of the peace;

2. To develop friendly relations among nations based on respect for the principle of equal rights and self-determination of peoples, and to take other appropriate measures to strengthen universal peace;

3. To achieve international cooperation in solving international problems of an economic, social, cultural, or humanitarian character, and in promoting and encouraging respect for human rights and for fundamental freedoms for all without distinction as to race, sex, language, or religion; and

4. To be a center for harmonizing the actions of nations in the attainment of these common ends.

Article 2   The Organization and its Members, in pursuit of the Purposes stated in Article 1, shall act in accordance with the following Principles.

1. The Organization is based on the principle of the sovereign equality of all its Members.

2. All Members, in order to ensure to all of them the rights and benefits resulting from membership, shall fulfill in good faith the obligations assumed by them in accordance with the present Charter.

3. All Members shall settle their international disputes by peaceful means in such a manner that international peace and security, and justice, are not endangered.

4. All Members shall refrain in their international relations from the threat or use of force against the territorial integrity or political independence of any state, or in any other manner inconsistent with the Purposes of the United Nations.

5. All Members shall give the United Nations every assistance in any action it takes in accordance with the present Charter, and shall refrain from giving assistance to any state against which the United Nations is taking preventive or enforcement action.

6. The Organization shall ensure that states which are not Members of the United Nations act in accordance with these Principles so far as may be necessary for the maintenance of international peace and security.

7. Nothing contained in the present Charter shall authorize the

United Nations to intervene in matters which are essentially within the domestic jurisdiction of any state or shall require the Members to submit such matters to settlement under the present Charter; but this principle shall not prejudice the application of enforcement measures under Chapter VII.

Article 33   The parties to any dispute, the continuance of which is likely to endanger the maintenance of international peace and security, shall, first of all, seek a solution by negotiation, enquiry, mediation, conciliation, arbitration, judicial settlement, resort to regional agencies or arrangements, or other peaceful means of their own choice.

2. The Security Council shall, when it deems necessary, call upon the parties to settle their dispute by such means.

Article 34   The Security Council may investigate any dispute, or any situation which might lead to international friction or give rise to a dispute, in order to determine whether the continuance of the dispute or situation is likely to endanger the maintenance of international peace and security.

Article 36   The Security Council may, at any stage of a dispute of the nature referred to in Article 33 or of a situation of like nature, recommend appropriate procedures or methods of adjustment.

2. The Security Council should take into consideration any procedures for the settlement of the dispute which have already been adopted by the parties.

3. In making recommendations under this Article the Security Council should also take into consideration that legal disputes should as a general rule be referred by the parties to the International Court of Justice in accordance with the provisions of the Statute of the Court.

Article 37   Should the parties to a dispute of the nature referred to in Article 33 fail to settle it by the means indicated in that Article, they shall refer it to the Security Council.

2. If the Security Council deems that the continuance of the dispute is in fact likely to endanger the maintenance of international peace and security, it shall decide whether to take action under Article 36 or to recommend such terms of settlement as it may consider appropriate.

Article 39   The Security Council shall determine the existence of any threat to the peace, breach of the peace, or act of aggression and shall make recommendations, or decide what measures shall be taken in accordance with Articles 41 and 42, to maintain or restore international peace and security.

Article 41   The Security Council may decide what measures not involving the use of armed force are to be employed to give effect to its decisions, and it may call upon the Members of the United Nations to apply such measures. These may include complete or partial interruption of economic relations and of rail, sea, air, postal, telegraphic, radio, and other means of communication, and the severance of diplomatic relations.

Article 42   Should the Security Council consider that measures provided for in Article 41 would be inadequate or have proved to be inadequate, it may take such action by air, sea, or land forces as may be necessary to maintain or restore international peace and security. Such action may include demonstrations, blockade, and other operations by air, sea, or land forces of Members of the United Nations.

Article 43   All Members of the United Nations, in order to contribute to the maintenance of international peace and security, undertake to make available to the Security Council, on its call and in accordance with a special agreement or agreements, armed forces, assistance, and facilities, including rights of passage, necessary for the purpose of maintaining international peace and security.

2. Such agreement or agreements shall govern the numbers and types of forces, their degree of readiness and general location, and the nature of the facilities and assistance to be provided.

3. The agreement or agreements shall be negotiated as soon as possible on the initiative of the Security Council. They shall be concluded between the Security Council and Members or between the Security Council and groups of Members and shall be subject to ratification by the signatory states in accordance with their respective constitutional processes.

Article 44   When the Security Council has decided to use force it shall, before calling upon a Member not represented on it to provide armed forces in fulfillment of the obligations assumed under Article 43, invite that Member, if the Member so desires, to participate in the decisions of the Security Council concerning the employment of contingents of that Member's armed forces.

Article 51   Nothing in the present Charter shall impair the inherent right of individual or collective self-defense if an armed attack occurs against a Member of the United Nations, until the Security Council has taken the measures necessary to maintain international peace and security. Measures taken by Members in the exercise of this right of self-defense shall be immediately reported to the Security Council and shall not in any way affect the authority and responsibility of the Security Council under the present Charter to take at any time such action as it deems necessary in order to maintain or restore international peace and security.

Article 55   With a view to the creation of conditions of stability and well-being which are necessary for peaceful and friendly relations among nations based on respect for the principle of equal rights and self-determination of peoples, the United Nations shall promote:

a. higher standards of living, full employment, and conditions of economic and social progress and development;

b. solutions of international economic, social, health, and related problems; and international cultural and educational cooperation; and

c. universal respect for, and observance of, human rights and fundamental freedoms for all without distinction as to race, sex, language, or religion.

Article 56   All Members pledge themselves to take joint and separate action in cooperation with the Organization for the achievement of the purposes set forth in Article 55.

signed, June 26, 1945

7

DOMESTIC CHANGE
AND WORLD PEACE

Introduction

Our readings on world government and the reform of the state system have focused on the global dimension of world peace. They have outlined alternative models of world order designed to minimize international violence and, at the same time, to promote other global values like social justice and economic welfare. These models are both analytic and prescriptive. They can help identify the dynamics of the present international system, pinpoint its deficiencies, and provide goals to inform immediate national policy choices. Nevertheless, such images of possible future international systems are open to the criticism that the choices they suggest, at least for the United States and in the short run, are unrealistic because of the facts of domestic political life. Many might agree on the abstract desirability of a world government that oversees disarmament and development, for example. But in practice, both projects would very likely meet with the concerted opposition of a variety of domestic interests. In a world without large armies and with a more equitable distribution of wealth, many would lose economic or political advantages. Clearly, another level of theorizing is required if a strategy for building a more peaceful world order is to succeed. This is the level of theories about domestic change, which deal with possible sources of resistance to world order change within the superpowers and explore ways of minimizing or eliminating those resistances. The articles in this section represent a range of approaches to such problems in the United States.

In the first, Richard Barnet argues that United States defense plans are based on three major misconceptions regarding the dominant threats to the national security. (All of these are reflected in the articles by Kissinger and McNamara in section 3.) The first of them, which, according to Barnet, led directly to the arms race, is the belief that the United States must be prepared to meet any conceivable nuclear attack with a more than equivalent retaliatory response. This "logic of deterrence" is fueled by a second misconception, that the United States' primary enemies in the world are communist states bent on world domination and willing to go to dangerous extremes to achieve their goal. Barnet contends that the United States contributed more to cold war tensions than the Soviets, and thus has itself to blame for what its security managers now see as communist aggressiveness. The third major misconception Barnet identifies is the belief that the communists sponsor third world revolutions as means of "indirect aggression" against the "free world." In reality, he says, these revolutions are more reflective of essentially local concerns for social reform than of any communist drive for world domination.

The consequence of these three faulty assumptions, according to Barnet, is a United States national security apparatus, that is much larger and more pervasive than necessary. In fact, he argues that this apparatus is itself a profoundly destabilizing force in world politics and may foster immense long-range security problems by enforcing a growing division between the rich, industrial minority of nations and the poor, agrarian majority. Even greater threats to America's long-range security are the "irrational and destructive patterns of development and consumption of resources that have evolved in the United States." They not only create tensions with the third world but place impossible strains on the common environment as well. What follows, according to Barnet, is that the United States can move in the direction of genuine security only by reducing its level of domestic consumption, supporting rather than opposing revolutionary movements aimed at achieving social justice, and drastically reducing its military spending in order to concentrate on urgent domestic needs.

While Barnet's critique of the United States' foreign orientation is telling in many respects, he gives no explanation of the forces that support these illusions or that would be likely to resist the substantial policy changes he suggests. The following article, by Marc Pilisuk and Tom Hayden, is a radical analysis of the "power elite," which allegedly determines United States security policy and benefits from it, both directly, in terms of military spending, and indirectly, in wealth extracted from "allies" and client states. The authors contend that available evidence leads to a "yes" answer to the question posed by their title, "Is there a military-industrial complex that prevents peace?"

Their detailed analysis begins with an examination of C. Wright Mills' contention in *The Power Elite* (New York: Oxford University Press, 1959) that corporate and military elites dominate the decision-making institutions of United States politics by their influence over virtually all positions of political power. In addition Mills argues that the dominant elites, through their control of the communications media, could manipulate public opinion to create indifference to their self-serving machinations. Opposed to Mills' view is the "pluralist" position that decisions are the outcome of competition among groups (corporations, unions, defense agencies, etc.), not of collaboration. Those who take this position contend that the conflict among such groups assures that no single group will be able to monopolize power or determine important decisions. This is called the "theory of countervailing power."

Although they do not accept Mills' analysis of a monolithic power structure, Pilisuk and Hayden are severely critical of the pluralistic point of view. They argue that "countervailing power," in reality, refers to a constant pattern of the rise and fall of irresponsible groups within a framework of generally accepted core beliefs about the legitimacy of the system. "Irresponsible" means that the groups contending for influence act primarily out of their own self-interest, and are not subject to significant regulation by other agencies representing the public interest. What is important is Pilisuk and Hayden's analysis of the core beliefs about foreign policy and domestic process that unite the groups competing for rewards within the military-industrial complex. They argue that these core beliefs are inimical to creation of an enduring world peace system.

The strategy of change dictated by this analysis of the obstacles to peace is quite thoroughgoing: since "American society *is* a military-industrial complex," a transformation of the social structure is called for, beginning with a change in elite attitudes.

The following selection, by the conservative economist Arthur Burns, expands the analysis of the relation of the military to American society, developed by Pilisuk and Hayden, but leads to less radical recommendations for change. Burns is less concerned about the core values represented by the "defense" establishment than about the cost, in money and energy, of maintaining it. He documents many of these costs, principally those that represent nonmilitary needs that have not been met because so many national resources have been committed to military purposes. At the same time, he believes that the military-industrial complex is here to stay, and that the debate over new priorities will produce, at best, relatively small changes in the allocation of national resources. He hopes that this debate will underline the fact that American security depends as much on domestic health and welfare as on a strong military establishment, and that this realization will help form a national consensus on new priorities.

Burns' position reflects that of many liberals, who do not criticize the beliefs and values on which United States security policy is based but feel that these values can be served more cheaply and efficiently than at present. The failure of "defense" planners appears as little more than a failure of proportion. The distinction between reformers such as Burns and radicals such as Pilisuk and Hayden is crucial in the choice of alternative change strategies. One side argues that the basic values supporting the United States' political and economics institutions must change before it can truly advance the cause of peace; the other, looking more toward domestic welfare than toward world peace, believes that the immediate problem is to reallocate the money and energy that has supported an increasingly pervasive military-industrial complex.

The last selection suggests a strategy for controlling the military that might be acceptable to both radicals and reformers. On the one hand, Galbraith considers the central fact of concentrated, irresponsible military and industrial power. This power, he contends, generates its own constituency and validates its own distorted image of national security needs. On the other hand, he holds that change is possible within the electoral process, and recommends a strategy that combines reduction of the defense budget with making defense contractors responsible to the public by nationalizing the major munitions and equipment manufacturers. He also believes that Congress needs its own independent staff of experts to evaluate the judgments of the national security managers with an eye toward eliminating unnecessary programs. If Pilisuk and Hayden's analysis of the strength of the military-industrial elite is accurate, it might be expected that Galbraith's program would have little chance of gaining congressional approval, since the military-industrial complex's outlook and values pervade Congress as well as other major political institutions. On one hand, it could be argued that Congress can be used as a forum for building public consciousness of past military excesses and for reinforcing the democratic claim that major institutions must be returned to the control of the people. In this way a change-oriented constituency could be built from the bottom up.

The issues raised by our selections in this section focus on two questions: What is the nature and extent of the military-industrial complex's resistance to peace, and what strategies will be most effective in minimizing this resistance? The second of these questions will be explored more fully in our two concluding sections.

SUGGESTIONS FOR FURTHER READING

Richard J. Barnet, *The Economy of Death*. New York: Atheneum, 1970.

————, *Intervention and Revolution*. Cleveland: Meridian, 1969.

John Kenneth Galbraith, *The New Industrial Complex*. New York: Houghton Mifflin, 1967.

Sidney Lens, *The Military Industrial Complex*. Philadelphia: Pilgrim Press, 1970.

Seymour Melman, *Pentagon Capitalism*. New York: McGraw-Hill, 1970.

C. Wright Mills, *The Power Elite*. New York: Oxford University Press, 1959.

The Illusion of Security

RICHARD J. BARNET

The crisis of national security now faced by the United States stems, in my view, from a fundamental misconception of the nature of the problem. For twenty-five years we have been building a Maginot Line against the threats of the 1930s while the threats of the 1970s are rapidly overwhelming us along with the rest of mankind.

United States national security policy is designed to deal with three classic threats. The first is a nuclear attack on the United States. In a world where nuclear weapons exist no one can say that such an attack could not happen. The question is whether American planners have (a) put that threat into proper perspective and (b) whether the strategy they have developed to deal with it has decreased or increased the threat. It seems likely that for much of the cold war period the United States has been running an arms race with itself. It was always *possible* that the Soviet Union would launch a nuclear attack on the United States; but everything we know about the nature of nuclear weapons, budgetary

From *Foreign Policy,* no. 3 (Summer 1971), pp. 71–90. Copyright 1971 by National Affairs, Inc. Reprinted by permission of the author and publisher. Richard Barnet is an author on questions of U.S. foreign and defense policy, and co-director of the Institute for Policy Studies, Washington.

constraints, political pressures in the Soviet Union, and Communist ideology suggests that it was *highly unlikely*. The United States has had an enormous superiority in numbers of nuclear weapons, a fact that has neither made the people of the United States feel more secure, nor provided the "strength" to intimidate Communists to negotiate on our terms. Indeed, as one might have expected, the Soviets have seemed to be more willing to negotiate as they have approached nuclear parity with the United States. At the same time, the U.S. attempt to maintain superiority has encouraged the Soviet Union and China to develop their own nuclear capabilities and has given them greater power of life and death over the people and territory of the United States. In an arms race, neither side will permit the other to continue amassing an ever-widening lead.

The United States has believed that it could promote security by preserving the "option" to use nuclear weapons not only to retaliate for a nuclear attack, but also to protect "vital interests" of a lesser sort, primarily in Western Europe. The unwillingness to renounce the first use of nuclear weapons has thus led to less security, not more. We have communicated to all countries the fact that the greatest power in the world must rely on nuclear weapons to promote its foreign policy interests. Weaker countries, such as France, have taken this cue and have concluded that no country can be "sovereign" unless it, too, commands a powerful nuclear arsenal.

During the Cuban missile crisis President Kennedy said that the chances were at least one in three that nuclear weapons would be used by the United States and that if they had been used, at least 150 million people would have been killed. In a later speech he said that as many as five hundred million would be killed in the opening hours of a nuclear conflict. Yet it was prestige, not military security, that was at stake in the Soviet-American confrontation of 1962. From a U.S. security standpoint, the resolution of the Cuban crisis was a disaster. Washington gave up everything it would have had to give in a negotiated settlement (Jupiter missiles in Turkey and Italy, and a pledge not to invade Cuba). And the 1962 humiliation of the Soviet Union led directly to a major rearmament program which has now made Moscow a far more formidable adversary than it was nine years ago.

There is no objective, including the survival of the United States as a political entity, that merits destroying millions or jeopardizing the future of man. The pretense that it is legitimate to threaten nuclear war for political ends creates an international climate of fear in which Americans will continue to have less security, not more.

GUARDIANS AT THE GATE

National security planners have been reluctant to renounce the "option" to destroy millions of human beings in a nuclear "first strike" because of a mistaken analysis of the second threat to national security. This is the problem of aggression, its causes and its cure. The official theory has been presented many times in presidential speeches: we must assure peace by preparing for war and by making governments believe that we will do exactly what we say we will do to protect our positions of strength in the world, including our alliances. Thus we fight in small wars now to prevent fighting in larger wars later.

These ideas are not mere rhetoric. They are deeply held beliefs of a generation of National Security Managers for whom the decisive learning experience was the Second World War. Staggered by the apocalyptic events of the war, the demonic Hitlerian vision of a world order, the death camps, the fire bombings, the saturation raids, and the nuclear attacks, this generation has believed with the first Secretary of Defense, James Forrestal, that "the cornerstone in any plan which undertakes to rid us of the curse of war must be the armed might of the United States." [1] Despite the standard denial that the United States is not the "policeman of the world," which has been inserted in presidential statements and State Department press releases since opposition developed to the Vietnam war, this is precisely the official image we have had of ourselves. "History and our own achievements have thrust upon us the principal responsibility for the protection of freedom on earth," [2] President Johnson declared at a Lincoln Day dinner in 1965. Earlier, President Kennedy called our nation "the watchman on the wall of world freedom." [3] Both expressed their generation's judgment of America's security role. "We did not choose to be the guardians at the gate," Johnson declared, but "history" has "thrust" that "responsibility" upon us. Imperial nations always have a view of their own unique destiny.

In the early postwar period American planners had a self-conscious notion that they were playing out for their generation the particular imperial roles that England and France had played in the last—filling "power vacuums" and picking up "responsibilities" for keeping order. Unless the forces of international "stability," so the argument went, were always ready, and, most important, *willing* to use whatever force was

---

[1] Quoted in Arnold Rogow, *James Forrestal* (New York: Boulevard, 1963), p. 125.

[2] Address of Lyndon B. Johnson, Feb. 12, 1965 quoted in *The New York Times,* Feb. 13, 1965.

[3] Quoted in Ronald Steel, *Pax Americana* (New York: Viking Press, 1967), p. 3.

necessary, aggressor nations would take over their weaker neighbors one by one. Unless nations with an impulse to upset the *status quo* were opposed at the outset, they would expand as far as their power permitted—even to the point of world domination. In this view of the world which has dominated American thinking on world affairs for a generation, there is an infinite supply of potential aggressors. Any "have-not" nation that can field an army will do. General Thomas Power of the Strategic Air Command, for example, warned in the mid-sixties of a possible "African Hitler" whom we might have to confront once we had disposed of the Communist threat.[4]

Because the principal threats to peace and security were foreign "aggressors" bent on world conquest, it was necessary for the United States as the world's most powerful country to attempt to organize an alliance of threatened nations to try to contain those threats. Postwar planners looked on their own time as a direct continuation of the pre-1945 period. The United States was spearheading a crusade against totalitarianism and militarism in behalf of a "free world" deemed to represent the forces of good, if only because of the evil of the Communist adversaries. Stalin was the postwar Hitler, the leader of an infinitely expansionist power who could be stopped only by the very show of strength England and France failed to make against Hitler. When President Truman enunciated the far-reaching doctrine that bears his name with its commitment to "support free peoples who are resisting attempted subjugation by armed minorities or by outside pressures," he defended this momentous change of policy as a protection of the investment already made in World War II.

MYTHS OF THE MANAGERS

A visitor from another planet in the early postwar days would have had a hard time reconciling the official American analogy, "Stalin is the Hitler of today," with the facts as they emerged. Indeed, the naive visitor might well have concluded that the problem of military aggression in the postwar period had its source in the United States. Soviet armies stopped at the point of their farthest advance in World War II and withdrew from adjacent areas such as Czechoslovakia only to return when political domination threatened to fail. The United States retained the major bases it had acquired in World War II and acquired more. Within

---

[4] Thomas S. Power, *Design for Survival* (New York: Coward-McCann, 1964), p. 216.

a few years the Soviet Union was surrounded by air and later missile bases from which devastating nuclear attacks could be launched—all at a time when the Soviet Union lacked a similar capacity to attack the United States. It has been the United States and not the Soviet Union that has stationed its military forces on every continent and spread nuclear weapons in the tens of thousands on the continents of Asia and Europe and on the high seas. It is the United States and not the Soviet Union that has intervened with its military and paramilitary forces almost every year since 1945 on the territory of other countries either to prevent local insurgent forces from taking power or displacing them from power.

Despite Stalin's monumental crimes against his own people, a kind of permanent internal war, Dean Acheson, along with most of the National Security Managers of his generation, now admits that the early postwar fears of a Soviet military invasion of Western Europe may have been exaggerated.[5] The problem of European security was whether the West European countries would move toward domestic Communism, not whether the Soviets would attack them. As in Vietnam almost twenty years later, the National Security Managers used military measures in an effort to give psychological support to allies facing domestic economic and political crises. In Europe the policy worked—but at the cost of perpetuating the myth of outside military aggression on which it was premised. A generation later, there is still no historical evidence that Stalin or his successors ever contemplated an invasion of West Germany, or that they were deterred, as Winston Churchill claimed in a speech at M.I.T. in 1950, only because of the American possession of the atomic bomb. Indeed, the Soviet Union in Stalin's day, as many historians now conclude, was following a highly cautious course, more conservative in most respects than that in the present "era of negotiations." Today's Soviet leaders play a more active and dangerous role in world affairs, for example in Cuba and the Middle East, than Stalin ever dared to do. Indeed, it is ironical that the strategy chosen by the U.S. to deal with the limited Soviet challenge to American supremacy may well have helped to create a Soviet Union with global interests and commitments.

Although there were very few objective reasons for believing that Stalin, with his country ruined, was about to embark on a campaign of Hitler-like aggression, U.S. National Security Managers did indeed feel insecure. It is important to try to understand the source of that insecurity,

---

[5] Dean Acheson, *Present at the Creation* (New York: W. W. Norton, 1969), p. 753.

which still persists. The United States will not change its role in the world as long as the official belief continues that the United States can be safe in the world only by running as much of it as possible.

Despite its unparalleled monopoly of power it was not surprising that the United States felt insecure at the close of the Second World War. The managers of the Number One Nation always feel the insecurity that comes with winning and having to defend the crown. Moreover, the floodgates of technological and political change were opened by the war and America's leaders felt the anxiety of being swept by unfamiliar currents, particularly when, because of the atomic bomb, the stakes were supremely high. It was natural that the managers of the new American empire should construct an analysis that justified their power and sanctified its use.

Thus the political analysis of security threats took on the character of military contingency planning. Many of the contingencies on which policies have been constructed have been highly implausible. During the whole postwar period there have been very few cases of World War II type "aggression," i.e., invasion of one state by another for the purpose of occupying it or dominating it. It must be said that a high percentage of the invasions of the last generation have been carried out by the United States in its self-appointed role as "guardian at the gates." The closest analogy to Hitler-type aggression from the Communist side was the invasion of South Korea by North Korea and the Soviet invasion of Czechoslovakia, neither of which was or looked like the first slice of a "salami" program of world conquest, or so U.S. intelligence agencies concluded at the time. Other examples of old-fashioned "aggression" include the 1962 incursions of Communist China into India, the 1965 India-Pakistan war, and the 1967 Israeli invasions of Egypt and Syria which the United States did not oppose with military power. Although the United States has sought to enlist many other countries in a network of alliances aimed at containing one or another "aggressive" or "expansionist" power, the nations whose security is much more directly threatened by such powers have tended to drag their feet. This is especially true in Southeast Asia where Thailand and the Philippines, supposedly among the next "dominoes" to fall, refuse to give more than token cooperation in the Vietnam war and exact major political and economic concessions for their participation. If they accepted the American analysis of the security threat, they would act as if their own security was gravely threatened.

There are two principal reasons why the problem of war and violence in the postwar world does not resemble the prewar problem of aggression. First, the development of technology has made the acquisition of strategic real estate for powerful nations much less important. Big powers like the United States and the Soviet Union can now hit any part of the globe with missiles launched from their own territory. The United States can dispatch powerful military forces by air transport anywhere within a matter of days, and the Soviet Union is developing its capacity to do likewise. Thus the pressure to achieve security by invading other countries is less than it used to be. The arms race has reduced the tactical incentive of both major powers to resort to territorial aggression.

Second, despite technology, the extension of formal physical and juridical control by a great power over other countries has become much more difficult because of the development of the techniques of partisan and guerrilla warfare, the ideology of self-determination and nationalism, and the resulting politicization of formerly colonized populations. The history of the last decade makes it clear that the entry of new countries into the Communist bloc involves heavy costs as well as benefits for the Soviet Union. Indeed, the extension of Soviet power into Cuba appears to have complicated life for Moscow. It has been a financial burden for the Soviet Union, has posed risk of conflict with the United States, and has involved conflict with the Cubans themselves. The same might be said of the Middle East. It has become more and more difficult to manage empires or to derive the prestige traditionally associated with empires. That is one reason why the United States does not officially admit to being an empire and prefers to conduct so many of its activities abroad by covert means.

THE COUNTERREVOLUTIONARY IMPULSE

The third major security threat which, in my view, has been misperceived in the official U.S. world-view is the problem that John Foster Dulles used to refer to as "indirect aggression." Most of the violence and instability in the postwar world has arisen not from confrontation between national states but from revolutions and internal insurgencies. Between 1958 and 1966, according to Robert McNamara, there were over 149 serious internal insurgencies.[6]

The counterrevolutionary impulse has been a cornerstone of American policy since the end of the Second World War. On an average of once every eighteen months the United States has sent its military or paramilitary forces into other countries either to crush a local revolution or

---

[6] Robert S. McNamara, Address to the American Society of Newspaper Editors, Montreal, Canada, May 8, 1966.

to arrange a coup against a government which failed to acquire the State Department seal of approval.[7]

Why has this been thought necessary to make the world safe for the United States? There have been essentially two theories about the connection between indigenous revolutionary change and American security. In the early days of the cold war it was assumed that any Communist revolutionary was a Kremlin agent. Ho Chi Minh's independence movement, Ambassador William C. Bullitt explained in 1947, was designed to "add another finger to the hand that Stalin is closing around China." [8] According to Dean Rusk, in a speech made twenty years ago, Mao's regime was "a colonial Russian government." [9]

It is now generally accepted that Communism is no longer "monolithic." Of course it never was in the Rusk-Bullitt sense. Far from being planned and initiated by the Soviet Union, the revolutionary movements in China, Indo-China, Greece, Cuba, and elsewhere were often at the outset opposed and discouraged by the Kremlin as embarrassments to the diplomatic relationships the Soviet Union was pursuing as a Great Power. The Soviet Union has barely disguised its reluctance at being sucked into the Vietnam war to oppose American intervention, although, as in the Cuban case, it has given aid to counter American military attacks. For years after the Geneva settlement of 1954 the Soviet Union acquiesced in the maintenance of a U.S. protected anti-Communist South Vietnam, which was contrary to the spirit of the settlement. The Soviets proposed the admission of North and South Vietnam as separate members of the United Nations as late as 1959.

As long as the myth of "indirect aggression"—the transformation of local revolutions into Soviet invasions by Trojan Horse—was credible, a counterrevolutionary policy could be defended as traditional balance of power politics. Every revolution was part of a pattern of world conquest emanating from a rival center of power. Thus the situation was sufficiently like Hitler's expansionism to justify a similar military response.

The Soviet Union sought to dominate every nation into which its troops marched in the Second World War and to establish subservient "revolutionary" governments. But every revolutionary government that has come to power without the Red Army has turned out to be ambiva-

---

[7] A few of the examples: Greece (1948), Iran (1953), Guatemala (1954), Indonesia (1958), Lebanon (1958), Congo (1964), British Guiana (1964), Cuba (1961), Dominican Republic (1965), Vietnam (1954–).

[8] Quoted in Carl Oglesby and Richard Shaull, *Containment and Change* (New York: Macmillan, 1967), p. 30.

[9] Quoted in Ronald Steel, *op. cit.*, p. 129.

lent, cool, or even hostile to the Soviet Union—Yugoslavia, Albania, North Vietnam, China, and Cuba. In each case the relationship is complex, but in none of them can it be said that the existence of the Communist regime necessarily makes the Soviet Union stronger or more threatening to the physical safety of the United States.

There is another connection between revolutionary change in other countries and American national security which is not military, but psychological. The United States has consciously sought to expand its system so that other countries will not only buy our products but accept our values. We have wanted to be accepted as the world's definition of the good society. To a considerable extent this has happened. Only a few revolutionary societies have held out a vision of the future different from the American model—what Walt Rostow called "the high mass consumption society." Even the Soviet Union has adopted as its goal the American model of the highly industrialized consumer society. Its brand of socialism is a means for "overtaking and surpassing the United States" on the way to the same Utopia.

"WE'RE NUMBER ONE?"

For almost fifty years, however, America has been experiencing a continuing national identity crisis. In the thirties, amidst depression, seemingly permanent unemployment, and great social unrest, there was a serious loss of faith in the American system as it then existed. The pretensions of the foreign "isms"—state capitalism, Communism, fascism, and others—that they, rather than "free enterprise America," represented the wave of the future caused shudders of doubt in the United States. Victory in the Second World War brought new confidence. Yet there was enough awareness that the war had transcended but had not solved the domestic crises of the thirties to make both managers and the public uneasy about the future at the very moment of America's supreme power. Thus the rhetorical claims of Communist ideologues that they were the new "wave of the future" struck a terror out of all proportion to the real strength of what the State Department called "international Communism."

Much of what the United States does in the name of national security is designed to allay the inner fears of America's leaders that the United States may be slipping from the pinnacle of power. They spend hundreds of billions of dollars and tens of thousands of lives to preserve their "credibility" for toughness so that no one would dare to think of the nation which they manage as a "pitiful, helpless giant." The principal argument in the government for persisting in Vietnam despite the obvious catastrophic political, economic, military, and social consequences has been based on reputation and prestige. It may have been an error to have made a commitment in Vietnam, but to back down would put the nation in a bad light. Reputation, as Thomas Schelling has said, is one of the few things worth fighting for. "We are the Number One Nation," Lyndon Johnson told a National Foreign Policy Conference at the State Department less than a year before he left office, "and we are going to stay the Number One Nation."

Like many empires before us we have used reputation abroad as the criterion of national success and as a diversion from intractable domestic problems. As long as our criteria of "development" and "progress"— such as the ratio of cars to bicycles on the main street of the capital— were accepted by other nations, this amounted to a kind of validation for the American system at home. American scientific achievements, American books, American magazines, American educational materials, American business techniques appeared to be changing the face of the world, making it look like an extension of America and hence giving the illusion that the globe was becoming a friendlier and more manageable place.

It is as illusory, however, to measure national security by the willingness of elites in other nations to imitate the United States as it is to do so by counting nuclear warheads. Whether American methods work elsewhere will not help solve the pressing security problem of a society unable to deal with its own internal violence. Indeed, there is now strong evidence that the export of American consumption values and American technology creates long-term security problems for the United States by encouraging economies of waste in the Third World which add to world pollution and resource allocation problems. It is in our own selfish interest, if we care about prolonging the life support systems of the planet, that the irrational and destructive patterns of development and consumption of resources that have evolved in the United States not be repeated elsewhere.

FACING THE REALITIES

The United States cannot achieve national security until we begin to accept certain realities of our age. The first is that poor countries will, and many probably must, experiment with revolution to solve political and economic problems fast enough to permit survival for their people. Whether a country in Asia, Africa, or Latin America chooses another political and economic system, whether it looks to another country as its model, does not threaten our national security unless we define such events (over which we have no effective control in any event) as "defeats."

Second, the United States must be prepared to live with a high degree of disorder and instability, which are characteristics of a world experiencing rapid political and technological change. To set as a national security goal the enforcement of "stability" in a world in convulsion, a world in which radical change is as inevitable as it is necessary, is as practical as King Canute's attempt to command the tides. Real stability can come only with the building of a legitimate international order which offers genuine hope for people, whatever their history and wherever they are located. That sort of stability requires change and not always the sort that can be easily controlled.

Third, it is in the real security interest of the United States to ease rather than complicate the life of people with whom we coexist on the planet, whatever the political ideology of their governments. It does not increase American national security, for example, for Castro to suffer economic reverses, whatever the U.S. may have done to help bring them about. The point would be equally true if Castro were a right wing military dictator. When governments oppress their own citizens, stepping up outside military pressure hardly creates a more liberal atmosphere.

There is no existing political solution to the major problems of human development that can be called "the wave of the future." The problems transcend all existing ideologies. It is in the interest of the people of the United States as a whole, although not in the short-term interest of those who fear change because it threatens privilege, to encourage a variety of experiments around the globe to find ways to solve the world-wide crisis of political order. Until Americans can begin to identify with the people of other countries as members of the same species with the same basic problems, we will continue to treat other countries as abstractions to be manipulated for our own psychological and political needs and will continue to build our power on their suffering. The attempt to isolate, contain, or overthrow revolutionary governments makes them more likely to resort to terror against their own people and to adopt a militant nationalism to protect themselves from American attack. No nation, including the United States, can enforce virtue, moderation, or justice in another country. Making war on Germany did not save the Jews. Indeed, the mass extermination did not begin until the war was on. All a nation can do is to help create an international political environment that will encourage other governments to permit freedom and a decent life for their own citizens.

A national security policy for the United States which can minimize the resort to violence and promote an international system for the resolution of the basic human problems of justice and order must see the United States not as the problem-solver of the world but as an integral part of the problem. America's extraordinarily disproportionate share of resources and power, which we have celebrated as proof of a messianic destiny, is itself a long-term threat to our own national security. The United States will become increasingly isolated from the rest of humanity if we continue to set as a national security goal the preservation of present power and economic relationships in the world rather than the rapid evolution towards world community. The *status quo,* which we call "stable," will come to be seen by more and more other peoples as intolerable. Vietnam shows that despite the massive employment of military power the United States cannot always maintain positions of domination that it has acquired around the world. Perhaps in the short term the strategy that succeeded in Greece and the Dominican Republic and failed in Vietnam may succeed elsewhere. But it is clear that we need new criteria for defining "success." A military dictatorship that supports the United States in the United Nations and welcomes its military mission but uses American aid to hold down its population and to forestall institutional change contributes to the sum of repression, misuse of resources, and misery in the world. It should not be counted an American success.

SURVIVAL ISN'T GUARANTEED

American security is inextricably linked with the problem of global security. For this reason much of the debate in the United States about "neo-isolationism" seems Orwellian. Those who favor continuation of the policy of military intervention around the world whenever the United States decides it is in America's interest to "project its power" advertise themselves as "internationalists." Those who wish to renounce the right to threaten nuclear war on behalf of American vital interests, to stop seeking American security by killing or assisting in the killing of Asians, Africans, and Latin Americans, are stigmatized as "isolationists."

The issue is not whether the United States should or can withdraw from the world but the character of American involvement. The development of technology and communication has multiplied international and transnational contacts of all kinds. Americans cannot and will not resign from the world. But they can renounce the myths on which their contact with the world has been so largely based: that the United States government can manage social and political change around the world; that it can police a stable system of order; that it can solve problems in other countries it has yet to solve for its own people; that there is no real conflict of interest between the people of the United States, with their high standard of living, and people in Asia, Africa, or Latin America, who make less than $100 a year; that the United States government, unlike all other governments, is capable of true philanthropy.

The United States cannot develop a national security policy that will improve the prospects for global survival until we seriously examine the extent to which a new foreign policy requires domestic changes. How much, for example, can we change America's present destructive definition of national security without dismantling the bureaucratic structures which promote a militarist definition of the national interest? Can we still have a military establishment anything like the present one without continuing to have an interventionist policy? I am virtually certain that the answer is no. Can we have relations with Third World countries that will close instead of further widen the gap between rich and poor countries without making major changes in the patterns of consumption in the United States and basic structural changes in the economy? On this question I am less clear. Both Marxists and the National Association of Manufacturers appear convinced that the standard of living cannot be maintained in the U.S. except through the continuation of imperialist policies. It is crucial to the building of a real national security policy to determine whether they are right or wrong. If they are right, then it is a prime security task to change consumption patterns in the United States. The alternative would be global class war.

No national security problem can ultimately be solved except within the context of planetary security. The overshadowing risk to mankind is the destruction of the earth through nuclear war or the collapse of life support systems as a consequence of pollution and maldistribution of resources. The policy of seeking national security through permanent war preparation and intermittent wars directly contributes to the crisis of planetary survival in a variety of specific ways. Military establishments preempt resources. They produce waste. They generate an atmosphere of conflict and competition in which the minimal measures of cooperation necessary to insure planetary survival become impossible.

There is nothing to suggest that achieving security in the final third of the twentieth century will be easy, or even that the survival of civilization is guaranteed. No one has yet developed a global security system that works.

But we do know what does not work.

Is There a Military-Industrial Complex That Prevents Peace?

MARC PILISUK AND TOM HAYDEN

The notion of a military-industrial complex as a potent force or even indeed a ruling elite is not new in American history. From FDR who attacked the "merchants of destruction" and campaigned in 1932 to "take the profits out of war" to a more restrained warning by Eisenhower against the "unwarranted" power of the military-industrial complex, American politics and scholarship have often entertained such a concept. Many scholars, however, have rejected the "power elite" concept implicit in the charge of a military-industrial complex capable of dominating the entire American scene. Implicit in the writings of such pluralist writers as Daniel Bell, Robert Dahl, and Talcott Parsons is the basis for a denial that it is a military-industrial complex that prevents peace. The argument is:

1. It is held that the *scope* of decisions made by any interest group is

Reprinted from *The Triple Revolution Emerging,* Robert Perrucci and Marc Pilisuk, editors (Boston: Little, Brown, 1971), pp. 73–94. An earlier version of this article was published under the title, "Is There a Military-Industrial Complex Which Prevents Peace?: Consensus and Countervailing Power in Pluralistic Systems." It also appears as a chapter in the book *International Conflict and Social Policy* by Marc Pilisuk (Englewood Cliffs: Prentice-Hall, 1972). Reprinted by permission of Marc Pilisuk and the Society for the Psychological Study of Social Issues. Pilisuk is Professor in Residence at the School of Public Health, University of California at Berkeley. Tom Hayden is a leader of the antiwar movement in the United States.

quite narrow and cannot be said to govern anything so broad as foreign policy.

2. It is held that the "complex" is *not monolithic, not self-conscious,* and *not coordinated,* the presumed attributes of a ruling elite.

3. It is held that the military-industrial complex does not wield power if the term *power* is defined as the ability to realize its will even against the resistance of others and regardless of external conditions.

Since the arguments of the pluralists have been directed largely to the work of C. Wright Mills, it is with Mills that we will begin to analyze the theories which claim there *is* a military-industrial complex blocking peace.

THE THESIS OF ELITE CONTROL

Mills is by far the most formidable exponent of the theory of a power elite. In his view, the period in America since World War II has been dominated by the ascendance of corporation and military elites to positions of institutional power. These "commanding heights" allow them to exercise control over the trends of the business cycle and international relations. The cold war set the conditions that legitimize this ascendance, and the decline and incorporation of significant left-liberal movements, such as the CIO, symbolizes the end of opposition forces. The power elite monopolizes sovereignty, in that political initiative and control stem mainly from the top hierarchical levels of position and influence. Through the communications system the elite facilitates the growth of a politically indifferent mass society below the powerful institutions. This, according to the Mills argument, would explain why an observer finds widespread apathy. Only a small minority believes in actual participation in the larger decisions that affect their existence and only the ritual forms of "popular democracy" are practiced by the vast majority. Mills' argument addresses itself to the terms of the three basic issues we have designated, i.e., scope of decision power, awareness of common interest, and the definition of power exerted.

By *scope,* we are referring to the sphere of society over which an elite is presumed to exercise power. Mills argues that the scope of this elite is general, embracing all the decisions which in any way could be called vital (slump and boom, peace and war, etc.). He does not argue that *each* decision is directly determined, but rather that the political alternatives from which the "deciders" choose are shaped and limited by the elite through its possession of all the large-scale institutions. By this kind of argument, Mills avoids the need to demonstrate how his elite is at work during each decision. He speaks instead in terms of institutions and resources. But the problem is that his basic evidence is of a rather negative kind. No major decisions have been made for twenty years contrary to the policies of anticommunism and corporate or military aggrandizement; *therefore* a power elite must be prevailing. Mills might have improved his claims about the scope of elite decisions by analyzing a series of actual decisions in terms of the premises that were *not* debated. This could point to the mechanisms (implicit or explicit) that led to the exclusion of these premises from debate. By this and other means he might have found more satisfying evidence of the common, though perhaps tacit, presuppositions of seemingly disparate institutions. He then might have developed a framework analyzing "scope" on different levels. The scope of the Joint Chiefs of Staff, for instance, could be seen as limited, while at the same time the Joint Chiefs could be placed in a larger elite context having larger scope. Whether this could be shown awaits research of this kind. Until it is done, however, Mills' theory of scope remains open to attack, but, conversely, is not subject to refutation.

Mills' theory also eludes the traditional requirements for inferring monolithic structure, i.e., consciousness of elite status, and coordination. The modern tradition of viewing elites in this way began with Mosca's *The Ruling Class* in a period when family units and inheritance systems were the basic means of conferring power. Mills departs from this influential tradition precisely because of his emphasis on institutions as the basic elements. If the military, political, and economic institutional orders involve a high coincidence of interest, then the groups composing the institutional orders need not be monolithic, conscious, and coordinated, yet still they can exercise elite power.[1] This means specifically that a military-industrial complex could exist as an expression of a certain fixed ideology (reflecting common institutional needs), yet be "composed" of an endless shuffle of specific groups. For instance, our tables show 82 companies have dropped out of the list of 100 top defense contractors and only 36 "durables" remained on the list from 1940 to 1960. In terms of industry, the percentage of contracts going to the automotive industry dropped from 25 percent in World War II to 4 percent in the missile age. At the same time, the aircraft companies went from 34 to 54 percent of all contracts, and the electronics industry from 9 to 28 percent (Peck and Scherer, 1962). Mills' most central argument is that this ebb and flow is not necessarily evidence for the pluralists. His stress is on the unities which underlie the procession of competition and

---

[1] See James H. Meisel, *The Myth of the Ruling Class,* for the best available discussion of the innovation in theorizing about elites.

change. The decision to change the technology of warfare was one that enabled one group to "overcome" another in an overall system to which both are fundamentally committed. Moreover, the decision issued from the laboratories and planning boards of the defense establishment and only superficially involved any role for public opinion. The case studies of weapons development by Peck and Scherer, in which politics is described as a marginal ritual, would certainly buttress Mills' point of view.

Making this institution analysis enables Mills to make interesting comments on his human actors. The integration of institutions means that hundreds of individuals become familiar with several roles: general, politician, lobbyist, defense contractor. These men are the power elite, but they need not know it. They conspire, but conspiracy is not absolutely essential to their maintenance. They mix together easily, but can remain in power even if they are mostly anonymous to each other. They make decisions, big and small, sometimes with the knowledge of others and sometimes not, which ultimately control all the significant action and resources of society.

Where this approach tends to fall short is in its unclarity about how discontinuities arise. Is the military-industrial complex a feature of American society which can disappear and still leave the general social structure intact? Horst Brand (1962) has suggested a tension between financial companies and the defense industries because of the relatively few investment markets created by defense. Others have challenged the traditional view that defense spending stimulates high demand and employment. Their claim is that the concentration of contracts in a few states, the monopolization of defense and space industry by the largest 75 or 100 corporations, the low multiplier effect of the new weapons, the declining numbers of blue-collar workers required, and other factors, make the defense economy more of a drag than a stimulant (Melman et al., 1963; Etzioni, 1964). Certainly the rising unemployment of 1970 in the midst of expansion of the ABM system and extension of the Vietnam war to Laos and Cambodia show the flaws of relying upon defense spending for an economic stimulant. Mills died before these trends became the subject of debate, but he might have pioneered in discussion of them if his analytic categories had differentiated more finely between various industries and interest groups in his power elite. His emphasis was almost entirely on the "need" for a "permanent war economy" just when that need was being questioned even among his elite.

This failure, however, does not necessarily undermine the rest of Mills' analysis. His institutional analysis is still the best means of identifying a complex without calling it monolithic, conscious, and coordinated. Had he differentiated more exactly, he might have been able to describe various degrees of commitments to an arms race, a rightist ideology constricting the arena of meaningful debate, and other characteristics of a complex. This task remains to be done, and will be discussed at a later point.

Where Mills' theory is most awkward is in his assertions that the elite can, and does, make its decisions against the will of others and regardless of external conditions. This way of looking at power is inherited by Mills, and much of modern sociology, directly from Max Weber. What is attributed to the elite is a rather fantastic quality: literal omnipotence. Conversely, any group that is *not* able to realize its will even against the resistance of others is only "influential" but not an elite. Mills attempts to defend this viewpoint but, in essence, modifies it. He says he is describing a tendency, not a finalized state of affairs. This is a helpful device in explaining cracks in the monolith—for instance, the inability of the elite to establish a full corporate state against the will of small businessmen. However, it does not change the ultimate argument—that the power elite cannot become more than a tendency, cannot realize its actual self, unless it takes on the quality of omnipotence.

When power is defined as this kind of dominance, it is easily open to critical dispute. The conception of power depicts a vital and complex social system as essentially static, as having within it a set of stable governing components, with precharted interests which infiltrate and control every outpost of decision-authority. Thereby, internal accommodation is made necessary and significant change, aside from growth, becomes impossible. This conception goes beyond the idea of social or economic determinism. In fact, it defines a "closed social system." A "closed system" may be a dramatic image, but it is a forced one as well. Its defender sees events such as the rise of the labor movement essentially as a means of rationalizing modern capitalism. But true or false as this may be, did not the labor movement also constitute a "collective will" which the elite could not resist? An accommodation was reached, probably more on the side of capital than labor, but the very term "accommodation" implies the existence of more than one independent will. On a world scale, this becomes even more obvious. Certainly the rise of communism has not been through the will of capitalists, and Mills would be the first to agree. Nor does the elite fully control technological development; surely the process of invention has some independent, even if minor, place in the process of social change.

Mills' definition of power as dominance ironically serves the pluralist argument, rather than countering it. When power is defined so extremely, it becomes rather easy to claim that such power is curbed in the contemporary United States. The pluralists can say that Mills has conjured up a bogeyman to explain his own failure to realize his will. This is indeed what has been done in review after review of Mills' writings. A leading pluralist thinker, Edward Shils, says that Mills was too much influenced by Trotsky and Kafka:

> Power, although concentrated, is not so concentrated, so powerful, or so permeative as Professor Mills seems to believe. . . . There have been years in Western history, e.g., in Germany during the last years of the Weimar Republic and under the Nazis when reality approximated this picture more closely. . . . But as a picture of Western societies, and not just as an ideal type of extreme possibilities which might be realized if so much else that is vital were lacking, it will not do. (Shils, 1961.)

But is Mills' definition the only suitable one here? If it is, then the pluralists have won the debate. But if there is a way to designate an irresponsible elite without giving it omnipotence, then the debate may be recast at least.

This fundamental question is not answered in the other major books that affirm the existence of a military-industrial complex. Cook's *The Warfare State* and Perlo's *Militarism and Industry* and several more recent works are good examples of this literature which is theoretically inferior to Mills' perplexing account.

Cook's volume has been pilloried severely by deniers of the military-industrial complex. At least it has the merit of creating discussion by being one of the few dissenting books distributed widely on a commercial basis. It suffers, however, from many of the same unclarities typical of the deniers. Its title assumes a "warfare state" while its evidence, although rich, is only a compilation of incidents, pronouncements, and trends, lacking any framework for weighing and measuring. From his writing several hypotheses can be extracted about the "face of the Warfare State," all of them suggestive but none of them conclusive:

1. The Department of Defense owns more property than any other organization in the world.[2]

2. Between 60 and 70 percent of the national budget is consistently allocated to defense or defense-related expenditures.

3. The military and big business join in an inevitable meeting of

---

[2] Swomley (1964) accounts for Department of Defense holdings equivalent in size to eight states of the U.S.A. Kenneth Boulding, including personnel as well as property criteria, calls the Department of Defense the world's third largest socialist state. (Personal discussion, 1963.)

minds over billions of dollars in contracts the one has to order and the other to fulfill.

4. The 100 top corporations monopolize three-fourths of the contracts, 85 percent of them being awarded without competition.

5. As much as one-third of all production and service indirectly depends on defense.

6. Business and other conservative groups, even though outside of the Defense establishment, benefit from the warfare emphasis because it keeps subordinate the welfare state that is anathema to them. (Pages 20–24, 162–202.)

There is no doubt about Cook's data holding up for the years since his book was written. The federal budget of $154.9 billion for the fiscal year 1971 assigns 64.8 cents of every tax dollar to the cost of past and present wars and war preparation. The Vietnam war costs are concealed in the 48.4 cents per dollar for current military expenditures. Veterans benefits and national debt interest are also sizable items. The Nixon administration claims 41 percent of its budget to be on human resources. The figure, however, includes trust funds like Social Security (for which the government is merely a caretaker), veterans benefits, and even the Selective Service System in this category. The actual human resources figure is 17 percent, indicating that welfare is still being crushed by warfare (Senator M. Hatfield, address, Feb. 10, 1970, Corvallis, Oregon).

Cook's work, much more than Mills', is open to the counterargument that no monolithic semiconspiratorial elite exists. Even his definitions of vested interests are crude and presumed. Moreover, he suffers far more than Mills from a failure to differentiate between groups. For instance, there is nothing in his book (written in 1962) that would explain the economic drag of defense spending, which Cook preceptively observed in a *Nation* article, "The Coming Politics of Disarmament," in 1963. One year he wrote that big business was being fattened off war contracts, but the next year the "prolonged arms race has started, at last, to commit a form of economic hara-kiri." "Hara-kiri" does not happen spontaneously; it is a culmination of long-developing abnormalities. That Cook could not diagnose them before they became common in congressional testimony illustrates the lack of refinement in his 1962 analysis. Cook's failure lies in visualizing a monolith, which obscures the strains that promote new trends and configurations.

It is in this attention to strains that Perlo's book is useful. He draws interesting connections between the largest industrial corporations and the defense economy, finding that defense accounts for 12 percent of the profits of the 25 largest firms. He adds the factor of foreign investment as one which creates a further propensity in favor of a large defense system, and he calculates that military, business, and foreign investments combined total 40 percent of the aggregate profits among the top 25. He draws deeper connections between companies and the major financial groups controlling their assets.

This kind of analysis begins to reveal important disunities within the business community. For instance, it can be seen that the Rockefellers are increasing their direct military investments while maintaining their largest foreign holdings in extremely volatile Middle Eastern and Latin American companies. The Morgans are involved in domestic industries of a rather easy-to-convert type, and their main foreign holdings are in the "safer" European countries, although they too have "unsafe" mining interests in Latin America and Africa. The First National City Bank, while having large holdings in Latin American sugar and fruit, has a more technical relation to its associated firms than the stock-owner relation. The Mellons have sizable oil holdings in Kuwait, but on the whole are less involved in defense than the other groups. The Du Ponts, traditionally the major munitions makers, are "diversified" into the booming aerospace and plutonium industries, but their overseas holdings are heavily in Europe. Certain other groups with financial holdings, such as Young and Eaton interests in Cleveland, have almost no profit stake in defense or foreign investments. On the other hand, some of the new wealth in Los Angeles is deeply committed to the aerospace industry.

Perlo makes several differentiations of this sort, including the use of foreign policy statements by leading industrial groups. But he does not have a way to predict under what conditions a given company would actively support economic shifts away from the arms race. These and other gaps, however, are not nearly as grave as his lack of analysis of other components of the military-industrial complex.[3] There is no attempt to include politicians, military groups, and other forces in a "map" of the military-industrial complex which Perlo believes exists. This may be partly because of the book's intent, which is to document profiteering by arms contractors, but, for whatever reason, the book is not theoretically edifying about the question we are posing. Nor does it refute the pluralist case. In fact, it contains just the kind of evidence that pluralist arguments currently employ to demonstrate the absence of a monolith.

The newer literature, since 1965, shows a somewhat more penetrating

---

[3] In an earlier book, *The Empire of High Finance* (1957), Perlo documented the close relations of the major financial groups and the political executive. He did not, however, carry this analysis to congressmen and senators, nor did he offer sufficient comparative evidence to demonstrate a long-term pattern.

glimpse into the extent of the merger of the military and the defense industry. Lapp, *The Weapons Culture*; Weidenbaum, "Arms and the American Economy"; Galbraith, *The New Industrial State*; and Knoll and McFadden, *American Militarism 1970,* all show the heavy involvement of the Department of Defense with the corporate giants. The two recent and most striking works which provide the most concrete detail on the operation of this military-industrial network are Seymour Melman's *Pentagon Capitalism* (1970) and Richard Barnet's *The Economy of Death* (1969). Both are well written and a must for any serious student of contemporary policy. *Pentagon Capitalism* describes the result of the defense-industrial merger as a giant enterprise controlled by the civilian defense establishment, or "state-management." Through the elaboration of government controls over the firms that carry out defense contracts, the Defense Department's role has changed from that of customer to that of administrator over a far-flung empire of defense production. The Pentagon is able to divert capital and scientific and technical manpower to its own purposes, drawing resources away from productive activity to, what Melman calls, economically "parasitic" activity. He holds that the prime goal of the "state-management" *is to enlarge its decision power.* Thus wars, once begun, tend to expand; "security gaps" are invented, causing weapons systems to grow in size and sophistication; and international arms sales increase.

Barnet (*The Economy of Death*) sees the military-industrial complex as more decentralized, like a machine with several separate parts that run together smoothly. Each institution within the complex acts for its own purposes, and all contribute to justifying and maintaining the irrational and dangerous growth of military capability. Barnet documents the interchangeability of personnel between industry and the military. A major strength of Barnet's work lies in his willingness to be specific, to name the key names from among those in his study of 400 top decision makers who come from a handful of law firms and executive suites "in shouting distance of one another in fifteen city blocks in New York, Washington, Detroit, Chicago, and Boston." Many of the names are commonly known (although the extent of their financial-world connections is not)—Charles Wilson, Neil McElroy, Robert Anderson, George Humphrey, Douglas Dillon, John McCone, Adolph Berle, Averell Harriman, William C. Foster, John McCloy, Robert McNamara, Roswell Gilpatric, James Douglas, William Rogers, and Nelson Rockefeller. Men such as these are systematically recruited into the top Cabinet posts and become "national security managers." Their common backgrounds, even membership in the same elite social clubs, assures a measure of homogeneity around their task of defining who or what threatens this nation and what should be done about it. Their views on the national interest reflect their own success in judicious management of risk in the business world. Barnet's assumption about the homogeneity of their club is supported by Domhoff's "Who Made American Foreign Policy, 1945–1963?" It is clear that a man like William Rogers with the right business background but no particular knowledge or background in foreign affairs can be made Secretary of State while a civil-rights leader, Martin Luther King, was admonished by official spokesmen for expressing a position against the Vietnam war.

Barnet believes it is the ongoing mechanisms of the system that keep it rutted in old paths. The evils are not incidental, he says, but built into the system. Military solutions to international problems seem more reliable, "tougher," than diplomatic solutions, and they are backed up by millions of dollars worth of "scientific research"; so military solutions are preferred even by civilian defense officials. The military, the civilian defense establishment, and defense contractors constantly work together to develop new weapons systems to meet defense "needs"; so they feed one another's ideologies, and costlier, more elaborate weapons result. It is difficult and expensive for military contractors to convert to peacetime production, so they have done virtually no planning for conversion and many have abandoned all interest in such planning. Perhaps most important for Barnet, those in power see America's chief purpose as consolidating and extending American power around the world; hence military technology is an indispensable tool. Whether this collection of civilian managers is really in control or whether they are merely serving more powerful military bureaucracy is the point at issue, and Barnet leans toward the view of the ascendance of relatively smooth-working military hierarchy. Dumhoff, using very similar evidence, places the aristocratic economic elite at the top of the pinnacle.

Melman, in particular, presents a strong case to suggest that militarism in the United States is no longer an example of civilian corporate interests dictating a military role to produce hardware for profit from the governmental consumer and to defend the outposts of capitalism. Instead, he sees the system as one led by the military managers for their own interests in power, a state socialism whose defense officials dictate the terms of policy, and of profits, to their subsidiary corporations. Melman supports his case by the observation that not only the personnel but the actual procedural ways of operation demonstrate that the Defense Department and the corporations which serve it have interpenetrated one another's operations—to such an extent that there is for all practical purposes really only one organization. The horrible example that comes to mind is the rise of Hitler, first backed and promoted by industrialists who later lost their measure of control over an uncontrollable military machine. Melman's thesis differs from both the pluralist doctrine which sees various groups competing for power and the Marxist doctrine which sees the greed of the capitalists as the prime mover. In Melman's convincing analysis the military is fast becoming the King.

Melman's analysis may yet prove true. For the present, however, corporate capitalism has fared too well to alleviate all suspicions of the hidden hand. The nature of the new interlocking industrial conglomerates like Lytton, Textron, or General Dynamics is that they and the main financial houses of the United States provide an inner core whose interests are permanently protected even as individual corporations prosper or falter. For such centers of elite power, which Barnet shows to be the main source of top Defense Department and other foreign-policy-appointed officials, the terms of the military merger have been highly beneficial. The benefits must be seen not only in profits but in the retention of the entire profit-making system against the demands of a hungry and impatient world. Melman speaks of the drive of the new technocratic military bureaucracy to increase its power and control but deemphasizes what interests this power is protecting. Barnet specifies the community of interest and outlooks among the corporate decision managers who are recruited into the inner circles of foreign policy but does not state explicitly what beliefs lie at the core of the practices that are promoted.

Both Barnet and Melman believe that American militarism is a function of institutions directly involved with defense. It can be argued, on the other hand, that a description of something called a military-industrial complex should include all of the power centers of American society. Directorates of the major defense contractors are not separable from those of industries geared primarily to the production of consumer goods. Neither are the consumer industries independent of military and diplomatic actions which protect international marketing advantages. Barnet himself notes that it is not merely the faction of the labor movement directly employed in defense industries, but organized labor in general which is a political supporter of military-industrial power. The universities are heavily involved in defense interests as is the complex of oils, highways, and automotives. Even in education the armed services Project 100,000 has inducted a large number of former draft rejects for resocialization and basic educational development (followed by two years of applied study abroad in Vietnam for the successful graduates) (Little, 1968; Pilisuk, 1968).

Barnet and Melman deal incompletely with the relationship of the sector they regard as the military-industrial complex to the rest of society. Both realize the tremendous power of the military, the civilian defense officials, and the defense industry combined. They are aware that the defense establishment has a powerful hold on public opinion through fear of enemy attack and through control over a large sector of the work force. Yet they seem to hope this power can be curbed by a loud enough public outcry. In the last analysis they too believe that the defense establishment has merely been allowed to get out of hand, and that now the exercise of some countervailing power may bring sanity back into American policy and make peace possible.

REVISING THE CRITERIA FOR
INFERRING POWER

After finding fault with so many books and divergent viewpoints, the most obvious conclusion is that current social theory is deficient in its explanation of power. We concur with one of Mills' severest critics, Daniel Bell, who at least agrees with Mills that most current analysis concentrates on the "intermediate sectors," e.g., parties, interest groups, formal structures, without attempting to view the underlying system of "renewable power independent of any momentary group of actors" (Bell, 1964). However, we have indicated that the only formidable analysis of the underlying system of renewable power, that of Mills, has profound shortcomings because of its definition of power. Therefore, before we can offer an answer of our own to the question, "Is there a military-industrial complex that blocks peace?" it is imperative to return to the question of power itself in American society.

We have agreed essentially with the pluralist claim that ruling-group models do not "fit" the American structure. We have classified Mills' model as that of a ruling group because of his Weberian definition of power, but we have noted also that Mills successfully went beyond two traps common to elite theories, viz., that the elite is total in the scope of its decisions, and that the elite is a coordinated monolith.

But we perhaps have not stressed sufficiently that the alternative case for pluralism is inadequate in its claim to describe the historical dynamics of American society. The point of our dissent from pluralism is over the doctrine of "countervailing power." This is the modern version of Adam Smith's economics and of the Madisonian or Federalism theory of checks and balances, adapted to the new circumstances of large-scale organizations. Its evidence is composed of self-serving incidents and a faith in semimystical resources. For instance, in the sphere of political economy, it is argued that oligopoly contains automatic checking mechanisms against undue corporate growth, and that additionally, the factors of "public opinion" and "corporate conscience" are built-in limiting forces.[4] We believe that evidence in the field, however, suggests that oligopoly is a means of stabilizing an industrial sphere either through tacit agreements to follow price leadership or rigged agreements in the case of custom-made goods; that "public opinion" tends much more to be manipulated and apathetic than independently critical; that "corporate conscience" is less suitable as a description than Reagan's terms, "corporate arrogance."

To take the more immediate example of the military sphere, the pluralist claim is that the military is subordinate to broader, civilian interests. The first problem with the statement is the ambiguity of "civilian." Is it clear that military men are more "militaristic" than civilian men? To say so would be to deny the increasing trend of "white-collar militarism." The top strategists in the Department of Defense, the Central Intelligence Agency, and the key advisory positions often are Ph.D.'s. In fact, "civilians" including McGeorge Bundy, Robert Kennedy, James Rostow, and Robert McNamara are mainly responsible for the development of the only remaining "heroic" form of combat: counterinsurgency operations in the jungles of the underdeveloped countries. If "militarism" [5] has permeated this deeply into the "civilian" sphere, then the distinction between the terms becomes largely nominal.

The intrusion of civilian professors into the military arena has been most apparent in more than 300 universities and nonprofit research institutions which supply personnel to and rely upon contracts from the Department of Defense. About half of these centers were created to do specialized strategic research. One of these, the RAND Corporation, was set up by Douglas Aviation and the Air Force to give "prestige-type support for favored Air Force proposals" (Friedman, 1963). When RAND strategy experts Wohlstetter and Dinerstein discovered a mythical "missile gap" and an equally unreal preemptive war strategy in Soviet post-Sputnik policy, they paved the way for the greatest military escalation of the cold war era, the missile race.

The civilian strategists have frequently retained an exasperating measure of autonomy from the services that support them. Such conflicts reached a peak when both the Skybolt and the RS 70 projects met their demise under the "cost effectiveness" program designed by Harvard

---

[4] For this argument, see A. A. Berle, *The Twentieth Century Capitalist Revolution*; and J. K. Galbraith, *American Capitalism*. For sound criticisms, but without sound alternatives, see Mills' and Perlo's books. Also see Michael Reagan, *The Managed Economy* (1963); and Bernard Nossiter, *The Mythmakers* (1964), for other refutations of the countervailing power thesis.

[5] We are defining the term as "primary reliance on coercive means, particularly violence or the threat of violence, to deal with social problems."

economist Charles Hitch (then with RAND, later Defense Department comptroller, now President of the University of California). That the civilian and military planners of military policy sometimes differ does not detract from the argument. What must be stressed is that the apparent flourishing of such civilian agencies as RAND (it earned over 20 million dollars in 1962 with all the earnings going into expansion and spawned the nonprofit Systems Development Corporation with annual earnings exceeding 50 million dollars) is no reflection of countervailing power. The doctrine of controlled response under which the RS 70 fell was one which served the general aspirations of each of the separate services; of the Polaris and Minuteman stabile deterrent factions, of the brush-fire or limited-war proponents, guerrilla war and paramilitary operations advocates, and of the counterforce adherents. It is a doctrine of versatility intended to leave the widest range of military options for retaliation and escalation in U.S. hands. It can hardly be claimed as victory against military thought. The fighting may have been intense but the area of consensus between military and civilian factions was great.

CONSENSUS

All that countervailing power refers to is the relationship between groups who fundamentally accept "the American system" but who compete for advantages within it. The corporate executive wants higher profits, the laborer a higher wage. The president wants the final word on military strategies, the chairman of the Joint Chiefs does not trust him with it, Boeing wants the contract, but General Dynamics is closer at the time to the Navy secretary and the president, and so on. What is prevented by countervailing forces is the dominance of society by a group or clique or a party. But this process suggests a profoundly important point; that *the constant pattern in American society is the rise and fall of temporarily irresponsible groups.* By *temporary* we mean that, outside of the largest industrial conglomerates,[6] the groups which wield significant power to influence policy decisions are not guaranteed stability. By *irresponsible* we mean that there are many activities within their scope which are essentially unaccountable in the democratic process. These groups are too uneven to be described with the shorthand term "class." Their personnel have many different characteristics (compare IBM executives and

---

[6] The term refers to industrial organizations like Textron and Ling-Temco-Vought which have holdings in every major sector of American industry.

the Southern Dixiecrats) and their needs as groups are different enough to cause endless fights as, for example, small versus big business. No one group or coalition of several groups can tyrannize the rest as is demonstrated, for example, in the changing status of the major financial groups, such as the Bank of America which grew rapidly, built on the financial needs of the previously neglected small consumer.

It is clear, however, that these groups exist within consensus relationships of a more general and durable kind than their conflict relationships. This is true, first of all, of their social characteristics. In an earlier version of this essay we compiled tables using data from an exhaustive study of American elites contained in Warner et al., *The American Federal Executive* (1963) and from Suzanne Keller's compilation of military, economic, political, and diplomatic elite survey materials in *Beyond the Ruling Class* (1963). The relevant continuities represented in this data suggest an educated elite with an emphasis upon Protestant and business-oriented origins. Moreover, the data suggest inbreeding with business orientation in backgrounds likely to have been at least maintained, if not augmented, through marriage. Domhoff, in *Who Rules America?,* has shown that elites generally attend the same exclusive prep schools and universities, and belong to the same exclusive gentlemen's clubs. The consistencies suggest orientations not unlike those found in examination of editorial content of major business newspapers and weeklies and in more directly sampled assessments of elite opinions.[7]

The second evidence of consensus relationships, besides attitude and background data indicating a pro-business sympathy, would come from an examination of the *practice* of decision making. By analysis of such actual behavior we can understand which consensus attitudes are reflected in decision making. Here, in retrospect, it is possible to discover the values and assumptions which are defended recurrently. This is at least a rough means of finding the boundaries of consensus relations. Often these boundaries are invisible because of the very infrequency with which they are tested. What are visible most of the time are the parameters of conflict relationships among different groups. These conflict relationships constitute the ingredients of experience which give individuals or groups their uniqueness and varieties, while the consensus relations constitute the common underpinnings of behavior. The tendency in social science has been to study decision making in order to study group differences; we need to study decision making also to understand group commonalities.

Were such studies done, our hypothesis would be that certain "core

---

[7] For some interesting work bearing upon the attitudes of business and military elites, see Angell, 1964; Bauer et al., 1963; Eells and Walton, 1961; and Singer, 1964.

beliefs" are continuously unquestioned. One of these, undoubtedly, would be that efficacy is preferable to principle in foreign affairs. In practice, this means that violence is preferable to nonviolence as a means of defense. A second is that private property is preferable to collective property. A third assumption is that the particular form of constitutional government which is practiced within the United States is preferable to any other system of government. We refer to the preferred mode as limited parliamentary democracy, a system in which institutionalized forms of direct representation are carefully retained but with fundamental limitations placed upon the prerogatives of governing. Specifically included among the areas of limitation are many matters encroaching upon corporation property and state hegemony. While adherence to this form of government is conceivably the strongest of the domestic "core values," at least among business elites, it is probably the least strongly held of the three on the international scene. American relations with, and assistance for, authoritarian and semifeudal regimes occurs exactly in those areas where the recipient regime is evaluated primarily upon the two former assumptions and given rather extensive leeway on the latter one.

The implications of these "core beliefs" for the social system are immense, for they justify the maintenance of our largest institutional structures: the military, the corporate economy, and a system of partisan politics which protects the concept of limited democracy. These institutions, in turn, may be seen as current agencies of the more basic social structure. The "renewable basis of power" in America at the present time underlies those institutional orders linked in consensus relationships: military defense of private property and parliamentary democracy. These institutional orders are not permanently secure, by definition. Their maintenance involves a continuous coping with new conditions, such as technological innovation, and with the inherent instabilities of a social structure that arbitrarily classifies persons by role, status, access to resources, and power. The myriad groups composing these orders are even less secure because of their weak ability to command "coping resources," e.g., the service branches are less stable than the institution of the military, particular companies are less stable than the institution of corporate property, political parties are less stable than the institution of parliamentary government.

In the United States there is no ruling group. Nor is there any easily discernible ruling institutional order, so meshed have the separate sources of elite power become. But there is a social structure which is organized to create and protect power centers with only partial accountability. In this definition of power we are avoiding the Weber-Mills meaning of *omnipotence* and the contrary pluralist definition of power as consistently *diffuse.* We are describing the current system as one of overall "minimal accountability" and "minimal consent." We mean that the role of democratic review, based on genuine popular consent, is made marginal and reactive. Elite groups are minimally accountable to publics and have a substantial, though by no means maximum, freedom to shape popular attitudes. The reverse of our system would be one in which democratic participation would be the orienting demand around which the social structure is organized.

Some will counter this case by saying that we are measuring "reality" against an "ideal," a technique which permits the conclusion that the social structure is undemocratic according to its distance from our utopian values. This is a convenient apology for the present system, of course. We think it possible, at least in theory, to develop measures of the undemocratic in democratic conditions, and place given social structures along a continuum. These measures, in rough form, might include such variables as economic security, education, legal guarantees, access to information, and participatory control over systems of economy, government, and jurisprudence.

The reasons for concern with democratic process in an article questioning the power of a purported military-industrial complex are twofold. First, just as scientific method both legitimizes and promotes change in the world of knowledge, democratic method legitimizes and promotes change in the world of social institutions. Every society, regardless of how democratic, protects its core institutions in a web of widely shared values. But if the core institutions should be dictated by the requisites of military preparedness, then restrictions on the democratic process, i.e., restrictions in either mass opinion exchange (as by voluntary or imposed news management) or in decision-making bodies (as by selection of participants in a manner guaranteeing exclusion of certain positions), then such restrictions would be critical obstacles to peace.

Second, certain elements of democratic process are inimical to features of military-oriented society, and the absence of these elements offers one type of evidence for a military-industrial complex even in the absence of a ruling elite. Secretary of Defense Robert McNamara made the point amply clear in his testimony in 1961 before the Senate Armed Services Committee:

> Why should we tell Russia that the Zeus development may not be satisfactory? What we ought to be saying is that we have the most perfect anti-ICBM system that the human mind will ever devise. Instead the public domain is already full of statements that the Zeus may not be satisfactory, that it has deficiencies. I think it is absurd to release that

level of information. (*Military Procurement Authorization Fiscal Year 1962.*)

Under subsequent questioning McNamara attempted to clarify his statement that he only wished to delude Russian, not American, citizens about U.S. might. Just how this might be done was not explained.

A long-established tradition exists for "executive privilege" which permits the president to refuse to release information when, in his opinion, it would be damaging to the national interest. Under modern conditions responsibility for handling information of a strategic nature is shared among military, industrial, and executive agencies. The discretion regarding when to withhold what information must also be shared. Moreover, the existence of a perpetual danger makes the justification, "in this time of national crisis," suitable to every occasion in which secrecy must be justified. McNamara's statement cited above referred not to a crisis in Cuba or Vietnam but rather to the perpetual state of cold war crisis. And since the decision about what is to be released and when is subject to just such management, the media become dependent upon the agencies for timely leaks and major stories. This not only adds an aura of omniscience to the agencies, but gives these same agencies the power to reward "good" journalists and punish the critical ones.

The issues in the question of news management involve more than the elements of control available to the president, the State Department, the Department of Defense, the Central Intelligence Agency, the Atomic Energy Commission, or any of the major prime contractors of defense contracts. Outright control of news flow is probably less pervasive than voluntary acquiescence to the objectives of these prominent institutions of our society. Nobody has to tell the wire services when to release a story on the bearded dictator of our hemisphere or the purported brutality of Ho Chi Minh. A frequent model, the personified devil image of an enemy, has become a press tradition. In addition to a sizable quantity of radio and television programming and spot time purchased directly by the Pentagon, an amount of service, valued to $6 million by *Variety*, is donated annually by the networks and by public-relations agencies for various military shows (Swomley, 1959). Again, the pluralistic shell of an independent press or broadcasting media is left hollow by the absence of a countervailing social force of any significant power.

Several shared premises, unquestioned by any potent locus of institutionalized power, were described as:

1. Efficacy is preferable to principle in foreign affairs (thus military means are chosen over nonviolent means).

2. Private property is preferable to public property.
3. Limited parliamentary democracy is preferable to any other system of government.

At issue is the question of whether an America protecting such assumptions can exist in a world of enduring peace. Three preconditions of enduring peace must be held up against these premises.

The first is that enduring peace will first require or will soon generate disarmament. Offset programs for the reallocation of the defense dollar require a degree of coordinated planning for the change inconsistent with the working assumption that "private property is preferable to public property" in a corporate economy.

If one pools available projections regarding the offset programs, especially regional and local offset programs, necessary to maintain economic well-being in the face of disarmament in this country, the programs will highlight two important features. One is the lag time in industrial conversion. The second is the need for coordination in the timing and spacing of programs. One cannot reinvest in new home building in an area which has just been deserted by its major industry and left a ghost town. The short-term and long-term offset values of new hospitals and educational facilities will differ in the building and the utilization stages, and regional offset programs have demonstrable interregional effects (Reiner, 1964). Plans requiring worker mobility on a large scale will require a central bank for storing job information and a smooth system for its dissemination. Such coordination will require a degree of centralization of controls beyond the realm which our assumption regarding primacy of private property would permit. Gross intransigence has already been seen even on the contingency planning for nondefense work by single firms like Sperry Rand which have already been severely hurt by project cutbacks. And the prospect of contingency planning will not be warmly welcomed in the newer aeroframe industry (which is only 60 percent convertible to needs of a peacetime society) (McDonagh and Zimmerman, 1964). Private planning by an individual firm for its own future does occur, but without coordinated plans, the time forecast for market conditions remains smaller than the lag time for major retooling. A lag time of from six to ten years would not be atypical before plans by a somewhat overspecialized defense contractor could result in retooling for production in a peacetime market. In the meantime, technological innovations, governmental fiscal or regulatory policies, shifts in consumer preferences, or the decisions by other firms to enter that same market could well make the market vanish. Moreover, the example of defense firms which have attempted even the smaller step toward diversification presents a picture which has not been entirely promising (Fearon and Hook, 1964). Indeed, one of several reasons for the failures in this endeavor has been that marketing skills necessary to compete in a private-enterprise economy have been lost by those industrial giants who have been managing with a sales force of one or two retired generals to deal with the firm's only customer. Even if the path of successful conversion by some firms were to serve as the model for all individual attempts, the collective result would be poor. To avoid a financially disastrous glutting of limited markets, some coordinated planning will be needed.

The intransigence regarding public or collaborative planning occurs against a backdrop of a soon-to-be increasing army of unemployed youth and aged, as well as regional armies of unemployed victims of automation. Whether one thinks of work in traditional job-market terms or as anything worthwhile that a person can do with his life, work (and some means of livelihood) will have to be found for these people. There is much work to be done in community services, education, public health, and recreation, but this is people work, not product work. The lack of a countervailing force prevents the major reallocation of human and economic resources from the sector defined as preferable by the most potent institutions of society. One point must be stressed. We are not saying that limited planning to cushion the impact of arms reduction is impossible. Indeed, it is going on and with the apparent blessing of the Department of Defense (Barber, 1963). We are saying that the type of accommodation needed by a cutback of $9 billion in R & D and $16 billion in military procurement requires a type of preparation not consistent with the unchallenged assumptions.

Even the existence of facilities for coordinated planning does not, to be sure, guarantee the success of such planning. Bureaucratic institutions, designed as they may be for coordination and control, do set up internal resistance to the very coordination they seek to achieve. The mechanisms for handling these bureaucratic intransigencies usually rely upon such techniques as bringing participants into the process of formulating the decisions which will affect their own behavior. We can conceive of no system of coordinated conversion planning which could function without full and motivated cooperation from the major corporations, the larger unions, and representatives of smaller business and industry. Unfortunately, it is just as difficult to conceive of a system which would assure this necessary level of participation and cooperation. This same argument cuts deeper still when we speak of the millions of separate individuals in the "other America" whose lives would be increasingly "administered" with the type of centralized planning needed to offset a defense economy. The job assignment which requires moving, the vocational retraining program, the development of housing projects to meet minimal standards, educational enrichment programs, all of the programs which are conceived by middle-class white America for racially mixed low-income groups, face the same difficulty in execution of plans. Without direct participation in the formulation of the programs, the target populations are less likely to participate in the programs and more likely to continue feelings of alienation from the social system which looks upon them as an unfortunate problem rather than as contributing members. Considering the need for active participation in real decisions, every step of coordinated planning carries with it the responsibility for an equal step in the direction of participatory democracy. This means that the voice of the unemployed urban worker may have to be heard, not only on city council meetings which discuss policy on the control of rats in his dwelling, but also on decisions about where a particular major corporation will be relocated and where the major resource allocations of the country will be invested. That such decision participation would run counter to the consensus on the items of limited parliamentary democracy and private property is exactly the point we wish to make.

Just as the theoretical offset plans can be traced to the sources of power with which they conflict, so too can the theoretical plans for international governing and peace-keeping operations be shown to conflict with the unquestioned beliefs. U.S. consent to international jurisdiction in the settlement of claims deriving from the nationalization of American overseas holdings or the removal of U.S. military installations is almost inconceivable. Moreover, the mode of American relations to less-developed countries is so much a part of the operations of those American institutions which base their existence upon interminable conflict with communism that the contingency in which the U.S. might have to face the question of international jurisdiction in these areas seems unreal. Offers to mediate, for example, with Cuba by Mexico, are bluntly rejected. Acceptance of such offers would have called into question not one but all three of the assumptions in the core system. International jurisdictional authority could institutionalize a means to call the beliefs into question. It is for this reason (but perhaps most directly because of our preference for forceful means) that American preoccupation in those negotiations regarding the extension of international control, which have taken place, deal almost exclusively with controls in the area of weaponry and police operations and not at all in the areas of political or social justice.

The acceptance of complete international authority even in the area of weaponry poses certain inconsistencies with the preferred "core beliefs." Nonviolent settlement of Asian-African area conflicts would be slow and ineffective in protecting American interests. The elimination, however, of military preparedness, both for projected crises and for their potential escalation, requires a faith in alternate means of resolution. The phasing of the American plan for general and complete disarmament is one which says in effect: prove that the alternatives are as efficient as our arms in protection of our interests and then we disarm. In the short term, however, the effectiveness of force always looks greater.

The state of world peace contains certain conditions imposed by the fact that people now compare themselves with persons who have more of the benefits of industrialization than they themselves. Such comparative reference groups serve to increase the demand for rapid change. While modern communications heighten the pressures imposed by such comparisons, the actual disparities revealed in comparison speak for violence. Population growth rates, often as high as 3 percent, promise population doubling within a single generation in countries least able to provide for their members. The absolute number of illiterates as well as the absolute number of persons starving is greater now than ever before in history. Foreign aid barely offsets the disparity between declining prices paid for the prime commodities exported by underdeveloped countries and rising prices paid for the finished products imported into these countries (Horowitz, 1962). All schemes for tight centralized planning employed by these countries to accrue and disperse scarce capital by rational means are blocked by the unchallenged assumptions on private property and limited parliamentary democracy. A restatement of the principle came in the report of General Lucius Clay's committee on foreign aid. The report stated that the U.S. should not assist foreign governments "in projects establishing government-owned industrial and commercial enterprises which compete with existing private endeavors." When Congressman Broomfield's amendment on foreign aid resulted in cancellation of a U.S. promise to India to build a steel mill in Bokaro, Broomfield stated the case succinctly: "The main issue is private enterprise vs. state socialism" (*The Atlantic,* September 1964, p. 6). Moreover, preference for forceful solutions assures that the capital now invested in preparedness will not be allocated in a gross way to the needs of underdeveloped countries. Instead, the manifest crises periodically erupting in violence justify further the need for reliance upon military preparedness.

We agree fully with an analysis by Lowi (1964) distinguishing types of decisions for which elite-like forces seem to appear and hold control (redistributive) and other types in which pluralist powers battle for their respective interests (distributive). In the latter type the pie is large and the fights are over who gets how much. Factional strife within and among military-industrial and political forces in our country are largely of this nature. In redistributive decisions, the factions coalesce, for the pie itself is threatened. We have been arguing that the transition to peace is a process of redistributive decision.

Is there, then, a military-industrial complex that prevents peace? The answer is inextricably embedded into the mainstream of American institutions and mores. Our concept is not that American society contains a ruling military-industrial complex. Our concept is more nearly that American society *is* a military-industrial complex. It can accommodate a wide range of factional interests from those concerned with the production or utilization of a particular weapon to those enraptured with the mystique of optimal global strategies. It can accommodate those with rabid desires to advance toward the brink and into limitless intensification of the arms race. It can even accommodate those who wish either to prevent war or to limit the destructiveness of war through the gradual achievement of arms control and disarmament agreements. What it cannot accommodate is the type of radical departures needed to produce enduring peace.

REFERENCES

Angell, Robert C., "A Study of Social Values: Content Analysis of Elite Media," *Journal of Conflict Resolution,* 8:4 (1964), pp. 329–385.

Bank Holding Companies: Scope of Operations and Stock Ownership, Committee on Banking and Currency (Washington: U.S. Government Printing Office, 1963).

Barber, Arthur, "Some Industrial Aspects of Arms Control," *Journal of Conflict Resolution,* 7:3 (1963), pp. 491–495.

Barnet, Richard, *The Economy of Death* (New York: Atheneum, 1969).

Bauer, Raymond A., I. Pool, and L. Dexter, *American Business and Public Policy* (Alberton, N.Y., 1963).

Bell, Daniel, *The End of Ideology* (Glencoe, Ill.: Free Press, 1959).

Benoit, Emile, and K. E. Boulding (eds.), *Disarmament and Economy* (New York: Harper, 1963).

Berle, Adolf A., *The Twentieth Century Capitalist Revolution* (New York: Harcourt, 1954).

Bluestone, Irving, "Problems of the Worker in Industrial Conversion," *Journal of Conflict Resolution,* 7:3 (1963), pp. 495–502.

Brand, Horst, "Disarmament and American Capitalism," *Dissent* (Summer 1962), pp. 236–251.

Burdick, Eugene, and H. Wheeler, *Fail-safe* (New York: McGraw-Hill, 1962).

Burton, John, *Peace Theory* (New York: Knopf, 1962).

Cartwright, Dorwin, "Power: A Neglected Variable in Social Psychology," in D. Cartwright (ed.), *Studies in Social Power* (Ann Arbor: Research Center for Group Dynamics, 1959).

Catton, Bruce, *The War Lords of Washington* (New York: Harcourt, 1948).

Coffin, Tristran, *The Passion of the Hawks* (New York: Macmillan, 1964).

Cohen, Bernard C., *The Press and Foreign Policy* (Princeton: Princeton Univ. Press, 1963).

Convertibility of Space and Defense Resources to Civilian Needs, 88th Congress, 2nd Session, Vol. 2, Subcommittee on Employment and Manpower (Washington: U.S. Government Printing Office, 1964).

Cook, Fred J., "The Coming Politics of Disarmament," *The Nation* (February 6, 1963).

Cook, Fred J., *The Warfare State* (New York: Macmillan, 1962).

Dahl, Robert A., *A Modern Political Analysis* (New York: Prentice-Hall, 1963).

Dahl, Robert A., *Who Governs?* (New Haven: Yale Univ. Press, 1961).

Dillon, W., *Little Brother Is Watching* (Boston: Houghton Mifflin, 1962).

Domhoff, G. William, "Who Made American Foreign Policy, 1945–1963?," in David Horowitz (ed.), *Corporations and the Cold War* (New York: Monthly Review Press, 1969), pp. 25–69.

Economic Impacts of Disarmament, U.S. Arms Control and Disarmament Agency, Economic Series 1 (Washington: U.S. Government Printing Office, 1962).

Eells, Richard, and C. Walton, *Conceptual Foundations of Business* (Homewood, Ill.: Irwin, 1961).

Etzioni, Amitai, *The Hard Way to Peace* (New York: Collier, 1962).

Etzioni, Amitai, *The Moon-doggle* (Garden City, N.Y.: Doubleday, 1964).

Fearon, H. E., and R. C. Hook, Jr., "The Shift from Military to Industrial Markets," *Business Topics* (Winter 1964), pp. 43–52.

Feingold, Eugene, and Thomas Hayden, "What Happened to Democracy?", *New University Thought,* 1 (Summer 1964), pp. 39–48.

Fisher, Roger (ed.), *International Conflict and Behavioral Science* (New York: Basic Books, 1964).

Fishman, Leslie, "A Note on Disarmament and Effective Demand," *Journal of Political Economy,* 70:2 (1962), pp. 183–186.

Foreign Assistance Act of 1964 (Parts VI and VII), Committee on Foreign Affairs, Hearings, 88th Congress, 2nd Session (Washington: U.S. Government Printing Office, 1964).

Friedman, S., "The RAND Corporation and Our Policy Makers," *Atlantic Monthly* (September 1963), pp. 61–68.

Frye, William R., "Characteristics of Recent Arms-Control Proposals and Agreements," in D. G. Brennan (ed.), *Arms Control, Disarmament, and National Security* (New York: Braziller, 1963).

Galbraith, J. K., *American Capitalism* (Boston: Houghton Mifflin, 1956).

Galbraith, J. K., "Poverty among Nations," *Atlantic Monthly* (October 1962), pp. 47–53.

Galbraith, J. K., *The New Industrial State* (New York: Signet, 1967).

Galbraith, J. K., *How to Control the Military* (Garden City, N.Y.: Doubleday, 1969).

Gans, Herbert J., "Some Proposals for Government Policy in an Automating Society," *The Correspondent*, 30 (January-February 1964), pp. 74–82.

Government Information Plans and Policies (Parts I–V), Hearings before a Subcommittee on Government Operations, 88th Congress, 1st Session (Washington: U.S. Government Printing Office, 1963).

Green, Philip, "Alternative to Overkill: Dream and Reality," *Bulletin of the Atomic Scientists* (November 1963), pp. 23–26.

Hayakawa, S. I., "Formula for Peace: Listening," *N.Y. Times Magazine* (July 31, 1961).

Heilbroner, Robert, "How the Pentagon Rules Us," *New York Review of Books*, 15:2 (1970), pp. 5–6, 8.

Horowitz, David, *World Economic Disparities: The Haves and the Havenots* (Santa Barbara: Center for Study of Democratic Institutions, 1962).

Horowitz, I. L., *The War Game: Studies of the New Civilian Militarists* (New York: Ballantine, 1963).

Humphrey, Hubert H., "The Economic Impact of Arms-Control Agreements," *Congressional Record* (October 5, 1962), pp. 2139–2194.

Impact of Military Supply and Service Activities on the Economy, Report to the Joint Economic Committee, 88th Congress, 2nd Session (Washington: U.S. Government Printing Office, 1963).

Isard, Walter, and E. W. Schooler, "An Economic Analysis of Local and Regional Impacts of Reduction of Military Expenditures," *Papers, Vol. 1, 1964 Peace Research Society International*, Chicago Conference, 1963.

Janowitz, Morris, "Military Elites and the Study of War," *Journal of Conflict Resolution*, 1:1 (1957), pp. 9–18.

Janowitz, Morris, *The Professional Soldier* (Glencoe, Ill.: Free Press, 1960).

Keller, Suzanne, *Beyond the Ruling Class* (New York: Random House, 1963).

Knebel, Fletcher, and C. Bailey, *Seven Days in May* (New York: Harper, 1962).

Knoll, Erwin, and Judith McFadden (eds.), *American Militarism 1970* (New York: Viking, 1969).

Knorr, Klaus, "Warfare and Peacefare States and the Acts of Transition," *Journal of Conflict Resolution*, 7:4 (1963), pp. 754–762.

Lapp, Ralph E., *Kill and Overkill* (New York: Basic Books, 1962).

Lapp, Ralph E., *The Weapons Culture* (New York: Norton, 1968).

Larson, Arthur, *The International Rule of Law*, a report to the Committee on Research for Peace, Program of Research No. 3, Institute for International Order, 1961.

Lasswell, Harold, *Politics: Who Gets What, When & How* (New York: Meridian, 1958).

Lipset, Roger W., "Basic Education and Youth Socialization in the Armed Forces," *American Journal of Orthopsychiatry*, 38:5 (1968), pp. 869–876.

Long Island Sunday Press (February 23, 1964).

Lowi, Theodore J., "American Business, Public Policy, Case Studies, and Political Theory," *World Politics* (July 1964), pp. 676–715.

Lumer, Hyman, *War Economy and Crisis* (New York: International Publishers, 1954).

Lynd, Robert S., and Helen Merrill, *Middletown* (New York: Harcourt, 1959).

McDonagh, James J., and Steven M. Zimmerman, "A Program for Civilian Diversifications of the Airplane Industry," in *Convertibility of Space and Defense Resources to Civilian Needs*, Subcommittee on Employment and Manpower, U.S. Senate, 88th Congress (Washington: U.S. Government Printing Office, 1964).

McNamara, Robert S., "Remarks of the Secretary of Defense before the Economic Club of New York," Department of Defense Office of Public Affairs, Washington, November 18, 1963.

Mannheim, Karl, *Freedom, Power and Democratic Planning* (London: Routledge and Kegan Paul, 1956).

Meisel, James H., *The Fall of the Republic* (Ann Arbor: Univ. of Michigan Press, 1962).

Meisel, James H., *The Myth of the Ruling Class* (Ann Arbor: Univ. of Michigan Press, 1958).

Melman, Seymour (ed.), *A Strategy for American Security* (New York: Lee Offset Inc., 1963).

Melman, Seymour, *The Peace Race* (New York: Braziller, 1962).

Melman, Seymour, *Pentagon Capitalism* (New York: McGraw-Hill, 1970).

Merbaum, R., "RAND: Technocrats and Power," *New University Thought* (December-January, 1963–64), pp. 45–57.

Michael, Donald, *Cybernation: the Silent Conquest* (Santa Barbara: Center for the Study of Democratic Institutions, 1962).

Milbrath, L. W., *The Washington Lobbyists* (Chicago: Rand McNally, 1963).

Military Posture and Authorizing Appropriations for Aircraft, Missiles, and Naval Vessels, Hearings No. 36, 88th Congress, 2nd Session (Washington: U.S. Government Printing Office, 1964).

Military Procurement Authorization Fiscal Year 1962, Hearings before the Committee on Armed Services, U.S. Senate, 87th Congress, 1st Session (Washington: U.S. Government Printing Office, 1961).

Mills, C. Wright, *The Causes of World War III* (New York: Simon & Schuster, 1958).

Mills, C. Wright, *The Power Elite* (New York: Oxford Univ. Press, 1959).

Minnis, Jack, "The Care and Feeding of Power Structures," *New University Thought*, 5:1 (Summer 1964), pp. 73–79.

Mollenhoff, Clark R., *The Pentagon: Politics, Profits, and Plunder* (New York: Putnam, 1967).

Nossiter, Bernard, *The Mythmakers: An Essay on Power and Wealth* (Boston: Houghton Mifflin, 1964).

Osgood, Charles E., *An Alternative to War or Surrender* (Urbana: Univ. of Illinois Press, 1962).

Parsons, Talcott, *Structure and Process in Modern Societies* (Glencoe, Ill.: Free Press, 1959).

Parsons, Talcott, *The Social System* (Glencoe, Ill.: Free Press, 1951).

Paul, J., and J. Laulicht, "Leaders' and Voters' Attitudes on Defense and Disarmament, *In Your Opinion,* Vol. 1, Canadian Peace Research Institute, Clarkson, Ontario, 1963.

Peck, M. J., and F. M. Scherer, *The Weapons Acquisition Process* (Boston: Harvard Univ. Press, 1962).

Perlo, Victor, *Militarism and Industry* (New York: International Publishers, 1963).

Piel, Gerard, *Consumers of Abundance* (Santa Barbara: Center for the Study of Democratic Institutions, 1961).

Pilisuk, Marc, "Dominance of the Military," *Science* (January 18, 1963), pp. 247–248.

Pilisuk, Marc, "The Poor and the War on Poverty," *The Correspondent* (Summer 1965).

Pilisuk, Marc, "A Reply to Roger Little: Basic Education and Youth Socialization Anywhere Else," *American Journal of Orthopsychiatry,* 38:5 (1968), pp. 877–881.

Progressive, The, "The Power of the Pentagon," 33:6 (June 1969).

Pyramiding of Profits and Costs in the Missile Procurement Program (Parts 1, 2 and 3), Hearings, Committee on Government Operations, U.S. Senate, 87th Congress, 2nd Session (Washington: U.S. Government Printing Office, 1962).

Pyramiding of Profits and Costs in the Missile Procurement Program, Report No. 970, 88th Congress, 2nd Session (Washington: U.S. Government Printing Office, 1964).

Rapoport, Anatol, *Fights, Games, and Debates* (Ann Arbor: Univ. of Michigan Press, 1960).

Rapoport, Anatol, *Strategy and Conscience* (New York: Harper, 1964).

Raymond, Jack, *Power at the Pentagon* (New York: Harper, 1964).

Reagan, Michael, *The Managed Economy* (New York: Oxford, 1963).

Reiner, Thomas, "Spatial Criteria to Offset Military Cutbacks," paper presented at the University of Chicago Peace Research Conference, November 18, 1964.

"Report on the World Today," *The Atlantic* (September 1964), pp. 4–8.

Rogow, Arnold A., *James Forrestal* (New York: Macmillan, 1963).

Satellite Communications, 1964 (Part 1), Hearings, Committee on Government Operations, 88th Congress, 2nd Session (Washington: U.S. Government Printing Office, 1964).

Scherer, Frederick, *The Weapons Acquisition Process: Economic Incentives* (Cambridge, Mass.: Harvard Business School, 1964).

Shils, Edward, "Professor Mills on the Calling of Sociology," *World Politics,* 13:4 (1961).

Singer, J. David, "A Study of Foreign Policy Attitudes," *Journal of Conflict Resolution,* 8:4 (1964), pp. 424–485.

Singer, J. David, *Deterrence, Arms Control and Disarmament* (Columbus: Ohio State Univ. Press, 1962).

Singer, J. David (ed.), "Weapons Management in World Politics," *Journal of Conflict Resolution,* 7:3; and *Journal of Arms Control,* 1:4.

Stachey, John, *On the Prevention of War* (New York: St. Martin's Press, 1963).

Strauss, Lewis L., *Men and Decisions* (Garden City, N.Y.: Doubleday, 1962).

Sutton, Jefferson, *The Missile Lords* (New York: Dell, 1963).

Swomley, J. M., Jr., "The Growing Power of the Military," *The Progressive* (January 1959).

Swomley, J. M., Jr., *The Military Establishment* (Boston: Beacon, 1964).

Toward Full Employment: Proposals for a Comprehensive Employment and Manpower Policy in the U.S., a report of the Committee on Labor and Public Welfare, United States Senate (Washington: U.S. Government Printing Office, 1964).

Toward World Peace: A Summary of U.S. Disarmament Efforts Past and Present, U.S. Arms Control and Disarmament Agency Publication 10 (Washington: U.S. Government Printing Office, 1964).

Warner, William Lloyd, and J. D. Abegglen, *Big Business Leaders in America* (New York: Harper, 1955).

Warner, William Lloyd, P. P. Van Riper, N. H. Martin, and O. F. Collins, *The American Federal Executive* (New Haven: Yale Univ. Press, 1963).

Watson-Watt, Sir Robert, *Man's Means to His End* (London: Heinemann, 1962).

Weidenbaum, Murray L., "Arms and the American Economy: A Domestic Emergence Hypothesis," *American Economic Review* (1968).

Westin, Alan, "Anti-Communism and the Corporations," *Commentary* (December 1963), pp. 479–487.

Wise, David, and Thomas Ross, *The Invisible Government* (New York: Random House, 1964).

Wright, Quincy, William Evans, and Morton Deutsch (eds.), *Preventing World War III: Some Proposals* (New York: Simon & Schuster, 1962).

The Defense Sector:
An Evaluation of Its Economic
and Social Impact

ARTHUR F. BURNS

In his famous farewell address, President Eisenhower warned the nation to remain vigilant of what he called "the military-industrial complex." This warning needs to be remembered and pondered by thoughtful citizens. An age of nuclear weapons leaves no time for assembling the military and industrial forces needed to repel an aggressor. Once a nation is attacked, it can be practically destroyed in a matter of minutes. For this reason as well as because of the unhappy state of our relations with the Communist bloc, "normalcy" for us has come to include since 1950 a formidable military establishment in a state of constant readiness, if need be, for war. But "the conjunction of an immense military establishment and a large arms industry," as President Eisenhower has observed, "is new in the American experience. The total influence—economic, political, even spiritual—is felt in every city, every statehouse, every office of the Federal government." My purpose . . . is to consider with you some of the ways in which the emergence of a massive and permanent defense sector has already changed and is continuing to change our economic and social life.

Originally delivered as the Moskowitz Lecture, New York University, November, 1967. Published in *The Defense Sector and the American Economy*, by Jacob K. Javits, Charles J. Hitch, and Arthur F. Burns (New York: New York University Press, 1968), pp. 59–87. Reprinted by permission of the author. Arthur F. Burns, an economist, is chairman of the Federal Reserve Board.

I.

To begin with, the defense sector has revolutionized governmental finances in our generation. In fiscal year 1948, Federal expenditures came to $36 billion. In fiscal 1964, well before Vietnam became a significant financial burden, spending on national defense alone amounted to $54 billion, or half as much again as the total budget in 1948. In the current fiscal year, the defense budget may amount to about $80 billion, but this huge sum still does not indicate the full financial cost of defense activities. The Federal government expects to spend another $5 billion on international programs and also $5.25 billion on space research and technology. These activities, of course, are mainly pursued in the interests of our national security. Moreover, the Federal budget allows $10.5 billion for interest on the public debt and over $6.5 billion for veterans' benefits, the former being preponderantly and the latter entirely a legacy of past wars. Thus, defense-related expenditures will probably come this year to over $100 billion—a sum that represents more than $500 for every man, woman, and child of our population.

The large and rising cost of defense activities would have caused financial problems even if other costs of government had not changed. In fact, as we all know, the range of governmental activities has greatly increased. Since the end of World War II, the American people have come to expect their government to maintain economic conditions that are generally conducive to full employment. The Federal government has been also under increasing pressure to enlarge social services—that is to say, improve the nation's schools, help support universities, improve hospitals and medical facilities, facilitate home ownership, reduce urban slums, promote safer and faster air travel, raise social security and related welfare benefits, train manpower for the needs of industry, seek ways of reducing air and water pollution, and even concern itself with problems of traffic congestion and police protection. These expanding interests of the Federal government are a political response to the increasing urbanization of modern life, the new opportunities opened up by advances in technology, and the growing impatience for better living on the part of many citizens who have been left behind by the march of progress. Thus, at the very stage of history when demographic, technological, and political trends have been releasing powerful forces to raise the costs of government, the defense sector likewise became an increasing burden on the Treasury. The inevitable result has been a vast growth of Federal spending—from $36 billion in fiscal 1948 to $120 billion in 1964, and probably $175 billion, if not more, this fiscal year.

The upsurge of Federal spending on defense and on civilian activities has naturally resulted in much higher taxes. To be sure, we have recently become accustomed to deficits when the economy is booming as well as when the economy is depressed. The role of deficits in governmental finance, however, is commonly exaggerated. From mid-1946 to June 1967, the cumulative revenue of the Federal government covered all but 2 percent of its expenditures, so that Federal taxes have in fact grown just about as rapidly as expenditures. Our economy has also grown substantially during this period, but not enough to prevent taxes from siphoning off an increasing portion of the national income. In fiscal 1940, Federal revenues came to about 7 percent of the gross national product, in 1950 to 15.5 percent, in 1960 to 19 percent, last year to 20 percent. Meanwhile, state and local taxes have also moved up—indeed, they have grown even more rapidly during the past ten or twenty years than Federal taxes. According to the national income accounts, the combined revenue of all governmental units amounted in the past fiscal year to about 29 percent of the gross national product and 32 percent of the net national product; and even the higher figure may understate the tax burden, since it makes inadequate allowance for the capital used up in the process of producing goods and services.

This year, with the war in Vietnam escalating and social expenditures also rising, the Federal budget deficit may well exceed $20 billion unless steps are taken to raise taxes and curb expenditures. To reduce the enormous deficit now in sight, President Johnson has proposed a 10 percent surcharge on income taxes, but the Congress has thus far failed to adopt the proposal. Some members of Congress feel that the tax burden is already so heavy that it would be wiser to cut governmental expenditures than to raise taxes. Others would be willing to accept higher taxes provided substantial reductions in expenditures were simultaneously made. With financial markets disturbed and interest rates rising above last year's abnormally high level, a great debate is now raging both within and outside governmental circles about the relation of the Federal budget to economic activity, interest rates, and inflation. What is critically at issue in this debate is not whether Federal spending should be permitted to rise, but the size of the reduction—if any—in the projected scale of spending on nondefense programs. No matter how this issue is resolved, spending in the aggregate will still go up and—if history is any guide—taxes will follow; so that we now face the prospect of higher income taxes, higher social security taxes, and assorted increases in state and local taxes.

We also face the prospect of paying more for foodstuffs, clothing, automobiles, and whatever else we buy. The causes of inflation are complex, and it is not strictly true that an increase in spending on defense or on business equipment or on any other category is the sole cause of inflation. In principle, the government can always adjust its monetary and fiscal policies to economic conditions so as to keep the price level reasonably stable. If the government had foreseen how rapidly the cost of the Vietnam War would mount, and if it had taken promptly the restraining measures necessary to keep the aggregate demand for goods and services from outrunning the nation's capacity to produce them, the new round of inflation that we have experienced since 1964 could have been prevented. But if we blame the government for its lack of foresight or courage in this instance, we should also bear in mind that the theoretical ideal of price stability has rarely, if ever, been closely approximated under wartime conditions.

When demand presses hard on a nation's resources, as it generally does at a time of war, it becomes very difficult to adjust tax, credit, and expenditure policies on the scale needed to prevent advances in the price level. The doubling of wholesale prices between 1940 and 1950 was obviously linked to the enormous expansion of military spending during World War II. Since then, the trend of prices has continued upward at a much slower pace, and no single factor stands out so prominently among the causes of inflation. Indeed, prices have risen less in our country since 1950 than in most others, despite our exceptionally large military burden. It is nevertheless true that the greater part of the recent advance in both wholesale and consumer prices came in three spurts— between 1950 and 1952 when the Korean War was raging, between 1955 and 1957 when a fairly rapid increase of military contracts for newly developed weapon systems paralleled a booming trend of business investment in new plant and equipment, and since mid-1965 when our ground forces shifted to an active role in Vietnam. It appears, therefore, that the sudden surges within the defense sector have contributed to the inflationary trend which has been gradually eroding all savings accumulated in the form of bank deposits, life insurance, savings bonds, and other fixed-income assets, besides complicating life for everyone whose money income fails to respond to the rising cost of living.

The defense sector has also contributed to the deficit in our balance of payments. Since 1950 the receipts from our sale of goods, services, and securities to foreign countries have run considerably below the sums that we need to pay foreign countries. One reason for this persistent deficit is the large expenditure that is required, year in and year out, to maintain our military forces abroad. Foreign assistance programs have also been adding to the deficit, although their foreign exchange cost is now much smaller. Since the revenue derived from our foreign transactions has been insufficient to cover the required payments, our stocks of gold have shrunk from $24.5 billion at the beginning of 1950 to about $13 billion at present. Meanwhile, the dollar balances that are held here by foreigners have also grown, so that the United States finds itself in the position of a banker whose short-term liabilities are steadily rising while his reserves keep dwindling. In order to check the deterioration in our international financial position, the Department of Defense has lately been favoring domestic over foreign suppliers even at cost differentials of 50 percent. More disturbing still, the government has found it necessary to impose restrictions on the outflow of capital—an interference with private investment that is contrary to our national traditions. Even so, the deficit in the balance of payments has persisted, and —at least partly as a result of the war in Vietnam—it is larger this year than last. International confidence in the dollar, which is of such immense importance to America's political leadership as well as to our economy and that of the rest of the world, is still strong, but we can no longer count on it as we did ten or twenty years ago.

II.

I have been concerned thus far with the financial aspects of national defense—its impact on governmental expenditures, taxes, the price level, and the balance of payments. Financial transactions and the price system, however, are merely mechanisms for putting a nation's resources to work and for distributing what is produced among people and their government. The resources that we devote to national defense are not available for making consumer goods or for adding to the stock of industrial equipment or for public uses in the sphere of education, health, or urban redevelopment. To the extent that we allocate labor, materials, and capital to national defense, we cannot satisfy our desires for other things. The civilian goods and services that are currently foregone on account of expenditures on national defense are, therefore, the current real cost of the defense establishment.

This cost has become very large, as my observations on governmental finance have already suggested. Its magnitude can perhaps be grasped best by considering the amount of labor devoted to national defense. In fiscal 1965, the armed forces numbered close to 2.75 million. They were supported by over 900,000 civilian workers attached to the Department of Defense and by another 2.1 million civilians employed in private industry who worked, directly or indirectly, on military supplies. Thus the total employment on defense goods and services amounted to 5.75 million, or to 86 out of every 1,000 employed workers in the country. Two years later—that is, during the fiscal year which ended June, 1967 —the number was nearly 7.5 million, or 103 out of every 1,000 employed workers. The employment currently attributable to national security expenditures is still larger; for the figures that I have cited, besides not being fully up to date, take no account of the activities of the Atomic Energy Commission, the National Aeronautics and Space Administration, or other defense-related efforts.

A mere count of numbers, moreover, does not convey adequately the drain of the defense establishment on the nation's work force. Men differ in quality, and we need to take account of the fact that those involved in the defense effort are, on the average, superior from an economic viewpoint to workers engaged in civilian production. Military technology and operations have become very sophisticated in our times. The armed forces now have a highly skilled core and are very selective in accepting men for service. Indeed, the proportion of personnel who completed high school is much larger in the armed forces than in the comparable age group of the civilian population, while the proportion of college graduates is not materially lower. Training and skill count even more heavily among the civilians involved in defense activities. Last year, professional workers accounted for nearly 16 percent and skilled blue-collar workers for 21 percent of the civilians employed on defense work, in contrast to about 13 percent for each of these groups in the total working population. One out of every five of the nation's electrical and mechanical engineers in civilian jobs, two out of every five airplane mechanics, two out of every five physicists outside of teaching, and three out of every five aeronautical engineers were employed on defense goods during the past year. And even these figures understate the skill dimension of defense employment, for they again leave out of account the highly technical activities originating in the Atomic Energy Commission and the Space Administration.

The heavy emphasis on skill and brainpower in defense employment reflects, of course, the explosion of military technology to which modern science has been contributing so much of its finest energy. Since the Korean War, defense contractors have been devoting themselves not only to the production of extremely complex weapons but also to developing entirely new weapon systems that no one as yet knew how to produce. Much of the defense sector of our economy has come to consist, therefore, of research and development work. The president's budget for this fiscal year, for example, allots about $16 billion to research and development, of which $9 billion is to be devoted to defense and another $5 billion to space activities. Since 1960 defense and space programs have consistently accounted for over 80 percent of the rapidly increasing Federal funds devoted to research and development. More important still, they have amounted to about 54 percent of the expenditure on research and development carried out in the entire nation—that is, by the Federal government, industry, universities and colleges, research centers affiliated with universities, and other nonprofit institutions. During the 1950s the proportion of the nation's research and development effort devoted to defense-related activities was only a little lower.

By diverting to its interest so much manpower, especially scientific and engineering skills, the defense establishment has left its mark on both the structure and the functioning of our economy. The effects are all around us. Some defense-oriented industries—notably, the aerospace group, electronics, and communications—have become a major factor in the economy, and their development has favored many communities— for example, Los Angeles, San Diego, Seattle, Baltimore. Some large firms have acquired marvelous technological competence from their work on defense or space contracts and this rather than any immediate profit has commonly been their chief reason for wanting the contracts in the first place. Not a few of the scientists and engineers who received their training in the more sophisticated enterprises have moved into traditional lines of activity, bringing something of the spirit of research and innovation with them. Many of the men released by the armed forces have been able to put the technical skills acquired during their military service to effective use in civilian jobs. Nondefense activities have shared in the increased supply of engineers, scientists, and technicians that has been stimulated by the defense-related demand. And not a few of the processes or products developed for the military have found application in civilian life—for example, jet transports, advanced computers, radar, miniaturized components, and nuclear power plants.

But if the defense sector has stimulated economic development in some directions, it has retarded growth in others. Many civilian-oriented laboratories of business firms have found it difficult to match the salaries or the equipment that subsidized defense firms offer to scientists and engineers. Research and development work in behalf of new products and processes for the civilian economy has therefore been handicapped. Small firms have derived little benefit from military or space contracts. The draft has added to the labor turnover of all businesses, large and small. The lack of opportunity in the defense sector for poorly educated and unskilled workers has not helped the rural Negroes who have flocked into the cities in recent years in search for jobs and a better life. More-over, a new class of business executives has arisen, consisting of men whose understanding of marketing and cost controls is often deficient, but who know how to negotiate effectively with government officials han-dling military or scientific problems. While knowing the right people or having friends in the right places can sometimes advance the interests of an enterprise better than plain business ability, the nation's economic efficiency is not likely to reap a corresponding advantage.

In any event, the economic growth of a nation is a blind concept unless we consider what is produced as well as the rate of growth of what happens to be produced. During the decade from 1957 to 1966, our nation spent approximately $520 billion on defense and space programs. This sum is almost two-and-one-half times as large as the entire amount spent on elementary and secondary education, both public and private. It is two-and-three-quarter times as large as the amount spent on the construction of new housing units. It exceeds by over a fourth the expenditure on new plant and equipment by the entire business community—manufacturing firms, mining concerns, transportation en-terprises, public utilities, and all other businesses. To be sure, an extra billion dollars' worth of bombs or missiles will increase current produc-tion just as much as an extra billion of new equipment for making civilian goods. Bombs or missiles, however, add nothing to the nation's capacity to produce, while new equipment serves to augment production in the future. The real cost of the defense sector consists, therefore, not only of the civilian goods and services that are currently forgone on its account; it includes also an element of growth that could have been achieved through larger investment in human or business capital. But even if we assumed that the conflicting influences of the defense sector on economic growth canceled out, its real cost is still enormous.

Unhappily, we live in dangerous times which make large national security expenditures practically unavoidable. Nevertheless, there are always some options in a nation's foreign and military policy, and we therefore must be alert to the opportunities that our military establish-ment forces us to forgo. For example, if the resources devoted to military and space activities during the past decade had been put instead to civilian uses, we could surely have eliminated urban slums, besides add-ing liberally to private investment in new plant and equipment as well as to both public and private investment in human capital.

III.

It follows from our analysis that the military-industrial complex, of which President Eisenhower spoke so perceptively in his farewell address, has not only been enlarging the scale of governmental operations and thereby complicating financial problems. By changing the thrust of economic activity and by making the economy more dependent on government, it has also been affecting profoundly the character of our society. Nor have the social effects been confined to the kinds of goods that we produce. Hopefulness about the future, optimism about success of new undertakings, impatience to complete satisfactorily whatever is begun—these psychological qualities have been peculiarly American characteristics, and they account in far greater degree than we may realize for the remarkable achievements of our economic system and the vigor of our political democracy. These qualities are deep-rooted in American experience and they continue to sustain us. Nevertheless, the development and spread of thermonuclear weapons, the frustrations of the cold war, and now the brutal struggle in Vietnam have left us, despite our awesome military power, more anxious about our national security than our fathers or grandfathers ever were.

Adults whose habits were formed in an earlier generation may put the dangers of nuclear catastrophe out of mind by losing themselves in their work or by seeking solace in religion. That is more difficult for our children who increasingly wonder what kind of world they have inherited by our doings. There can be little doubt that the lively competition among the great powers in devising instruments of terror is one of the underlying causes of the restlessness of modern youth.

Moreover, young men of military age are bearing a disproportionately large part of the defense burden. That is unavoidable at a time of war, but our generation has institutionalized compulsory military service even when the nation is at peace. It is undoubtedly true that many young men derive deep satisfaction from helping to protect their country by serving as soldiers, sailors, or aviators. Not only that, many have also found useful careers in the armed forces, or have benefited in their civilian jobs from the skills and discipline acquired during military service, or have gained a larger understanding of life by associating with men of widely different backgrounds or by being stationed abroad for a time. But just as these benefits deserve recognition, so too does the fact that the draft has by and large proved to be a seriously upsetting factor in the lives of young people. Not knowing when they would be called up for military service or whether they would be accepted, many have found themselves marking time. Those who are accepted have often had to interrupt their schooling or careers, perhaps alter plans with regard to marriage, and in any event be content with substantially lower pay than they could earn as a rule in civilian work. Moreover, the administration of the draft over the years, particularly the handling of student deferments, has raised troublesome moral questions in the minds of young people—and, for that matter, in the minds of older citizens as well.

The emergence of our country as a great military power, having world-wide political responsibilities, has also affected our educational system. Greater emphasis on science, mathematics, and modern languages in secondary schools and colleges; new area institutes and schools of international affairs in the universities; advanced courses in the esoteric languages and customs of the Far East and Africa—these educational developments not only reflect the widening scientific and geographic interests of modern business; they are also a response to urgent requirements of national security. But it is in the area of research, rather than teaching, where the impact of the defense establishment on our universities has been particularly felt. Colleges, universities, and research centers associated with universities spent in the aggregate $460 million on the performance of research and development in 1953, with something over half of this sum financed by the Federal government. Last year, the sum so spent was six-and-one-half times as large, and the federally financed portion rose to 70 percent. Clearly, Federal funds are mainly responsible for the extraordinary growth of research activities in universities, and the chief—although by no means the sole—reason for this governmental involvement is the intensive search for new knowledge on the part of defense-related agencies. During 1963–1966, the Department of Defense, the Atomic Energy Commission, and the Space Administration together accounted for five-eighths of the dollar value of Federal grants for research and development to institutions of higher learning, and their proportion in immediately preceding years was even larger.

The huge influx of governmental research funds has served to enrich the intellectual life of numerous colleges and universities, especially in the larger institutions where the grants have been mainly concentrated. By virtue of research grants, professors have better equipment to work with and more technical assistance than they had in former times. They also travel more, keep in closer contact with their counterparts in other universities, and mingle more freely with government officials, business executives, and scientists working for private industry. The gulf that previously separated a university from the larger interests of the community and the nation has therefore narrowed very significantly.

However, governmental research grants have created problems for universities as well as new opportunities for useful service. The greater interest of a faculty in research is not infrequently accompanied by lesser devotion to teaching. No little part of the time set aside for research may in practice be consumed by travel and conferences of slight scientific value. However welcome grants from military and space agencies may be, their concentration on the physical and engineering sciences makes it more difficult for a university to maintain the balance among various branches of learning that is so essential to the intellectual and moral improvement of man. Some military contracts involve classified research, and the secrecy which attends such work introduces an entirely foreign note in institutions that have traditionally taken a strong pride in completely free and uninhibited communication among scholars. Not less serious is the tendency, which appears to be growing among university scholars, to forsake the research to which they are drawn by intellectual curiosity in favor of projects that have been designed by, or contrived to suit the tastes of, government officials or others who take care of the financing. All universities and many of our colleges are struggling with this and other problems that the defense sector has created or accentuated.

The danger of diminished independence is not confined to research activities. If college or university presidents no longer speak out as vigorously on national issues as they did a generation or two ago, one major reason is that the institutions over whose destiny they preside have become heavily dependent on Federal contracts and subsidies. Even professors who are benefiting from Federal research grants or consulting relationships, or who expect to be able to do so in the future, have been learning the occasional value of studied reticence. And if discretion is tempering the spirit of forthright questioning and criticism in our universities, its power is all the stronger in the business world. It is hardly in the interest of businessmen to criticize their customers publicly, and by far the largest customer of the business world is clearly the Federal government itself. Some firms sell all and many sell a good part of what they produce to the Federal government, and there are always others that hope to be in a position to do likewise in the future.

To be sure, the great majority of business executives, even those who manage very large enterprises, prefer commercial markets to governmental business; but they have become so sensitive nowadays to the regulatory powers of government that they rarely articulate their thoughts on national issues in public. Trade union leaders are typically more candid and outspoken on governmental issues than business executives; but they too have become dependent in varying degrees on the goodwill of government officials and therefore often deem tact or reticence the better part of wisdom. Not only that, but it is no longer unusual for the government in power, whether the administration be in Democratic or Republican hands, to suggest to prominent businessmen, trade union leaders, attorneys, journalists, or university professors that they support publicly this or that administration proposal. And men of public distinction at times comply regardless of their beliefs, perhaps because they are flattered by the attention accorded them, or because they vaguely expect some advantage from going along, or simply because they feel that they dare not do otherwise. Thus the gigantic size to which the Federal government has grown, for which the defense sector bears a heavy but by no means exclusive responsibility, has been tending to erode perceptibly, although not yet alarmingly as the open discussion of the war in Vietnam indicates, the spirit of rational and constructive dissent without which a democracy cannot flourish.

The huge size of military budgets and incomplete disclosure concerning their management carry with them also the danger of political abuse. Since money spent in the interest of national security necessarily has economic effects, the government in power may sometimes be tempted to ease domestic problems by adjusting the scale or direction of military spending. For example, raw materials may be stockpiled beyond the minimum military target, or the target itself may be revised upward, in order to grant some relief to a depressed industry. Or at a time of general economic slack, the government may begin to look upon military spending as if it were a public works program. Worse still, considerations of political advantage may play a role in deciding whether contracts are placed in one area rather than another, or with this firm instead of that. Such practices confuse military officers, lead to waste, and might even exacerbate international relations. Nevertheless, they are not entirely unknown to history, including our own. Fortunately, our government officials have generally been reluctant to tamper with something so fundamental to the nation as its defense establishment; and even on the rare occasions when they have strayed from virtue, the sluggishness of a governmental bureaucracy in carrying out any plan has kept down the scale of mischief. But if politics is ever effectively computerized, as some students believe it will be, we may have less protection against political abuse within the defense sector in the future.

Any enlargement of the economic power of government, whether brought about by military expenditures or through other causes, can eventually result in some infringement of liberty. However, because of the sense of urgency in troubled times, the requirements of national security may lead more directly to restriction of freedom. Necessary though the draft may be, it still constitutes compulsion of the individual by the state. Necessary though security clearances may be, they still constitute an invasion of privacy. Necessary though passport regulations may be, they still restrict the freedom of individuals to travel where they choose. Fortunately, the vitality of our democracy has thus far proved sufficient to limit restrictions of freedoms such as these. Not only that, it has enabled us to put an end to the nightmare of McCarthyism, to suppress the interest of the Central Intelligence Agency in our colleges and universities, and even to fight the war in Vietnam without imposing price and wage controls. We cannot take it for granted, however, that our formidable defense establishment will not give rise to more serious dangers to our liberties and the democratic process in the future.

IV.

Throughout the ages, philosophers and religious teachers have lamented the horrors of war and searched for the keys to peace. Yet their noblest thought has been frustrated by the course of human events. Our country has been more fortunate than most, but we have had our share of the destruction of life and property that is the universal coin of warfare. Every American of age fifty or over has lived through two world wars, the Korean War, and now the smaller but still very costly and protracted struggle in Vietnam. When this war ends, military expenditures will probably decline for a while, as they have in fact after every war in our history. We cannot look forward, however, to demobilization on anything like the scale experienced after World War I or World War II, when the military budget was reduced by about 90 percent within three years.

The reason for the difference, of course, is that the cold war is still with us, just as it was when the Korean hostilities ended. After the cessation of that conflict, the defense budget was reduced merely by a fifth. If the cost of the Vietnam War remains at approximately the current rate, it is doubtful whether a ceasefire will be followed by a reduction of even the Korean magnitude. A return to the defense budget of fiscal 1964 or 1965 would indeed involve a cut of roughly 35 percent from this year's expenditure; but in the absence of a dramatic change in our international relations, this is quite unlikely. In the first place, prices are higher at present than they were in 1964 or 1965, and they will probably be higher still when the war phases out. In the second place, it may well be necessary for us to keep many more troops in Vietnam after a ceasefire than was the case in Korea and also to become more heavily involved in the task of reconstruction. In the third place, while stocks of military equipment were built up during the Korean War, they have been seriously depleted—particularly for the Reserve and National

Guard units—by Vietnam. They will need to be rebuilt when hostilities come to an end, and this demand will be reinforced by the deferred procurement of newer models to replace equipment now in inventory.

Nevertheless, a sizable reduction of military spending will take place in the year or two after the ceasefire, and we will have the opportunity to concentrate more of our resources on the arts of peace. In the past, the American economy has demonstrated a remarkable ability to adjust speedily to cutbacks in military spending, and we can be confident of doing so again. After World War I the conversion from war to peace was carried out with only a mild and brief setback in total economic activity. The like happened after World War II, despite the fact that more than two-fifths of our nation's resources were devoted to military uses at the peak of the war. Between 1945 and 1946, spending on the manufacture of defense goods dropped drastically and the number of men in the armed forces declined from 11.5 million to 3.5 million. Nevertheless, the unemployment rate remained below 4 percent. The termination of the Korean War was followed by a recession but the return of peace was not its sole cause. In any event, unemployment during this recession was less serious at its worst than during the recession which came just before or just after it. With the experience that our country has gained during the past two decades in coping with economic fluctuations, with both the Executive and the Congress obviously eager to prevent unemployment, and with plans for dealing with post-Vietnam problems already beginning to take shape, there should not be much difficulty in adjusting Federal tax, expenditure, and credit policies so as to maintain aggregate monetary demand at the level needed to assure reasonably full employment when hostilities cease. Some sizable adjustments will still need to be made by numerous communities and industries; but even they should prove manageable since the military cutbacks are likely to be largely concentrated on items produced by business firms that are closely oriented to our diversified and resilient civilian markets.

The highly specialized aerospace, electronics, and communications industries will probably not bear much of the burden of post-Vietnam cutbacks. Indeed, once the curve of military spending turns upward again, as it well may two or three years after the ceasefire, these are the very industries that are likely to benefit most from the dynamism of modern technology. To maintain a sufficient strategic superiority to deter any aggressor, we have been devoting vast sums to research and development, as I have already noted. The fantastic new weapons and weapon systems devised by our scientists and engineers soon render obsolete some of the existing devices, which themselves were new and revolutionary only a short time ago. But until the new devices are ready, those that were only recently new cannot be abandoned and may even need to be augmented. Meanwhile, strategic concepts may shift, as they did during the sixties from reliance on massive nuclear deterrents to developing a capability for limited warfare and counterinsurgency operations. One way or another, therefore, costs tend to multiply all around. The Soviet Union, of course, will not stand still while our military prowess increases. On the contrary, it is striving through a remarkably enterprising and inventive military-industrial complex of its own to establish military parity, if not actual supremacy. For example, we have recently learned of the deployment of an antiballistic missile system around Moscow and Leningrad, of a novel ship-to-ship missile of Russian origin fired in the Mediterranean, and of the apparent development of an orbital bomb capability by the Soviet Union. Communist China has also been developing, and with greater speed than was generally anticipated, the ability to make and deliver sophisticated weapons. In turn, our military establishment, besides innovating vigorously on its own, keeps devising countermeasures to what the Russians or Chinese have or may have in hand. Both its reaction and its fresh challenge to potential aggressors can be expected to become stronger once Vietnam no longer requires top priority.

As we look beyond the cessation of hostilities in Vietnam, we therefore need to recognize that the scale of defense expenditures has, to a significant degree, become a self-reinforcing process. Its momentum derives not only from the energy of military planners, contractors, scientists, and engineers. To some degree it is abetted also by the practical interests and anxieties of ordinary citizens. Any announcement that a particular defense installation will be shut down, or that a particular defense contract will be phased out, naturally causes concern among men and women who, however much they abhor war and its trappings, have become dependent for their livelihood on the activity whose continuance is threatened. With a large part of our economy devoted to defense activities, the military-industrial complex has thus acquired a constituency including factory workers, clerks, secretaries, even grocers and barbers. Local politicians and community leaders may not find it easy to plead for the extension of activities that no longer serve a military purpose. Many, nevertheless, manage to overcome such scruples. Indeed, candidates for the Congress have been known to claim that they are uniquely qualified to ward off military closings or even to bring new contracts to their districts, and their oratory has not gone unrewarded by the electorate. The vested interest that numerous communities have acquired in defense activities may therefore continue to run up costs on top of the rising budgets generated by the momentum of competing military technologies.

If this analysis is at all realistic, the military-industrial complex will remain a formidable factor in our economic and social life in the calculable future. It will continue to command a large, possibly even an increasing, part of our resources. It will continue to strain Federal finances. It will continue to test the vigor of our economy and the vitality of our democratic institutions. It will continue to confuse understanding by suggesting to many foreign citizens, as it sometimes does even to our own, that our national prosperity is based on huge military spending, when in fact we could be much more prosperous without it. For all these reasons, while we need to recognize the high and honorable national purpose of our military-industrial complex, we also need to remain continually vigilant of its activities and seek to protect ourselves against its possible abuses, just as we long ago learned to guard the public interest against business monopolies and as we are beginning to protect ourselves against labor monopolies.

V.

The scale and activities of our defense sector are now being subjected to a searching public discussion. Two major schools of political thought have become locked in a contest for the mind and soul of America. One school draws much of its strength from the revolution of military technology, the other from the revolution of rising expectations. One school tends to regard communism as a centrally directed conspiracy that threatens our survival as a free people. The other school believes that communism is breaking up into independent national movements, and sees the main threat to free institutions in the deterioration of our cities and the sickness of our society. One school seeks overwhelming military power to deter fresh communist adventures, and is willing to risk war in order to prevent the geographic expansion of communism. The other school seeks wider social justice and better economic conditions for Negroes and others who have not participated fully in the advance of prosperity, and holds that the force of moral example can contribute more to our national security than additional bombs or missiles.

Both schools have focused attention on the Federal budget and neither has been satisfied by the treatment accorded its claims. From 1955 to 1965, Federal spending on nondefense activities increased faster than spending on defense. Since then, defense expenditures have gone up more rapidly, though not much more rapidly. Looking to the future, professional economists never tire of pointing out that our growing economy will make it possible to have more butter and, if they are needed, also more guns, even as we have been managing to do while the war in Vietnam is being waged. Their reassurance, however, does not satisfy those who feel that our national security requires not just more guns, but many more guns, and that we therefore need to give up some of our butter. Nor does it satisfy those who feel that we need not just more butter, but much more butter, and that our statistics of the gross national product are misleading us by their failure to allow for the pollution of our water, the poisons in our air, the noise of our streets, the rats in our slums, the rioting in our cities, and the destruction of life on our highways. Debate along these lines has reached a high pitch of intensity and even bitterness as the war in Vietnam has dragged out. It has become a divisive force, and it has brought anguish to our people. Its effect on the conduct of the war, however, is likely to count for less than its effect on the general direction of our foreign and military policy in the future.

For the debate is demonstrating to thoughtful citizens that our national security depends not only on awesome military forces. It depends also on the strength of our economic system, on the wholesomeness of our social and political life, and particularly on how well governmental objectives express the national will and purpose. As this lesson sinks in, we will want to try far harder than we ever have, both in our personal capacity and through our government, to bring the armaments race under decent control. And if the cracks of freedom within the communist system of tyranny widen, as they well may in coming decades, we can count on being joined in this quest by the people of the Soviet Union and eventually by the people of mainland China as well. That, at any rate, is the only real basis for hope of saving ourselves and the entire human family from catastrophe.

Controlling the Military

JOHN KENNETH GALBRAITH

The importance of military spending in the economy—half the Federal budget, about one-tenth of the total economic product, I need not stress. Though much attention is focused upon it, this bloodless economic side is not, I venture to think, the important feature. The important feature is the peculiar constitutional and bureaucratic arrangements which govern this economic activity.

In our ordinary economic arrangements we think of the individual as instructing the market by his purchases, the market, in turn, instructing the producing firm. Thus economic life is controlled. This the textbooks celebrate. And where public expenditures are concerned, the young are still taught that the legislature reflects the will of the citizen to the Executive. The Executive, in turn, effects that will.

I have argued that with industrial development—with advanced technology, high organization, large and rigid commitments of capital—power *tends* to pass the producing organization—to the modern large corporation. Not the consumer but General Motors tends to be the source of the original decision on the modern automobile. If the consumer is reluctant he is persuaded—to a point at least.

This part of my case has not escaped argument. Dissent raises its head

Testimony before the Subcommittee on Economy in Government Joint Economic Committee of the U.S. Congress, June 3, 1969. Reprinted by permission of the author. John Kenneth Galbraith, formerly Ambassador to India and an advisor to President Kennedy, is professor of economics at Harvard.

everywhere these days. But where military goods are concerned one encounters little or no argument. Here, it is agreed, the historic economic and constitutional sequence *is* reversed. The citizen does not instruct the legislature and the legislature the Pentagon and its associated industries. No one wants to be that naive. Vanity becomes the ally of truth. It is agreed that the services and the weapons manufacturers decide what they want or need. They then instruct the Congress. The Congress, led by the military bureaucrats and sycophants among its members, hastens to comply. The citizen plays no role except to pay the bill. As I say, these matters are not subject to serious dispute, those with a special capacity to believe in fairy tales apart.

The power that has brought this remarkable reversal—has assumed this authority—has, of course, been well identified. It is the military services acting individually or in association through the Department of Defense and the large military contractors. The latter, an important point, are few in number and highly specialized in the service to the military. In 1968, a hundred large firms had more than two-thirds (67.4 percent) of all defense business. Of these, General Dynamics and Lockheed had more than the smallest fifty. A dozen firms specializing more or less completely on military business—McDonnell Douglas, General Dynamics, Lockheed, United Aircraft—together with General Electric and A.T.&T. had a third of all business. For most business firms defense business is inconsequential except as it affects prices, labor and material supply—and taxes. The common belief that all business benefits from weapons orders is quite wrong. For a few it is a rewarding source of business. The great multitude of business firms pay. The regional concentration, I might add, is equally high; in 1967 a third of all contracts went to California, New York, and Texas. Ten states received two-thirds. And no one should be misled by the argument that this picture is substantially altered by the distribution of subcontracts.

One must not think of the military power—the association of the military and the defense firms—in conspiratorial terms. It reflects an intimate but largely open association based on a solid community of bureaucratic and pecuniary interest. The services seek the weapons; the suppliers find it profitable to supply them. The factors which accord plenary power of decision to the military and the defense plants, and which exclude effective interference by the Congress and the public, are quite commonplace. Nothing devious or wicked is involved. The following are the factors which sustain the military power.

First: There is the use of fear. This, of course, is most important. Anything which relates to war, and equally to nuclear weapons and nuclear conflict, touches a deeply sensitive public nerve. This is easily played on. The technique is to say, in effect, "Give us what we ask, do as we propose, or you will be in mortal danger of nuclear annihilation." In this respect one must pause to pay tribute to Secretary of Defense Laird. He has shown himself, on this matter, to have a very high learning skill.

Second: There is the monopoly, or near monopoly, of technical and intelligence information by the services, their suppliers, and the intelligence community. This monopoly, in turn, is protected by classification. This allows the military power to exclude the lay critic, including the legislator, as uninformed. But even the best scientist can be excluded on the grounds that he is not fully informed on the latest secret technology—or does not have the latest knowledge on what the Soviets or the Chinese are up to. Here too the new administration has been very apt. If Secretary Laird deserves a special word of commendation on the way he has learned to use fear, Under Secretary Packard must be congratulated on the speed with which he has learned to discount criticism as inadequately informed of the latest secrets.

Third: There is the role of the single-firm supplier and the negotiated contract. These are largely inevitable with high technology. One cannot let out the MIRV to competitive bidding in the manner of mules and muskets. In fiscal 1968, as the work of this committee has revealed, 60 percent of defense contracts were with firms that were the sole source of supply. Most of the remainder were awarded by negotiated bidding. Competitive bidding—11.5 percent of the total—was nearly negligible. With single-firm supply, and in lesser degree with negotiated supply, opposition of interest between buyer and seller disappears. The buyer is as interested in the survival and well-being of the seller as is the seller himself. No one will enter this Elysium to cut prices, offer better work, earlier deliveries or cry favoritism. That is because there is no other seller. The situation, if I may be permitted the word, is cozy.

Fourth: There is the fiction that the specialized arms contractor is separate from the services. The one is in the public sector. The other is private enterprise. As Professor Murray Weidenbaum (the notable authority on these matters), as well as others, have pointed out, the dividing line between the Services and their specialized suppliers exists mostly in the imagination. Where a corporation does all (or nearly all) of its business with the Department of Defense; uses much plant owned by the government; gets its working capital in the form of progress payments from the government; does not need to worry about competitors for it is the sole source of supply; accepts extensive guidance from the Pentagon on its management; is subject to detailed rules as to its accounting; and is extensively staffed by former service personnel, only the remarkable flexibility of the English language allows us to call it a private enterprise. Yet this is not an exceptional case, but a common one. General Dynamics, Lockheed, North American-Rockwell and such are public extensions of the bureaucracy. Yet the myth that they are private allows a good deal of freedom in pressing the case for weapons, encouraging unions and politicians to do so, supporting organizations as the Air Force Association which do so, allowing executives to do so, and otherwise protecting the military power. We have an amiable arrangement by which the defense firms, though part of the public bureaucracy, are largely exempt from its political and other constraints.

Fifth: This is a more subtle point. For a long period during the fifties and sixties during which the military power was consolidating its position, military expenditures had a highly functional role in the economy. They sustained employment; they also supported, as no other expenditures do, a high technical dynamic. And there was no wholly satisfactory substitute. More specifically, a high federal budget, supported by the corporate and progressive personal income tax, both of which increased more than proportionally with increasing income and reduced themselves more than proportionally if income faltered, built a high element of stability into the system. And the scientific and technical character of this outlay encouraged the expansion of the educational and research plant and employed its graduates. It was long a commonplace of Keynesian economics that civilian spending, similarly supported by a progressive tax system, would serve just as well as military spending. This argument which, alas, I have used myself on occasion was, I am now persuaded, wrong—an exercise in apologetics. Civilian spending does not evoke the same support on a large scale. (Even in these enlightened days I am told that Representative Rivers prefers naval ships to the Job Corps.) And although it is now hard to remember, the civilian pressures on the federal budget until recent times were not extreme. Taxes were reduced in 1964 because the pressures to spend were not sufficient to offset tax collections at a high level of output—to neutralize the so-called fiscal drag. And civilian welfare spending does not support the same range of scientific and technical activities, or the related institutions, as does military spending. On a wide range of matters— electronics, air transport, computer systems, atomic energy—military appropriations paid for development costs too great or too risky to be undertaken by private firms. They served as a kind of honorary non-socialism.

Sixth and finally: There is the capacity—a notable phenomenon of our time—for organization, bureaucracy, to create its own truth—the truth that serves its purpose. The most remarkable example in recent times, of course, has been Vietnam. The achievements of bureaucratic truth here have been breathtaking. An essentially civilian conflict between the Vietnamese has been converted into an international conflict with a rich ideological portent for all mankind. South Vietnamese dictators of flagrantly repressive instincts have been converted into incipient Jeffersonians holding aloft the banners of an Asian democracy. Wholesale larceny in Saigon has become an indispensable aspect of free institutions. One of the world's most desultory and impermanent armies —with desertion rates running around 100,000 a year—was made, always potentially, into a paragon of martial vigor. Airplanes episodically bombing open acreage or dense jungle became an impenetrable barrier to men walking along the ground. An infinity of reverses, losses and defeats became victories deeply in disguise. There was nothing, or not much, that was cynical in this effort. For, for those who accept bureaucratic truth, it is the unbelievers who look confused, perverse, and very wrong. Throughout the course of the war there was bitter anger in Saigon and here in Washington over the inability of numerous people— journalists, professors, and others—to see military operations, the Saigon government, the pacification program, the South Vietnam army in the same rosy light as did the bureaucracy. Why couldn't all sensible people be the indignant instruments of the official belief—like Joe Alsop? (If I may pay tribute to the Edward Gibbon of the Vietcong.)

An equally spectacular set of bureaucratic truths has been created to serve the military power—and its weapons procurement. There is the military doctrine that whatever the dangers of a continued weapons race with the Soviet Union, these are less than any agreement that offers any perceptible opening for violation. Since no agreement can be watertight this largely protects the weapons industry from any effort at control. There is the belief that the conflict with communism is man's ultimate battle. Accordingly, no one would hesitate to destroy all life if communism seems seriously a threat. This belief allows acceptance of the arms race and the production of the requisite weapons no matter how dangerous. The present ideological differences between industrial systems will almost certainly look very different and possibly rather trivial from a perspective of fifty or a hundred years hence if we survive. Such thoughts are eccentric. There is also the belief that national interest is total, that of man inconsequential. So even the prospect of total death and destruction does not deter us from developing new weapons systems if some thread of national interest can be identified in the outcome. We can accept 75 million casualties if it forces the opposition to accept 150 million. We can agree with Senator Richard Russell that, if only one man and one woman are to be left on earth, they should be

Americans. (Not from any particular part of the country, just Americans.) We can make it part of the case for the Manned Orbiting Laboratory (MOL) that it would maintain the American position up in space in the event of total devastation from Maine to California. Such is the power of bureaucratic truth that these things are widely accepted. And being accepted they sustain the military power.

What now should be our response? How do we get the power under control?

Our response must be in relation to the sources of power. Again for purposes of compressing this discussion, let me list specific points:

1. Everyone must know that fear is deployed as a weapon. So we must resist it. I am not a supporter of unilateral disarmament. I assume that the Soviets also have their military power sustained by its bureaucratic beliefs. But we must look at the problem calmly. We must never again be stampeded into blind voting for military budgets. These, as a practical matter, are as likely to serve the bureaucratic goals of the military power and the pecuniary goals of the contractors as they do the balance of terror with the Soviets. And we must ascertain which.

2. That part of the military budget that serves the balance of terror can be reduced only with negotiations with the Soviets. As Charles Schultze and others have pointed out, however, this is a relatively small part of the military budget. The rest serves the goals of the military power and the interests of the suppliers. This can be curtailed. But it can only be curtailed if there is a vigorous reassertion of congressional power. Obviously this will not happen if sycophants of the military remain the final word on military appropriations. The Congress has the choice of serving the people in accordance with constitutional design or serving Senator Russell and Representative Rivers in accordance with past habit.

3. Informed technical and scientific judgment must be brought to bear on the foregoing questions. This means that the Congress must equip itself with the very best of independent scientific judgment. And the men so mobilized must not be denied access to scientific and intelligence information. I believe that on military matters there should be a panel of scientists, a Military Audit Commission, responsible only to the Congress—and not necessarily including Edward Teller—to be a source of continuing and informed advice on military needs—and equally on military non-needs.

4. We must, as grown-up people, abandon now the myth that the big defense contractors are something separate from the public bureaucracy. They must be recognized for what they are—a part of the public

establishment. Perhaps one day soon a further step should be taken. Perhaps any firm which, over a five-year period, has done more than 75 percent of its business with the Defense Department, should be made a full public corporation with all stock in public hands. No one will make the case that this is an assault on private enterprise. These firms are private only in the imagination. The action would ensure that such firms are held to strict standards of public responsibility in their political and other activities and expenditures. It would exclude the kind of conspiracy uncovered in the Lockheed case. It would help prevent private enrichment at public expense. In light of the recent performance of the big defense contractors, no one would wish to argue that it would detract from efficiency. And the 75 percent rule would encourage firms that wish to avoid nationalization to diversify into civilian production. Needless to say, the 75 percent rule should be applicable to the defense units of the conglomerates. Perhaps to press this reform now would direct energies from more needed tasks. Let us, however, put it on the agenda.

5. Finally, it must be recognized that the big defense budgets of the fifties were a unique response to the conditions of that time. Then there were the deep fears generated by the cold war, the seeming unity of the communist world, and, at least in comparison with present circumstances, the seeming lack of urgency of domestic requirements. All this has now changed. We have a wide range of tacit understandings with the Soviets; we have come to understand that the average Soviet citizen —in this respect like the average American voter—is unresponsive to the idea of nuclear annihilation. The communist world has split into quarrelling factions. I am enchanted to reflect on the Soviet staff studies of the military potential of the Czech army in case of war. Perhaps, as I have said elsewhere, we have here the explanation of their odd passion for the Egyptians. And as all philosophers of the commonplace concede, we have the terrible urgency of civilian needs—of the cities, the environment, transportation, education, housing, indeed wherever we look. It is now even agreed as to where the danger to American democracy lies. It is from the starvation of our public services, particularly in our big cities, here at home.

Let me make one final point. Our concern here is not with inefficiency in military procurement. Nor is it with graft. These divert attention from the main point. And this is not a crusade against military men— against our fellow citizens in uniform. Soldiers were never meant to be commercial accessories of General Dynamics. It would horrify the great captains of American arms of past generations to discover that their successors are by way of becoming commercial accessories of Lockheed Aircraft Corporation.

The matter for concern is with the military power—a power that has passed from the public and the Congress to the Pentagon and its suppliers. And our concern is with the consequences—with the bloated budgets and bizarre bureaucratic truths that result. The point is important for it suggests that the restoration of power to the Congress is not a sectarian political hook. It is one for all who respect traditional political and constitutional processes.

8
CIVILIAN DEFENSE AND NONVIOLENCE

Introduction

The approaches to war prevention discussed so far aim at producing a change in the world order system that minimizes the threat of war by anticipating possible conflicts and providing mechanisms for their avoidance or nonviolent resolution. In this section we focus on a different way of responding to the war threat, the belief that the advocates of military deterrence are wrong in insisting that military defense guards against armed aggression. Advocates of civilian or unarmed defense believe that it is possible to organize systems of nonviolent resistance that will prevent potential aggressors from attaining their goals at a cost in lives and treasure far below that of military defense.

The opening selections from the writings of Ghandi provide a background in the nature of his thought, and suggest the hopes that he had for nonviolent tactics. It is this outlook that has established the framework within which much subsequent speculation on nonviolence has taken place. Ghandi's outlook was essentially religious and moral. He believed that every human life is sacred and that it is never morally permissible to take a life, even in defense of a just cause. Violence is always evil; to respond to violence merely multiplies the evils incurred. Ghandi's feeling that suffering was the most honorable response to injustice reflects his belief that the moral salvation of all the parties to a conflict was at least as important as the victory of innocent victims against violent aggressors. At the same time, he thought it dishonorable not to respond to injustice, and he thought it cowardly and irresponsible to respond in a weak or ineffective way. Since his position effectively prohibited resort to violence, he was forced to devise nonviolent tactics for resisting injustice.

The article by Gene Sharp outlines specific plans for a civilian, nonmilitary defense system. His assumptions are that the just purpose of military power is to defend populations; that today's military technology makes it impossible to defend a population without incurring unacceptable and probably catastrophic losses; and that, when used offensively, military power does not guarantee control of an invaded country, but merely provides the means to destroy it, an eventuality that presumably neither side would want. Since he believes people have a right to be concerned about their security, an alternative to military defense must be devised. Sharp envisions a civilian defense system in which most of the population would participate. Mass education programs would teach people techniques of nonviolent resistance, so that an invading army would be faced with people who would not only refuse to cooperate, but actively interfere with the invader's activities. While it is not clear from Sharp's article, it seems reasonable to assume that he would not rule out sabotage of the invader's installations, supplies, and weapons. Thus, for him, civilian defense is not necessarily totally nonviolent. For this reason, many believe that Sharp's approach is bolder and more practical than Ghandi's. Certainly there are differences between their conceptions of nonviolent tactics and strategies, and one needs to consider which is more likely to be effective and which requires greater courage. Nevertheless, both share the same moral vision of confronting injustice with justice, mass violence with nonviolence. For both, one of the most compelling reasons for adopting nonviolent tactics is that the tactics themselves tend to reinforce basic values of justice, nonviolence, and democracy. As Sharp says, "Civilian defense is . . . a democratic defense of democracy," since it relies on the active participation of the populace in its own defense (although it might be asked how such a rationale differs from that advanced for a "people's" conscript army in the Second World War). Unlike the preparations for military defense, preparations for civilian defense would probably not interfere with the values and needs of domestic society.

The short article by Thomas Schelling, the deterrence theorist, expresses several doubts about the concept and practicality of civilian defense. It will be seen that Schelling's remarks are based on the understanding of the functions of modern warfare expressed in his article in section 3. He questions whether civilian defense could be used to fulfil the threat functions of contemporary military strategies, even when these are enlisted in the service of acceptable diplomatic goals. What would happen to global stability if a major power "transarmed" from military to nonmilitary defense? Schelling also wonders whether civilian defense could "win" a war in any conventional sense. It could deny control of a country to an aggressor, but the aggressor could respond by cutting off trade and communications and thus prevent a country from normal functioning. Although Sharp denies it, one might ask whether civilian defense can be made to appear fully acceptable only if a positive value is attached to human suffering as a response to injustice (following Ghandi), since civilian defense would inevitably involve periods of intense suffering for many people who would be denied their normal living conditions because of the absence of military defense. Finally, Schelling questions the assumption that civilian defense is always associated with democratic values. Is it really morally neutral? Conceivably, Schelling argues, civilian defense could be used as an offensive tactic if it were to be supported against the regime of a country by an external power. Then it would not be unlike guerrilla warfare with external support. In all of this, Schelling is interested more in raising questions for examination than in invalidating the concept of civilian defense. It is interesting to note that such a radical departure from conventional strategic thinking should receive so sympathetic a hearing from a leading strategist of deterrence.

In the concluding brief excerpt from an article by Barbara Deming, an answer is suggested to the question about the suffering that would follow from a posture of nonviolent resistance. Deming argues that suffering could of course be expected in any such situation, and that people must be prepared to accept it as the price of their resistance. But the appropriate way to consider the problem is to compare the casualties that could realistically be expected in an exercise of civilian defense with those that would certainly be sustained in a military war. Unquestionably, Deming says, the military casualties would be far more numerous, serious, and inhumane. In addition, they are likely to be far more indiscriminate. In civilian defense, the defenders could retain greater control of the situation by conducting themselves in an honorable, largely nonviolent way, thus regulating the aggressor's level of violence. Deming believes an armed aggressor would probably not resort to indiscriminate slaughter when confronted by such nonviolent tactics.

While the theoretical case for civilian defense may be sound, it is clear that many questions remain to be answered, especially with regard to a modern population's ability to accept the concept and all that it implies. Beyond this, it is important to ask two further questions. First, what would be the effect on the rest of the world if one nation adopted civilian defense? How might civilian defense help bring global peace? Second, how do proposals for civilian defense fit into a strategy for changing public opinion and national policies to make them more compatible with those attitudes and policies required for a more peaceful world order? How could civilian defense be combined with plans for general and complete disarmament to offer a new, nonmilitary kind of national security?

SUGGESTIONS FOR FURTHER READING

American Friends Service Committee, *In Place of War*. New York: Grossman, 1971.

Joan V. Bondurant, *Conquest of Violence: The Ghandian Philosophy of Conflict*. Berkeley: University of California Press, 1969.

Barbara Deming, *Revolution and Equilibrium*. New York: Grossman, 1971.

H. J. N. Horsburgh, *Non-Violence and Aggression: A Study of Ghandi's Moral Equivalent of War*. London: Oxford University Press, 1968.

G. Ramachandran and T. K. Mahadevan, eds., *Ghandi: His Relevance for Our Times*. Berkeley: World Without War Council, 1967.

Adam Roberts, ed., *Civilian Resistance as a National Defense*. Harrisburg, Pa.: Stackpole Books, 1968.

Gene Sharp, *Exploring Nonviolent Alternatives*. Boston: Porter Sargent, 1970.

On Nonviolence

MOHANDAS K. GANDHI

Up to the year 1906, I simply relied on appeal to reason. I was a very industrious reformer. I was a good draftsman, as I always had a close grip of facts, which was the necessary result of my meticulous regard for truth. But I found that reason failed to produce an impression when the critical moment arrived in South Africa. My people were excited and there was talk of wreaking vengeance. I had then to choose between allying myself to violence or finding out some other method of meeting the crisis and stopping the rot, and it came to me that we should refuse to obey legislation that was degrading, and let them put us in jail if they liked. Thus came into being the moral equivalent of war. I was then a loyalist, because I implicitly believed that the sum total of the activities of the British Empire was good for India and for humanity. . . . The disillusionment came in 1919 after the passage of the Black Rowlatt Act and the refusal of the government to give the simple elementary redress of proved wrongs that we had asked for. And so, in 1920, I became a rebel. Since then the conviction has been growing upon me that things of fundamental importance to the people are not secured by reason alone but have to be purchased with their suffering. Suffering is the law of human beings; war is the law of the jungle. But suffering is infinitely

Selected passages from pp. 153–167 of *Selections from Gandhi*, 2d ed., edited by N. K. Bose, Navajivan Publishing House, copyright 1957 by the Navajivan Trust. Reprinted by permission. Omissions have not been indicated.

more powerful than the law of the jungle for converting the opponent and opening his ears, which are otherwise shut, to the voice of reason. Nobody has probably drawn up more petitions or espoused more forlorn causes than I, and I have come to this fundamental conclusion that if you want something really important to be done you must not merely satisfy the reason, you must move the heart also. The appeal of reason is more to the head, but the penetration of the heart comes from suffering. It opens up the inner understanding in man. Suffering is the badge of the human race, not the sword.

Nonviolence is the law of the human race and is infinitely greater than and superior to brute force.

In the last resort it does not avail to those who do not possess a living faith in the God of Love.

Nonviolence affords the fullest protection to one's self-respect and sense of honour, but not always to possession of land or movable property, though its habitual practice does prove a better bulwark than the possession of armed men to defend them. Nonviolence in the very nature of things is of no assistance in the defence of ill-gotten gains and immoral acts.

Individuals and nations who would practice nonviolence must be prepared to sacrifice (nations to the last man) their all except honour. It is therefore inconsistent with the possession of the other people's countries, i.e., modern imperialism which is frankly based on force for its defence.

Nonviolence is a power which can be wielded equally by all—children, young men and women or grown up people, provided they have a living faith in the God of Love and have therefore equal love for all mankind. When nonviolence is accepted as the law of life it must pervade the whole being and not be applied to isolated acts.

It is a profound error to suppose that whilst the law is good enough for individuals it is not for masses of mankind.

No human being is so bad as to be beyond redemption, no human being is so perfect as to warrant his destroying him whom he wrongly considers to be wholly evil.

A *satyagrahi* must never forget the distinction between evil and the evil-doer. He must not harbour ill-will or bitterness against the latter. He may not even employ needlessly offensive language against the evil person, however unrelieved his evil might be. For it is an article of faith with every *satyagrahi* that there is no one so fallen in this world but can be converted by love. A *satyagrahi* will always try to overcome evil by good, anger by love, untruth by truth, *himsa* by *ahimsa*. There is no other way of purging the world of evil.

Nonviolence is not a resignation from all real fighting against wickedness. On the contrary, the nonviolence of my conception is a more active and real fight against wickedness than retaliation, whose very nature is to increase wickedness. I contemplate a mental and therefore a moral opposition to immoralities. I seek entirely to blunt the edge of the tyrant's sword, not by putting up against it a sharper-edged weapon, but by disappointing his expectation that I would be offering physical resistance. The resistance of the soul that I should offer would elude him. It would at first dazzle him and at last compel recognition from him, which recognition would not humiliate him but would uplift him.

Revolutionary crime is intended to exert pressure. But it is the insane pressure of anger and ill-will. I contend that nonviolent acts exert pressure far more effective than violent acts, for that pressure comes from good will and gentleness.

I do not blame the British. If we were weak in numbers as they are, we too would perhaps have resorted to the same methods as they are now employing. Terrorism and deception are weapons not of the strong but of the weak. The British are weak in numbers, we are weak in spite of our numbers. The result is that each is dragging the other down. It is common experience that Englishmen lose in character after residence in India and that Indians lose in courage and manliness by contact with Englishmen. This process of weakening is good neither for us two nations, nor for the world.

Good brought through force destroyed individuality. Only when the change was effected through the persuasive power of nonviolent non-cooperation, i.e. love, could the foundation of individuality be preserved, and real, abiding progress be assured for the world.

History teaches one that those who have, no doubt with honest motives, ousted the greedy by using brute force against them, have in their turn become a prey to the disease of the conquered.

I do not deny the revolutionary's heroism and sacrifice. But heroism and sacrifice in a bad cause are so much waste of splendid energy, and hurt the good cause by drawing away attention from it by the glamour of the misused heroism and sacrifice in a bad cause.

I am not ashamed to stand erect before the heroic and self-sacrificing revolutionary, because I am able to pit an equal measure of nonviolent men's heroism and sacrifice untarnished by the blood of the innocent. The self-sacrifice of one innocent man is a million times more potent than the sacrifice of a million men who die in the act of killing others. The willing sacrifice of the innocent is the most powerful retort to insolent tyranny that has yet been conceived.

I am more concerned in preventing the brutalization of human nature than in the prevention of the sufferings of my own people. I know that people who voluntarily undergo a course of suffering raise themselves and the whole of humanity; but I also know that people who become brutalized in their desperate efforts to get victory over their opponents or to exploit weaker nations or weaker men, not only drag down themselves but mankind also. And it cannot be a matter of pleasure to me or anyone else to see human nature dragged to the mire. If we are all sons of the same God and partake of the same divine essence, we must partake of the sin of every person, whether he belongs to us or to another race. You can understand how repugnant it must be to invoke the beast in any human being, how much more so in Englishmen, among whom I count numerous friends.

The doctrine of violence has reference only to the doing of injury by one to another. Suffering injury in one's own person is on the contrary of the essence of nonviolence, and is the chosen substitute for violence to others. It is not because I value life low that I can countenance with joy thousands voluntarily losing their lives for *satyagraha,* but because I know that it results in the long run in the least loss of life, and what is more, it ennobles those who lose their lives, and morally enriches the world for their sacrifice.

The beauty of *satyagraha,* of which noncooperation is but a chapter, is that it is available to either side in a fight; that it has checks that automatically work for the vindication of truth and justice for that side, whichever it may be, that has truth and justice in preponderating measure. It is as powerful and faithful a weapon in the hand of the capitalist as in that of the labourer. It is as powerful in the hands of the government as in that of the people, and will bring victory to the government, if people are misguided or unjust, as it will win the battle for the people if the government be in the wrong.

National Defense Without Armaments

GENE SHARP

Now, more than ever, we need to question some of our basic assumptions about defense, security and peace, and to examine possible new policies that might help achieve those goals. The dangers and limitations of modern military means—conventional, nuclear, and chemical-bacteriological—are too obvious to need repetition. What has not been clear is what alternative we have. This article is focused on one alternative system of defense, which is most commonly called civilian defense.

The often-posed choice between the acceptance of tyranny and the waging of war has been aggravated by developments in weapons technology, communications, and transportation. The technological changes in methods of war have brought about the concentration of large-scale military power in the hands of a few countries which possess scientific know-how, a technological and industrial base, and vast resources. In particular, the supremacy of the United States and the Soviet Union in capability for large-scale conventional and nuclear warfare cannot yet be seriously challenged.

In consequence, most countries have found that their capacity for self-defense has been drastically reduced or destroyed altogether. This

From *War/Peace Report,* vol. 10, no. 4 (April 1970), pp. 3–10. Copyright © 1970 by Gene Sharp. Reprinted by permission of the author and publisher. Gene Sharp teaches at Southeastern Massachusetts University and is an associate of the Harvard Center for International Relations.

is true even for highly industrialized Western European countries, and the matter is more extreme for less developed countries.

At the same time, local conflicts have gained worldwide significance and led to direct involvement in one form or another by the superpowers. This gravitation of deterrence and defense tasks to the most powerful and most technologically developed countries has had a variety of undesirable results for the other countries.

For example, alliance with a superpower is no sure guarantee of national security. The ultimate defense decision lies in foreign hands, and despite treaties a small power may be left helpless when the chips are down, as the fate of Czechoslovakia in 1939 illustrated. In 1968, Czechoslovakia was attacked by its own allies!

Likewise, military help from a superpower can be highly dangerous for the people being "defended." Witness Vietnam. And what would happen to West Berlin, or even West Germany, in case of powerful American military help to throw back a Russian invasion?

Dependence on stronger powers for defense may have other disadvantages. For example, do not the very people who want American military support frequently resent being dependent on it? Does not dependence on others for defense sometimes lead to reduced willingness to contribute to one's own defense? Does not such dependence often lead to an unwise stifling of one's own political judgment and autonomy in both domestic and foreign policies?

This shift of responsibility for the security of many nations to the superpowers has more than doubled the latter's defense tasks. Military commitments of the U.S. extend far beyond its own defense. Dozens of countries around the world depend on American support and pledges for their security. A similar situation exists on a smaller scale for the Soviet Union. Someday China may have a comparable status.

These foreign commitments (assuming good motives behind them) are for the United States an extraordinarily difficult and often thankless task. Even from a military perspective, there are severe problems involved in carrying out this world role, as is illustrated by the war in Vietnam and the tensions in Korea.

The political problems are also severe. It is hard, for example, to pose as a defender of freedom when that role seems to require alliances with reactionary dictatorships. Great sacrifices intended to help people avoid dictatorial rule are sometimes seen as unwanted efforts of Uncle Sam to be the world's policeman. Or, less flatteringly, as ruthless attempts to impose a new imperialism.

It is hardly necessary to mention that the local involvement of a superpower carries with it the additional danger of escalation into a

larger international war. All this is to say nothing of the drain of resources on the United States, the killing of American soldiers, the effects
of such violence abroad on the society at home, or the distraction from
other important domestic and international tasks.

This could all be changed if countries fearing military aggression or
the imposition by violence of minority dictatorships had the capacity to
defend themselves—in other words, if countries throughout the world
were able, primarily by their own efforts, to defeat domestic or foreign-
aided dictatorial groups of *any* political stripe, and also were able to
deter and defeat international aggression against themselves.

The world security situation would then be very different, and would
not "require" global American military involvement. There would then
be neither the need nor the excuse for worldwide military commitments
of the United States or any other country. The superpowers could instead concentrate on their own defenses and devote their technical and
financial superiority to constructive humanitarian ends.

But is this possible? How can the capacity for self-defense be restored, if it has been destroyed by the very nature of modern military
technology? We need to ask: Can there be a new concept of defense
which is *not* dependent on military technology, but which could nevertheless be effective against real dangers? That could only happen if defense could be provided *without* military means—an idea which to most
people has been inconceivable.

Defense has almost always meant military defense. I will argue that
this need no longer be true. The main question is: How can there be a
nonmilitary defense?

We must start with basics. We have usually assumed that defense
capacity and military power are identical, and that military occupation
means political control. But these assumptions are not valid:

Military power today often exists without real capacity to *defend* in
struggle the people and society relying upon it. Often it only threatens
mutual annihilation. More importantly—and this is the main argument
of this article—defense capacity can today be provided without military
means.

Military occupation does *not* necessarily give the invader political
control of the country, and the occupation can be destroyed *without*
military resistance.

Since military technology in most cases has abolished the possibility
of effective geographical defense, we are thrown back to the people for
the defense of their freedoms and society. This approach is called *civilian
defense* (not to be confused with civil defense).

Civilian defense aims to defeat military aggression by using resistance by the civilian population as a whole to make it impossible for the enemy to establish and maintain political control over the country. This is a direct defense of the society by the citizens. The priorities of action are crucial. The maintenance of a free press, for example, or keeping the invader's propaganda out of the schools is each of more direct importance to democracy than, say, possession of a given mountain or the killing of young conscripts in the invader's army. Large-scale preparations and training would be necessary to maximize the effectiveness of social, economic, and political power against an invader or an internal take-over.

The citizens would prevent enemy control of the country by massive and selective refusal to cooperate and to obey, supporting instead the legal government and its call to resist. For example, police would refuse to locate and arrest patriotic opponents of the invader. Teachers would refuse to introduce his propaganda into the schools—as happened in Norway under the Nazis. Workers and managers would use strikes, delays, and obstructionism to impede exploitation of the country—as happened in the Ruhr in 1923. Clergymen would preach about the duty to refuse to help the invader—as happened in the Netherlands under the Nazis.

MAINTAINING CONTROL

Politicians, civil servants, and judges, by ignoring or defying the enemy's illegal orders, would keep the normal machinery of government and the courts out of his control—as happened in the German resistance to the Kapp *Putsch* in 1920. Newspapers refusing to submit to censorship would be published illegally in large editions or many small editions—as happened in the Russian 1905 Revolution and in several Nazi-occupied countries. Free radio programs would continue from hidden transmitters—as happened in Czechoslovakia in August, 1968.

In civilian defense struggles, the general citizenry and the society's institutions are themselves combatants. When successful, civilian defense of the society would lead to the collapse or withdrawal of the invader or internal usurper. But the victory would follow from the successful direct defense of the society, not from battles over the control of geography.

In addition, in case of invasion, civilian defense would set in motion restraining influences both in the invader's own country (stimulating dissension at home, splits in the regime, and, in extremes, even resistance) and in the international community (creating diplomatic pressures, political losses, and sometimes economic sanctions) that would be inimical to the invader's interests and to his attempts at consolidating an occupation.

This may sound unlikely. But there is more evidence that civilian defense can work than there was 30 years ago for the practicability of nuclear weapons, intercontinental rockets, and trips to the moon.

Nevertheless, the idea that national defense may be exercised more effectively by the vigilance and trained nonviolent resistance of citizens than by military means seems startling to some and ridiculous to others. There is no denying that there would be risks and dangers involved in such a policy. But these need to be measured against the risks and dangers of military deterrence policies.

Contrary to present assumptions, there is a long history of nonviolent political struggle. Despite lack of knowledge of its requirements, and in the absence of training and preparations, this technique has produced some impressive results, even against high odds.

There are as yet no cases in which prepared civilian defense has caused an invader to withdraw—because there has never yet been a case of prepared civilian defense being used as a country's official defense policy. (There are, of course, cases of effective unprepared resistance in occupied countries, such as colonial India and World War II Norway.) The formulation of a civilian defense policy is a deliberate attempt to advance beyond where we are now, an attempt based upon a serious calculation of political realities and possibilities.

Given the resources and the commitment, there is reason to believe progress can be made in devising political strategies of nonviolent action calculated to control tyrants and preserve political freedom. With political research and analysis, it seems to me that we could locate and come to understand the weaknesses of occupation regimes and of totalitarian systems. Then we could concentrate resistance against them on their weak points, using what might be called a form of "political karate."

Even *without* advance preparations, the people of Czechoslovakia provided an experiment in the use of nonviolent struggle in their response to the Russian invasion and occupation. Given the options open to them, their successes, while moderate, were temporarily impressive. The Russians have not yet withdrawn; they have won important points, although at greater cost than expected. The Dubcek regime held out from August until April, while the Russians expected to be able to overcome possible Czech military resistance within days. We need to learn from the strengths and weaknesses of this case.

Civilian defense ought to be subjected to an examination and consideration at least as rigorous as that devoted to any proposal for a

major change in defense policy. Concrete examination has to be given
to the many practical problems involved in waging civilian defense, to
possible strategies, to types of repression that would need to be anticipated, and to the question of the casualties. My plea, therefore, is not
for the adoption of civilian defense now, but for research, investigation
and official consideration. My intent is not to win converts, but to pro-
voke thought.

BEGIN WITH THE KNOWN

As a first step, civilian defense must draw upon the known experience
of nonviolent struggle, without being limited by it, in order to develop
viable strategies to deter and defeat attacks on a country.

The study of cases of nonviolent action has been largely neglected by
strategists, historians, and social scientists. Serious research to correct
this neglect has only begun. Moreover, the situation has been aggravated
by a series of misunderstandings about the nature of nonviolent action
which need to be corrected.

Nonviolent action, the major instrument of a civilian defense policy,
is the opposite of passivity and cowardice. It is not simply persuasion,
but the wielding of power. It does not assume that man is inherently
"good." It has been mostly used by "ordinary" people. It does not absolutely require shared principles or a high degree of common interest
between the contending groups. It may work by "nonviolent coercion."
At least as "Western" as it is "Eastern," the technique is designed for
struggle against a repressive violent opponent. It may be used to defend
as well as to change a government, and has been widely applied against
foreign occupations and even against totalitarian systems.

There are many instances of effective nonviolent action, including:
the early resistance by American colonists, 1763–1775; Hungarian passive resistance vs. Austrian rule, especially 1850–1867; Finland's disobedience and political noncooperation against Russia, 1898–1905; the
Russian 1905 Revolution, and that of February 1917 (before the October Bolshevik coup); the Korean nonviolent protest against Japanese
rule, 1919–1922 (which failed); the Indian 1930–1931 independence
campaign; German government-sponsored resistance to the Franco-
Belgian occupation of the Ruhr in 1923.

Later examples include: resistance in several Nazi-occupied countries,
especially Norway, the Netherlands, and Denmark; governmental and
popular measures to nullify anti-Jewish measures in several Nazi-allied
and Nazi-occupied countries, such as Bulgaria, Italy, France, and Den-

mark; the toppling by popular noncooperation and defiance of the dictators of El Salvador and Guatemala in 1944; the 1963 and 1966 campaigns of the Buddhists against the Saigon regimes in South Vietnam.

Other recent cases involve resistance, uprisings, and less dramatic pressures for liberalization in communist-ruled countries, including the 1953 East German uprising, strikes in the Soviet political prisoner camps in 1953, major aspects of the 1956 Hungarian revolution, Polish popular pressures for reforms, efforts for de-Stalinization in the Soviet Union, popular pressures for liberalization in Czechoslovakia early in 1968, and popular and governmental noncooperation following the Russian invasion in August.

Thus, it is evident that nonviolent resistance has occurred even against totalitarian systems, on an improvised basis and despite the absence of training, preparations, and know-how. It should be noted that totalitarians like Hitler deliberately sought to promote the impression of their regime's omnipotence, both domestically and internationally, to discourage any potential opposition. Such systems contain critical weaknesses in the form of inefficiencies, internal conflicts and tendencies toward impermanence. It is precisely these features that offer themselves up for exploitation by civilian defense strategies. However, the basic reason why civilian defense can be effective against totalitarian systems is that even such extreme political systems cannot free themselves entirely from dependence on their subjects. As an articulated strategy, civilian defense is designed to deny totalitarian rulers the compliance, cooperation, and submission they require.

Over 146 specific methods of nonviolent action have been identified (defined, with examples, in my forthcoming *The Politics of Nonviolent Action*).[1] These methods are classified under three broad categories: protest, noncooperation, and intervention.

The methods of nonviolent protest are largely symbolic demonstrations, including parades, marches, and vigils (40 methods). Noncooperation is divided into four subcategories: a) boycotts of social relations (six methods), b) economic boycotts (24 methods), c) strikes (24 methods), and d) acts of political noncooperation (34 methods). "Nonviolent intervention," by psychological, physical, social, or political means, includes 18 methods (such as the fast, nonviolent occupation and parallel government).

The use of a considerable number of these methods—carefully chosen, on a large scale, persistently, with wise strategy and tactics, by trained civilians—is likely to cause any illegitimate regime severe problems.

---

[1] Philadelphia and Boston: Pilgrim Press, September 1970.

Nonviolent action resembles military war more than it does negotiation; it is a technique of struggle. As such, nonviolent action involves the uses of power, but in different ways than military violence. Instead of confronting the opponent's apparatus of violence with comparable forces, the nonviolent actionists counter with political weapons. The degree to which noncooperation itself will threaten the opponent's power position will vary, but its potentiality is illustrated most obviously in the disruptive effects of massive strikes and in mutinies of the opponent's own troops.

The violent antagonist's repressive measures are hardly insignificant, but *in themselves* they are not decisive. In fact, the opponent's repression is evidence of the power of nonviolent action, and is no more reason for despair than if, in a regular war, the enemy shoots back.

If the civilian defenders maintain their discipline and persist despite repression, and if they involve significant sections of the populace in the struggle, the opponent's will can be retarded and finally blocked. If leaders are arrested, the movement may carry on without a recognizable leadership. The opponent may declare new acts illegal, only to find that he has opened up new opportunities for defiance.

There is a strong tendency for the opponent's violence and repression to react against his power position. This is called "political jujitsu." Against disciplined and persistent nonviolent actionists, his violence can never really come to grips with the kind of power they wield. Under certain conditions repression may make more people join the resistance. The opponent's supporters may turn against him; uneasiness may lead to disobedience in his own camp. The numbers of resisters may become so large that control becomes impossible. His police may give up, his officials occasionally resign, and sometimes his troops may even mutiny. Massive nonviolent defiance by the population has by then made the enemy government powerless. This is the potential. But it will not be easy to achieve. Defeat of the nonviolent actionists is always possible, just as defeat occurs in traditional war. Victory with this technique will come only to those who have developed it into a refined and powerful political tool.

Thus, civilian defense depends primarily on a trained civilian population to defend the country's freedom and independence by social, psychological, economic, and political means. The population could be prepared through regular democratic processes and government decisions. Long before the change-over from military defense to civilian defense—a process called *transarmament*—considerable research, investigation, and analysis would be needed. Highly important, too, would be widespread public study, thinking, discussion, and debate on the nature, feasibility, merits, and problems of civilian defense and all of the forms its exercise might take.

After the decision to transarm, a Department of Civilian Defense might be set up to provide planning, analysis, coordination, and some leadership. All this would probably be more complex than planning for military defense.

No country is going to abandon military defense without confidence in a substitute defense policy. Therefore, for a significant period, civilian defense preparations would be carried out alongside military measures, until the latter could be phased out as no longer needed. Because of their different natures, however, the two policies would probably require separate institutional arrangements. During the transarmament period, personnel and money would be needed for both.

A major educational program for the whole country on the nature and purpose of civilian defense would be required. Federal, state, and local governmental bodies, assisted by independent institutions such as schools, churches, trade unions, business groups, newspapers, television, and the like could undertake this. People would be informed about the broad outlines of the new policy, the ways it would operate, and the results expected.

Certain occupational groups, including those wishing to participate in advanced aspects of the policy, would need specialized training. Such training would vary in its character and purpose, ranging from that required by local neighborhood defense workers to specialist education at civilian defense counterparts of West Point. This is not to say that there is no role for spontaneity within the scope of civilian defense, but that it is a limited role and even then needs to be self-disciplined and rooted in thorough understanding of the requirements of nonviolent action and the chosen civilian defense strategies.

In crises, specialists in civilian defense would play an important role in initiating resistance, especially at the beginning of an occupation or a coup. In various situations they could serve as special cadres for particularly dangerous tasks. Some specialists might be kept in reserve to guide the later stages of the resistance. However, they could not—and should not be expected to—carry out the resistance *for* the general population. Responsibility for the main thrust of civilian defense must be assumed by the citizenry. Since the leaders generally would be among the first imprisoned or otherwise incapacitated by the usurper, the population must be able to continue on its own initiative.

MAXIMIZING IMPACT

Preparations for civilian defense would not consist simply of instructions arrived at by a centralized leadership and carried out at the lower levels. An effective strategy would require an analysis of the potentialities of many factors—means of transportation, government departments, schools, and so forth—to identify the specific points at which non-cooperation might have a maximum impact in preventing any illegal group from seizing control. Ordinary people in jobs at those places would often be the best sources of the intelligence information needed to make these decisions. To make accurate tactical judgments, however, one would need knowledge of the forms and strategies of nonviolent resistance, the enemy's weaknesses, the kinds of repression to expect, the crucial political issues on which to resist, and many practical questions of how to implement the resistance.

The setting up of an underground system of contacts would probably have to wait until a crisis, to make it harder for the opponent to know the exact personnel and structure of the resistance organization. However, "war games" and civilian defense maneuvers could offer the specialists a chance to examine the viability of alternative strategies and tactics for dealing with various types of threats. Training maneuvers in which imaginary occupations or takeovers would be met by civilian resistance could be acted out at levels ranging from local residential areas, offices, or factories to cities, states, and even the whole country.

Technical preparations would also be necessary for civilian defense. For example, provisions and equipment would be required for communication with the population after the enemy had occupied key centers and seized established newspapers, radio stations, and other mass media. Equipment to publish underground newspapers and resistance leaflets and to make broadcasts could be hidden beforehand. It might be possible to make advance arrangements for locating such broadcasting stations or printing plants in the territory of a friendly neighboring country as part of a civilian defense mutual aid agreement.

Since an enemy might seek to force the population into submission by starvation, and since certain resistance methods (e.g., a general strike) would disrupt distribution of food, emergency supplies of staples should be stored locally. Alternative means of providing fuel and water during emergencies could also be explored. For certain types of crises, plans might be considered for the dispersal of large groups of people from big cities to rural areas where the oppressor would find it more difficult to exercise control over them.

Because civilian defense requires the active support and participation of the populace (*not* necessarily unanimity, however), the citizens must have both the *will* and *ability* to defend their society in crises. For citizens to have the will to defend their democratic system does not imply that they believe the system is perfect. But it does mean that the system is preferable to any regime likely to be imposed by internal take-over or by foreign invaders, and that any necessary changes in the system should be made by democratic decision. For effective civilian defense, people have to *want* to resist threats to their freedom and independence. They must genuinely cherish the democratic qualities of their society.

Measures to increase the effectiveness of civilian defense (including the decentralization of control in order to make citizens more self-reliant in facing emergencies) are likely to contribute to the vitality of democratic society, and to increased participation in it. With civilian defense, therefore, there is no rivalry or contradiction between defense requirements and domestic needs; they are complementary. In the case of the U.S., this would be a considerable advance over present military policy, which has delivered us into exactly that contradiction.

Civilian defense is thus a democratic defense of democracy. Just as tyranny and war, in their cyclical appearances, may be mutually reinforcing causes, so political freedom and peace may be intimately connected. A civilian defense policy may provide concrete means for producing a condition of life that allows for the interplay and perpetual renewal of the last two qualities in place of the first two.

AGGRESSOR'S CONSIDERATIONS

An aggressive regime deciding whether or not to invade another country will usually consider: 1) the expected ease or difficulty of the invasion and subsequent control of the country, and 2) the anticipated gains as compared to costs (human, economic, political, ideological, prestigial, military, and other). Except in the case of a nation acting on a huge gamble or pure irrationality, the likelihood of considerably greater losses than gains will probably deter the invader.

Invasion is not an objective in and of itself. It is a way to achieve a wider purpose, which almost always involves occupation of the invaded country. If, however, a successful invasion is followed by immense difficulties in occupying and controlling the country, its society and population, the invasion's "success" becomes for its perpetrators a dangerous mirage. Certainly the Russians invading Czechoslovakia encountered at the early stages great and unanticipated difficulties. Advance civilian defense preparations and training could have considerably increased these. Where preparations and training are thorough, a would-be invader might perceive that he will not be able to rule successfully the country that he might easily invade. Civilian defense has at that moment revealed itself as a powerful deterrent.

There are other contingencies a would-be aggressor would need to think through. A population's spirit and methods of resistance could well spread to other countries and again be applied against his tyranny. In such a light, civilian defense has to be considered as a possible post-nuclear deterrent to conventional attack.

Could civilian defense deter a nuclear attack? It is sometimes argued that civilian defense is nonsense in the nuclear age, since it would provide no defense should nuclear bombs start falling. The question, however, is whether the conditions likely to be produced by transarmament to civilian defense will encourage or discourage a decision to launch a nuclear attack on the country involved.

Who fears and expects a nuclear attack the most today, and who the least? It is precisely the nuclear powers who most fear nuclear attack, partly because each side is afraid of the other. Brazil, Mexico, Indonesia, Canada and Australia—all *without* nuclear weapons—fear and expect nuclear attack far less than the U.S. and U.S.S.R.

Fear of nuclear attack, then, or fear of military defeat in a major conventional war, may be a strong reason for launching a nuclear attack on the enemy. Civilian defense, which can only be used for *defensive* purposes, would remove that motive, and hence, if not cancel out the danger, at least greatly reduce it. It is certainly significant that several military men to whom this problem has been presented do not see much likelihood of a nuclear attack against a country employing only civilian defense as a deterrent.

No deterrent can ever be *guaranteed* to deter. And, of course, the failure of the nuclear deterrent could permanently end all talk of alternative deterrents as well as the talkers and nontalkers. But the failure of the civilian defense deterrent would still permit human life to continue and long-range hope for a just solution to remain, while the struggle against tyranny would enter a new stage with a more direct confrontation of forces. When the deterrence capacity of civilian defense fails, a series of contingency plans to deal with the new situation comes into operation with the potential to win a real political and human victory.

Although resistance is never easy, it is less difficult to resist a tyrannical regime while it is seeking to establish itself than after it has succeeded. George Kennan points out that for a successful seizure of power by a totalitarian regime "a certain degree of mass bewilderment and passivity are required." Advance preparations and training for civilian defense are designed specifically to prevent that condition. The invader will encounter a population well prepared to fight for its freedom with methods which, precisely because they are nonviolent, will be especially insidious and dangerous to the occupation regime. And in the end, the invader may well lose.

Of course, civilian defense cannot keep enemy troops from entering the country. But the enemy's entry is an illusion of easy success; it operates as a political ambush. The people will not have allowed themselves to succumb to the psychological condition that Hitler prescribed for successful occupation; they will not have admitted defeat and recognized the occupation regime as their conqueror and master.

Under civilian defense, the country and the defense capacity would not have been defeated. The combat strength would not yet have been applied. The citizenry, trained and prepared, would not feel dismayed or confused. They would understand that the distribution of enemy soldiers and functionaries throughout the country did not mean defeat but instead was the initial stage of a longer struggle at close range. This would be difficult. But the civilian defenders would hold advantages. Setbacks might occur; these could lead, however, to rebuilding strength for future campaigns. There are no white flags of surrender in civilian defense.

Although civilian defense cannot defend the geographic borders, some limited action could be taken even at the initial stage. The deployment of troops could be delayed by obstructionist activities at the docks (if troops came by sea), by refusal to operate the railroads, or by blocking highways and airports with thousands of abandoned automobiles.

Such acts would make clear to the individual enemy soldiers that, whatever they might have been told, they were not welcome as an invasion force. As other symbolic actions the people could wear mourning bands, stay at home, stage a limited general strike, defy curfews, or urge the invading soldiers not to believe their government's propaganda. Such actions would give notice to friend and foe that the occupation will be firmly resisted and at the same time build up the people's morale so as to prevent submission and collaboration.

The invader's parades of troops through the cities would be met by conspicuously empty streets and shuttered windows, and his public receptions would be boycotted. Efforts would be made to undermine the loyalty of his individual soldiers and functionaries. They would be informed that there will be resistance, but that the resistance will be of a special type, directed against the attempt to seize control but without threatening harm to them as individuals. If this could be communicated, the soldiers might be more likely to help the resisting population in small ways, to avoid brutalities, and to mutiny at a crisis point, than they would if they expected at any moment to be killed by snipers or plastic bombs.

FORMS OF NONCOOPERATION

There would be early forms of more substantial political and economic noncooperation. For example, the invader might meet a blanket refusal by the government bureaucracy and civil servants to carry out his instructions. Or, these officials might continue the old policies, ignore his orders, and disrupt the implementation of new policies. The police might refuse to make political arrests for the invader, warn people of impending arrests, selectively refuse certain orders, or carry them out with great inefficiency.

Attempts to exploit the economic system might be met with limited general strikes, slow-downs, refusal of assistance by or disappearance of indispensable experts, and the selective use of various types of strikes at key points in industries, transportation, and the supply of raw materials. News of resistance might be publicized through prearranged channels throughout the world, and also be beamed at the invader's homeland. These are only illustrations. Since each case is different, and the enemy's objectives are crucial, obviously there can be no one blueprint for all situations. And it would be important to plan different possible types of strategies for dealing with diverse threats.

Over the long run, both injuries and deaths are to be expected, though they are likely to be much fewer than in military struggles. If the citizens are unwilling to face the prospect of such casualties in their defense action, the resistance will surely collapse; similarly, in a conventional war defeat is certain if the troops when fired upon run the other way or surrender. In this, as in any struggle, casualties must be seen in the context of the campaign as a whole. It is remarkable how many people who accept as natural millions of dead and wounded in a military war find dangers of execution and suffering in civilian defense a decisive disadvantage; this is especially puzzling when there is evidence that casualty rates in nonviolent struggles are vastly smaller than in regular warfare.

As the occupation develops, the enemy may try to gain control of various institutions, such as the courts, schools, unions, cultural groups, professional societies, and the like. If that control is achieved, the future capacity for resistance will be weakened for a long period. Therefore, civilian defense must firmly resist any efforts of the invader to control the society's institutions. A few examples will show how this could be done.

The courts would declare the invader's bureaucracy an illegal and unconstitutional body; they would continue to operate on the basis of pre-invasion laws and constitutions, and they would refuse to give moral support to the invader, even if they had to close the courts. Attempts to control the schools would be met with refusal to change the school curriculum or to introduce the invader's propaganda, explanations to the pupils of the issues at stake, continuation of regular education as long as possible, and, if necessary, closing the schools and holding private classes in the children's homes.

Efforts to dominate trade unions or professional groups could be met by persistence in abiding by their pre-invasion constitutions and procedures, denial of recognition to new organizations set up by or for the invader, refusal to pay dues or attend meetings of any new pro-invader organizations, and the carrying out of disruptive strikes and economic and political boycotts.

In considering the possibility of failure of civilian defense, or of only very limited success, two factors need to be kept in mind. First, even failure after an heroic struggle by civilian defense would be preferable to any outcome of a major nuclear war. At worst, it would mean a long, difficult, and painful existence under severe tyranny, but life would go on, and with life the hope for eventual freedom. Nonviolent action is not a course for cowards. It requires the ability and determination to sustain the battle whatever the price in suffering, yet it would, in the most disastrous case imaginable, still allow a future for mankind. And secondly, in this kind of struggle, failure to achieve total victory would not mean total defeat. Even if the population were unable to drive out the invader, it could maintain a considerable degree of autonomy for the country, and for its institutions upon whose independence any country's freedom largely depends.

The other side of the argument for civilian defense is that under present international and technological conditions this system offers a greater chance of real success in opposing occupation or regaining political freedom than does military defense. When the usurper fails to bring the occupied country to heel, a miasma of uncertainty and dissent would grow within his regime and among his soldiers and officials. International pressures would further weaken the oppressor and strengthen the civilian defenders. Very likely, the usurper would find that he faced not only the opposition of world opinion but significant diplomatic moves and economic embargoes. Continued repression in the occupied country would feed further resistance. The multiplication of noncooperating and disobedient subjects would thus be calculated to defeat the would-be tyrant and bring about a restoration of liberty, enhanced with new meaning, vitality, and durability.

The exact way that victory would come would vary from one situation to another. In one case it might coincide with a change of government in the invading country. Or there might be negotiations, with some face-saving formula for the invader. In extremes, the occupation force itself might be so near disintegration and mutiny that with or without such a formula the troops and functionaries would simply go home. In any case, the real meaning would be clear: the occupation would have been defeated.

Another way of looking at civilian defense is to realize that it is *not* disarmament, if disarmament means the reduction or abandonment of defense capacity. Instead, the change-over to civilian defense is *transarmament*—the substitution of a new defense capacity that provides deterrence and defense without conventional and nuclear military power. It also contributes to world peace, since unlike military means civilian defense cannot be used for, or misperceived as intended for, international aggression.

A POLICY, NOT A CREED

Nor is civilian defense a new doctrine for which unquestioning "believers" are sought. It is a defense policy, not a creed. The stage of development of civilian defense, in theory and practice, is still primitive. Those who have examined the idea differ in their judgments of the types of defense problems, and of enemies, for which it might be suitable. For example, some say it is not possible against a Nazi-type regime, but that it would work against occupation regimes of medium severity. I hasten to add that there is also anything but uniformity of opinion about military defense policies!

Another crucial point about civilian defense is that it is possible for only one or a few countries to adopt the policy initially, without treaties and while most countries remain militarily armed. When convinced of its effectiveness and advantages, other countries too may transarm. Aggressive regimes may well have to be taught lessons in the resistance capacity of civilian defense countries.

The first nations to adopt civilian defense are likely to be those that most want self-reliance in defense but which lack the ability to do this with their own military means. The superpowers may well follow far behind. It does not, of course, have to be that way, and surprises may occur. A considerable period would doubtless exist in which some countries had transarmed to civilian defense while many others retained military defense—and some of the latter might never change over.

There would inevitably be strongholds of resistance to adoption of this policy. Democratic countries with large military establishments are unlikely, and probably unable, to eliminate these in a short span of time. They might, however, add a civilian defense component, if its effectiveness could be convincingly demonstrated. They might increasingly rely on this component, gradually phasing out the military sector, until the substitution was completed. Some military personnel could no doubt be retrained to fit into the new civilian defense system.

Dictatorial regimes and unstable governments probably would cling hardest to military capacity for both domestic and international purposes. However, even dictatorships could be influenced toward civilian defense, both by removal of fear of foreign military attack (contributing to internal political relaxation) and by nonviolent pressures for change from their own population.

It is impossible to predict with certainty the international consequences of the initial cases of transarmament. A nation's decision to adopt a policy of civilian defense and its effectiveness in carrying it out will depend on the state of knowledge of this kind of struggle, the adequacy of the strategic planning, the quality and extent of preparations and training, the geographical location of the country, the nature of its enemies, and the determination, skill, and heroism of the people.

The successful defeat of a seizure of power or an occupation by a systematic civilian defense policy might make a significant contribution toward the adoption of such a policy by other countries. Initial successes of this policy are likely to lead more and more countries to investigate it and finally to transarm.

Countries that had already adopted civilian defense could directly encourage other nations to transarm. Under "Civilian Defense Mutual Assistance Pacts" several countries could share knowledge, research results, and experience. They could provide certain aid in emergencies (such as food, supplies, finances, diplomatic and economic pressures, a haven for refugees, safe printing and broadcasting facilities). They could give technical advice to countries considering civilian defense, and undertake joint activities to deter aggression by this means.

In contrast with military planning, a sharing of results of civilian defense research, planning, and training would not endanger future combat effectiveness. It would instead accelerate the rate at which countries transarmed to civilian defense. This would be of major importance in a step-by-step removal of war from the international scene, and in increasing world security. It is important to note also that even if some countries never abandon military capacity, this would not be a reason for abandoning civilian defense, but rather for expanding it and improving its effectiveness.

Some of the important consequences of civilian defense will be social and economic. For example, transarmament to civilian defense by poor developing countries would probably mean that a large percentage of their present inordinate military budgets could be spent on dealing with poverty and development. Likewise, the developed countries would be able to give more help to the developing world after they convert to civilian defense.

Civilian defense can also deal with domestic or foreign-aided coups d'etat against the legal government, for which military defense is not designed. (Furthermore, it is usually the military establishment which overthrows the legal government, as in Greece in 1967.)

In the long run, civilian defense would be significantly cheaper than military defense, although it would not be inexpensive. And the transition period, with both military and civilian defense preparations, might be quite expensive.

Another side benefit of civilian defense is that it is likely to make the means of defense serve democratic political ends positively, rather than requiring a foreign policy and alliances that violate a country's avowed democratic principles. No longer would it be necessary in the name of "defense" to make military alliances with dictatorships or to give tacit support to oppressive governments in order to keep military bases. In short, civilian defense would very likely become a potent force around the world for liberalizing or overthrowing tyrannical regimes.

But most importantly, civilian defense could be expected to restore a very high degree of self-reliance in defense to all countries. It would do this by shifting the source of defense power from modern technology to the people themselves, to their determination and ability to act. If the nations of the world were able, predominantly by their own efforts, and above all without military assistance from the superpowers, to defend themselves from internal usurpation by violent minorities and from foreign invasions, the security problems of the world would be altered fundamentally.

THE LARGE ASSUMPTION

All of this discussion, of course, is based upon a large assumption: that today's elementary idea of civilian defense can be refined and developed to produce a new kind of defense policy at least as effective as military means. A considerable period of time given over to specific problem-oriented research will be needed to develop the general principles and theoretical frameworks of this policy, to produce models that may lend themselves to adaptation to a particular country's needs, and to complete planning, preparations, training, and other difficult tasks for the trans-armament period.

Certainly all would agree that no reasonable possible solution to the problems of modern war and tyranny, and of effective defense against aggression and internal take-overs should be left uninvestigated. It is important now to start the exploration, thought, discussion, and research that are needed to make possible a fair evaluation of this concept, and, if it turns out to be workable, to provide the basic knowledge necessary for transarmament, which could be completed within our lifetimes. We are now at a stage in the development of civilian defense at which major advances could be achieved relatively quickly.

Increased confidence in civilian defense and liberation by nonviolent action could produce a chain reaction in the progressive abolition of both war and tyranny. If this happened, the whole course of history would be altered. Some of the gravest fears and insecurities of the modern world would be lifted. Civilian defense could make it possible to face the future realistically, without fear or panic, but with courage, confidence, and hope.

Some Questions on Civilian Defence

THOMAS C. SCHELLING

One has to admit that it could work.

> Structures of power (governments, social organizations) always depend upon the voluntary co-operation of great numbers of individuals even when the structures seem to rely on physical force. The chief wielders of power, in other words, must have the assistance and co-operation of hundreds or even thousands of persons for the administration of physical force. The task of those who oppose a structure having physical force at its command is, therefore, to persuade hundreds of men to refuse any longer to co-operate with the tyrant or other administrator of violence . . .[1]

This is the starting point, whether our concern is resisting the tyrant or promoting his regime, frustrating a military victor or helping to establish his control. The fruits of conquest—nearly all of them, though not quite all—depend on *affirmative* action by large numbers of people. Force cannot procure it directly. You can drag a horse to water, but only he can make his muscles work; and if he won't drink, you'll shortly have no horse.

This essay appears in *Civilian Resistance as a National Defense,* edited by Adam Roberts. Harrisburg: Stackpole, 1968, pp. 302–308. Reprinted by permission of the publisher. Schelling teaches at Harvard University and has published extensively on questions of strategic theory.

[1] Mulford Q. Sibley (ed.), *The Quiet Battle,* Doubleday, New York, 1963, p. 9.

It is the *threat* of pain, privation, and loss that may induce people to cooperate. Inflicting the pain and damage gives the tyrant, or the military victor, nothing directly. If people can be made immune to threats—because they cannot comprehend what is wanted of them, because they cannot comprehend what will be done to them, or because they are motivated to refuse compliance even in the face of threats—violence will get you nowhere unless you want merely to exterminate or to immobilize or to impoverish the population, to expel it from its territory, to carry away its physical assets, or to make an example that will appeal to some other people in some other territory.

Fiction may prove the point better than historical documentation. We can imagine a militarily defenceless people thoroughly confounding a conqueror by sitting quietly, perhaps not eating, threatening to deprive him of any subjects by dying on his hands. He may let them die; he may even kill them; but exploit them he cannot. And if his subjects truly believe that life on this earth is but a chance to earn access to paradise after death, if they believe that nonviolent noncooperation earns entrance, and especially if suicide is permitted to avoid involuntary collaboration under the stimulus of pain or hunger, the people may quietly die, to the embarrassment and frustration of their conqueror.

If he anticipates it, perhaps he will not even conquer them. He can still take their belongings, eliminate them as a military threat, deny their territory to some other opponent, or achieve whatever else comes from the extinction of these people who will not become his subjects; but if he wants to rule a viable economy populated by human beings this can be denied him.

At least, in fiction it can, and in science fiction chemical or electronic substitutes might be found for the beliefs and values that would otherwise do the trick. Whether actual human beings, the residents of an actual contemporary country, can take advantage of this principle in frustrating a tyrant (or, better still, in deterring his conquest before it occurs) is the question to which this [essay] is addressed. And the answer, as I discern it . . . is that we do not know. The principle is undeniable, but we have not yet been given evidence that live human beings in today's world can so embody the principle in their organized behaviour as to make the tyrant quit the effort, to disarm him of his bureaucrats and soldiers, or to dissuade him in advance.

Of course, the principle may work unintentionally. If nobody seems terribly eager to recolonize the former Belgian Congo, it may be because some societies appear incapable of responding to authority or of submitting even to a benevolent effort at discipline. Impotence may be as impressive as the threat of disciplined nonviolent resistance in dissuading conquerors. The world is full of animals that enjoy freedom because no-body knows how to domesticate them. As Russell Baker has pointed out, the dolphins should take a lesson from the cats, not from the dogs and the monkeys; dogs have to come to heel and monkeys to work for hurdy-gurdy men because people know that dogs and monkeys can understand what is demanded of them and what the consequences of rebellion are, while the cats have got a reputation for indiscipline and poor learning, and are accorded privacy and freedom. If the dolphins, in their conceit, show that they can hear what is said to them and can evaluate conse-quences, they will become prime candidates for slavery.

Disciplined nonviolence—an overriding unwillingness to comply—has this unique defensive quality: if you successfully communicate it, it makes you totally immune to threats. If it is known that no sanctions, no penalties, no inducements can make one behave, then *purposive* threats are of no avail. One may still be punished for spite or revenge, or in disbelief that noncompliance can persist; but when the tyrant is convinced that no sanctions will work, that he can no more successfully command his defenceless populace than he can command vegetables, his authority is gone, he knows it, and even punishment becomes a chore, not a source of authority. Xerxes whipped the waters of the Hellespont for their turbulence when he wanted to cross his army over; an objective of nonviolent resistance—indeed, of completely inactive submissiveness —would be to persuade the dictator that punishment and blandishments would be of no more avail than whipping the waters or pouring jars of honey into them.

Technically, though, the tyrant and his subjects are in somewhat symmetrical positions. *They* can deny *him* most of what *he* wants—they can, that is, if they have the disciplined organization to refuse collabora-tion. And *he* can deny *them* just about everything *they* want—he can deny it by using the force at his command. They can deny him the economic fruits of conquest, he can deny them the economic fruits of their own activity. They can deny him the satisfaction of ruling a disci-plined country, he can deny them the satisfaction of ruling themselves. They can confront him with chaos, starvation, idleness, and social break-down, but he confronts them with the same thing and, indeed, most of what they deny him they deny themselves. It is a bargaining situation in which either side, if adequately disciplined and organized, can deny most of what the other wants; and it remains to be seen who wins.

Mr. Sternstein's [essay] on the *Ruhrkampf* of 1923[2] makes this bar-

---

[2] Roberts, Adam (ed.), *Civilian Resistance as a National Defense.* Harrisburg: Stackpole, 1968, pp. 119–135.

gaining relation clear. His essay suggests that the side with the better organization and the better access to outside resources may in the end have the stamina to hold out and win. My immediate point is not that the tyrant is bound to win, merely that the best-organized and best-disciplined resistance, if it takes the form of refusal to collaborate, only converts what would have been an asymmetry of force into a two-sided bargaining situation, with no guarantee that the "resisters" will win.

And note that *win* is what they have to do if "civilian defence" is to work. Compromise is not enough. This [essay] is not about nonviolence and organized civilian resistance as a method of protest, as a method of alleviating conditions, as a method of denying a conqueror *some* of what he wants and of coming to terms with him. [It] is not about how to improve the terms of surrender, how to live better under military occupation, or how to make a tyrannical regime become gradually more civilized. It is . . . about defence and deterrence; and the proposition is that disciplined, organized civilian nonviolent resistance can actually make the conqueror withdraw (or at least make his military occupation utterly nominal) or dissuade him from conquest in advance.

The proposition is not merely that the Danes—had Hitler won his war and covered Europe with his Nazi regime—might have ameliorated that regime by skilful use of nonviolent resistance. The proposition is not merely that the Dutch could sabotage Hitler's military effort by some acts of nonviolent opposition. The proposition has to be that a regime could actually be overthrown, or made to retire, or dissuaded from conquest in the first place, by the use or the prospect of nonviolent resistance. Otherwise we are dealing not with "defence" but with protest, with political action, with a bargaining technique that leads to compromise and accommodation.

The proposition is easy to establish in its weaker form. If one merely proposes that nonviolence can be an effective bargaining technique, whether used by striking workers, by an oppressed minority, or by the bulk of a population against a nonrepresentative government; or if it is proposed that a good way to deal with a military conqueror, after one has been defeated militarily, is to revert to disciplined nonviolence; the case is a strong one. If it were proposed that a conqueror could be weakened in his conduct of war elsewhere by some organized nonviolent sabotage, so that his eventual military defeat would come more quickly, a good case could be made for some countries at some times.

And perhaps if one is willing to allow unlimited time to seduce a conqueror or his local representatives, to impress him and to teach him, even to negotiate eventual decolonization, the case for nonviolence is surely substantiated by history, though perhaps often with the threat of violence lurking in the background. (Considering the abortive result of so many revolutions that supplant one tyranny with another, one can wish that more rebellious cliques and revolutionary movements around the world had the patience and the discipline to rely on "civilian defence," not only because it might minimize violence but because it might improve the quality of the regimes that succeed those that are overthrown.)

But the proposition [here] is a stronger one. It is that a country—in particular, a country that has a real alternative of military defence, and by implication a country of western Europe or North America—can successfully substitute "civilian defence" altogether for its military effort to deter or to defend itself. And this must be a hard case to make; otherwise [it] would have [been] made. . . .

A critical question is whether nonviolent methods are compatible with the threat or the actual use of violence. The answer seems to depend on at least three circumstances. First, are the morale, discipline, and leadership that nonviolence requires compatible with the exercise of violence? Second, in dealing with the adversary, does the occurrence of violence undermine much of what nonviolence is trying to achieve, by providing an excuse for revenge, by abandoning the claim to moral superiority, and by exacerbating relations between the subject people and the bureaucracy of the tyrant? Third, can the violence be handled by some third party, as in the case of the Allies against Hitler, while other dissidents harass the regime "nonviolently"?

The case for pure nonviolence is stronger if the object is protest rather than defence. If one is trying to reach accommodation with a tyrant, resort to violence may spoil a nonviolent bargaining campaign; but if one is actually trying to make a tyrant retreat or withdraw, it is not clear that nonviolence by itself is up to the job, at least within the time span that the word *defence* suggests.

A more intriguing question is raised by the term *defence*. In the West we have got used (and perhaps in the East as well) to a good many euphemisms for words like *war, military,* and other (euphemisms) that are neutral or symmetrical in their moral implications. What about civilian *offence?* Are the techniques of "civilian defence" equally available to an aggressor, who needs only to support a disciplined dissident group to cause the downfall of a regime? Was not the original conception of Communist conquest one of "civilian offence"? Are not the techniques of "civilian defence" against a tyrant or against any regime that one wishes to overthrow just as pertinent to revolution as to defence, and as susceptible to aggressively and externally inspired revolution as to purely indigenous revolt?

. . . "Non-Violent Resistance Against Communist Regimes" by Theodor Ebert[3] is bound to raise the possibility that Western nations, wishing to overthrow Eastern regimes, might promote, facilitate, stimulate, and find ways of supporting "civilian offence" in those regimes, just as Western countries themselves have feared both violent and nonviolent rebelliousness inspired by some kind of international communism.

Let me raise an even more serious question. Is there any reason to suppose that the techniques of nonviolent resistance are more available to good people than to bad, to right causes than to wrong, to democrats than to demagogues, or to defence than to offence? There is of course reason to suppose that these techniques are *comparatively* more available to the dispossessed than to the wealthy, to the weak than to the strong; those who have a capacity for violence have an alternative; those who have not, lack the alternative. Nonviolence has a *comparative* advantage for the defeated that it does not have for the victor, because the victor has the alternative of force. Nonviolence thus sometimes has a comparative advantage for the poor, the weak, the disfranchised, because they lack the trappings of power and force. (They do not necessarily lack the capacity for violence against people and property, so nonviolence has to compete with terrorism; I wish it competed better.) There may also be an argument that nonviolence demands moral qualities that are usually absent in the more vicious regimes, like those that have worn black shirts or boots and belts and masks.

Still, terror may be most effective when disciplined; and if the discipline is present, nonviolence may be an alternative. Passive resistance has been notoriously the technique by which nonintegrating southern states have frustrated the federal government in America. Civil rights in America is a good case to keep in mind, because it lacks the bilateral simplicity of so many adversary relations. There are two minorities, a Negro minority and a white minority; both have used nonviolence and passive resistance, one of them against the military forces of the United States.

The movement of M. Poujade in France suggests that nonviolence is as pertinent, say, to the rich who prefer not to pay income taxes as to the poor who prefer not to be taxed for the conduct of foreign wars, as pertinent to the well-to-do farmer as to the poor one who wants better credit, better legal aid, more land, or more education for his children.

Mulford Sibley's words can be inspirational or frightening, according to *whose* noncooperation you have in mind and what kind of regime

---

[3] *Ibid.*, pp. 173–194.

the nonviolent resisters wish to impose. "Structures of power" and "wielders of power" may indeed sound like tyrants, oligarchies, and military occupation forces, but they may also include the United Nations, the Supreme Court of the United States, or a regime trying desperately to become democratic in a country with a military or authoritarian tradition.

The most disturbing question raised by all these discussions of nonviolence is, which target is more vulnerable? Is it a military rampant Hitler or the Weimar Republic? Is it the segregated south or the Supreme Court of the United States? Is it France under the Fifth Republic or France under the Fourth? Is it the University of Peking or the University of California?

It would be nice if all good things clustered together, and nonviolence (which sounds so much better than violence) had a necessary affinity for the good and the right and the pure—for the meek and all those who should inherit the earth. Maybe it does, but we do not know it yet. The potential of nonviolence is enormous. Mulford Sibley has quietly pointed out that it knows almost no limits. In the end it could be as important as nuclear fission. Like nuclear fission it has implications for peace, war, stability, terror, confidence, and international and domestic politics that are not easy yet to assess.

Nonviolence and Casualties

BARBARA DEMING

In any violent struggle one can expect the violence to escalate. It does so automatically, neither side being really able to regulate the process at will. In nonviolent struggle, the violence used against one may mount for a while (indeed, if one is bold in one's rebellion, it is bound to do so), but the escalation is no longer automatic; with the refusal of one side to retaliate, the mainspring of the automaton has been snapped and one can count on reaching a point where deescalation begins. One can count, that is, in the long run, on receiving far fewer casualties.

Nothing is more certain than this and yet, curiously, nothing is less obvious. A very common view is that nonviolent struggle is suicidal. This is, for example, Andrew Kopkind's view: "Turn-the-other-cheek was always a personal standard, not a general rule: people can commit suicide but peoples cannot." The contention that nonviolent struggle is suicidal hardly stands up under examination. Which rebels suffered more casualties—those who, under Gandhi, managed to throw the British out of India or the so-called Mau Mau who struggled by violence to throw the British out of Kenya? The British were certainly not "nice guys" in their response to the Gandhians. They, and the Indian troops who obeyed their orders, beat thousands of unarmed people, shot and killed hundreds. In the Amritsar Massacre, for example, they fired into an

Excerpts from Barbara Deming's article "On Revolution and Equilibrium," *Liberation,* February 1968, pp. 7–9. Reprinted by permission of Liberation Collective. Barbara Deming is an author and poet who lives near New York City.

unarmed crowd that was trapped in a spot where no one could escape and killed 379 people, wounding many more. There was a limit, nevertheless, to the violence they could justify to themselves—or felt they could justify to the world. Watching any nonviolent struggle, it is always startling to learn how long it can take the antagonist to set such limits; but he finally does feel constrained to set them—especially if his actions are well publicized. In Kenya, where the British could cite as provocation the violence used against them, they hardly felt constrained to set any limits at all on their actions, and they adopted tactics very similar to those the Americans are using today against the Vietnamese. In that struggle for independence, many thousands of Africans fighting in the forest and many thousands of their supporters and sympathizers on the reserves were killed. Many were also tortured.

One can, as I say, be certain if one adopts the discipline of nonviolence that in the long run one will receive fewer casualties. And yet very few people are able to see that this is so. It is worth examining the reasons why the obvious remains unacknowledged. Several things, I think, blind people to the plain truth.

First, something seems wrong to most people engaged in struggle when they see more people hurt on their own side than on the other side. They are used to reading this as an indication of defeat, and a complete mental readjustment is required of them. Within the new terms of struggle, victory has nothing to do with their being able to give more punishment than they take (quite the reverse); victory has nothing to do with their being able to punish the other at all; it has to do simply with being able, finally, to make the other move. Again, the real issue is kept in focus. Vengeance is not the point; change is. But the trouble is that in most men's minds the thought of victory and the thought of punishing the enemy coincide. If they are suffering casualties and the enemy is not, they fail to recognize that they are suffering *fewer* casualties than they would be if they turned to violence.

Actually, something seems wrong to many people, I think, when—in nonviolent struggle—they receive any casualties at all. They feel that if they are not hurting anybody, then they shouldn't get hurt themselves. (They shouldn't. But it is not only in nonviolent battle that the innocent suffer.) It is an intriguing psychological fact that when the ghetto uprisings provoked the government into bringing out troops and tanks—and killing many black people, most of them onlookers—observers like Kopkind decided that the action had been remarkably effective, citing as proof precisely the violence of the government's response. But when James Meredith was shot, just for example, any number of observers editorialized: "See, nonviolence doesn't work." Those who have this reaction overlook the fact that nonviolent battle is still battle, and in battle of whatever kind, people do get hurt. If personal safety had been Meredith's main concern, he could, as the saying goes, have stayed at home.

Battle of any kind provokes a violent response—because those who have power are not going to give it up voluntarily. But there is simply no question that—in any long run—violent battle provokes a more violent response and brings greater casualties. Men tend not to think in long-run terms, of course; they tend to think in terms of isolated moments. There will always be such moments that one can cite, in which a particular man might have been safer if he had been armed. If Meredith had been carrying a loaded pistol, he might well have shot his assailant before the man shot him. (He might also well have been ambushed by still more men.) Whatever one can say about overall statistics, some men will always *feel* safer when armed—each able to imagine himself the one among many who would always shoot first.

To recognize that men have greater, not less control in the situation when they have committed themselves to nonviolence requires a drastic readjustment of vision. And this means taking both a long-range view of the field and a very much cooler, more objective one. Nonviolence can inhibit the ability of the antagonist to hit back. (If the genius of guerrilla warfare is to make it impossible for the other side really to exploit its superior brute force, nonviolence can be said to carry this even further.)

And there is another sense in which it gives one greater leverage— enabling one both to put pressure upon the antagonist and to modulate his response to that pressure. In violent battle the effort is to demoralize the enemy, to so frighten him that he will surrender. The risk is that desperation and resentment will make him go on resisting when it is no longer even in his own interest. He has been driven beyond reason. In nonviolent struggle the effort is of quite a different nature. One doesn't try to frighten the other. One tries to undo him—tries, in the current idiom, to "blow his mind"—only in the sense that one tries to shake him out of former attitudes and force him to appraise the situation now in a way that takes into consideration your needs as well as his. One is able to do this—able in a real sense to change his mind (rather than to drive him out of it)—precisely because one reassures him about his personal safety all the time that one keeps disrupting the order of things that he has known to date. When—under your constant pressure—it becomes to his own interest to adapt himself to change, he is able to do so. Fear for himself does not prevent him. In this sense a liberation movement that is nonviolent sets the oppressor free as well as the oppressed.

9

INDIVIDUAL ACTION
AND SOCIAL CHANGE

Introduction

These readings have examined the war system in both political and moral terms and have suggested a variety of approaches to change in the system. While the ultimate goal must be change at the level of the global system, several authors have urged the necessity of beginning with attempts to revise in one way or another the foreign and military policies of the United States. Presuming one agrees that some change is necessary, where does one begin, and what strategies does one adopt?

The choice of strategy depends on the short-term goals to be attained, on one's political and moral values, and on one's understanding of the possibilities and limitations of the change process in this time and place. Although they are united by a concern for building a more peaceful and just world, the selections in this concluding section differ from each other in all three respects.

The opening selection, by historian W. Warren Wagar, reviews several conventional approaches to world order change and concludes that none in itself is an adequate response to the problem. All the standard approaches—the peace movement in all of its forms, the scientist and social scientists, and the New Left—lack a vision of global culture comprehensively different from the global present. Such a vision, Wagar claims, must emerge from a perception of the "totalizing" nature of the present crisis. He argues that the next step in the development of civilization must be a world culture and a world government: a truly global framework for responding to supranational problems of war, environmental deterioration, and poverty. By this he means something more than the minimal federal authority proposed by Clark and Sohn. According to Wagar, nothing short of a "world revolution" will be required to create such a new world order, but clearly he has in mind a revolution quite different from the violent revolutions of the past. Intellectuals have the responsibility of leading the search for designs for a satisfactory future, and in so doing, of creating the foundations of a world culture.

Wagar's vision is bold. But how different are its immediate, practical implications from the strategies already being pursued by people working for change? How, for example, can those of us who are not among the world's intellectual elites work for change toward a world culture? Aside from such strategic questions, several substantive questions are important as well. For example, Wagar claims that the dream of a peaceful world is inconsistent with the hope of preserving many distinct cultural traditions, since the conflict of cultural values often leads to war. Is the hope for cultural pluralism indeed a myth? How many would genuinely prefer a future in which the diversity of cultures are fused together into a single, dominating global culture? How important are deep-seated attitude changes in the turn toward peace? For example, must we wait until most people accept such concepts as respect for all human life or the brotherhood and sisterhood of all men and women?

While such critical and imaginative thinking is important in devising a strategy of peace, it is also important to look more carefully at the potential of the movement for change that already exists. Despite Wagar's criticisms of the peace movement and the New Left, it remains true that these groups—loosely, "the movement"—represent most of the public energy recently exerted outside of official channels for change toward a peaceful world. The selections by Walzer, Murphy, and members of the Movement for a New Society, suggest alternative views of "movement" strategy.

Walzer, a former student activist who is now a professor of politics, argues that the only real choices for a movement of citizen activists is between pressure politics and electoral politics. "Revolution" and "making the system work" are both myths that serve only to detract energy from the real need of the movement, which is to win public office and thus change public policy. According to Walzer, the goals of the movement (and the requirements of a peaceful world, according to Pilisuk and Hayden in section 7) conflict fundamentally with the core values of the governing elites of the United States. Thus pressure politics is unlikely to produce significant change. Since Walzer thinks "revolution" is impractical and unlikely, the only remaining option is to attempt to change policies through electoral politics.

Murphy's article examines the effectiveness of student power in the 1970 elections. He was a member of the Princeton University group (Movement for a New Congress) that attempted to channel into electoral action the student energy released at the time of the Cambodia invasion and Kent and Jackson State shootings in May 1970. His article reports the result of a research project that collected data on the effects of this effort. The data clearly show that organized, committed citizen activists can influence the outcomes of elections in which the candidates' positions on peace are at issue. Murphy argues that it was not important that the citizen activists in this case were students. They could have been workers and had the same impact. What is important is that there were many of them, that they cared strongly about the issues, and that they were well organized.

Quite as significant is what Murphy's data indicate about apathy and nonparticipation. Even in a year of crises and, at times, of near hysteria among antiwar students, the number who actually worked in political campaigns against the war was only a small percentage of the total number of students theoretically available for such work. In times of noncrisis, nonparticipation might be expected to be even greater. This supports Walzer's claims that any tactics for radical change that depend on mass participation are unrealistic and that the only realistic avenue of policy change available is through electoral politics.

For those with a vision of creating a new society in a new world order, the path of change through electoral politics often seems virtually endless. Even if a large number of "citizen activists" could be marshaled to work in every federal election for the next twenty years, there would still be doubt about their ability to bring about fundamental change unassisted by less political forms of change-oriented activism. There is also the problem of building a reform-oriented consciousness in order to counteract the influence of the establishment media—a problem that cannot be dealt with solely through electoral action. The selection by Sue Carroll, George Lakey, William Mayer, and Richard Taylor seeks to provide a strategy for "conscientization"—for introducing the perspectives of a new society into present political debate. The authors are a working party of the Movement for a New Society, a Quaker group centering in Philadelphia. In the book from which this selection comes, they develop a model of a "new society" based on a ruthless critique of present United States society as war-prone, militarist, and socially unjust. The authors argue that any strategy for building a peaceful world order would have to deal first with these aspects of pervasive social ill-health.

Unlike Walzer, Carroll, Lakey, Mayer, and Taylor argue in favor of creating a mass movement for change outside the political system. Its purpose would be more to raise consciousness than to win office; more to teach values than, in the early stages, to change policies. Presumably electoral change would come later, after the movement had gathered sufficient strength and a coherent program. To sustain the movement, they propose creation of a chain of "nonviolent revolutionary groups" (NRGs) to carry out various social action projects, and by their very existence, to give witness to the values of a new society. With radical caucuses, "counter-institutions," and other elements of a change-oriented counterculture, the NRGs would give organizational form to a mass democratic movement.

The issues raised by these solutions bring into focus much that has gone before in this book. Tactics can be chosen only after one has a coherent idea of the roots of war and the most appropriate ways of coming to grips with them. Like Wagar, Carroll, Lakey, Mayer, and Taylor believe that the core values of United States culture are somehow inconsistent with those required for a peaceful world. For them, it follows that a movement for radical change is the most reasonable mechanism for working for peace. Walzer and Miller, on the other hand, represent the view that there is something significant to be gained by the attempt to win power within the framework of existing institutions. Are these views inconsistent, or can they be understood as complementary approaches to the problem of change?

A third position—possibly taken by most people in the United States —is that U.S. foreign and defense policies are not, in themselves, threats to world peace. While many who agree with this claim also believe that some change is necessary to make war less likely, they generally hold that these changes must take place at the global or regional level and that the U.S. government can be induced to support such changes when they are possible. How deep, it must finally be asked, are the necessary changes? And at what level? What action by concerned citizens makes these changes most likely? These questions are the most crucial in facing the problems of peace and war.

Half Measures and Red Herrings

W. WARREN WAGAR

THE PROJECT OF A WORLD CIVILIZATION

An intelligent species in deep distress does not permit itself to be para-
lyzed by poor odds. The greater the challenge, the greater the response.
In light of the gravity of our predicament, it is not surprising that millions
of able and powerful men throughout the world devote most of their
waking hours to the struggle against war and social disintegration. The
campaign for world government, with its peace chest of more than ten
billion dollars and its twenty-five thousand political candidates contesting
seats in all national parliamentary elections; the antiwar strikes, boycotts,
and insurrections; the systematic harassment of ecocidal maniacs by mail,
telephone, and citizen's arrests; the unnumbered best-selling books on
world order that crowd the lists of every major publisher; the civil disobedience of most of the world's clergymen, who refuse any longer to
play puppet to national establishments—all of this was to be expected.
In every corner of the planet, the people are marching. More than five
hundred million signatures were obtained for the recent world petition
against nationalism and militarism. Everywhere taxes go unpaid, econ-

From W. Warren Wagar, *Building the City of Man*. San Francisco: W. H.
Freeman and Company, 1972. Copyright © 1971 by World Law Fund. Reprinted
by permission of the publisher. Wagar is an historian and author. He teaches at
the State University of New York at Binghamton.

omies are strangled by consumer resistance, frontier guards have lost control of international checkpoints.

Don't bother to pinch yourself. You wouldn't feel a thing. End of dream! Wake up.

If there is anything more dispiriting than the immensity of the threat to mankind's survival, it is the insignificance of mankind's response. Our "millions of able men" have not yet been born. In the real world, the full-time workers for world integration unbeholden to national power structures could all be accommodated in a Vermont village. Their expenditures in the cause would not provide for the annual needs of Mrs. Jacqueline Onassis. The difference they have made in world affairs is too small to be weighed on any historian's scale.

. . . the twentieth-century world crisis in civilization involves every aspect of our lives. It is a "totalizing" crisis. Although we must—for sanity's sake—allow ourselves some hope of survival, we have not yet resolved to make a "totalizing" response. Our solutions have been piecemeal, provisional, parochial, uncoordinated, and unsubstantial. They are too often conceived on a national scale, although the real problems are all planetary. They are directed at immediately burning issues, in the unfortunate tradition of American pragmatism, which refuses to see life whole and has no sense of the organic unity of past, present, and future. Above all, they lack prophetic moral vision. Separately or in combination, our responses to the twentieth-century crisis project no sense of world purpose or direction. They are innocent of ultimate objectives. They tinker, when they should forge.

Let us confront our situation manfully. The crisis is too vast to yield to segmental solutions. No repairs can salvage the existing international system. No half measures will prevent ecocide and technological dehumanization. Nothing can stay the evaporation of faith in the old gods. In the language of Arnold J. Toynbee, what we see before us is the socioethical breakdown of all the civilizations of mankind—their death as entities capable of sustaining further organic growth. Wherever growth still does occur, it is most often cancerous and self-destructive. The local civilizations no longer function as organisms.

The circumstances give us two options: either to preserve the shells of our diseased civilizations as long as possible, or to try consciously and concertedly to build a new world civilization. A third possible choice, to abandon civilization and revert to primeval anarchy, contradicts the social nature of man. *Homo sapiens* is a civilization-forming animal. For the past six thousand years, wherever material conditions have been favorable, he has faithfully obeyed the impulse to create civilizations.

And a civilization—let us be quite clear—is not simply a human community. It is always an effort to unify the *ecumene,* to bring the whole known world under one law and one cultural configuration. A civilization is a world order. It seeks, although it does not always succeed, to pacify the earth. It is the most effective of mankind's social inventions for subjecting the state of nature to the rule of art, reason, and will.

But when a civilization loses its power to grow and thrive organically, it must be replaced. Toynbee identifies three distinct generations of civilizations since earliest antiquity, each built on the ruins of its predecessor. Some civilizations, like the Mohenjo-Daro society of northern India, disappeared without a trace. Most have transmitted extensive portions of their culture to their successors. None is necessarily immortal. But the inescapable task before mankind at the present juncture in its history is the formation of a new civilization, constructed from the viable and compatible components of all its dying local societies, and scaled to the new dimensions of the *ecumene*—the planet itself. For the first time, the "known world" is the planet earth. The local societies are no longer ecumenical. They can no longer keep the peace, give justice, or solve the most urgent material problems of our communal life. World history has served notice upon them. They must go.

It is at once obvious that the new world civilization will not come into existence, if it comes into existence at all, in the "normal" and "historical" way, by a process of gradual evolution. In certain superficial respects, a world civilization already exists, a world technical order that works unpurposefully toward a common planetary way of life. If we could afford the violence and waste that would accompany such an unpurposeful drift toward integration, if we were not faced with enormous demographic pressures, with weaponry of total destruction, and with a degree of mass consciousness unprecedented in history, it might be just as well to sit back and wait.

Unhappily, the tempo of technological progress does not permit historical patience. If we are to make the transition safely to a unified world civilization, we must accelerate all the natural processes of civilization building. Whole ages must be telescoped into less than a century. What was largely unpremeditated in the past must become deliberate in the future.

We must totalize the search for world order. We must become architects and builders of civilization. Anything less is too little.

How to begin? Although the experience will be painful, and will force us to deal harshly with good men, I suggest that we can best begin by weighing the past efforts of liberals and radicals to resolve the twentieth-century world crisis. Let us analyze what has been attempted by men who understand, at least in part, the seriousness of the crisis and who are not mindless apologists for the existing order. Their efforts have seldom been exposed to frank criticism. They have enjoyed the same patronizing immunity as the very old and the very young in a well-regulated modern family. But we owe them the courtesy of candor. As pioneers in a desperate undertaking, they have much to teach us. From their failures, and also their successes, we have much to learn.

DEMYTHOLOGIZING THE PEACE MOVEMENT

The German existentialist theologian Rudolf Bultmann must accept the heavy responsibility for bringing into the language of twentieth-century man a useful but unlovely new word: demythologization. To demythologize is to winnow the chaff of pagan mythological imagery from the good grain of the Christian *kerygma*, or "message." But Christianity is not the only system of ideas enveloped by mythology. The peace movement also stands in need of demythologizing. Of all liberal efforts to respond to the twentieth-century world crisis, the struggle against war is the most direct and the most ambitious. Yet it operates on the basis of illusions that render it almost impotent.

The "peace movement" is an omnibus phrase for many different, but intimately related activities. It started early in the nineteenth century. Its most spectacular achievements before 1914 were the great international conferences held at The Hague in 1899 and 1907. During its long history, it has developed three distinct strategic concepts: resistance to war making by civil disobedience (either violent or nonviolent); collective security through diplomatic conferences; and world federalism.

Each of these strategic concepts is flawed by utopian premises. The most ingenuous is the first—the idea of civil disobedience—although in one respect it is also the most shrewd. At least it does not go cap in hand to the "guv'nor." It recognizes that war makers will not stop making war unless they are strenuously resisted. Projects for civil disobedience range from the plans of the Second International, just before 1914, to call a general strike by the working men of all countries at war, to the current refusal of many young people to accept induction into national armed forces on any terms. In the same category are the campaign for unilateral nuclear disarmament launched in Great Britain in 1958, the demonstrations in the United States against the war in Indochina, the student protests against militarism and nuclear testing in Japan, and the militant religious pacifism of the International Fellowship of Reconciliation. Following the example of Buddhist monks in Vietnam, some war resisters have resorted to self-immolation. American pacifists have attacked selective service offices and physically threatened the Pentagon.

But civil disobedience directly aimed at national war machines cannot prevent wars. War is an accepted instrument of national policy in all countries, to which all governments turn when they judge that vital national interests can be served in no other way. A sovereign state cannot protect its sovereignty without being prepared to go to war or to accept the military aid of a friendly power. It follows that the decision to make war is a public decision, tacitly or actively supported by the majority of politically responsible citizens in the state. They seldom demand war for the sheer love of blood. But they choose war, and readiness for war, in preference to the surrender of vital national interests. Direct attacks on war machines make little sense, then, because they are attacks on the instrumentalities freely chosen by bodies politic for the pursuit of their interests. To stop war by civil disobedience, one must attack the whole state; one must disavow the sovereign-state system, and persuade others to do likewise. For the same reason, campaigns for general or nuclear disarmament accomplish little. Wars are not made by armies, and much less by arms—only sovereign polities make wars.

It is still more unrealistic to ask men to abjure physical violence in any or all circumstances. The doctrinaire nonviolent pacifism of modern times is a counsel of perfection which arbitrarily prohibits one remedy for an intolerable situation while endorsing others that may inflict or cause the infliction of more harm than violence itself. Man is spirit, as well as flesh. Destroying the flesh is only one way of injuring our fellow men. There are situations in human conflict where violence is necessary; in other types of conflict, nonviolent solutions work very well. Gandhi and Martin Luther King chose appropriate tactics for the struggles they had to lead; so also did Winston Churchill in 1940 and Joseph Stalin in 1941. It would be far better, no doubt, not to injure our fellow men at all, to resolve all conflict by never permitting conflict to arise in the first place. But this is to suggest that men become gods, or robots.

The second strategic concept of the peace movement is collective security through diplomatic conferences. The post-Napoleonic Quadruple Alliance and its "system" of international congresses, which lasted from 1814 until about 1822, was an early example of this strategy in actual operation. It returned to life after the First World War in the Covenant of the League of Nations, and later in the United Nations. Although international collective security arrangements can be made only by states, their strongest defenders today are the various national citizens' associations established to offer them popular support.

But organizations such as the United Nations are only councils of ambassadors. The nations have surrendered and given nothing. The United Nations, like the League before it, has not even replaced the regular system of embassies and consulates by which countries negotiate with one another bilaterally. The United Nations has no power of taxation or legislation, no army, no police force, no judicial authority over persons, and no citizenry. H. G. Wells once called the League of Nations "a homunculus in a bottle." The United Nations is its twin. Proposals to "strengthen" or "improve" it are merely grotesque.

In any case, all schemes for the prevention of war through diplomatic conferences lack realism, whatever temporary relaxation of tensions they may sometimes afford. Diplomats have no power to determine national policy. Even when nations are prepared to seek peaceful settlements of their disputes, the vast polyglot lecture halls of the United Nations are often the worst places in the world to conduct serious negotiations. They could disappear one night in thick Manhattan smog, never be seen again, and never be missed.

The last major strategic concept developed by the peace movement, world federalism, escapes some of the criticisms that must be aimed at civil resistance and diplomatic conferences. It does not limit its attention to war making as such, and it recognizes that the decision to resort to war is political. It demands the voluntary democratic surrender of the "external" sovereignty of nations to a world political authority. Such a world federal government would assume the responsibilities now shouldered by foreign offices and ministries of defense. In most plans, it would also have certain limited legislative and judicial powers. At the same time, it would zealously protect the "internal" sovereignty of nations, allowing them to manage their domestic affairs as they pleased, while safeguarding their sociocultural integrity. The model of world order envisaged is a pluralistic community of autonomous nations.

Most projects for a democratic world federal government feed on a wide assortment of deadly illusions, which appeal strongly to middle-class and middle-aged liberal opinion because they seem to promise security without the need for radical change. The most obvious of these, the myth of "minimalism," is the working premise of all the others. It argues that the only way to convince nation-states of the relative harmlessness of world government is to require the transfer of the fewest possible powers from national to federal authority. The essence and most of the substance of national sovereignty—as minimalists reassure uneasy statesmen—is preserved.

The theory of divisible sovereignty has long ago been demolished by Hans Morgenthau. Sovereignty means full power. Divided sovereignty is a contradiction in terms. Subtract 10 percent or 25 percent from 100 percent and you no longer have 100 percent. Notice, too, that the one power which, above all, the minimalists hope to wheedle away from national governments is the power of self-defense. This is no ordinary 10 percent or 25 percent: it is the keystone of all sovereignty, which alone guarantees to states the possibility of effective exercise of authority in any form. States may agree to more extensive international controls over world trade, transport, communications, and tourism. One can even imagine a world currency, health service, customs union, or space program. But the last power the nation-states will surrender is their power to make war, and the last way to persuade them to surrender it is to send politically impotent humanitarians to beg respectfully at their doors. It is not for nothing that world federalists rarely interest national intelligence agencies. Their doings are so harmless that governments let them continue unmolested and unnoticed.

Federalism itself is something of a myth. This is the constitutional formula by which "minimal" powers will be delegated to the world authority, and all others reserved to the self-governing states. The classical federalism of the eighteenth century, to which this formula nostalgically alludes, is so much cold mutton in the second half of the twentieth. It survives here and there, in attenuated forms and unusual local circumstances, but all the tendencies of the age fight against it. In modern practice, certain powers are delegated to the component states of the federal union, and ultimate authority rests with the people as a whole, acting as a whole through their federal government. Such federal states as the Soviet Union, West Germany, and the United States do not differ markedly from such unitary states as the United Kingdom and France. The logic of technique and the social and psychic needs of mass democracy demand centralization of power. Federalism on a global scale is ludicrous; in a world of nations so greatly unequal in population and wealth, in a world faced with so many urgent problems requiring drastic public solutions, from population control to imminent race war in South Africa (and perhaps North America), a classically federalist world government would be almost as powerless as the General Assembly of the United Nations.

Yet minimalism and federalism are not urged upon us by world government enthusiasts merely because minimalism and federalism would be hypothetically easier to sell to existing national establishments. Minimalists do not want a maximalist government even if they could get it, because it attacks another of their cherished myths, the idea of cultural pluralism.

Nothing better illustrates the decadence and world weariness of modern Western civilization. The myth of cultural pluralism has captivated every pedestrian liberal mind on both sides of the Atlantic. Its immediate origins are obvious: remorse for the blood-stained imperialism of the past and the economic imperialism of the present; the Wilsonian concept of national self-determination; and the anthropological relativism of the school of Franz Boas. Westerners who cannot contribute 1 percent of their national income to rectify the economic imbalance of East and West are nonetheless perfectly happy to subscribe to the theory of the complete relativity of sociocultural values. It is a seductive theory, if only because it is scientifically and philosophically impeccable, and costs nothing to espouse. It makes no demands upon others, and—more to the point—no demands upon one's own culture. Nothing need be done except to practice "toleration" or "mutual appreciation."

One of the few times in recent history when cultural pluralism received a definitive public challenge occurred in 1946. Julian Huxley, then executive secretary of the Preparatory Commission for the United Nations Educational, Scientific, and Cultural Organization (UNESCO), warned the commission that UNESCO could not function effectively unless it adhered to an overarching philosophy—which in his judgment should be scientific humanism. At once Huxley encountered implacable criticism. As the American delegate William Benton pointed out, the adoption of any binding credo by the organization would violate its pledge to respect the democratic freedom of every culture to develop along its own lines. Benton's point of view prevailed. UNESCO adopted no credo, and the homunculus in the bottle was spared all embarrassment. Another, somewhat less historic confrontation between cultural pluralism and the concept of a world civilization took place at a meeting of British world federalists which I addressed in Belgravia in 1964. During the question period, a prominent federalist spokesman (Patrick Armstrong) rose to wonder if I did not see "that world government will be created for the express purpose of *preventing* a world civilization! A federal world government must protect the existing national societies, not replace them."

At least this lays the issue plainly and openly on the table. The program of cultural pluralism is to preserve business as usual, except for the imposition of a minimalist world government on the community of nations, a tin hat to be worn in case of emergency, so light and so cheap that it will annoy no one.

Also implicit in the myth of pluralism is the myth of "politicism," the notion that politics itself is the prime determinant of public policy. I have already suggested that the decision to go to war is a political decision, and that sometimes it is a purely political decision. But other influences have their due effect. In the last analysis, the acts of a body politic are determined by its values, mores, class structure, economy, institutions, and historical experience. The political decision is a product of the whole life of the society. Political decisions may generate from their own logic certain other political decisions, but the ultimate source of their authority in either case is the public will.

It is this organic quality of politics that "politicism" chooses to ignore. Politicism contends that states may form and statesmen may govern without a supportive sociocultural context. By such reasoning a world government can flourish without a world civilization or a world public will. Whether such a concept is utopian or dystopian, I could not say; it is certainly not practicable in the real world. But it suits the needs of the cultural pluralists, who must persuade themselves that a seemingly minor adjustment in the structure of world politics will save mankind from Armageddon.

There are other myths, of course. One especially cheerful delusion ("functionalism") proposes that national governments can be drawn willy-nilly into effective union through the spinning of a world-web of governmental and nongovernmental international service organizations. All this will happen, so to speak, behind the backs of the politicians. One fine morning they will all wake up and find themselves guests in the same silken parlor of the same spidery world bureaucracy.

One fine morning! But it will never come. Politicians are not so easily fooled. Even if the sovereign states miraculously did agree to some kind of world administration of international affairs, I have no confidence that such an agreement would be enough to save mankind from disaster. We need much more than a planetary dose of Nixonian "law and order."

Clearly the men and women of the peace movement have hearts where hearts belong. I cannot possibly quarrel with their hope for a planet at peace. We can learn much from the tactics of nonviolent civil disobedience employed by pacifists. Good diplomacy can buy mankind badly needed time. The publicity already given to the idea of a federal world government has helped to create the moral atmosphere in which stronger initiatives and further progress toward world order become feasible.

But the peace movement has tended to lose itself in narrow and doctrinaire byways. A movement whose only real goal is peace (*i.e.,* the absence of war) will never achieve it. One might as well start a happiness movement. Peace is the bliss and felicity that we may live to earn if we create a new world civilization; yet, in and of itself, it is nothing at all.

SALVATION BY SCIENCE

The peace movement pleads to the moral and social conscience of mankind. It is essentially a movement of the heart. But we have omitted one school of pacifist thought whose appeal is mostly intellectual. In recent years one of the few newsworthy developments in the peace movement has been a proliferation of institutes for "peace research." Other centers have sprung up for research into the ecocidal crisis. Both have quite different intellectual origins from the traditional peace movement. They belong to the equally venerable Baconian and Saint-Simonian tradition of "salvation by science" or—in Alfred Korzybski's phrase—"human engineering."

One of the major documents in the new scientism is Kenneth Boulding's book *The Meaning of the Twentieth Century*. Boulding is a professional economist and former director of the Center for Research in Conflict Resolution at the University of Michigan. Unlike many contemporary scientist-prophets, he has a firm grasp of the dynamics of world history. He defines "civilization" as a necessary but uncomfortable interlude of one hundred centuries between the million years of prehistory and the era of "postcivilization," the pacified, prosperous world society of the future. In his prognosis, such a postcivilized society is easily within our reach if only we can avoid the three great "traps" of world war, international poverty, and social entropy brought about by premature exhaustion of the earth's resources. How may these traps be avoided? What we must have, writes Boulding, is knowledge. Social scientists studying conflict and population control and natural scientists and engineers discovering how to make limited resources meet expanding material needs, will save mankind. Boulding's concept of a "great transition" from civilization to postcivilization, he tells us, is more "like the multiplication table than it is like an ideological position." Our crisis, as Wells once wrote, is "a race between learning and disaster." We require no new religion, ideology, or party of evangelists, since wise and honest men need only repair to "the standard of the truth itself."

In short, once research workers learn how to resolve conflict scientifically, control human reproductive behavior scientifically, and manage the earth's biological and mineral resources scientifically, mankind at large will soon accept their answers. The greatest obstacle to world integration is lack of adequate technical know-how. The same concern prompts the biophysicist John R. Platt to call for the mobilization of scientists in "task forces for social research and development," to produce thousands of "social inventions." We need "peace-keeping mechanisms with stabilization feedback-designs," advances in "biotechnology" and "game theory," and more research in "management theory." John Fischer in *Harper's* advocates an experimental "Survival University" staffed by "emotionally committed" specialists in the sciences of survival, such as biology, geology, engineering, and government. The motto of the new university "—emblazoned on a life jacket rampant—will be: 'What must we do to be saved?' "

There are few limits to the imagination of working scientists. For them, the deserts can be reclaimed, billions of people can be fed from algae and yeast farms, ample construction materials can be extracted from ordinary sand and rock, and surplus populations can live in giant seagoing or airborne skyscrapers made of aluminum and plastic. For several trillion dollars, it should even be a simple matter to "terra-form" the moon and the planet Mars, thereby almost doubling the *Lebensraum* of the species. Going beyond mere imagination, Buckminster Fuller (the inventor of the geodesic dome) has begun the building of a Centennial World Resources Center at the Edwardsville campus of Southern Illinois University, which will house an international data bank and a computer-feeding facility enabling scientists to "predict in advance, and solve before eruption, potential world problems associated with world resources and bearing on human poverty and suffering." The only real obstacle to an age of peace and abundance, Fuller complains, is "politics," an obsolete mode of human interaction that substitutes passion and violence for reason and scientific management. Scientists who use the facilities at Edwardsville will be forbidden to play politics or import ideologies into their work.

It may seem rather impudent for a nonscientist to say it, especially in view of the relatively lower scores on I.Q. tests of nonscientists, but the solutions to the twentieth-century world crisis of men like Buckminster Fuller are unintelligent. In spite of their mental powers, these men behave stupidly. Perhaps because they have deliberately and irrationally shut off the flow of the most relevant data into their brains, they fail to take into account the nature of the beast whose survival they hope to make possible.

One question alone is enough to bring these soaring promises of salvation back to mother earth. If only scientist-saviors would bother to read the fables of Aesop! Contrive the most ingenious technical solutions you can. Develop new machinery, methods, schemes of organization and control. Hook all the computers in the world together, end to end. Then ask yourselves: who will bell the cat?

How can societies and governments be induced to implement technical solutions? We know enough already to renovate the whole human race and all its civilizations. Many technical solutions no doubt still elude us, and much more can be learned. But the knowledge already exists to solve many of our greatest problems. The difficulty is that men and their societies act only on the urging of beliefs and desires given effect by will. Such beliefs and desires often conflict with one another, leading also to clashes of will. As Leslie A. White pointed out long ago in *The Science of Culture,* will and struggle determine social outcomes, not knowledge; moreover, the choices available to men in any society are circumscribed by the culture of that society. It is impossible to break out of one's culture and historical situation and become transcendentally or abstractly free. "No amount of development of the social sciences," White insisted, "would increase or perfect man's control over civilization by one iota." This does not mean that progress is impossible. In a later chapter of the same book, he even expressed hope for the eventual organization of "the whole planet and the entire human species within a single social system." But such organization will be the responsibility of willing, struggling, and historically conditioned men, not of social scientists acting as *dei ex machina.*

Above all, what we must have are changes of will, which knowledge can help to guide and enlighten, but only if we willingly permit knowledge to do so. The great questions of the future are not questions of "how" but of "who" and "how much." That is, who gets how much of what is left? Who will decide to postpone or modify "unnegotiable" demands? Who will agree to alter his whole way of life and thought? Who will find it possible to sacrifice nearly everything he has, for the sake of others? Who will consent to refrain from imprudent growth or wolfish aggression? How much time will it take to accomplish how much change? Can whole societies surrender their immediate advantage or tolerate their present disadvantages for the sake of the long-term progress of mankind? Will there some day be a politics and religion of human survival? Although we have little reason for hopefulness at the moment, the only thing indispensable to real progress is human will. Knowledge, like science, is in itself entirely neutral and can be turned to any purpose whatsoever.

Some behavioral scientists, needless to add, would object that human behavior, too, can be controlled. Mechanical engineers can build the technical apparatus for survival, and behavioral engineers can ensure that men will use it. We have already explored . . . the logic of technique, and the prospects for a planetary anthill. A solution achieved by behavioral engineering would throw out the baby with the bath water. No doubt techniques of advertising, pedagogy, medicine, and whatnot can be invented that will "humanely" induce men to work together more efficiently than they now do. Aggressive impulses can be damped, and tender feelings elevated, without any intervention by the willing subject.

But even if one could stomach its inevitable diminution of human freedom, behavioral engineering entails intolerable risks. *Quis custodiet machinatores?* Who will watch over the engineers? Who will engineer them? How can populations that have submitted to behavioral engineering change or entirely replace a given system of conditioning, after they have lost their wills? How can any science, no matter how subtle and thorough, foresee all the major consequences of an experiment in behavioral engineering involving an intelligent race of three or twelve or thirty billion souls?

Our criticisms of "salvation by science" are not meant to imply that science has nothing to offer suffering humanity. Scientists should be persuaded to enlist *en masse* in the struggle for world integration. But they must school themselves (despite their scores on intelligence tests) to function as yeomen, not field marshals.

THE NEW RADICALISM

If the peace movement is too narrowly political and scientism not political enough, consider the New Left. It disavows the established order; it is thoroughly, and yet not exclusively, political; it is not middle-aged; it has partisans in every country; it promises to make a new civilization. What more could be asked?

Of all the political events since the Second World War, none has generated greater excitement than the arrival in the mid-1960s of the New Left. For anyone who came of age between 1940 and 1955 (*peccavi*), excitement is mingled with incredulity. We had just settled down, so we believed, to a long winter's nap of consensus politics, the welfare state, economic miracles, and the "Free World"; of Eisenhowerism, Adenauerism, and de-Stalinization. Daniel Bell wrote *The End of Ideology,* and Judith Shklar *After Utopia.* Scholars agreed that the "radical impulse" and the "utopian imagination" were dead. But the New Left has given the lie to these obituary notices. The new young refuse to join their older brothers in anti-ideological slumber. They want causes and programs. They want revolutions.

In a representative manifesto of New Leftism, published in the *Berkeley Barb* in the late spring of 1969, a coalition of "liberation committees" promised the conversion of Berkeley's schools into training grounds for revolution, the destruction of the University of California unless it became "relevant to the Third World, workers, women and young people," the protection and expansion of "our drug culture," direct seizures of real estate, the liberation of women, armed self-defense against political repression, a "soulful socialism," the formation of a people's democracy, and solidarity with Black Panthers and other movements "throughout the world to destroy this motherfucking racistcapitalistimperialist system."

Many New Leftists would use more temperate language or less overt tactics, but the vital ingredients of New Leftism are all here: socialism, internationalism, populism, a strong identification with the cause of oppressed minorities, and a militant revolutionary ethos. The slogan of the New Left everywhere, and the last line of the Berkeley manifesto, is "All power to the people."

The instincts of the New Left are sound. In a collapsing civilization, we need such instincts. At last there are young men and women who will not play the sordid games of official nationalism and militarism! But at the same time, the New Left has been a disappointment. The poverty of its imagination, the superficiality of its diagnosis of the twentieth-century world crisis, the sentimentalism and infantilism of its revolutionary strategy, and its self-defeating absorption in purely local and educational issues have gravely impaired its effectiveness. It may have set other forces in motion that no one can yet see; but in its present form, it cannot build the City of Man. Despite its claims to revolutionary leadership, the New Left is not revolutionary enough.

Its first and most profound error has been to shackle itself emotionally and intellectually to the Old Left. In spirit the New Left is only another Jacobin-Marxist-Anarchist defense of "the People" against oppression. The ranks of the so-called oppressors have widened, however, to include the whole middle class, whose eventual precipitation into the proletariat can no longer be seriously expected, and great segments of the rural and urban working class, whose relative affluence and fierce loyalty to the established order have rendered them *plus bourgeois que les bourgeois* —more middle class than the middle classes themselves. In this way "the People," which means the socioeconomically disadvantaged or oppressed, have dwindled in numbers until they constitute a minority of the population (at least of the male population) in most Western countries. But they remain the rallying point of the Left. It is the *reductio ad absurdum* of sentimental populism. What becomes of populism when most of the people are not "the People"?

New Leftists are nonetheless resolute in their attachment to the cause of "the People." They agree that conspiratorial corporate-bureaucratic elements in all countries but those with young revolutions (China, Cuba,

North Vietnam) foment wars, manufacture an artificial "commodity culture," battle movements of national liberation, and ruthlessly oppress the poor. Modern life reduces, in the twentieth century as well as in the nineteenth, to a straight fight between exploiters and their victims. If the poor did not exist, the New Left would have to invent them.

Such innocence takes the breath away. In New Leftist mythology, the oppressed are virtuous because they are oppressed. Societies can dispense with elites, which alone are capable of selfishness, stupidity, and barbarism. The masses are relieved of all blame for the dumb ferocity of world wars and the ecocidal greed of modern civilization. One is asked to forget that all the major political movements of the century (including German national socialism) have drawn their strength from the masses and have taken as their program the pacification of class warfare.

To be sure, poverty and social injustice still thrive, intolerably, in parts of the Western world, and throughout the underdeveloped countries. I make no excuses for the machinations of the capitalist or the feudal landowner. They bear far more responsibility for the ills of the twentieth century than the masses. But our crisis goes much deeper: it is the death-agony of whole civilizations. Radicals betray their own cause when they imagine that all the problems of the present age result from the oppression of masses by a single devil class or devil race. On the contrary. In the developed countries, doctrinaire populism plays directly into the hands of the national orders themselves. Their willingness to satisfy popular demands for a rising material standard of life is perhaps the foundation of their remaining strength. While resources hold out, reformist elements in the national orders will go on trying to distribute national wealth ever more democratically, following tendencies of societal evolution that started in the developed countries in the nineteenth century. When resources are exhausted, no class will prove more generous or self-sacrificing than any other.

This is no time for romanticism. Mankind needs a whole new civilization, not merely a redistribution of power or income within existing structures. Although the new world civilization must be democratic, both in its system of government and in its socioeconomic life, all classes in the present-day civilizations are equally obsolete, and equally capable of leading the human race to oblivion. Witness the sorrowful history of Soviet Russia, where a new governing class, drawn almost exclusively from the popular masses, pursues domestic and foreign policies no more enlightened, and in some respects less enlightened, than those of non-revolutionary Western states. "All power to the people!"—in the usage of many New Left romantics—is the death rattle of the old civilization, not the lusty wail of the new.

The same must be said of New Leftist efforts to link arms with the neo-nationalist movements of the late twentieth century, such as Afro-American and Mexican-American nationalism in the United States, the Catholic cause in Ulster, French separatism in Canada, the National Liberation Front in South Vietnam, and Palestinian nationalism. These are all movements representing the interests of groups victimized to some degree by larger or more powerful groups. But every neonationalist program labors competitively for the liberation of its own people. When the disadvantaged group begins to enjoy the same privileges and benefits as its former oppressors, it loses its revolutionary ardor and becomes reconciled to the world of things-as-they-are. All establishments need do is open their gates.

The lesson to the New Left should be clear. Neonationalism is not basically revolutionary. Except in the already independent countries of Asia, Africa, and Latin America, whose poor are too numerous (and whom New Leftists often ignore anyway), disadvantaged ethnic minorities may easily be bought off by any establishment capable of enlightened self-interest. If establishments do not act quickly enough, the disadvantaged group may become more militant, but in such instances it will probably move toward fascism, rather than toward revolutionary social democracy. For the New Left, nothing is gained except embarrassment. By forcing establishments to accelerate the assimilation (and hence the *embourgeoisement*) of their dissident minorities, the New Left temporarily strengthens the establishments. By supporting neonationalism, it may also help to promote neofascism. The New Left cannot win. No matter how just the cause, nationalism by its very nature turns inward upon itself and therefore provides no firm basis for cosmopolitan world revolution. It has no place at all in the revolution unless it can be totally integrated into a larger and more powerful movement. Given the present actual strength of the New Left, the prospects for New Leftist absorption into neonationalism are better than for neonationalist absorption into the New Left.

But democratic socialism has always been an easy prey for tribal passions. It succumbed to them in 1914 and again in the 1930s in Germany and Russia and again in the national welfare states of the 1950s. When nationalism overwhelms paramount loyalty to mankind, the result is always the emasculation of socialism.

The New Left has also diverted too many of its meager resources into struggles directly affecting young people of college age: the fight against compulsory military service, against the legal prohibition of marijuana, and against authoritarianism in higher education. This is the most easily forgiven of all its strategic errors, since the New Left draws most of its tangible support from young people. Some attention to these problems is imperative. But for many New Leftists, incredibly, the success of the whole revolution is hinged on plans for the "liberation" of the universities. The universities take the place of the mountains in guerrilla warfare. They become the staging areas and training grounds of revolution. Students also erect barricades during confrontations with civil authorities, in the self-conscious role of citizens of Paris in 1848–49. "If one day one hundred campuses were closed in a nationally-coordinated rebellion," writes Jerry Rubin, "we could force the President of the United States to sue for peace at the conference table." With massive worker support, rare in recent times, French students did very nearly overthrow the government of General de Gaulle in May 1968.

Because universities are relatively easy to "occupy" for at least short periods of time, and most of the "natives" are friendly, they seem to make ideal centers for romantic revolutionary exploits. Faculty and administrations tend to be liberal and eager to appease dissent. But the difficulty is that universities are neither power centers nor impregnable mountain retreats. Despite their undoubted usefulness to government and industry, any society can survive without most of their services for months or years at a time. In any event, the established order—supported by the majority of "the People" themselves—has no intention of financing or protecting self-declared instruments of its own overthrow. The expropriation of the universities for overtly revolutionary purposes will be met, sooner or later, with crushing force and a wave of counter-revolutionary terror far more powerful than anything that could be mounted by the New Left. For milder offenses, the simple expedient of the established order will be to cut the purse strings. Although the universities may offer the prospective builders of a new world civilization opportunities to find one another, any hope of using them as sanctuaries from which to launch guerrilla warfare is, at least for the time being, misguided.

Still more pointless are the anarcho-terrorist adventures of extremist elements in the New Left, both on and off campus. Like the civil disobedience of nonviolent pacifism, the use of terrorism—bombings, kidnappings, assassinations—is efficacious only when revolution is near and public opinion ripe for radical change. In a country such as the United States, where a recent poll disclosed that only 2 percent of the population describes itself as "radical," terrorism can do nothing except unleash the counterrevolution.

Even the new public anxiety over the environment may turn out to be a red herring for unwary New Leftists. The issue is real enough, as is the issue of Afro-American or women's liberation, but the reigning social orders can readily exploit it to their own advantage. Overpopulation, pollution, and exhaustion of resources are, after all, not in the self-interest of any national economy. It follows that governments themselves must show increasing concern about the problem, from their various national points of view. The more vigorously the New Left complains about "the rape of the environment," the easier it will be to persuade electorates to tax themselves to fight environmental spoliation. The more public money flows into the fight, the less will corporate profits suffer. The more the New Left is diverted from revolutionary politics, the less of a nuisance it will be to the established order. If the New Left could, by collaborating in this way with the old order, actually save the environment, at least something very important to mankind would have been won; but where public funds and governmental influence are involved, we may be sure that the fight against spoliation will be waged on a national scale, for short-term gain, and that it will have only a palliative effect, delaying but not preventing world ecocide.

Let me say again: any true believer in the idea of a world civilization must rejoice in the emergence of a new radical conscience. To the extent that capitalism and feudalism, as well as racism and male sexism, support the nation-state system, they are enemies of peace and enemies of mankind. Even if one ignores their involvement in the defense of national political power, they breed injustice which must not be allowed, under any circumstances, to survive into the coming world society.

But a movement that seeks to build a new world civilization must concern itself with much more than the problem of social justice in existing national orders. For the world integrationist, many of the causes of the new radicalism are red herrings, well calculated to throw him off the scent. They become useful to him only when they fall into place in a carefully designed master strategy for world revolution.

THE POLICY OF THE WHOLE HOG

Unfortunately master strategists of world revolution are in chronically short supply. It is easier to attend to selected small problems ready at hand. The general public, and most intellectuals as well, dither from one issue to another. Now it is Korea, now Algeria, now Vietnam. Petitions for world government are followed by civil rights demonstrations, which in turn give way to bomb shelter building and emigration to New Zealand. Everyone rallies around the Common Market; next the Peace Corps; then campus revolution. Every year brings its new approved activity: marches on nuclear installations, silent vigils, ghetto riots, draft card burnings, ecology crusades. The current persuasion or obsession of every man, woman, and child over the age of nine is readily identifiable by his dress, hair, ornamentation, and insignia, which undergo complete stylistic metamorphoses at least twice a decade. But nothing ever really changes. We do not give one hour or one dollar in a thousand to the solving of world problems, and only one of every thousand that we do give is not dissipated in haphazard, uncoordinated, miscellaneous philanthropy.

All the movements taken to task in this chapter have something to contribute to the search for a new world. I lament only their lack of broader visions and more versatile strategies. We must pull ourselves together, in spite of everything. Developing a master strategy for world revolution means a drastic simplification of purpose, and at the same time a drastic complexification of effort.

Our goal must be, quite simply, a new organic world civilization, a new sociocultural, economic, and political environment for the species *Homo sapiens,* with a new organic relationship to the larger environment of earth and cosmos. Such a goal simplifies our world view, but it does not make our task any easier or smaller, just the opposite. The search for social justice, personal freedom, truth and meaning, peace, well-being, and the good life are not superseded by the search for a new civilization, but are assimilated directly into it. Civilization building requires disciplined attention to all the needs of progressive mankind . . . therefore, we shall have to discuss politics, law, religion, philosophy, culture, human rights, economics, education, ecology, the universe itself— all in relationship to our vision of the desirable future for mankind.

Nothing can be left out, because everything is collapsing. Proposals to repair the old civilizations, or replace them piece by piece, are madness in reason's mask. H. G. Wells relates an appropriate parable in one of his last books on world order. The survivors of a vessel lost at sea have found refuge on a desert island, where the most likely source of food is a wild pig. The pig, of course, objects. Despite their great hunger, the survivors put forward reasonable suggestions for satisfying their needs without causing too much discomfort to the pig. One man will be content with a loin chop, another with the left ham, a third will settle for chitterlings. The cabin boy, however, points out that the animal is unlikely to agree to any diminution of himself whatsoever. In such a situation, the only policy that makes sense is to kill the whole hog and be done with it.

Strategic Choices

MICHAEL WALZER

Quiet men and women often exaggerate the importance of their own outrage, their long delayed decision to *do something*. If they are moved, how can the rest of the world stand still? But it is always best to plan one's moves on the supposition that most of the world will stand still, that established institutions and social practices will survive the shock. All that has changed is that some group of people has decided to use the pronoun "we," and to act together. Nor is it the case in a democratic society that this decision challenges the political system. Quiet citizens are the resources of a democracy, saved up, we are told, for those moments when professionalism fails. They may feel unconventional; they may behave unconventionally; but their intermittent forays into the political arena are by now one of the conventions of democratic politics. That doesn't mean that what they do isn't important, nor that it isn't sometimes dangerous. Using democratic rights puts them at risk: now there are men and women—now there are enemies—threatened by that use. For this reason above all, it is important for activists to know what they can and cannot do, and never to indulge themselves (or frighten their enemies) with fantasies of social and political changes they cannot actually bring about.

From *Political Action: A Practical Guide to Movement Politics*, by Michael Walzer. Chicago: Quadrangle Books, 1971, pp. 23–27. Reprinted by permission of Quadrangle Books. Walzer, who was active in the civil rights movement as a student, is now a political scientist teaching at Harvard.

Revolution is such a fantasy, less common than is often thought, but worth dealing with early on. Citizen activists may aim at this or that fundamental change, but they cannot hope to make a revolution. It is not very often that anyone actually *makes* a revolution. Revolutions happen, and all sorts of people find themselves, unexpectedly, participants in the happening. Ordinary citizens will be among them (often yearning not to be), but at such moments it is the professionals, newly recruited professionals perhaps, who take charge. Power of the ultimate sort is at stake, and no one contends for such power in a part-time way, or carries on simultaneously a nonpolitical career, or retires casually from the struggle once some point of special interest has been won. But these are the characteristics of citizen activists; simply listing them helps explain why amateur politics is most often parasitic on the routines of a more or less stable democratic system. The crises and outrages that set off the political activity of ordinary citizens are serious enough, but they occur within a system that is not yet in a state of total crisis and that protects even the irregular responses of its members. Most men and women join the movement counting on that protection. It isn't absolute, as they will learn, but it is a great deal more than revolutionaries have any right to expect.

Giving the system a "last chance" is another fantasy. This suggests that revolution is the next step if citizen activism in general, or this particular citizens' campaign, fails to carry the cause to victory. But activists have no business imagining that they will win right away; they are a minority, probably a small minority, of the country. They must risk failure, and they ought to be aware that the most likely consequence of failure is not revolution at all, but the fragmentation of their movement and the retreat of many citizens from politics. Small bands of sectarian militants may then experiment with disruption and violence, fantastically imitating Jacobins and Bolsheviks. But this is rarely a serious business. One day, hopefully, there will be a new mobilization of activists, a reorganized movement, and another citizens' campaign—that is, another "last chance" for the system. *There is nothing else to do but try again.*

The real choice faced by the men and women who plan these successive attempts is between two kinds of politics, both of which have conventional names, though they can each be pursued in a variety of irregular ways. The two kinds are pressure politics and electoral politics, and I am inclined to think that there are no other kinds. To choose pressure politics means to try to influence those people who already hold power, who sit in official seats, who may even be responsible for the outrages against which the movement is aimed. To choose electoral politics is to try to dislodge those people and plant others in their seats, not necessarily or even probably the leaders of the movement, more likely whatever alternative set of professional politicians the system provides. Of course, the two choices overlap in important ways; they are often pursued simultaneously, with stress being put on the first only until some group of professionals adopts the cause. But it is worth emphasizing the two simply because they exhaust the range: changing the policies men make and changing the men who make policies. Changing the political system within which policy is made is rarely a real option for citizen activists.

It is never easy to know when to shift from pressure to electoral politics, whether at any given moment (and the moments are recurrent) to enter or to avoid the campaign of this or that candidate or party. On the one hand, electioneering is the sort of politics citizen activists are most familiar with, know best, probably do best. On the other hand, they often feel that their break with the routines of the system precludes it. They have come to distrust the promises of professional politicians. They are in search precisely of a politics that does not require them to support candidates who are only barely better than their opponents and who have, most likely, weak and vacillating positions on what the activists believe is the crucial issue. Sentiment of this sort is entirely justified. It is, after all, what makes the movement possible in the first place.

But assuming that pressure politics (petitions, mass meetings, marches, and so on) doesn't lead to a change in government policy, electoral politics is a necessary next step. The movement can't avoid it, even if supporting conventional candidates and parties involves some compromise of its principles. It is only a question of when, and to that there is no specific answer. The general answer is: not until the movement is strong enough to force fairly clear positions upon the professionals and to exercise some control over them once they have won.

This general rule sometimes suggests to activists that they must run their own candidates or that they must join in a new political party. A single-issue educational campaign, even with victory inconceivable, may be a useful activity; whether it is or isn't in any particular case is a tactical decision. A new party is something quite different. It involves the movement in a coalition with many other groups and so defines its position on many other issues; it requires a commitment to an elaborate program and to broad social change. That is a commitment many of the activists would probably like to make, but it is not what first brought them together, and it is not what holds them together with other activists in the movement. Nor is it at all clear that a new party and a struggle for social change on a wide front is the best (the easiest or the quickest) way to carry their own cause to victory. There are, in fact, two very different strategies entangled here, which will have to be separated out in the course of movement debate and action. Two questions are crucial: Should the citizens' movement be committed to single-issue or to multi-issue politics? Should the movement be organized as a single constituency or a coalition?

Student Power in the 1970 Elections:
A Preliminary Assessment

WILLIAM T. MURPHY, JR.

The Cambodian invasion and the tragedies at Jackson and Kent State this spring led to explosions on college campuses all across the country. There was a great deal of talk of massive student intervention in the fall congressional elections and universities adopted various measures in response to the crisis. Some abandoned institutional neutrality by taking positions condemning the president's actions, others scheduled fall courses on elections and "practical politics," while others opted for some variant of the two week "Princeton Plan" pre-election recess.

Most observers assumed that student political interest would remain high and that the student impact would be significant. By early summer university-based groups had been set up to lobby congressmen to support "end the war amendments," to raise money for antiwar candidates, and to supply student volunteers to work actively for such candidates.[1]

The largest of these organizations, the Movement for a New Congress, which attempted to harness student energies on behalf of antiwar candidates, had chapters on 417 campuses by June. Heavy nationwide press coverage was given to the student role in early primaries—especially the

From *P S* (published quarterly by the American Political Science Association) vol. 4, Winter 1971, pp. 27–32. Reprinted by permission. Murphy teaches at Princeton, where he helped organize the Movement for a New Congress.

[1] Lobbying groups included the Continuing Presence in Washington and the Academic and Professional Alliance; most of the fund raising was done by the Universities Anti-War Fund; the Movement for a New Congress supplied campaign volunteers.

attempts to unseat entrenched hawks Edward Patten (N.J.15) and John Rooney (N.Y.14). The primary season ended with twenty-five of the thirty candidates who received substantial student aid victorious. These were not easy victories. Five of these doves beat incumbents with from twenty to twenty-eight years seniority.

Yet on November fourth newsmen were saying that the student input had been minimal and many academics were regretting their support of much of the strike-induced legislation. In an attempt to find out what the students' real effect had been we decided to examine the attitudes of the voters in areas where students were involved, the campaign staffs with whom they worked, and the students who participated.[2] We surveyed over 4000 voters in eight congressional districts[3] to ascertain their opinions of student workers and how, if at all, student involvement affected their voting decision. We are interviewing twenty campaign managers to find out what the "professionals" thought of the students who worked with and for them. Finally, we are in the process of polling a nationwide random sample of 2000 students who actively took part in last fall's elections to find out who they were in both socioeconomic status and attitudinal terms; why they participated; what they thought of the experience; and what their plans are for future political involvement.

Much of these data are still being accumulated or processed. Nevertheless, because of the timeliness of the subject we will venture some observations on the role of students in the 1970 congressional elections. These are, of course, only tentative being based on the data presently available and impressions from participant observation.[4]

YOUTHLASH

Public opinion polls in recent years consistently have shown a high level of distaste for "students" by the general public. When these attitudes are probed more deeply, however, it becomes apparent that the public has transferred its antipathy towards campus violence and drug abuse to

---

[2] I would like to thank The Twentieth Century Fund for its valuable financial assistance.

[3] We surveyed voters in Maryland's 4th (Paul Sarbanes) and 7th (Parren Mitchell) congressional districts; New Jersey's 4th (Frank Thompson) and 9th (Henry Helstoski); New York's 27th (John Dow); Massachusetts' 3d (Robert Drinan); Wisconsin's 1st (Les Aspin); and Michigan's 6th (Charles Chamberlain). Doves were victorious in the first seven districts. In the Michigan district dove challenger John Cihon lost to Chamberlain.

[4] In my case, as National Co-Director of the Movement for a New Congress.

the group it most closely associates with these problems. Our interviews with voters have shown that this generalized negative reaction towards "students" is not carried over to young people working door-to-door in political campaigns.

An overwhelming proportion of voters favors such involvement on the part of young people. Seventy-eight percent of the respondents in our voter sample thought it was a good idea for college students to work in a campaign, with the rest split fairly evenly between "not sure" and "not a good idea." The most frequent reasons given for approving student involvement were: "everyone has the right," "it keeps them within the system," "it lets them learn how politics really works." While most people do object to demonstrations and riots, they do not resent young people engaging in activities that the general society considers legitimate.

For "youthlash" to occur voters who originally favored the candidate associated with students would have to have switched their vote to his opponent after contact with student workers. Of those who reported that they had been contacted only 2 percent said that student support had influenced them to vote against the student supported candidate while about 18 percent reported that the student contact had "had some effect in making me want to vote for their man."

Most people, however, said that the student workers had had little effect on their voting decision. Our surveys were conducted in precincts we knew to have been canvassed exclusively by students. However, most respondents (64 percent) did not perceive the young volunteer who came to their door as a student.[5] Rather they usually identified him as a regular party worker. Among those who had been contacted the proportion voting for the students' candidate was much higher than among those who reported that they were not contacted (See Table 1). Among those with a low issue orientation this difference between the percentage of contacted and noncontacted voters favoring the peace candidates was even more pronounced.[6]

This, of course, is not overly surprising in light of what we know about how the introduction of some information about the candidate radically

---

[5] A study done for Senator Philip Hart of Michigan gave evidence that the physical appearance of the canvassers was unimportant. Two groups of young canvassers, one clean-cut in coat and tie, the others in "hippie" regalia, were put into two sets of similar precincts. A before and after survey was taken which showed that the percentage favoring Senator Hart had risen about 15 percent in both sets of precincts.

[6] In each area the students canvassed only Democratic and Independent voters. For that reason the percentage of the vote totals are inflated in comparison with the totals for all voters.

TABLE 1
Effect of Contact by Student
Canvassers on Voters' Preferences

Voted for	Contacted	Not contacted†
Thompson*	67%	58%
Costigan	14%	25%
Sarbanes*	72%	59%
Fentress	12%	24%
Aspin*	66%	56%
Schadeberg	18%	29%

* Student-supported candidate.
† Column figures do not add to 100%
because "don't remembers" and "won't
says" are not included.

changes the probabilities of voting for him.[7] It is, nevertheless, important in explaining to young, strongly issue-oriented volunteers why it is best simply to get information about the candidate before the voter and then run an identification canvass and election day "pulling" operation to get most of his voters to the polls.

VOTER TURNOUT AND PREFERENCE

In areas where the students worked they made a tremendous difference. They were most effective when they were used on an organized, precinct basis. In most cases they were able to increase significantly both the turnout and their candidates' percentage of the vote.

In the September Maryland primary Paul Sarbanes unseated twenty-six-year veteran George Fallon of Baltimore. About 40 percent of Sarbanes' precincts were managed entirely by students. In these precincts they raised the turnout 30 percent over 1968 primary. Sarbanes' percentage of the vote was 12 percent better than that of another insurgent, J. Joseph Curran whom Fallon had narrowly defeated two years earlier. With heavy student support again, Sarbanes went on to win the general

---

[7] See for instance, Donald Stokes and Warren Miller, "Party Government and the Saliency of Congress," in Angus Campbell et al., *Elections and the Political Order* (New York: John Wiley, 1967), p. 205.

election easily. In Les Aspin's general election victory in the 1st congressional district of Wisconsin the same marked rise both in turnout and preference in the student worked areas can be observed. Students worked twenty-four wards in seven small towns for Aspin who was running against eight-year incumbent Henry Schadeberg. In these wards the Democratic turnout was raised an average of 50 percent (up in twenty-four of twenty-four wards) compared to 1966 and 26 percent (up in nineteen of twenty-four) compared to 1968. In the rest of the district the Democratic vote was up 11 percent over 1966 and 10 percent over 1968.[8]

We realize that these examples can be criticized as procrustean. We have used them because, though we do not have complete voting statistics for all eight districts as yet, the scattered returns we do have bear out this trend. In almost every student-worked precinct the percentage voting Democratic[9] was higher than both 1966 and 1968 while turnout was higher in almost every case than 1966 and in a majority of precincts greater than the presidential election year.

It would seem then that student volunteers can make a significant difference through their efforts. However this optimism must be tempered by the cold reality that only a tiny fraction of the nation's college students actually worked in a meaningful way this fall.

APATHY

Thousands of students worked in the 1970 congressional elections. Millions of students, and more generally, young people, did not work. Because so many did not work, the media and many candidates talked about student apathy, both before and during the elections.

During the spring, forecasts of student involvement ran up to 500,000. With a week remaining Congressional Quarterly estimated that 70,000 were working the last week of the campaign. There is no way of telling exactly how many students worked, though certainly no more than half the CQ estimate probably worked on a steady basis (i.e., more than

---

[8] These incomplete statistics are used merely for illustration. The complete voting and survey data will be subjected to more sophisticated quantitative analysis including scaling and multiple regression.

[9] Although, of course, not all the peace candidates were Democrats, those in the eight districts we surveyed were. Peace Republicans Daniel Button, Ogden Reid, Don Riegle, Tom Railsback, and Paul McCloskey had substantial student support. In addition, James Buckley claimed to have over 4,000 students working for him. Whether most did more than clean-cuttedly pose for pictures in "Buckley for Senate" hats is doubtful.

the last week of the campaign). Although many groups had long rosters a check of their records showed that many of their "members" worked only once or twice then declined further assignments. In many areas of the country, most notably most of the South, where there were neither peace candidates nor close races, no more than a handful of students were involved in congressional elections.

Moreover, estimating how many students actually worked is very misleading. A more politically meaningful unit of analysis is "man-hours worked." In a survey undertaken by the Princeton administration to assess the effect of the two-week recess, 24 percent of those polled claimed to have engaged in some campaign activities. Yet only 4 percent said they had worked more than a week and even in this "most active" group the average total "man-hours worked" was only slightly over twelve hours. The results from our nationwide student survey should tell us if this was typical of most workers. From what we personally observed, it probably was.

The whole apathy question is exacerbated by the high visibility of students in our present society. This visibility of students as a group and the attention they have received since the major campus disruption of the mid-1960s have led people to be extremely sensitive to their political impact.

The gap between rhetoric and action is much greater on the campus than in the larger society. On the campus, the level of political awareness in terms of candidate knowledge and issue discussion is very high, while the level of actual participation[10] is relatively low. For most other people the level of political awareness and the level of political participation are both low.

In general, a high proportion of the people who regularly discuss politics and hold strong political opinions become engaged in political activities. This is not true of students. There is simply no denying the fact that most students who became politically visible after the invasion of Cambodia were doing what students usually do: they attended meetings; passed resolutions; talked to each other. For the most part, this activity was rather easily accomplished. Because the circumstances were dramatic, because there are so many students, because there are excellent communications on campuses and between them, and because youth is an "issue," there was a great public awareness of what was occurring. These factors led many to believe mistakenly that vast num-

---

[10] We use participation here to mean electoral activities such as canvassing, literature distribution, poll watching, and not merely voting which, of course, was also very low.

bers of students would somehow depart from their normal pattern of low participation and poorly sustained interest in electoral politics.

It would be a great mistake to focus only on the gap between the events of May and the actualities of November. Vast numbers of volunteers are not needed to be effective. As shown above, the contributions of those who did turn out to work in campaigns were significant. Their contributions were significant not because students have some mystical political ability but rather because a well-organized volunteer effort can have a tremendous effect on almost any political contest below the presidential and senatorial levels.[11]

The venerable door-to-door canvass is still one of the most effective electoral techniques ever devised. But the personnel to carry out such a canvass have to come from somewhere. Except for Chicago and a few other places the local political organizations are moribund and unable to turn out campaign workers. At present, the only three groups which are both identifiable and accessible for campaign work are union workers,[12] housewives, and students. In addition, with campaigns becoming increasingly expensive a volunteer effort that can save candidates thousands of dollars becomes doubly important.

Students, then, constitute most of the pool of potential workers. If volunteers are so important, and can be so effective, we should examine some of the factors that inhibit wider student participation.

WHY DIDN'T MORE STUDENTS WORK?

Students are people. Despite everything voter surveys have told us of people's participation in politics many continue to adduce normative propositions of democratic theory calling for wide participation as though they reflected empirical reality. They manifestly do not. Young people do not participate in greater proportion than un-young people. In moments of perceived noncrisis to their lives they can be expected to continue that way. The major issues of the campaign—inflation/unemployment versus "law and order" or the "social issues"—were only marginally interesting to the young. Accordingly, the rates of youth participation reflected the rates for the society as a whole.

---

[11] Although volunteer efforts are also important in these races media plays a much greater part. In congressional races manpower is relatively much more important.

[12] The only unions that turned out workers in any amount were the United Auto Workers and, in some areas, the Steelworkers.

Two other general factors which affected how well the volunteer effort would be in a particular area came up repeatedly. If a college was primarily residential the recruiting task was eased considerably. People were geographically proximate, getting in touch with them was easy, and there was a greater awareness of campus activities. At the city schools and commuter colleges people were on campus at different times, often lived far from school, and took little interest in nonscholastic matters.

The second, and probably more important, factor was the ability of the local leadership of the volunteer effort. Because the MNC was a decentralized organization local chapter heads were essentially self-selected. They were often simply those students who got there first. Unfortunately, getting there first and being politically effective were not highly correlated. Equally bad, getting there first and being able to stay there were. Around the country the range of political expertise ran from some who were better than most professional politicians to some who were utterly inept. Most produced at least some volunteers for the local candidates. Many took over the major role in their candidates' campaigns, both supplying and directing the volunteers. Some, however, did nothing more than crank out endless newsletters foretelling all the wondrous things they were going to do.

Several other factors were also important. Tensions existed between what was most helpful in terms of recruitment and what was best for the candidate and his campaign. In their fear of "youthlash" many candidates and/or their staffs, like the Duffey campaign organization in Connecticut, publicly downplayed the role of students while privately asking for all the students they could get. This, of course, dampened the enthusiasm of many students. In some instances liberal candidates thought students would be a strong constituency, that the candidates could move to the center, downplay the role of the students, and still retain large-scale student support. This did not prove to be the case. Students, in fact, are a rather fragile constituency precisely because they are motivated often by idealism rather than material interest. The hard core of the electoral activists did continue to work. But many of those with lesser commitments fell by the wayside as candidates failed to embrace them openly and sullied their purity on the issues by moving to the center.

There can also be little doubt that the decline in the saliency of the Vietnam War as an electoral issue contributed to the fall-off in student interest. While there were clear-cut differences in their positions on the war between many candidates there was no Cambodian invasion to arouse the less committed and send them flocking to the standards of antiwar candidates.

Finally, for a large segment of the student population electoral politics is an irrelevant exercise—the politics of Tweedledee and Tweedledum. For them it made no difference in 1968 who was elected president, who was appointed attorney general, who was appointed chief justice of the Supreme Court. For the most part this group was not susceptible to recruitment in 1970.

FUTURE PROSPECTS

In order to make any judgments about the future direction and activities of young people in electoral politics, we must have more information about those already participating than is presently available.

Very little work has been done by political scientists on volunteer efforts in politics. The literature on the effects of canvassing on voter preference, for instance, consists of a handful of articles.[13] It is difficult to generalize from them since they deal with different locales, levels of party activity, and types of elections. Our surveys of the voters and campaign staffs in the eight districts listed above should give us good indexes of the degree of voter contact and level of party activity in these areas.

This information will be combined with voting data to assess the effect of the students by means of multiple regression analysis, on voter turnout and preference.

The data derived from our survey of this year's activists will not only tell us what their personal and political backgrounds were, but also how they compare with other similar groups[14] on a series of standard

---

[13] Peter H. Rossi and Philips Cutright, "The Impact of Party Organization in an Industrial Setting," in Morris Janowitz, Editor, *Community Political Systems* (New York: Free Press, 1961), pp. 81–116; Daniel Katz and Samuel J. Eldersveld, "The Impact of Local Party Activity upon the Electorate," *Public Opinion Quarterly*, Vol. 25, 1961, pp. 1–24; Philips Cutright, "Measuring the Impact of Local Party Activity on the General Election Vote," *Public Opinion Quarterly*, Vol. 27, 1963, pp. 372–386; Raymond Wolfinger, "The Influence of Precinct Work on Voting Behavior," *Public Opinion Quarterly*, Vol. 27, 1963, pp. 387–398; Gerald Kramer, "The Effects of Precinct-Level Canvassing on Voting Behavior," unpublished manuscript, Yale University, July 15, 1969; Edward Schneier and William T. Murphy, Jr., *Vote Power* (Englewood Cliffs, N.J.: Prentice-Hall, 1970) chap. 11.

[14] Both nonstudent activists reported on in previous research and student nonparticipants who were surveyed as a control group.

political attitudinal indexes.[15] Further, their opinions on items such as why they participated, how worthwhile they considered the activity, their willingness to participate in the future, what presidential candidate they favor, should give some indication of what we can expect, in terms of student participation, in future elections.

In the foregoing we have tried to cover, albeit briefly and incompletely, a few of the more salient questions connected with last fall's student effort. We believe that our project and the more refined research which will come out of it will not only tell us a great deal about what happened last fall but also about the future course of youth involvement in politics.

---

[15] These include indexes of Political Awareness, Political Efficacy, Citizen Duty, System Support, and University Support.

Organizing for Social Transformation

SUE CARROLL, GEORGE LAKEY, WILLIAM MAYER,
and RICHARD TAYLOR

CONSCIENTIZATION

The success of the struggle for fundamental change in America depends upon the extent to which a large number of people develop both a conscious will for a new society and an understanding of the need for a rapid social transformation. Assuming there can be no radical change without radical consciousness, the primary goal of the movement is to win a majority of the people, over time, to demand that the present social system of corporate capitalism be replaced by an entirely new society which might best be described as nonviolent, democratic, eco-socialism.

In order to develop such mass conscientization, the perspectives of the new society must be introduced into the political debate. The vision of what life would be like under the new society must be continually projected so that people will become increasingly aware of the difference between life as it is in America today and life as it can be under a new social organization of the political economy and a new set of social values.

This model for fundamental social change is a drastic departure from most traditional humanitarian efforts in the United States which have

From a forthcoming book tentatively titled *Revolution: A Quaker Prescription for a New Society*. Reprinted by permission of the authors, who are a working party of the Movement for a New Society in Philadelphia.

assumed that successive incremental changes within the present social system would eventually bring about the good society. It is, however, much more firmly supported by social change theorists. James C. Davies, for example, in his historical study of radical social change, concludes that social change requires new consciousness—people demand change only if their perceived actual social conditions do not meet their expectations.[1] And Thomas Kuhn, in *The Structure of Scientific Revolutions,* found that people will continue to believe in the old, "accepted" model, even if it no longer makes any sense to them, until an entirely new system is clearly presented to them as a viable alternative so they can (1) compare the presently accepted system to reality, (2) compare the new alternative system to reality, and (3) compare the present and alternative systems to each other.[2]

Mass Education Movement   One important method to develop mass conscientization is direct education. Such an effort will require a nationwide movement consisting of perhaps thousands of educational programs focused on the "big picture" of political economy, ecology, and social change—tailored to fit various individuals, groups, and organizations. The topics might include: (1) the values and social objectives of humanitarians; (2) the present United States political-economic system; (3) possible alternative political-economic systems for the United States; (4) the natural environment and its relevance to humanitarian efforts; (5) the international impact of the United States political economy, especially regarding the Third World; (6) ideas and theories of revolutionary change; and (7) the practical relevance of the above for people interested in working for a new society. Seminars, games, and audiovisual aids are already being developed which cover these topics. Also, speaking tours could be arranged for persons from nations such as Sweden, China, Yugoslavia, Chile, Cuba, and Tanzania. These would be augmented by "experiential" educational methods such as street speaking, speakers' bureaus, and work-learn visits within and outside the United States.

Key Groups   In the long run, direct education programs must be aimed at a broad cross-section of the population. At the beginning, however,

---

[1] James C. Davies, "The J-Curve of Rising and Declining Satisfactions as a Cause of Some Great Revolutions and a Contained Rebellion," in *Violence in America,* National Commission on the Causes and Prevention of Violence, June 1969.

[2] Thomas S. Kuhn, *The Structure of Scientific Revolutions* (Chicago: University of Chicago Press, 1962).

the programs will be geared to those individuals, organizations, and constituencies which are most interested and open to this approach. Especially important are population groups which play a critical role in maintaining the system but whose long-run interests require change. Groups such as . . . blacks and other Third World people, the peace movement, students, ecologically oriented scientists and ecology groups, radicals in various professions, prophetically oriented people from religious bodies, consumers' groups, poor people, blue collar workers, etc., are among those who most need to be reached.

BUILDING ORGANIZATION

> The revolt [of the American colonists] against the British government was not a vast, spontaneous movement. Instead, it was carefully planned by shrewd men and laboriously and sagaciously executed by some of the most active spirits on the continent. *It could never have succeeded if it had been left unorganized.* It was in part because the patriots were well organized, and because the Tories or loyalists were not, that the former won the day.[3]

Power Power is necessary for change to a new society. Changed attitudes alone will not change institutions: no matter how many individuals "green," the structures they participate in will remain essentially oppressive and unyielding.

The characteristic mistake of idealists is to think that ideas by themselves have power. It is helpful to remember the phrase, "Nothing is more powerful than an idea whose time is come." Much depends on the gradual change of public opinion that comes with time, but there must also be *organization* of large numbers of people to incarnate an idea and give it a form which can sustain struggle against the idea whose time came years ago.

A majority of Americans were in favor of strong gun control measures in 1936, according to a Gallup poll. Today we are still endangered by millions of loose guns in the U.S. The gun lobby has power, and unorganized public opinion does not.

Sometimes an aroused public taking action in the streets can force change. In May 1970 widespread protests against the invasion of Cambodia and shooting of students at Kent State and Jackson State Uni-

---

[3] Allan Nevins and Henry Steele Comager, *A Pocket History of the United States* (New York: Washington Square Press, 1967), p. 71. Emphasis added.

versities forced President Nixon, against his will and against clear military logic, to withdraw U.S. troops from Cambodia. This is probably the first time in recent U.S. history that antiwar sentiment forced a major reversal of wartime strategy in midstream.

Almost a year later, however, the president invaded Laos by means of Vietnamese footsoldiers and American helicopters, undeterred by the largely disorganized and passive antiwar movement. Even large-scale direct action provides lasting power only when it is backed by organization.

Organization of power makes possible democratization of power. A spontaneous rising is liable to manipulation by a vanguard elite or by a charismatic leader. A mass of people who are not organized into small communities of trust and political discussion results in demagoguery, not democracy. Democracy requires consensus, which requires discussion, which requires ground rules, which requires structure. We can structure a movement to be elitist or to be populist, depending on whether or not we stress open communication, rotation in leadership roles, explicit conflict mechanisms, and education. While all organization tends, under the "iron law of oligarchy," toward bureaucratization, checks can be built in and decentralist structures devised. When power is organized, democracy is at least possible; when decision making is left to impulse and circumstance, democracy is impossible.

Why a Mass Movement   We advocate a mass movement, operating outside the conventional framework, as the agency for fundamental change. Some people argue for a strategy of *permeation*—that radicals should join existing structures in order to bore from within. Permeation assumes a more hardy human being than we are familiar with, however. Individuals bombarded each day in their work situation entirely by pressures to conform would have to be moral giants to avoid co-optation; so many sad examples of sold-out left liberals dot our political landscape that we need hardly argue further.

Another alternative is keeping our own base clearly *outside the framework,* and using that point of moral clarity to speak truth to power. Unfortunately, that alternative assumes that ideas have more impact than they actually do in the rough-and-tumble of politics. People practicing this alternative sometimes adopt the establishment's basic framework to communicate with establishment representatives, and over time find themselves accommodated to the status quo as it basically is.

We might hope that the route to fundamental change lies through one of the major *political parties,* since these are highly legitimate in our society. The parties, are, however, controlled by the rich who support them, and are therefore unlikely agencies for change which eliminates wealth as well as poverty.[4]

Social movements in the United States which have been *mass movements* have, however, made broad changes: the woman suffrage movement and industrial trade unions are examples. The civil rights movement also achieved specific though nonrevolutionary goals, having its greatest successes where the movement was strongest—in the South.

Mass movements can be more democratic than other ways of organizing for change because the masses are themselves involved in the change and are sometimes taught powerfully by that process. Popular control of power means popular exercise of power, and this requires popular participation in the struggle for change. While some might argue for many small-scale campaigns rather than large-scale struggles, the latter provide a multiplier effect because of the greater publicity around them. People in other parts of the country (and outside the country) are more likely to be inspired to act by major conflict, as when the 1936 industrial sit-downs in France touched off similar sit-downs in Michigan.

We are urging that power is necessary for fundamental change and that power should be channeled by mass democratic movements. The question remains: in what forms might the revolutionary movement productively be organized?

Organizational Forms Organization is already occurring in the consciousness-raising stage, in study circles, street speaking groups, and travel seminars. We suggest four local and immediate organizational forms which serve educational needs as well as being units for struggle: NRG's, radical caucuses, counter-institutions, and training centers.

Nonviolent Revolutionary Groups (NRG's) arise from already existing friendships or ties or workplace or religion, and range in size from three to twelve individuals. They grow as cells grow, by division, and can proliferate rapidly when conditions are ripe. They seek to live the revolution *now,* sharing simple life-styles even while preparing for the emergence of a mass revolutionary movement. The groups serve the people, teach a revolutionary perspective, and develop their ability to use direct action.

The Nonviolent Revolutionary Groups should have enough analysis and broad strategy in common that they can help each other at critical points. They are not directed by a central committee, however, and they develop their own particular strategies in the light of their varying circumstances. Some will want to work within the coalition of poverty and

---

[4] See the writings of G. William Domhoff and Ferdinand Lundberg.

antiwar groups, helping in that way to build a mass movement with radical goals. Other NRG's may focus on issues not yet in the popular consciousness, such as the destructive impact of U.S. foreign aid on Third World nations, or gay liberation.

The team as the building-block of a mass movement makes sense because it meets the dilemma of collectivism versus individualism. Unlike some of the old communist cells it is not secret or conspiratorial; therefore, it cannot hold individuals to it rigidly with implicit threats. On the other hand, there is sufficient community to help the individual overcome his excessive attachment to self.

The often criticized tendency in mass movements for a kind of mob hysteria to sweep people away is not likely in a movement made of teams. On the other hand, the positive movement feelings of joy and celebration of community can be captured by teams. The solidarity which enables people to withstand the terror of repression is even more likely in teams than in an unstructured mass facing waterhoses or bullets. Studies of combatants in battlefield conditions have shown that the solidarity of the small unit is crucial in conquering fear and withstanding attack. Fear, of course, is the central weapon of repression. In a movement of small groups we may hold hands against repression and continue to resist.

Another form which serves the movement is the *radical caucus.* Many occupational groupings now have radical caucuses within them: social workers, miners, scientists, teachers, auto workers, health workers, lawyers, and so on. The radicals function as what the British call a "ginger group": they combine to press the group to take more advanced stands on political and social issues. The pressure often includes direct action at the national conventions.

The importance of the radical caucus is the close linkage to the non-radicals in the occupation; this ensures a dialogue and reduces the chance of isolation. Revolutionary ideas can in this way influence important elements of society, especially if the radical caucuses do not get distracted into mere power games with the leadership of the association or union.

Counter-institutions provide another fertile area for organizing. Free schools, community medical clinics, and producers' and consumers' cooperatives teach people that we can change things by our own work; discovering that we have untapped power has revolutionary implications. As long as the counter-institutions are seen as means to fundamental change rather than wholly as ends in themselves, they can provide a source of discipline and solidarity for sustained struggle.

Training communities are springing up in the United States, taking the form of schools for social change, nonviolent training and action centers, and Life Centers. Like Gandhi's ashrams they can provide "staging areas" for action campaigns, in which the necessary skills, strategies, and solidarity are developed. These centers can also reach across national lines to do transnational community building, looking toward the mass transnational movement of the future.

Propaganda of the Deed   Propaganda of the word is not enough. We also need to propagate our message through action. In the drama of action and counteraction the people see more clearly the brutality of the old order and the humanity of the new.

The Nonviolent Revolutionary Groups, radical caucuses, and other vehicles of change will test out their understanding and their strategies in the real world of struggle. Campaigning has been described as a "one-through-seven" process. It begins with preparatory activities, like research, fact-finding, and negotiations—then moves up to public education, organization, and the winning of allies. If its goals have not yet been reached, it moves into "step seven" of direct bodily confrontation with injustice and oppression.

Choosing Actions   The best kind of action is that which puts the guardians of the status quo in a dilemma—whichever response they make helps the movement. If they allow the demonstration to proceed, we gain that opportunity to educate the people. If they repress the demonstration, the people are awakened further to the underlying nature of the regime.

AQAG's *Phoenix* voyages to North Vietnam in 1967–1968 with medical supplies put the United States government into a dilemma about how to respond. The decision was finally made in the White House. The *Phoenix* was not physically prevented from reaching Haiphong and our act of compassion strengthened the antiwar movement. If the government had actually stopped the *Phoenix* on the high seas, it would have shown still more clearly the inhuman nature of its Vietnam policy.

As the movement develops its capacity to confront the oppressive institutions with the truth, it will grow. When the government strikes back in an effort to hide the truth, the people will see more clearly what is at stake. If the movement is prepared, it will maintain a nonviolent spirit which even more strongly contrasts with the violence of the repression.

Unifying the Movement   A scatter of organizations is not enough to contest the power of the ruling elite. Since the mid-sixties in the United

States there has been a growth in the tendency toward unity, taking the form of coalitions. One major effort was the Poor People's Campaign of 1968, which brought native Americans, blacks, poor whites, Chicanos, and others into alliance for a short period. Another was the antiwar coalition which currently embraces a variety of issues including poverty, the war, and racism.

The growth of coalitions is a welcome development, but it does not yet reflect a very high degree of unity, and therefore cannot communicate a fundamental analysis of our society nor a vision of a better one.

We look forward to the development of a revolutionary movement which can articulate clearly a radical analysis and vision. The movement would link the NRG's, radical caucuses, and other revolutionary groups, and coordinate the struggle in its mass phase. Linkage could take place in this way: as a local group, moving through the "one-through-seven" process, neared step seven on a significant issue, resources from the network of groups and communities could be put into the struggle to make it successful. Sometimes the struggle would achieve national or even international proportions. The groups working at the local level would define problems in terms of the way society is organized at the national level. Solutions to local problems would be defined in terms of a new political economy—a new society.

The organization of the movement should be bottom-up rather than top-down, as in the council system, in which groups send representatives who in turn elect representatives who make coordinating decisions. With frequent rotation of representatives and discussion of major decisions at every level, the councils are less likely to lose touch with the rank-and-file than the bureaucratic structure of American trade unions or the celebrity leadership of some of the social movements.

A Revolutionary Party?   We are not in this writing group agreed on the value of a revolutionary party. Certainly there is a strong legitimacy to the party as a means of organization, and the party could enter election campaigns as an educational tool. It could speak with a clearer voice about fundamental analysis than can a coalition. Traditionally, parties easily develop a deadening bureaucracy of their own, as noted by Robert Michels in *Political Parties*. Parties tend to get co-opted by the electoral process once they enter it, and soft-pedal their radicalism in order to get a larger proportion of the votes. They may finally go the pathetic way of the German Social Democrats, selling out first to nationalism and then to capitalism. While we are not clear about the value of the revolutionary party, we do agree that it is a question for a later stage in the struggle; the agenda now is building a revolutionary movement based on grass roots communities committed to struggle and new institutional life.

Issues   In a healthy body politic the private troubles of people are frequently translated into public issues. In America, as C. Wright Mills pointed out, the prevailing ideology insists on the reverse: we should see public issues such as ecological disaster as private troubles, and buy air filters to keep the filth out of our homes.

Working for social change means trying to restore that process of health by creating issues out of the private American's troubles. The troubles proliferate, however, and the potential issues multiply. An organizer must choose. What should he or she tackle?

The issue needs to relate to where the organizer is as a person. We have little confidence in a dogmatic approach, which, in the name of revolutionary discipline, insists that a person work on an issue which is alien to his inner concern. Personal concern is not a sufficient guide, however, for many of us care about far more matters than we can handle. Revolutionary issues are those through which it is easy to educate about "the big picture." Some issues lend themselves better to this than others. But a great deal depends on how the issues are *defined*. A war such as Vietnam can be defined simply as a blunder within an otherwise basically sound foreign policy, or it can be seen as part of the normal functioning of America's political economy.

Poverty issues can be defined in terms of the poor themselves, treating their characteristics (unemployment, low income, high birth rate, etc.) as the *cause* of their poverty. The resulting programs are then geared to rehabilitate the poor, as in job training, birth control, family counseling, self-help, etc. By contrast, we see poverty as a lack of resources *relative* to others in the society. We notice the rich as well as the poor, and see that 2 percent of the U.S. population holds 85 percent of all stock, 100 percent of state and local bonds, 32 percent of privately owned wealth, 29 percent of cash, and 36 percent of the mortgage notes. The problem then becomes the *gap* between the rich and the poor, and the cause lies in the basic social organization. We assume that the social institutions of the political economy are the primary distributors of both social benefits (employment, profits, etc.) and social costs (slums, unemployment, etc.). Defining poverty this way translates private troubles into basic issues which must be faced if social justice is ever to inhabit our country.

Ecological crises are often defined in such a way that their causes are traced to activities of individuals or "other" groups. Remedial programs are then proposed such as picking up trash along highways, buying unleaded gas, and recycling containers; and the world's poor are urged to reduce their birth rates in order to conserve dwindling world resources and end their poverty. Programs such as these, however, direct attention away from the real structural causes of ecological crises: a political economy of technological and industrial overdevelopment, overproduction, and overconsumption. Our skyrocketing GNP and the very burning of fuel, regardless of additives, are *ipso facto* villains of the ecological crises. And the problem of dwindling world resources is not the result of Third World population growth—200 million U.S. citizens consume an equivalent of 10.5 billion Indians. We need to choose our issues and define them in such a way that it becomes obvious that individual solutions are no longer sufficient and we need structural change.

Index